HUAORANI TRANSFORMATIONS IN TWENTY-FIRST-CENTURY ECUADOR

LAURA RIVAL

HUAORANI TRANSFORMATIONS IN TWENTY-FIRST-CENTURY ECUADOR

Treks into the Future of Time

The University of Arizona Press
TUCSON

*To Blanca Muratorio (1930–2014), Bogueney (193?–2013),
and Hélène Rival (1932–2013)*

The University of Arizona Press
www.uapress.arizona.edu

We respectfully acknowledge the University of Arizona is on the land and territories of Indigenous peoples. Today, Arizona is home to twenty-two federally recognized tribes, with Tucson being home to the O'odham and the Yaqui. Committed to diversity and inclusion, the University strives to build sustainable relationships with sovereign Native Nations and Indigenous communities through education offerings, partnerships, and community service.

© 2016 The Arizona Board of Regents
All rights reserved. Published 2016
First paperback edition published 2025

ISBN-13: 978-0-8165-0119-9 (cloth)
ISBN-13: 978-0-8165-5540-6 (paper)
ISBN-13: 978-0-8165-3371-8 (ebook)

Cover designed by Nicole Hayward
Cover photo by Romelia Angelica Papue Mayancha

Unless otherwise noted, all photographs are by the author.

Publication of this book is made possible in part by the proceeds of a permanent endowment created with the assistance of a Challenge Grant from the National Endowment for the Humanities, a federal agency.

Library of Congress Cataloging-in-Publication Data
Names: Rival, Laura M., author.
Title: Huaorani transformations in twenty-first-century Ecuador : treks into the future of time / Laura Rival.
Description: Tucson : The University of Arizona Press, 2016. | Includes bibliographical references and indexes.
Identifiers: LCCN 2015034538 | ISBN 9780816501199 (cloth : alk. paper)
Subjects: LCSH: Huao Indians—Ecuador.
Classification: LCC F3722.1.H83 R57 2016 | DDC 986.6/01—dc23 LC record available at http://lccn.loc.gov/2015034538

Printed in the United States of America
♾ This paper meets the requirements of ANSI/NISO Z39.48-1992 (Permanence of Paper).

CONTENTS

List of Illustrations — vii
Acknowledgments — ix

Introduction — 3

PART I: AMONG FOREST BEINGS — 37
1. Domesticating the Landscape, Producing Crops, and Reproducing Society in Amazonia — 47
2. Naming Trees — 73
3. Historical Ecology in Amazonia — 91

PART II: IN THE LONGHOUSE — 113
4. Human Birth: Hosting a New Life — 123
5. Living Well: Huaorani Sensuality and Happiness — 147
6. Femininity and Masculinity in Huaorani Land — 169

PART III: IN THE MIDST OF ENEMIES — 197
7. Forests of Abundance — 205
8. Prey at War — 223
9. Inside President Correa's Citizen Revolution — 244

Appendix A. Letter to President Correa   262

Notes   *267*
References   *303*
Index   *333*

ILLUSTRATIONS

FIGURES

1	Taromenani necklace	8
2	Well-known leader on a museum visit in Manaus	9
3	Women singing at a meeting	9
4	Teacher watching on his tablet pictures of a massacre taken on a smart phone and sent to him via e-mail	10
5	Young men running from tree to tree	40
6	Trekkers in their forest camp	40
7	Two brothers resting in the forest	41
8	Going home with chonta palm fruit	42
9	Visit to a manioc and plantain garden	43
10	A well-known shaman	44
11	Well-known leader preparing curare poison	45
12	Giving birth today	116
13	Mother and daughter resting in a hammock	117
14	The good life, the Huaorani way	117
15	Girl sharing her sweet with her pet monkey	118
16	Little girl in forest camp with pet monkey	119
17	Tamed deer	120
18	Guests resting at a festival	120

19	Bameno villagers getting ready to present their traditions at the Amazon State University, Puyo	199
20	Young men at a school festival	199
21	Leader preparing a conservation management plan for his community	200
22	Use of the tribal leader's picture by government officials	200
23	Housing along an oil road	201
24	Author in conversation with secondary school pupils	201
25	Participatory workshop	202

MAPS

1a	Huaorani territory within Ecuadorian Amazon	6
1b	Huaorani communities within the old protectorate created by the Summer Institute of Linguistics	7

TABLES

1.	Comparison of Ka'apor and Guajá names for nine species of the Inga genus	76
2.	Comparison of Ka'apor and Guajá names for three species of the Theobroma genus	77
3.	Huaorani and Quichua names for twenty-one species of the Inga genus	83
4.	Huaorani and Quichua names for seven species of the Theobroma genus	84
5.	Huaorani names for plants growing in alluvial and high forests	85

ACKNOWLEDGMENTS

THIS BOOK IS DEDICATED to three exceptional women who departed this world before I had a chance to say goodbye. Each taught me in their unique ways that thinking for oneself and refuting conventions that do not stand up to scrutiny are key ingredients of a life well lived. My mum, Hélène Rival, died when I was still in Ecuador, trying to make sense of the attack in which Bogueney lost her life. I owe much of what I know about Huaorani existential values to Bogueney and her kin. Blanca Muratorio, who introduced me to social and cultural anthropology at the University of British Columbia, changed the course of my life when she asked me to spend the academic year 1986–87 with her in Ecuador as her research assistant.

I have accumulated many debts over the years with so many Huaorani friends and collaborators that naming them individually would be impossible. I am particularly grateful to the inhabitants of Dayuno, Quihuaro, Zapino, Damointaro, QuehueireOno, and Bameno, who welcomed and sheltered me in the late 1980s and early 1990s for months at a time. As their children and grandchildren are to be found in every Huaorani community throughout the ethnic territory today, I feel at home everywhere I go! I keep a special thought deep in my heart for all the Huaorani friends—young and old—who have left this earth for heavenly abodes. I have used pseudonyms throughout the book to refer to friends, informants, and collaborators, except when talking about well-known public figures.

I have many Ecuadorian friends and colleagues to thank as well, whose conversations and company have enriched my life. I would like to thank more particularly Father Juan Bottasso and Jose Juncosa from the Salesian mission, who created Abya Yala, one of the most innovative publishing houses in Latin America; Jorge Leon, Andres Guerrero, and Luci Ruiz, who helped me understand their country's history and values; Maria Ulcuango, Alicia Torres, Esperanza Martinez, and FLACSO's teaching staff and students; Carlos Larrea and his team at the Simon Bolivar Andean University, as well as former rector Enrique Ayala; and Gabriela Zurita, Kati Alvarez, and Eduardo Pichilingue, who are part of a new generation of young Ecuadorian scholars dedicated to promote the welfare of Huaorani people.

The Amazonianist anthropology community may be small, but its buoyancy is unrivalled. The SALSA (Society for the Anthropology of Lowland South America) network has been a continuous source of intellectual support and collegiality. I wish to extend my warmest thanks to fellow Amazonianists Bill Balée, Audrey Butt-Colson, Lewis Daly, Philippe Erikson, Elizabeth Ewart, Theresa Miller, Istvan Praet, Peter Rivière, Anne-Christine Taylor, and Harry Walker for rich debates and stimulating conversations.

I am extremely grateful to a number of institutions and funding bodies for their generous support, in particular the Wenner-Gren Foundation, the ESRC, the University of Oxford, the Firebird Foundation for Anthropological Research, GIZ (Deutsche Gesellschaft für Internationale Zusammenarbeit, the German Organization for International Development), Pachamama, and Amazon Watch. I wish also to thank the publishers who have allowed me to use previously published materials:

- For Chapter 2: "Amazonian Historical Ecologies." In *Ethnobiology and the Science of Humankind. A Retrospective and a Prospective*, edited by Roy Ellen, 97–116. Special issue of *Journal of the Royal Anthropological Institute* # 1 (2006).
- For Chapter 3: "Huaorani Ways of Naming Trees." In *The Ethnobiology of Mobility, Displacement and Migration in Indigenous Lowland South America*, edited by Miguel Alexiades, 47–68. Oxford: Berghahn Books (2009).
- For Chapter 5: "Androgynous Parents and Guest Children: The Huaorani Couvade." Curl Essay Prize. *Journal of the Royal Anthropological Institute* 5(4): 619–42 (1998).
- For Chapter 6: "What Kind of Sex Makes People Happy?" In *Questions of Anthropology. Festschrift for Maurice Bloch*, edited by R. Astuti, J. Parry, and C. Stafford, 167–96. Oxford: Berg (2007).

- For Chapter 7: "Proies meurtrières et rameaux bourgeonnants. Masculinité et féminité en terre Huaorani (Amazonie équatorienne)." In *Une maison sans fille est une maison morte. La personne et le genre en sociétés matrilinéaires et/ou uxorilocales* (ed.) Claude-Nicole Mathieu, 125–54. Paris: Ed. de la Maison des Sciences de l'Homme (2007).
- For Chapter 8: parts in: Marginality with a Difference: "How the Huaorani Remain Autonomous, Preserve their Sharing Relations and Naturalize Outside Economic powers." In *Hunters and Gatherers in the Modern World: Conflict, Resistance and Self-determination*, edited by Peter Schweitzer, Megan Biesele, and Robert K. Hitchcock, 244–60. New York: Berghahn Books (2000).

I owe special thanks to Allyson Carter, Editor-in-Chief at the University of Arizona Press for her enthusiasm about my book project, to Jerryll Moreno for her excellent job as copyeditor, and to Michael Athanson for his beautiful maps.

My deepest thanks, finally, go to Martin and Léa, without whose love and companionship I could not have written this book.

HUAORANI TRANSFORMATIONS IN TWENTY-FIRST-CENTURY ECUADOR

INTRODUCTION

NECKLACES IN THE RAIN FOREST

OVER THE YEARS, we have traveled together quite extensively, Omari and me, in the Ecuadorian Amazon, to Quito, or even Brazil. This is how we became friends, sharing stories while waiting for a boat or a bus, or lying in a hammock when the darkness of the night has already settled around us, but when it is still too early to go to sleep. An accomplished jewel maker, Omari has often mentioned the Taromenani necklaces to me with awe and admiration.[1] Like all Huaorani girls, she learned with older female kin from an early age the art of twisting the palm fiber thread and of knotting it into all the items that make up the material culture repertoire of her people.[2] When she moved *a fuera* (outside the ethnic territory) to work in an internationally funded ethnobotanic project in the town of Puyo, she continued to knot the palm fiber thread. By then, she had learned new patterns and designs, which she incorporated in the necklaces and bracelets she was making for herself and her *cohuori* ("cannibal other," enemy, or simply non-Huaorani) friends or to sell to tourists. Being one of the most enthusiastic participants in various conservation and biocultural diversity programs promoting indigenous handicrafts in Ecuador in the 1990s and in the 2000s, she has received additional training, and over time her artistic talents have deepened.[3] I have vivid memories of a week we spent once in Manaus. There was no stopping Omari from returning to the Museu do Indio or to the market, where I had to photograph everything that interested her and that we could not afford to buy. It is perhaps not surprising, then, that when Omari speaks about the Taromenani (and they have been on her mind often in the last few years), their extraordinary necklaces inevitably come up in the conversation.[4]

I doubted for many years, I must confess, the objective existence of the men, women, and children known as Taromenani. I knew that the Tagaeri really existed; Tagae was the brother or classificatory brother of several of the villagers who had welcomed me in Dayuno in the late 1980s, and in QuehueireOno in the early 1990s. Their versions of oral history were unanimous on the split that took place between Tagae and his brothers shortly before the Summer Institute of Linguistics (SIL) missionaries incited the latter to move to their mission base (Tihueno). Those who became known as the Tagaeri had resolved that they would not surrender, but continue to fight for a vital space away from all external influences. The Tagaeri were *pïï*, or "bravos," as I was often told. Tales of the Taromenani, by contrast, seemed to indicate that they belonged to the vast constellation of ghostly and dangerous beings that people the cosmic forest. Despite all my ethnological attentiveness, I found myself listening to these exaggerated tales as any Westerner would: as phantasmagorical. For example, one summer in Damointaro, a man whose wife was related to Tagae told me that Taromenani meant "unknown and invisible," that is, "coming from the other side," or "living exclusively in the high forest." He then added that the Taromenani's way of killing is different from the Tagaeri's. "They start by pinching the heart, then go all the way to the extremity of one hand, then all the way back to the heart, and from the heart, all the way down to the final section of the foot." Rereading this hermetic statement today, I am able to imagine the electrifying presence the Taromenani have had in the Huaorani world; whereas in the past I could not even imagine that Omatoque, who had been forced to spend a week or so with the Babeiri in Tigüino, was a Taromenani.[5] My blind incredulity was essentially due to the extraordinary features with which my companions endowed the beings they called Taromenani. The more flowery the descriptions of the Taromenani's appearance were the greater my conviction that these imaginary beings could not possibly be real or be contemporary human inhabitants of the forest (their size—at least four meters high, the color of their skin—whiter than mine, their ability to fly from one tree to the next, and many other extraordinary characteristics). Then there were the violent deaths of Huaorani and Taromenani in March and April 2013, followed by weeks of intense public debate in Ecuador. Who could still doubt the Taromenani's existence? I reread my field notes once again, trying to find elements that would help me understand the status of these strange forest dwellers, at once so imaginary and so real, so very human (in the Western acceptation of the word), but unlike true human beings (in the Huaorani vision of humanity). The Taromenani had lived a parallel existence at the interstices between various regimes of truth, interstices that the geographic inconsistencies of the Zona Intangible Tagaeri Taromenane had rendered more complex and more perilous.

I arrived in Coca (Francisco de Orellana) two weeks after the murder of Ompure and Bogueney (two Huaorani elders) at the hands of Taromenani warriors. A short video recording Bogueney's cries for help and showing from different angles Ompure's head and torso pierced with long spears had been sent to me by e-mail two days after the attack had taken place. The video, now accessible on YouTube, had been shot on a mobile phone by one of their grandsons. I wept at my desk, at a loss, while listening to the general commotion and digitalized shouts. Omari had traveled to the village where Ompure's and Bogueney's siblings and children lived, urging the men not to take revenge.[6] However, as I heard at a workshop organized by the women's association, Asociación de Mujeres Waorani del Ecuador ([AMWAE] Women's Association of Ecuador), retaliation against the Taromenani had already been planned. We sat in groups, all quietly learning to master new macramé stitches and knots, as well as new designs for a range of "traditional" palm fiber products. The AMWAE had received a large order from Muji, a global Japanese brand, as a drawing of three small hanging baskets with their lids at the center of the main table certified. The description under the drawing read, "Set of hanging baskets for the kitchen. Technique: woven *chambira* palm fiber. Color: natural. Prototype: number one, Muji, Japan. Date: March 26, 2013."[7] While I was applying myself to stitching palm fiber into a thin bracelet, I overheard women related to Bogueney and to Ompure. Some had received phone calls about the departing expedition, and others were commenting on text messages sent to their mobile phones. The Ecuadorian woman who was teaching macramé had also been informed about the imminent attack. With a pounding heart and the mind full of racing thoughts, I was struggling to make sense of the situation, including my powerlessness. No one, not even Omari, had been able to prevent the massacre from taking place. Whose will was being exercised? Whose interests were being served?

My thoughts wandered about. In the heart of the Yasuní National Park, some of the extraordinarily beautiful necklaces that Omari had described to me

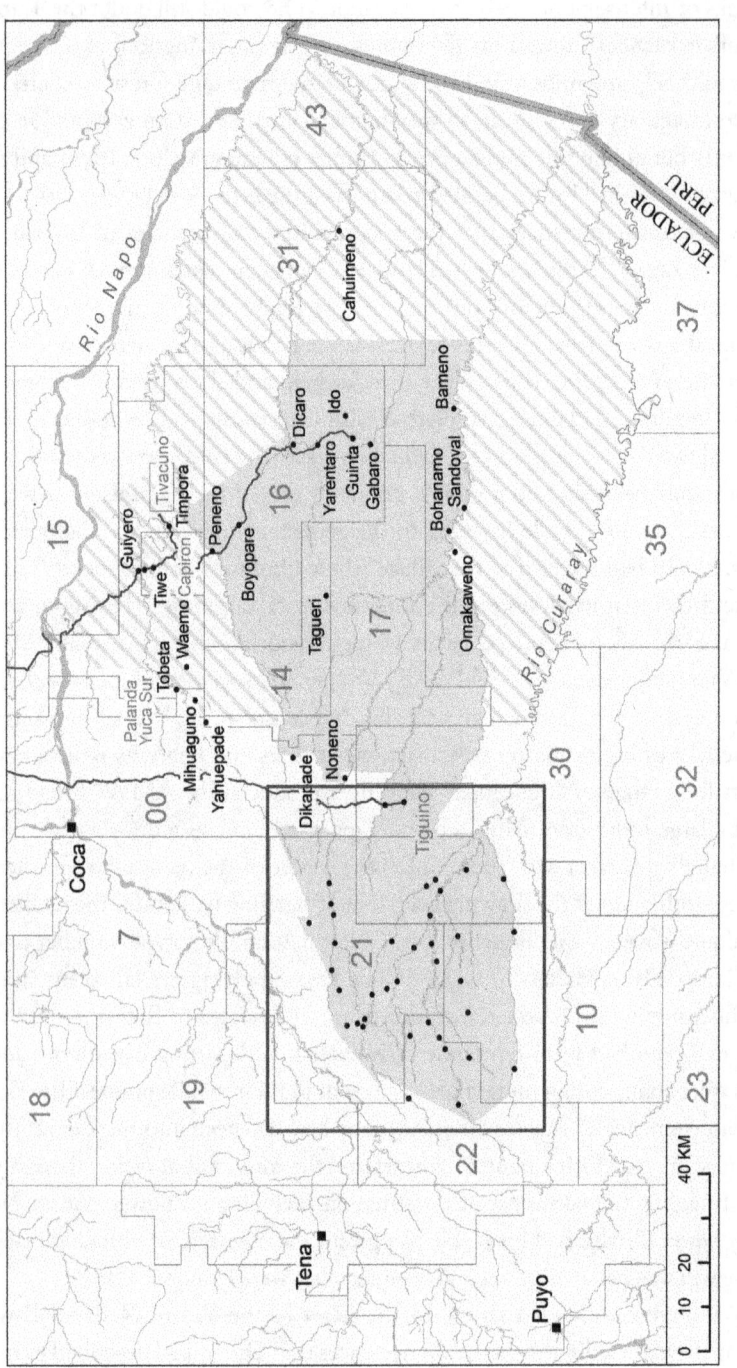

MAP 1A. Huaorani territory within Ecuadorian Amazon, by Michael Athanson.

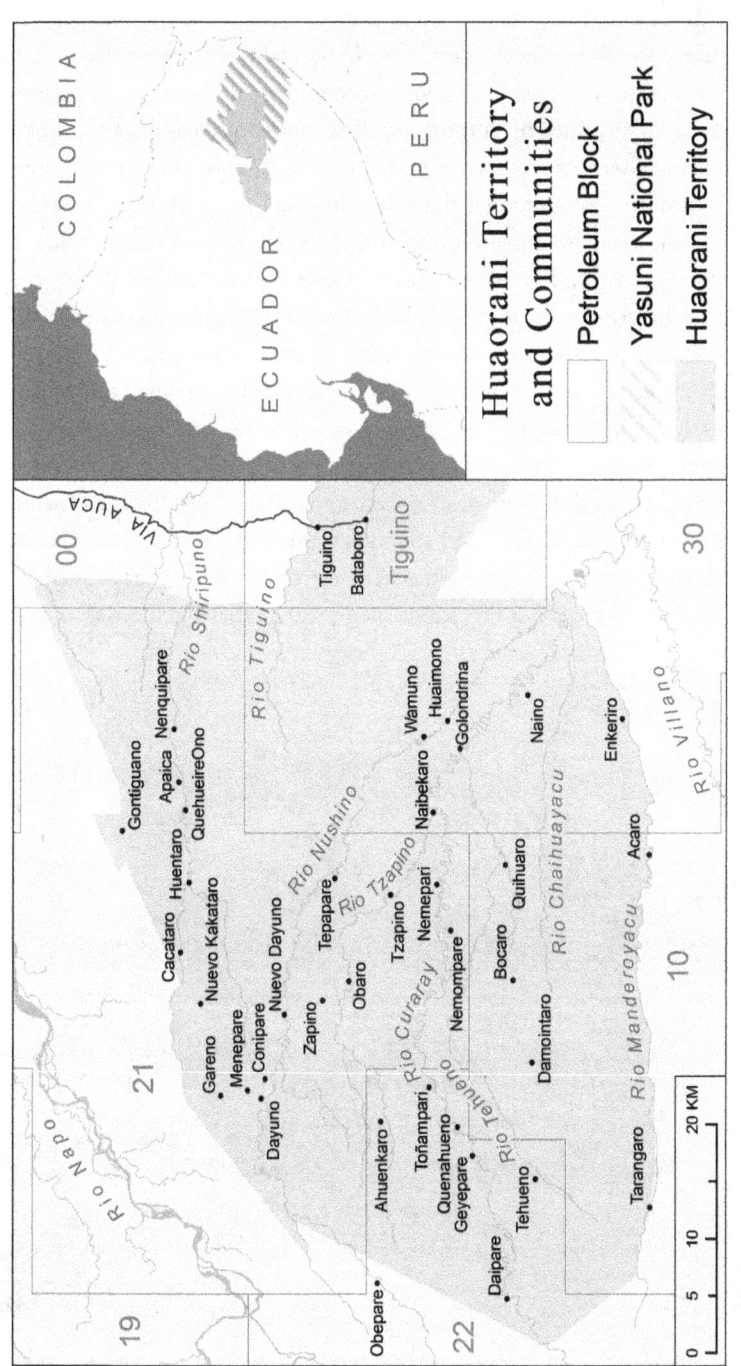

MAP 1B. Huaorani communities within the old protectorate, by Michael Athanson.

so many times were being made with bits of wire, bottle caps, plastic bags, and other refuse encountered in the rainforest. Omari admired the regularity of the "beads," so carefully carved from plastic-coated electric wire and arranged in multiple strings all joined up at the nape of the neck with palm fiber. The beads came in many alternating colors, but what she admired the most was the free-floating nylon threads added on the side, where animal teeth were inserted in between bottle caps. How many Taromenani women were occupied at this task right at this instant, and not very far from where we were seated? What struck Omari was the use the Taromenani made of leftovers from industrial activities and the value they seemed to grant to waste materials encountered in the forest. It had never occurred to me to ask Omari whether she owned one of these necklaces, but I suddenly felt the burning desire to see one, rather than simply trying to imagine it from her descriptions. Perhaps it is because I wondered whether the Taromenani women who were about to be killed by the Huaorani warriors wore such necklaces that I so much wanted to hold one in my hands.

Conversing with the macramé teacher over the course of the workshop, I got to know more about her life, and came to realize that she too was an artist.

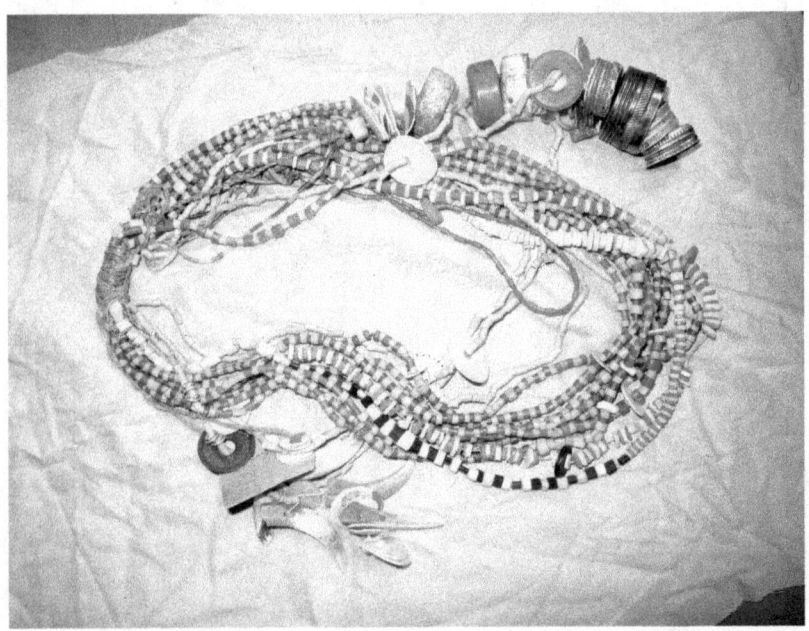

FIGURE 1. A Taromenani necklace, from a raided longhouse, 2003.

FIGURE 2. A well-known leader on a museum visit in Manaus, Brazil, June 2010.

FIGURE 3. Women singing at a meeting, April 2013. Photo by Romelia Papue.

FIGURE 4. A teacher watching on his tablet pictures of a massacre taken on a smart phone and sent to him by e-mail, April 2013.

She showed me some of the amazing objects she makes with recycled plastic bottles (bags, picture frames, jewelry, and more). She also showed me pictures of the arrangements she makes for weddings, Christmas dinners, or birthday parties, all with recycled materials. To this day, I cherish and often wear the pair of dangling earrings made with small bits of brown and transparent plastic carved out of soft drink bottles that she gave me so generously. Like other new settlers in the Oriente (Ecuador's Amazon region), she had arrived here at a very young age from a distant province after working for years as a waitress. She had been married twice to violent men before meeting her current husband, a retired oil engineer. They lived in Shushufindi, halfway between Coca and Lago Agrio, where the wells are over forty years old, and the oil is dwindling. She told me she loved the Yasuní. Her dream was to buy some land, reforest it, study tourism and conservation, and open an ecotourist resort.

When I finally caught up with Omari a couple of weeks later, we were both extremely sad; the Taromenani deaths had been officially confirmed, as well as the capture of two little girls (Rival 2015).[8] I asked Omari whether I could see the Taromenani necklaces she had in her possession. She invited me to her flat. The sitting room, filled with the crowns, bags, belts, and more objects she had made looked like a museum, or a handicraft shop. Delicately, she took out of a large box containing a necklace that she had received from her *maapo* (father's brother) ten years earlier. While putting the necklace around her neck, she told me she had cut her hair in mourning after the 2003 killing. I noticed that her hair had been cut again recently. I cannot really describe the emotions I felt on that day, or during that trip for that matter. The ironies of the collisions I have just described, collisions between forms of life, forms of being, and forms of death, were just too overwhelming. It is at that time that I decided to prepare this new collection of essays. I had spent too many years thinking about Omari's culture and society as if these could be decoded or encoded as logical adaptations or predictable practices. Yet, the oil frontier is more than a series of arguable policies, and the men and women that have made it what it is have made it into more than a collection of quantifiable facts. The essays, I decided, would not be aimed at presenting a new clever twist on Amazonian ontologies or a new theory of sociality or morality. Rather, they would clarify past generalizations, make recent ethnographic data available, and hopefully, inspire a new generation of Amazonianists, as well as young Huaorani researchers.

A NEW COLLECTION OF ESSAYS

In nine chapters grouped in three parts, these collected essays explore the Huaorani's unique way of relating to humans, to nonhumans, and to the forest landscape. Each part is introduced by an overview, which summarizes the main points in each chapter while showing the connections between them. "Among Forest Beings," the first part, offers a broad theoretical discussion of landscape domestication from a historical ecology perspective. Chapters 1, 2, and 3 look at how the Huaorani have trekked across vast stretches of the Amazon Basin in past and contemporary times with a set of broad questions: how does human action shape nature? How does nature shape human action? How does environmental change relate to the historical development of human societies? To provide some answers to these questions, I treat ecology and culture as interdependent variables and the rain forest as the biophysical manifestation of a long history of human and environmental interactions. For historical ecologists, if the natural environment conditions cultural creativity, it is also true that cultural creativity sets new environmental possibilities. Chapter 1 presents historical ecology as I have approached it in making sense of indigenous mobility. I argue that Northwest Amazon trekkers, who are not easily classifiable as devolved agriculturalists, may have had a historical trajectory different from that of the Tupi-Guarani. In an effort to grasp the particularities of Huaorani trekking, I put forward the thesis that nomadism and a hunting and gathering way of life need not be postcolonial phenomena. This leads me to conclude that mobility and the social forms it engenders are best envisaged as part of the historical development of distinct modes of life. Chapter 2 examines some of the peculiarities of the Huaorani plant naming system. I argue that Huaorani people value ecological relations over taxonomic ones. It follows that if the ability to recognize an order that exists in nature depends on embodied ecological knowledge, it may also be induced by aesthetic preferences. I propose that we need to rethink the thesis according to which the more a population intervenes in the reproduction of plants, the more its ethnobotanical inventory will expand for both wild and domesticated plants, as well as for plants and animals. I conclude with general remarks on the great fluidity found in Amazonia between horticulture and foraging and point out that historical ecology broadens and enriches both archaeological and anthropological studies of indigenous historicities. Chapter 3 engages the work of William Balée on the history of human occupation of the Amazon Basin at a more theoretical level to show that if there are continuing tensions between competing approaches within Amazonianist anthropology, Balée's work has left a legacy on which new, nondualist agendas can now develop.

The second part, "In the Longhouse," focuses on the intimate relations through which human persons are created and kinship relations enacted. Family and gender relations unfold within the primary unit of Huaorani society, the longhouse, which, it goes without saying, in no way means that forest beings are reduced to mere background scenery. The three chapters contained in Part II address core issues in Amazonianist anthropology (such as the nature of sociability, violence, death, sexuality and humanity, differences based on gender, and marriage and residence patterns) by looking at them in the light of wider anthropological debates about the sharing ethos and social values of hunter-gatherers. Chapter 4 discusses birth as a process of creation through which new human beings come to life, and new social relationships are forged. I pay particular attention to men's participation in the birth of their children and discuss the ritual prohibitions that accompany birth. This leads me to examine a number of theories concerning partible paternity in Amazonia, as well as the detachability and unconfinability of the soul. In Chapter 5, which explores further Huaorani personhood, I focus on the particular style of sociability that characterizes longhouses and discuss the fact that people who coreside under the same roof are understood to be sharing the same substance. As I illustrate, this conceptualization relates to particular understandings of happiness and sexual pleasure. In Chapter 6, coparenthood and the institutionalized complementarity existing between men and women is discussed further. I show that when some cosmological aspects are taken into consideration, the perfect symmetry between husband and wife, which mirrors the balanced reciprocity of brother-sister marriage exchanges, and more generally, the ideal equivalence of female and male, does in fact deviate into asymmetry. I then show that the rules regulating postmarital residence play a central role in structuring gender relations.

"In the Midst of Enemies," the third part, builds on the insights derived from Part II to examine further the insider/outsider dialectics in the light of contemporary cultural constructions of predation and enmity. The three chapters in Part III attempt to make sense of Huaorani life projects (Blaser 2004) by bringing together the political and economic concerns of hunter-gatherer studies with a prime interest in cultural meanings found in much Amazonianist anthropology, especially since the popularization of the perspectivist paradigm (Viveiros de Castro 1998). Chapter 7 engages the theorizations of Amazonian societies put forward by Joanna Overing, Peter Gow, and Eduardo Viveiros de Castro, among others, to argue that the social philosophies discussed by these authors correspond exactly to what the Huaorani imagine their enemy to be: societies of predators that depend on alterity and its successful incorporation to reproduce themselves. The Huaorani, by contrast, imagine themselves to be prey on the run. They constantly move to escape their enemy's cannibalistic forays. Freedom of movement, however, is not constructed as a retreat. Instead of choosing to stress their symbolic and material dependence on enemies and predators, people prefer to live in relative isolation, consuming the forest's bountiful resources, which they see as resulting from past human activity, as Chapter 7 illustrates. Chapter 8 discusses Huaorani encounters with the oil industry diachronically. It focuses in particular on the agreement signed by the ethnic association Organización Huaorani de la Amazonía Ecuatoriana ([ONHAE] Huaorani Organization of the Ecuadorian Amazon) with a Texas-based oil company, Maxus Energy Corporation. This legal document, which has bounded companies operating in Block 16 to provide education, health, and community development assistance to the Huaorani nation from 1992 onward, has shaped community dealings with both the private sector and the state ever since. The chapter, while providing evidence of the ambivalent, if not complacent, attitude of many villages toward oil companies, discusses as well a number of contemporary strategies aimed at preserving a certain degree of control and autonomy. Chapter 9 draws on recent work with Huaorani leaders involved in the design of policies to protect the rights of Huaorani groups living in voluntary isolation. Rich ethnographic vignettes are used in a somewhat exploratory fashion. Issues relating to citizenship, political change, and social transformation, as well as clashes between various regimes of indigeneity, are discussed at length.

DEBATING ANTHROPOLOGY FROM A HUAORANI PERSPECTIVE

The chief aim of *Trekking Through History* (Rival 2002), which insisted on the Huaorani relegation of horticulture to the ambiguous realm of feasting with the enemy, was to renew the anthropological understanding of agricultural regression in lowland South America. Ever since the publication of the monograph, I have contended that a culturally sensitive approach to the indigenous societies of the Upper Amazon requires a critical engagement with both environmental and historical determinisms. Let me summarize the main features of Huaorani society when examined in the ethnographic present before I take up the themes of "sharing economy" and "giving environment."

HUAORANI FOREST SOCIETY

Huaorani forest society is characterized by the fact that men, women, and children spend a great deal of time slowly exploring the ever-evolving network of paths that becomes their land as they "walk the forest" (*ömere gomonipa*), observing with pleasure and interest animal movements and the progress of fruit maturation or vegetation growth. With a subsistence economy that depends chiefly on hunting and gathering and restricts the use of cultivated products to festive and ceremonial occasions, the Huaorani have developed a unique way of knowing nature and of understanding the ecosystem of which they are a part. Huaorani relational epistemology, rooted in the recognition of the shared physicality and biological unity of beings that grow, mature, and decay, connects persons across species' boundaries—including the supernatural entities that control the release of game and those that prey on humans. The life force or vital energy that causes plants and other organisms to be born, to grow, and to mature is central to Huaorani social life and knowledge of the world. Vigorous growth irradiates the lived world with its aesthetic qualities to the point of saturation. What no longer grows, decays. The power to (re)generate vitality is associated with spontaneous plant growth. Processes of maturation and growth are key biological phenomena through which the socionatural world is ordered. Reproduction and continuity do not depend on the acquisition of, nor can they be appropriated by, external political or religious powers. The forest's natural bounty is understood to result from the interlocking of animal, plant, and human life cycles. The world gets made as it is through ongoing interactions between people and other forms of life. It is the relationship between living people, the forest, and past generations that makes forest resources bountiful. The longhouse sharing economy links present and past generations with the forest islands where people have dwelled, married, and died.

Trekking in the forest, thus, is like walking through a living history book in which natural history and human history seamlessly merge. People actively participate in the patterning of species distribution through ongoing living, foraging activities, and residential mobility. The forest, far from being a pristine environment external to society, exists as the product of the productive and consumptive activities of past peoples. Forest and society are regenerated through the business of ordinary life without need for accumulation, surplus, stealing, or the transfer of life energy from one sphere to another. As the dead ask nothing from the living, the relation between past and present people is not founded on the kind of exchanges that take place in societies where forebears are remembered, honored, or feared. What the dead "give" to the living is not strictly speaking a gift but, rather, a by-product of their own past living, that is, of the times they spent giving to and receiving from each other. While the fruit of slow-growing palms are used to celebrate endogamous alliances, diplomatic feasts with the enemy require large quantities of drinks made with fast-growing, short-lived crops. Game animals are kept in plentiful supply through thoughtful management and shamanic practices. Great men whose daughters attract sons-in-law and whose sons marry virilocally partake in the uncertain power of giant canopy trees. Old women who died alone in abandoned longhouses become the center of plant regrowth and social regeneration. It is through the lifecycles of their house groups and the death of their women that the Huaorani reach into the enduring form of energy that uses itself over and over again to make life out of what dies. A child who learns how to walk, a youth who gets married, a man who kills, a dreamer who lets the jaguar in, an old woman who lets herself die, or a house-group that splits are all irreversibly changed in the process. Of those transformations, only those that are associated with developmental processes are talked about in terms of plant growth. Huaorani ideas about growth are best understood with reference to the cosmological matrix in which they work as a counterdiscourse. By anchoring their society within the forest ecosystem and its cycles of growth, decay, and regeneration, the Huaorani have found ways of countering the timeless transformational whirlpool that engulfs their predatory enemies. The "true humans" or "real people" (literal translation of Huaorani) live in close association with forest groves where they grow, reproduce, and die along with fruit-bearing trees, birds, monkeys, and other species, protected from the "othering" calls of powerful predatory forces. In consciously assuming the subjective identity of "prey at the center," the Huaorani see themselves as succeeding in the continuous battle against those who take rather than give.

As this summary indicates, I may have succeeded in undoing some of the most entrenched nature/society dualisms that prevent us from understanding fully Amazonian forest societies. Yet, I am still at pains to transcend sociocentric constructions of what these societies really are. My failure, perhaps, can only be overcome through embracing the biosemiotic approach espoused by Eduardo Kohn (2013). In any case, this summary will suffice to show that combining the insights of historical ecology with those emerging from a cultural understanding of hunting and gathering economies, as *Trekking Through History* did, although insufficient, still represents a progress on the devolution thesis. The fundamental argument of the monograph is that the Huaorani have historically chosen to exist as a highly mobile network of economically independent house groups filling interstitial gaps between larger, more sedentary, and more powerful societies. In accordance with their mobility and with their preference for evasion (contact with powerful neighbors being avoided on the ground of their being predatory), they have traditionally developed a forest economy based on sharing the products of hunting, gathering, and horticulture. These activities, however, are combined in a unique way. Hunting is restricted to very few animal species, and cultivation to only a handful of crops (whose economic importance, moreover, is primarily linked to ceremonial purposes), which gives a very large place to gathering activities. Moreover, the food so obtained is subjected to transfers and exchanges that seem akin to those discussed in the literature on hunting and gathering societies, which, therefore, I decided to engage particularly closely.

HUNTER-GATHERER SOCIETIES "DEMAND SHARE"

The study of hunter-gatherer societies gained momentum in the 1970s when the results of multidisciplinary research teams, such as Richard Lee's Kalahari Research Project (1963–76), began to be discussed comparatively. Awareness increased as to how much was to be learned from focused studies on hunting and gathering—or foraging—as a way of life about both human nature and world history. The realization that humans had lived on earth as hunter-gatherers for 99 percent of their history brought primatologists, biological anthropologists, archaeologists, and evolutionary psychologists to collaborate in the writing of new scientific narratives about the past of humankind. The realization that at least 30 percent of the world's population still lived as foragers when Europeans started building their overseas empires (Wolf 1982) led anthropologists bent on undoing the nineteenth-century evolutionary models the discipline had inherited to collaborate with historians and literary critics. Last, but not least, the living presence in the contemporary world of communities of hunter-gatherers on every continent renewed possibilities for cross-cultural comparisons and opened up new theoretical avenues. Of course, the validity of the concepts of hunter-gatherer or forager in the modern context was also questioned. Alan Barnard (2004, 2012), for instance, has argued that the concept of hunter-gatherer society, quintessentially connected with the rise of the European Enlightenment, is both rooted in Western dualism (nature versus culture) and predicated on an economistic theory of society. In any case, the ethnographic evidence marshaled in the lively debates that took place around definitional issues revealed the originality of modes of life that had so often been dismissed as archaic survivals or discounted as nonrepresentative adaptations to the sweeping changes brought by modernization. The purpose of these debates was to establish the following: (1) the degree to which foragers depend on wild resources; (2) the extent to which their subsistence economy lies outside the market economy; and (3) whether core traits shared by all hunter-gatherer societies can be identified.

Because lowland South America had been discounted as a region of true, contemporary hunter-gatherers (Lee and DeVore 1968), I looked at Huaorani society and culture through the lens offered by modern studies of hunter-gatherer societies; I was determined to contribute to issues of definitions and comparability issues. My aim was also to show the relevance of recent historical ecology research on the anthropogenic nature of large tracks of the Amazon forest. These findings, as I make plain in Part I, were critical in my view to research on native Amazonians' cosmologies. I thus hoped to reach an understanding of Huaorani worldview and ethos that seemed closer to the native point of view than I would have reached had I relied exclusively on theories and analyses commonly used at the time in Amazonianist anthropology. For instance, I was able to shed light on the seemingly contradictory strategies of resistance and accommodation in the advent of petroleum development in their territory by looking at Huaorani culture in terms of a foraging ethos, or so it seemed to me at the time (see Chapter 8). Moreover, *pace* Bessire (2014) or Gordillo (2014), I am still convinced that this lens opens new doors onto indigenous understandings of the processes by which Amerindian foragers transform themselves into "civilized people."

In line with modern studies of hunting and gathering societies, I pointed out that a subsistence economy cannot be neatly determined on the basis of whether domesticated plants and animals are present and used in a given environment. Philippe Descola (1986) had already established that the domestication of animal species was technically possible in Amazonia. Native Amazonians could have chosen, like Melanesians, to domesticate wild boars (peccaries). They had instead preferred to remain pure hunters, who bring the young of some of their prey back to their homes to raise them as children. Carlos Fausto (2007), who has developed and generalized this insight, speaks of "familiarization," a form of sociability widely found throughout indigenous Amazonia. The fact that native Amazonians hunt rather than raise animals for food should, therefore, be understood primarily as a cultural choice, and not as a type of adaptation to a limiting environment. Applying the same argumentative logic to cultivation systems, Descola also contended that indigenous plant domestication and horticulture are best understood as resulting from aesthetic choices, rather than environmental constraints or historical accidents. Achuar gardening and agroforestry practices, for example, create a living landscape; they operate a "transfiguration" of the rain forest, understood by the Achuar as the garden of their demiurge, Shakaim. In other words, garden and forest are two cultivated spaces; the difference between the two is that the former, cultivated by humans, reproduces on a smaller scale and in a simplified manner the values and the properties of the latter.

Insights from the study of hunting-gathering societies (in particular, the reconceptualization of a host of terms, such as demography, material base, self-sufficiency, autonomy, egalitarian politics, sharing economy, social organization, ethos, ideology, and so forth) combined with Descola's insights on the sophisticated nature of indigenous worldviews would allow me, I thought at the time, to analyze with emic empathy the way of life of indigenous groups who, like the Huaorani, crucially depend on wild resources. Whereas Descola was bent on demonstrating that no part of the Amazon Basin is symbolically pristine (wilderness being a concept entirely alien to Achuar and to other native Amazonians, who imagine the forest as already domesticated), my interest lay, rather, in understanding what makes the Huaorani unique and different from their indigenous neighbors. Moreover, and although the notion of "natural abundance" appears today somewhat naïve or superficial (see Chapter 7), it did help me and other researchers to make sense of the ways in which oil wealth and state revenues have been culturally perceived (see Chapter 8). Furthermore, combining the insights of historical ecology with those of modern studies of hunting and gathering societies continues to be the most powerful approach to account for the striking contrasts existing in the cultural orientation of rainforest cultivators and foragers (see Barker and Janowski [2011] for the Southeast Asian context).

The main difference, ultimately, between the Huaorani and their indigenous neighbors is that the Huaorani have absolutely no interest in subordinating themselves, hence their preference for sharing and their relatively higher mobility. This has become clearer to me now that younger scholars, inspired by my work, have examined the "prey at the center" perspectivist position in other native Amazonian societies (e.g., Bonilla 2007; Costa 2009; Walker 2013). The Huaorani's rebellious spirit is unmistakably visible today in various sensitive spots dotting the Yasuní National Park where groups with symmetrically opposed positions vis-à-vis infrastructural and oil development confront each other. As Part III of this book makes clear, such confrontations over the structure and the composition of a forest world deemed worth inhabiting emerge from a shared ethos of insubordination. The Huaorani have remained fierce *demand sharers*, who force their leaders to give away the spoils of the project economy and spend every penny they lay hands on to the despair of international development advisers but to the delight of local traders. It is because power is embedded in relational matrices through which perspectives may shift, that the Huaorani continue to articulate their identity around the subject position of "prey" in their dealings with a hostile world. Trekking, which corresponds to a search for lands left unoccupied or abandoned, is neither a retreat nor an escape but an active form of looking for the traces of past human lives. I am thus struck by the number of studies to have appeared in recent years that present the rubber boom as an overwhelming, irresistible frontier. Old and new forms of hierarchy and of symbolic and physical violence are embraced as inevitable—if not welcomed—expressions of what makes humans human, that is, asymmetrical dependency. Such reasoning is not only extended back in history (e.g., Santos-Granero 2009), but also used to imagine the pre-Columbian past (e.g., Heckenberger 2005). Only a history and sociology of anthropological ideas will allow us to comprehend fully how and why in a world dominated by globalism a field long marked by the anarchist political philosophy of Pierre Clastres has become bent on demonstrating that native Amazonians have had a talent not so much for not being governed (Scott 2009) but, instead, for soliciting servitude. I do not doubt for one second the usefulness of exploring the diversity of structures of conjuncture in the tribal zone. However, and as Chapter 8 illustrates, the weirdest sociocultural forms that exist at the confluence of industrial and tribal forays are more often than not the Euro-American ones.

Some of the most interesting anthropological debates about hunter-gatherer societies have concerned the links between mobility, absence of property, and the nature of sharing relations, which is why the concept of *immediate return* (Woodburn 1982) remains seminal. As Widlok (2013, 14) discusses so convincingly, sharing is not limited to a particular mode of subsistence, even if sharing practices continue to be prevalent among hunter-gatherers, and former hunter-gatherers who also pursue other subsistence activities. Sharing is always culturally instituted as a form of *demand sharing*; this is why it is qualitatively different from other forms of exchange and other types of transfer (Widlok 2013, 22, 28). I entirely agree with Widlok that the demands of sharing create entirely new articulations between value and action. As he rightly puts it, "through its particular framing of transfers, sharing may be said to pluralize (economic) value creation [while also singularizing] the (moral) values involved" (Widlok 2013, 26). There is much about Huaorani sharing that one could describe more accurately using Widlok's fine analytical grid, including new situations that arise out of the uncertain service economy in which so many Huaorani men and women find themselves working today. There is much that an anthropology of value cognizant of the specificities of sharing can bring to Amazonianist anthropology. Not only may it renew discussions of productivity, work, materialism, compensation, and solidarity, but it also promises to facilitate the rethinking of relationships among economy, ecology, and the morality of exchange. In short, there is much scope for considering the Amerindianization of modes of sharing (Rival and Whitehead 2001).[9]

HUAORANI LANGUAGE

Catherine Peeke from the SIL correctly established that the Huaorani language is an isolate that had wrongly been classed in the Urarina family, or treated as a Zaparoan language. Thanks to her studies, we know that it is not attached to any known phylum, and bears no relation to the Aushiri language. It is, however, close to the Ssabela language, which might be extinct. There were significant dialectal differences between the Huaorani groups living along the Tivacuno, Shiripuno, and Tiputini rivers, dialectal differences that have persisted to this day, although perhaps attenuated through intermarriage, mixing, mobility, and above all, wide exposure to Spanish (Kelley 1988; Peeke 1973). Older native speakers say that their language has changed dramatically over the last fifty years or so, and I have myself witnessed a great deal of change and variation in the last twenty years. Catherine Peeke told me several times that familiarity with Spanish has affected the tonal qualities of spoken Huaorani. Phonologically, there is a radical attenuation of nasalization, and syntactically, a direct influence of Spanish. Huaorani people say they can communicate with the Taromenani and the Tagaeri, although these groups in voluntary isolation speak too fast to be fully comprehensible. Variation in the naming of common plants, animals, and objects is also mentioned. I have detected amazing language games among Huaorani speakers when they, for example, inverse word phonemes. These games may be intended to create confusion and to secure a kind of ad hoc linguistic autarchy, or simply as a source of entertainment. Huaorani linguistic dynamism and the ways in which it is perceived and interpreted by a number of actors (native speakers, school teachers, in-marrying non-Huaorani who have learned the language, and other actors) is a truly fascinating subject, which deserves to be thoroughly studied.

In addition to the generalization of bilingualism, efforts by a number of actors to standardize the language and create a written system have also added to the speed of linguistic modern change. Huaorani teachers and education specialists have talked for years about "finishing the dictionary," and "finally agreeing on a single spelling system" but to no avail. Bilingual education texts are continuously being revised. A teacher told me recently, "Do not waste time reading these 2005 textbooks. The translation is old. It's all wrong. We are redoing it. The new textbooks will not be ready for another two or three years at least." The difficulty of standardizing the language is, of course, compounded by dialectical differences. In fact, the Huaorani constitute the largest monolingual indigenous group in Ecuador. I have often wondered whether such fierce monolingualism, beyond an obvious pride in maintaining one's mother tongue, is not also a manifestation of isolationism or, at least, a form of political mastery. If most Huaorani would rather learn English than Spanish as a second language, they are more often than not reluctant to share linguistic and mythical knowledge with outsiders. Whereas they revel in finding clever expressions to translate foreign concepts and ideas into Huaorani, they are much more reserved—or impatient—when it comes to conveying native metaphysics across linguistic boundaries.

A number of spelling systems have been developed over the last fifty years. Some use a North American English alphabet (e.g., Waorani), others a Spanish alphabet (e.g., Huaorani), and others internationally agreed upon phonemic transcriptions (e.g., waodädi). In the 1990s, linguists from SIL and linguists working for the Dirreción Nacional de Educación Indígena Intercultural y Bilingüe ([DINEIIB] National Directorate of Bilingual Intercultural Indigenous Education) in the Ministry for Education established a standard orthography for Huaorani spelling consisting of ten vowels (a, e, ae, i, and o, and their nasalized equivalents, ä, ë, äë, ï, and ö), and twelve consonants (b, c, d, g, m, n, ñ, p, qu, t, w, and y). Recently, [qu] was changed to [k]. Whereas earlier alphabets tended to use a phonemic translation system (e.g., bädöbaï), more recent ones have adopted a phonetic system (e.g., manomain), which is simpler and clearer given that vowel nasalization is phonemic in Huaorani, but consonant nasalization is not.

When I started my doctoral fieldwork, only a handful of individuals—mainly men—could speak some Spanish, and if there are today about twenty-five young graduates with a Master's in Education, the population is still largely monolingual. In the years 1989–90 I worked mainly with informants trained by the Catholic University of Quito in partnership with the Capuchin Mission and with schooled children, who had learned to read and write in Spanish. I have spelled Huaorani words as my informants wrote them down. When more than one spelling was used for a word (this is a common occurrence, even for a same individual), I selected the most common spelling. For example, *cohuori*, "cannibal other," "enemy," or simply "non-huaorani" was also often spelled co-wode, kowori, or kowodi. During my doctoral fieldwork, the common way of spelling Huaorani was *Huaorani*; today, people tend to use *Waorani* or *Waodani*. The spelling used by Huaorani literates is highly variable and often inconsistent. *Huao terero*, or "language," is often spelled *wao tededo*, as well as any combination of [hu] or [w] with [r] or [d]. The same occurs with the sound [k], often spelled [c] in front of [o], [a], or [u], or [qu] in front of [e]. As for the short [e], it is often spelled [i]. A literate native speaker may decide to spell Taromenani as *Tadomenane*, or *Tadomenani*, or *Taromenane*. This spelling inconsistency applies to named villages as well. For instance, Toñampari may be spelled *Toñäpade* by individuals familiarized with the early phonemic system used by SIL missionaries. Given that there is no agreed upon spelling system, I have decided to continue to use the Spanish spelling system that was used by the DINEIIB at the time of my doctoral fieldwork.[10] I have on the whole used random Huaorani names and surnames to refer to men and women whose conversations I directly quote in the text. A study of Huaorani onomastics is overdue. Huaorani proper names often derive from the names of plants, flowers, fruits, animals, or other natural elements, but I opted to keep these in the original language rather than to offer capitalized translations.

WRITING ANTHROPOLOGICALLY ABOUT THE HUAORANI PEOPLE

As all academic disciplines with the intellectual mission of deepening our knowledge of social processes and cultural differences, anthropology has been a vast, ongoing experiment. Empirical facts have been continuously confronted with concepts, whose origin and development have too often been cast in the mold of their Western origins. Since its inception, however, anthropology's mission has always been to engage radically and critically with its evolutionary roots. Every anthropological text may thus be read as a new critical engagement with the discipline's history, as well as with analyses arising from other social sciences. What the essays presented in this book capture of Huaorani life can only be assessed in terms of their overall consistency and in relation with the findings of other ethnographers. Rereading some of my published work today in the light of more recent visits to Huaorani communities, I am struck by a somewhat naïve desire to identify core, essential, and timeless properties that crystalize stylistically into the "ethnographic present" (Sanjek 1991). There is also, at times, the rushed attempt at simplistic generalizations, even when one knows perfectly well that the social life of cultures is full of complexity and diversity of outcomes. Moreover, some theoretical constructions produce unwarranted generalizations, and this is certainly the case with early studies on hunting and gathering societies. Yet, as discussed in the previous section, I still think that the hunter-gatherer paradigm has opened up the ethnographic imagination. As anthropological knowledge cannot exist without generalization or comparison, the challenge is to come up with the right kind of anthropological question, as well as the right kind of generalization. Much has changed since my first prolonged stay in Huaorani land, but I have no doubt that people's collective will to orient and control the changes that are affecting them remains what the Huaorani life project is all about. There are many more aspects to this project than I am able to cover here. Moreover, and as always, such a project remains opened to interpretation, not least by the young Huaorani intellectuals who have begun to write about their own cultural traditions (Nenquimo 2011; Omene Ima 2012).

Despite current efforts to "globalize" anthropological knowledge, a project which, for a number of authors, involves engaging the sociology of cosmopolitanism (e.g., Kendall, Skribis, and Woodward 2009; Werbner 2008), as well as postcolonial studies (e.g., Mignolo and Tlostanova 2008), Latin American anthropological and sociological traditions have yet to be fully documented, especially in the context of the role played by "internal others" in the development of national and regional traditions (Peirano 2008). Amazonianist anthropology is unique in having involved a dialogue between Euro-American and Latin American scholarship from the start, especially in Brazil, Colombia, Peru, and Mexico (Rival 2010). In Ecuador, however, few anthropologists or sociologists have chosen the Amazon region as an area of specialization. With the exception of the work of Ecuadorian social and natural scientists who have focused on specific aspects of Huaorani culture and society, such as botany (Cerón and Montalvo 1998), health (Fuentes 1997), architecture (Izquierdo Peñafiel 2000), or community and oil company interactions (Narvaez 1996), often in the context of applied research relating to development or conservation projects, Huaorani studies have mainly involved Euro-American researchers.

I wish therefore now to turn to a rapid examination of some of the most representative publications I am aware of. My goal is not to be exhaustive, but to review works that illustrate the complexity and dynamism of the Huaorani life project while bringing insights and perspectives that complement, and sometimes challenge, my own analyses.[11] For ease of presentation, I have somewhat artificially grouped the works reviewed here under four headings: "Interethnic contacts"; "Ecology and conservation"; "State and oil development"; and "Mythology and oral traditions."

INTERETHNIC CONTACTS

The Huaorani are often described as "the most violent society on earth" (e.g., Robarchek and Robarchek 1998, vi), a society which, thanks to contact with evangelical missionaries, has learned to live at peace both within and with its neighbors. The Huaorani are also often talked about as the victims of ethnocide, whose society and culture have irremediably been lost to the oil development frontier (e.g., Kimerling 2013). Given the wide range of views expressed in the literature on the ills and benefits of contact, it is not surprising that many anthropological studies continue to focus on the nature of the changes and transformations that have taken place since the "true human beings" (*huaorani*) have stopped fearing as *cohuori* those they have come into contact with. A number of publications featuring the collaboration of Jim Yost, Stephen Beckerman, James Boster, and other researchers (Beckerman et al. 2009; Beckerman and Yost 2007; Boster, Yost, and Peeke 2004) have revisited the issues raised by the Robarcheks in their comparative analysis of Huaorani violent and semipeaceful ethos (Robarchek and Robarchek 1998). Based on the life histories of over one hundred elders of both sexes and on interviews with ninety-five warriors, these publications claim that the Huaorani have "the highest rate of homicide of any society known to anthropology" while offering a new explanation for such a dismal record. In contrast to Chagnon's findings for the Yanomamo, Beckerman and colleagues have found that "more aggressive warriors have lower indices of reproductive success than their milder brethren," a finding they relate to the greater spacing of revenge raids among the Huaorani. This has led them to conclude that the Yanomamo situation, in which "the more aggressive men had elevated indicators of individual fitness," applies neither to the Huaorani, nor to other warlike tribal societies. In another publication (Boster, Yost, and Peeke 2004) the research team has made use of evolutionary theories and cognitive analyses of religious beliefs to explain how contact with SIL missionaries has brought lasting peace to Huaorani society by committing its members to nonviolence. For these authors, the Huaorani, through their long history of inter- and intraethnic violence came to lack an effective means of stopping the cycles of revenge killing in their cultural repertoire. Adhering to Christian religious beliefs enabled them to develop emotions, which they could use to signal their commitment to social contracts.

Casey High's various contributions to the theme of Huaorani aggressive masculinity offers an important corrective to essentialized portrayals of male fitness and violent emotions (High 2006, 2009, 2012, 2015). Building on my earlier accounts of Huaorani moral values and self-identification as victims of cannibal predators, High sees violence as an aspect of social memory that can be deployed politically and used rhetorically in present-day situations. He argues that the "prey at the center" model reveals the indigenous appropriation of the biblical message of Christ's sacrifice and symbolically articulates the recent historical experience of real persecution by outsiders. The model is then politically instrumentalized as a tool to build peaceful communities through the prevention of further revenge killing. Looking more specifically at multiethnic festive public performances at which young male Huaorani act as "wild" Indians, a category that we are told evokes both their own ancestry and the wider cultural repertoire of potent savagery, High goes on to stress the importance of generational differences in cultural transmission and memory construction. Adults who have lived and experienced violence talk about it within family circles to impress on the young and the community at large the need to put an end to the cycles of revenge killing and to build a peaceful society. Young men, by contrast, use their parents' and grandparents' performed narratives to display their skills and identity as potential killers to affirm to the outside what has been suppressed as negative behavior within (High 2009). An analysis of young men's consumption of karate films leads the author to discuss the construction of manhood with reference to generational and intercultural relations, leading him to the conclusion that contemporary Huaorani men experience their masculinity through a multiplicity of role models that include not only their elders or ancestors, but also Ecuadorian nationals and even Bruce Lee (High 2010). Having pointed at the speed at which interethnic relations and urban migration have transformed Huaorani lives and possibilities, High stresses the emergence of new forms of interethnic male fraternity in urban areas, as well as of new generational differences. Young Huaorani men, we are led to conclude, remake themselves by drawing on indigenous notions of gendered agency, but in a social world saturated with global media imagery and intercultural relations, they are also increasingly influenced by broader Latin American constructions. In the same vein, Alvarez's (2009) ethnography of the funeral of an old warrior and powerful shaman vividly illustrates how new death rituals equally draw on concepts acquired from dominant society and on indigenous forms of self-representation.

Such ethnographic accounts illustrate the multiplicity of possibilities that peaceful contact has historically opened up for the children and grandchildren of the men and women with whom I did my doctoral fieldwork. They also give a broad hint as to the complex changes that have occurred between the late 1980s (when I first lived in a Huaorani community) and the early 2000s (when Casey High was in Toñampari), not to mention the current situation. Many young Huaorani couples today live more or less permanently along oil roads and in jungle towns. Authors that have stressed the historical importance of interethnic relations, particularly with lowland Quichuas (Cipoletti 2002; Reeve and High 2012), may be read as questioning my account of Huaorani isolationism as somewhat exaggerated. I would still contend, however, that historical transformations are far from representative of one single, homogenous passage from generalized warfare to uniform, peaceful, and globalized conviviality. The mounting tensions and sorcery accusations that divide interethnic villages (High 2015), on the one hand, and the violent clashes between Huaorani and Taromenani warriors (Rival 2015) on the other, are more than sufficient to evidence an unabated commitment to the values of nonmixing and autonomy.

ECOLOGY AND CONSERVATION

Understanding cultural diversity in the light of biological diversity has been a popular theme of research in the last fifteen years, especially with young Ecuadorians involved in the development of management plans for the Yasuní National Park. These have also included mitigation plans for groups in voluntary isolation (see in particular Rivas and Lara 2001; Rivas 2003, 2005, 2006, 2007a, 2007b, 2012). North American anthropologist Flora Lu pioneered this specialized contribution to Huaorani studies in her doctoral dissertation in 1999.[12] Conducted under the direction of Bruce Winterhalder, a renowned evolutionary ecologist, Flora Lu's work has investigated Huaorani behavioral ecology of resource use and common property management. Her theoretical framework, which combines a forager-prey population model with economic analyses of household budgeting, has allowed her to analyze shifts in rules governing communal management of property and resources, as well as increased participation in the market economy. By viewing change as simultaneous on an ecological, economic, and social plane, Lu stresses the interconnection of a number of factors and processes: demography, hunting and fishing patterns, time allocation, income sources, common property, dietary intake, and mobility (Lu 1999). Unfazed by the pessimist conclusions of her doctoral thesis (resource base depletion, ineffectiveness of the traditional property regimes, dependency on handouts from oil companies, and a cultural orientation that prevents the adoption of a pro-conservation property and management regime), Lu has continued to publish—and to inspire—work that not only offers empathic analyses of Huaorani responses to the destruction of their environment, but that also proposes policy solutions to the ongoing conundrum of development versus conservation.

Lu's findings about unsustainable hunting rates, especially of monkey species, have been discussed in relation to studies in other parts of the Huaorani ethnic territory (Franzen 2006; Franzen and Eaves 2007; Mena et al. 2000; Suárez et al. 2009; Suárez et al. 2012), as well as in relation to the hunting practices of other indigenous groups (e.g., Sirén 2012). Moreover, Lu (2010, 2013) has recently adopted a complex socioecological, systems resilience approach to revise the linear forager-prey model she had previously used in assessing the impact of hunting on the faunal prey populations of the Ecuadorian Amazon. Finally, in addition to broadening her human ecology interest in the ripple effect of entrance into the market economy on human welfare (Albán 2008; Houck et al. 2013; Lu 2007; Doughty, Lu, and Sorenson 2010; Lu, Bilsborrow, and Oña 2012), Lu has pursued her study of common property regimes (Doughty, Lu, and Sorenson 2010; Lu 2001; Lu Holt 2005; Lu and Wirth 2011). These studies have shown that conservation is a sociopolitical process that requires an understanding of the organization and government processes structuring resource use within and among communities. These studies have convinced me that the effective protection of the Yasuní will depend on the development of an endogenous form of environmental stewardship, in accordance with Huaorani ways of knowing the world, Huaorani values and practices, and, last but not least, Huaorani understanding of quality of life and its betterment.

Anthropological studies of biodiversity conservation projects involving Huaorani communities have multiplied in recent years with several doctoral projects on the way. I have revisited in a recent article (Rival 2014) some of the observations made in Chapter 2, and have raised a number of issues that concern the nature of indigenous knowledge and its relation to scientific knowledge practices. Papworth, Milner-Gulland, and Slocombe (2013) have contributed to this growing research topic with a study of contemporary Huaorani ways of categorizing primates. They have found out, somewhat unsurprisingly, that monkeys as a group (i.e., an order) are no more important than other groups of mammals and that cultural salience is best observed at the species level.[13] Kelly Escobar (2012), who has also worked in the vicinity of the Estación Científica Yasuní ([ECY] Yasuní Scientific Station), has just completed a doctoral dissertation using Latour's action network theory to analyze biodiversity research in terms of mediated constructions of the world's biophysical reality. Her rich ethnography of participatory environmental management offers a vivid portrayal of the tension between science, conservation, and development in the Yasuní Biosphere Reserve, as well as an insightful description of Huaorani engagements with competing knowledge systems. Finally, Gabriella Zurita (2014) has revisited "natural abundance" and other cultural perceptions of the forest. She has uncovered deeper dimensions of the Huaorani's ethos, historical ecology, and management of trees and cultivated landscapes, which I discuss in Chapters 3 and 7.

STATE AND OIL DEVELOPMENT

As discussed in Chapter 8, and as acknowledged by most researchers who have written on the Ecuadorian Amazon, large-scale oil extraction is by far the external pressure that has loomed largest on Huaorani lives (Kimerling 2012; Lu 2012; Narvaez 2007, 2009; Rivas 2005; Viteri 2008). Industrial activities linked to petroleum development have shaped the creation of both the Huaorani ethnic territory and the Yasuní National Park. To this day, oil continues to determine the evolution of the legal status of both to the point of rendering their future uncertain (Rival 2011; Rivas and Rommel Lara 2001). Given the legal and ethical issues raised by the economic intervention of large corporations in indigenous communities, many studies have taken up my initial analyses and given equal weight to social and cultural aspects when assessing the impacts the oil industry has had on the Huaorani people or their responses to these impacts (e.g., Alvarez 2005, 2012; Aviles 2008; Pappalardo, de Marchi, and Ferrarese 2013).

Particularly worthy of attention is Ziegler-Otero's (2004) ethnographic study of the ONHAE, the first Huaorani political organization created as a direct response to the growing threat posed by oil extraction.[14] In trying to identify the most effective way for indigenous peoples to organize in the face of capitalist penetration, the author stresses the specificities of petroleum development in Ecuador, in particular its economic rationality rooted in "a vast outlay of capital in the form of machinery and technology," economies of scale, and little need for unskilled labor (Ziegler-Otero 2004, 162). It would be easy, yet simplistic, to see in ONHAE no more than a puppet organization, whose sole purpose is to create an institutional framework for the implementation of development projects. True, ONHAE legitimizes the oil industry's extractive activities and promotes the projects agreed upon by oil companies and state agencies. However, Ziegler-Otero argues, ONHAE's positions, policies, and relationships with other political actors are "contingent, shifting, and flexible, in a manner analogous to the flexibility and pliancy of roles and positions within Huaorani society" (Ziegler-Otero 2004, 160). It is noteworthy that in the concluding chapter, the author seems to assimilate ONHAE's flexibility to the characteristics of Latin American new social movements and vanguardist left rather than to Huaorani social values per se.

Colleoni, whose doctoral thesis is in progress, agrees with Ziegler-Otero that indigenous politics are poorly explained in terms of manipulation, co-optation, or patronage. She then pushes Ziegler-Otero's argument further and interprets Huaorani political tactics in cultural terms. According to her analysis, which creatively builds on Fausto's (2008) theory of mastery, we should look at the political practices of Huaorani organizational leaders in terms of their cultural propensity to seek to control contact situations and to influence others. Colleoni thus interprets political leaders as morally equivalent to traditional shamans, warriors, and *ahuene* (feast owners/leaders). The role and mission of all these "great men," according to her, is to establish beneficial relations with outsiders so as to generate an abundance of wealth, which can then be gifted, shared out with kin, and widely redistributed to allies. Colleoni's analysis of the ONHAE–Maxus treaty thus emphasizes the indigenous valorization of the capacity to influence powerful forces.[15] According to her, Huaorani political leaders, who deploy a particular understanding of friends as both benevolent masters and potential prey, actively work at acquiring the skills needed to familiarize pets. In other words, whereas High puts the emphasis, as we saw earlier, on processes of cultural change and discontinuity with the past through intergenerational and intercultural processes of memory construction that lead to the prevalence of peacefulness in contemporary community building, Colleoni shows, on the contrary, that contemporary political practices are continuous with traditional fierceness and shamanic power. Taken together, these two separate ethnographic contributions illustrate the lasting importance of the split, bifocal nature of Huaorani malehood (see Chapters in Part II), as well as the dynamics of intra-ethnic diversity within wider regional cultural systems.

Whether, and how, Huaorani "binary ideology" (Maybury-Lewis 2009) will interact over time with other dualisms present on the oil frontier remains to be seen (see Chapter 9). Chapters 8 and 9 indirectly refer to the Yasuní Initiative and the intense debate caused by the modern alienation from nature through economics (Larrea 2011; Rival 2011). Whereas officials continue to present Ecuador's recent decision to extract oil from the Tambococha and Tiputini fields as a "win-win solution" combining the responsible exploitation of natural resources in a small section of the Yasuní Biosphere Reserve with the conservation of the rest (thanks to the revenues generated by petroleum development), hence avoiding any "trade-off," many experts and commentators have challenged the utilitarian logic that underlies the official vision of *both* biodiversity conservation and economic exploitation (e.g., Larrea 2011). Future studies will tell whether the Huaorani perceive oil extraction and biodiversity conservation as generated by the same cultural logic, a logic not only foreign to them (and thus amenable to the politics of mastery described above), but also deeply contrary to their life project or whether they see one as closer to their collective interests than the other. From the works reviewed in this section and the previous one, as well as some of the ethnographic discussions presented in Chapters 8 and 9, it seems that Huaorani communities have sought to confront oil extraction and biodiversity conservation as opposed, yet complementary, "civilizatory" (i.e., modernizing) projects, which they must equally embrace in their search for an ideal, timeless "bifurcated" social order (Maybury-Lewis 2009, 913).

MYTHOLOGY AND ORAL TRADITIONS

All that is currently published indicates that Amazonianist anthropology, having come of age, is now set to make a major contribution to contemporary anthropological theory (see Overview to Part II). In lowland South America, where historiographic records are rare and indigenous cosmologies impervious to linear time or progressive change, what is meant by history—ideological, ethnocentric, or otherwise—has been the topic of much discussion. Time is often conceptualized as a physical property of space; "timescapes," or memory landscapes, become indistinguishable from the cosmos of which they form a part. Like other native Amazonians, the Huaorani "are acutely aware of historical change, yet they insist on the timeless nature of their systems, while at the same time struggling hard to protect them from erosion" (Maybury-Lewis 2009, 911). Although I do not doubt that Huaorani people are continuously working at readjusting systems of ideas with social institutions (and vice versa), we lack a full picture of their mythology and, therefore, of the specificities of the articulations between the physical and the metaphysical dimensions of life to which they have chosen to give salience. Many of the works cited here, including mine, contain fragments of myths, exegeses of chants, pieces of poetic oratory, and snippets of ritual and shamanic discourse, but these are too sketchy to allow the depth of analysis reached for in, for instance, Quichua cultures (e.g., Kohn 2013; Uzendoski and Calapucha-Tapuy 2012). There are a number of reasons for such a state of affairs. As Huaorani language is an isolate, making semiological inferences within a linguistic family, as Viveiros de Castro (1992) does, for instance, is not possible. Although the study of Amazonian languages is more advanced today than it was twenty years ago, it is still hampered by a lack of funding and a paucity of specialized researchers. Moreover, and as mentioned earlier, there is still no dictionary, complete grammar, or, for that matter, agreed upon spelling for this beautiful and mysterious language.

However, two recent developments are noteworthy. They both involve the active participation of young Huaorani literates in documenting their cultural traditions. The first group of collaborative projects includes coauthored publications funded by governmental and nongovernmental organizations. *Tededanipa, Las Voces de la Mujeres* (2009) comprises a series of life histories and testimonies collected during participatory workshops by women's rights activist Ariadna Reyes Avila, who wrote the overall synthesis. The book, richly illustrated, is structured and presented as a collective self-study. It was funded by three Ecuadorian organizations: Corporación Humanas, AMWAE, and the Ministry of Culture. With its maps of Huaorani land and communities (drawn by the women themselves), cosmological maps, explanations for the origin of village names, photographs, drawings, and census data, *Tededanipa* offers fascinating insights in contemporary understandings of Huaorani history, myths, material culture, and values. *Tome Waorani Ponino. Nenki Wenga Itota tono Waorani Beye* (2011), written by Ima Fabian Nenquimo and beautifully illustrated by photographer Peter Oxford, was funded and published by the Ministry of the Environment. This book, the first ever written by a Huaorani, is exceptional. Moreover, it is the first time that the myth of origin is presented in written form in its entirety. Of course, this is one version among many of the cultural hero's saga, but it is fascinating to see the account laid out according to indigenous logic. Moreover, for once, Bameno villagers are photographed not as perennial savages, but as impersonators of mythical characters, thus offering new insights in Huaorani cosmology. Ima Fabian Nenquimo has since published another book, which tells the story of how the Tagaeri separated from his family and intermarried with the Taromenani, a theme that both fascinates the budding writer, and challenges his many talents. If it is hard enough for the native ethnographer to overcome hostile feelings under normal circumstances, the deaths of Ompure and Bogueney, and the ensuing tensions, have made interviewing key actors particularly difficult (Rival 2015).[16]

The originality of the second collaborative project, the Waorani Documentation Project (WDP), lies in its effort to provide a comprehensive documentation of the Huaorani language through the transcription and trilingual translation (Huaorani, English, and Spanish) of video recordings. The project includes a searchable electronic lexical database in the three languages, which, over time, will also act as a dictionary and a descriptive grammar. It is led by North American linguist Connie Dickinson, a specialist of Tsafiki linguistics (e.g., Dickinson 2002), in collaboration with Casey High, Ramón Uboye Gaba, and a number of other young Huaorani researchers of both sexes. The project is funded by the Hans Rausing Endangered Languages Project at the School of Oriental and African Studies, University of London, and hosted in Quito by Facultad Latino-Americana de Ciencias Sociales (Latin American Social Sciences Institute), Ecuador.[17] Key to the methodology used is the collection of video recordings of diverse discourse contexts, including storytelling, everyday conversations, and other speech events the young Huaorani researchers deem interesting to document in their home communities. Such a project would not be possible without technological innovation, in particular new, powerful open-source software, and versatile and affordable recording equipment. Fawcett (2012, 7) explains that:

> The WDP is of interest to various members of the Waorani community for different reasons. The elders seem to be interested in the project because it will aid in giving their language more cultural value and help in passing down ancestral

knowledge and language to the younger generations. Meanwhile, younger people seem to be interested because it gives them an opportunity to acquire technological skills (such as operating a computer, video camera, etc.), as well as learn more about their culture and past through the stories told by elders or a demonstration of how to make a hammock, for example.

No doubt, this collaborative project will help document mythology and shamanic beliefs more holistically (e.g., Wierucka 2012). One additional exciting prospect is that this collaborative tool will, over time, become a general digital repository to which other researchers will donate their own visual and audio recordings of Huaorani culture, in everyone's interest and for the benefit of all. As mentioned earlier, interesting and sometimes surprising linguistic variations exist, which can only be accounted for through careful comparative analysis. The research tools provided by the WDP will greatly facilitate such an endeavor. A two-way dialogue between indigenous and nonindigenous researchers, accompanied by the sustained and systematic comparison of native thought categories and social meanings with key anthropological concepts (such as descent, affinity, marriage, hierarchy, gender, body, soul, or spirit), will allow the development of bolder and more ambitious cross-cultural analyses of the unique social structures and cosmological systems found in the Amazon region. Connie Dickinson's thrilling new project will, no doubt, shed light on many aspects of the language, including phonological, semantic, syntactic, philological, and sociolinguistic—to name a few.

MODERNITY, ETHNIC IDENTITY, AND FOREST SOCIETIES

As the nine essays collected in this book illustrate, Huaorani recent history is a testimony to the inventiveness with which indigenous peoples have sought to grasp and seize the social and economic possibilities that an expanding world society offers. By presenting work that has been written over a span of almost twenty years (1996–2014), I wish to share with a wider public what I have learned from Huaorani life in the hope of fostering a better understanding of how indigenous people not only aspire to be valued by dominant society as different citizens living in a distinct collectivity, but also seek the recognition of their rights on their own terms. All cultures form part of the common heritage of humankind, and indigenous peoples contribute to this ongoing legacy from their own distinct perspectives. Huaorani people, like other indigenous peoples in Ecuador, in Latin America, and globally, have shown that they are not invisible victims of progress or part of a poverty-stricken, marginalized underclass that will eventually benefit from development through assimilation within a modernizing national society. As Fine-Dare so rightly puts it, "a central if not primary frustration of indigenous people anywhere in the world is that they are often asked to make a choice between retaining their cultural values and characteristics and achieving access to justice and resources" (Fine-Dare 2013, 16–17). In their struggle to control "development" and to challenge all forms of domination, especially forms that use an evolutionary scale to cast them as less developed, indigenous peoples have called on nation-states to respect their subsistence rights, even in regions where they are numerically inferior. Finally, they have learned to use their indigenousness to add political and economic significance to claims for legal and state recognition of their land and resource rights. By arguing that respect for culture difference can promote viable alternatives to integrationist development, indigenous peoples have shown that groups need not renounce their identities in order to participate actively and democratically in the planning of social and economic change for the enhancement of human welfare. If Huaorani politics have often puzzled, if not dismayed, those who have tried to interpret them (e.g., Kane 1995; Ziegler-Otero 2004), perhaps it is time to look at it as *indigeneity*, that is, as a particular form of political subjectivity now well recognized in international law (e.g., Barsh 1994; Kirsch 2012). This would allow us to recognize that a majority of Huaorani have retained their own sense of identity and of social solidarity, on the basis of which new forms of political subjectivities are unfolding, and will, no doubt, continue to unfold in the future. If difference can assume many different meanings (Peirano 2008), so does cultural openness to others, which explains why Ecuadorianists debate with such vigor the "plurinationalist" nature of this small and diverse country. At stake is a proper understanding of interculturality as politics beyond cultural politics (e.g., Becker 2013; Whitten 2008). Time will tell whether, how, or to what extent Huaorani political values are feeding into the "transculturative praxis of ethnogenesis" (Fine-Dare 2013), through which indigeneity is being constituted as shared political subjectivity in the Ecuadorian Amazon.

Although numbering less than 4,000, the Huaorani have played an important role in Ecuador's national consciousness, not least because Ecuador, like many Latin American countries, faces the momentous challenge of developing economic activities that enhance the well-being of its people while ensuring the maintenance of integrated social and ecological systems. Some progress has been made in recent years toward addressing the problems caused by entrenched poverty and environmental degradation (e.g., Larrea 2011). However, to conciliate economic development with the preservation and enhancement of the wealth that already exists in the form of biological and cultural diversity calls for an entirely new paradigm. There is growing awareness in Ecuador that by fully embracing its diverse forms of multiculturalism, the country will derive the strength it needs not only to adapt creatively to economic globalization, but also to imagine and to realize new articulations between national values, economic action, and political organization (Barnard 2011; Dayot 2014; Rival 2011). It is my hope that Huaorani studies will continue to develop as a domain of research that, in all its collaborative, comparative, and multidisciplinary forms, will not only continue to shed light on one of Amazonia's most fascinating indigenous cultures, but also open a dynamic intellectual space for continuing the intercultural dialogue that has started to shape Ecuador's political imaginary. Finally, I hope that this collection of essays will inspire a new generation to engage anthropological knowledge practically and theoretically in the search for better ways to inhabit the Oriente and, indeed, the rest of the planet.

PART I

AMONG FOREST BEINGS

OVERVIEW

WHAT KINDS of people occupied the Amazon Basin in the past, before and after Columbus? How similar were these native Amazonian formations to the relatively small and egalitarian tribes studied by anthropologists today? How did they adapt to, and what impact did they have on, their natural environment? These questions were hotly debated during my undergraduate student years in the late 1980s and the early 1990s. The predominant thesis at the time was that, as evidenced by the contemporary presence in Amazonia of small groups of shifting cultivators living in marginal isolation, environmental constraints had prevented the full development of social, economic, and political complexity. This thesis, however, was revisited by archaeologists who began to challenge the use of contemporary indigenous societies to reconstruct the past. Documentation of the existence of much larger ancient settlements in various parts of the region, including away from the main rivers, led to new models that suggested denser social groupings of greater permanency and complexity. Moreover, the thesis that large sections of the tropical rainforest had undergone substantial changes at the hands of humans for millennia was gaining momentum. It is in this context that my ethnographic research on the Huaorani became part of the debate over the anthropogenic nature of Amazon landscapes.

During the first months of fieldwork, when I was too scared to venture far from the school village where I was residing, my hosts' passion for walks in the forest was a mystery to me. *Ömere gobopa* (am going to the forest, bye), the greeting announcing a sudden departure, meant that I would not see some of my new companions for a while, a while being anything between one day and several weeks. The animated conversations that followed their return did not fully satisfy my curiosity or put an end to my speculations. Little by little, as I felt confident enough to accompany people on hunting and gathering expeditions, trek with them to distant villages, and even organize visits to remote settlements, I came to learn the many facets of Ömere gobopa. Sharing the joys of trekking with traveling companions was like going to the pub with British acquaintances, as if the forest, not the village, was the place where a Huaorani revealed one's true self. A number of my early publications have tried to convey the feelings of aliveness and freedom, the relational qualities, and the forms of knowing that make forest trekking such a core Huaorani experience (e.g., Rival 1996a, 2002).

The chapters in this section take a more theoretical approach to the particularities of Huaorani trekking. They show that Huaorani interactions with their forested homeland have much to tell us about the nature and the extent of human occupation in Amazonia over the last 11,000 years. Together, the three chapters support the thesis that nomadism and a hunting and gathering way of life need not be postcolonial phenomena. In each chapter, Huaorani trekking is apprehended in more general terms with a set of broad questions: how does human action shape nature? How does nature shape human action? How does environmental change relate to the historical development of human societies? To provide some answers to these questions, I treat ecology and culture as interdependent variables, and the rain forest as the biophysical manifestation of a long history of human and environmental interactions. Looking at trekking across vast stretches of the Amazon Basin in both past and contemporary times allows us to see that if the natural environment conditions cultural creativity, it is also true that cultural creativity sets new environmental possibilities.

In Chapter 1, I argue that landscape domestication necessarily involves the dynamic combination of evolutionary, historical, and symbolic processes. I stress the fact that domestication needs to be understood at the scale of an ecosystem rather than at the level of individual species. Contrastive identities are formed and unfold through numerous actions that transform the forest into dwelling places to which people return over time. This leads me to argue that the dynamics of social and environmental change, both historically and in the contemporary context, as well as the interactions between foragers and cultivators, have involved contrastive, competing, and coexisting modes of sociality for centuries. The archaeological literature on domestication, including in lowland South America, is much richer today than the literature reviewed in this chapter. Envisaging domestication as a nonlinear continuum comprising many different types of direct and indirect action is no longer controversial. However, the concept of landscape domestication is still in debate, and so are the historical trajectories of specific modes of forest living in Amazonia, especially the fact that foragers and cultivators may have coexisted with their contrastive ways of life for very long periods of time.

In Chapter 2, I develop further the argument that Huaorani trekking constitutes a unique mode of reproducing society across time and space by showing that, unlike the "devolved agriculturists" studied by Balée, the Huaorani have a rich nomenclature to name plants. Moreover, their plant classification system reveals a clear cultural preference for ordering nature according to ecological relations. I conclude that we need to rethink the thesis according to which the more a population intervenes in the reproduction of plants, the more its ethnobotanical inventory will expand for both wild and domesticated plants, as well as for plants and animals. This chapter underlines the relevance of ethnobotanical research in the Amazon context. Structuralist approaches, which still dominate Amazonianist anthropology, offer symbolic analyses of landscape domestication heavily based on the interpretation of myths too often detached from concrete practices and empirical ways of knowing. This is even the case, I wish to argue, of wonderfully detailed studies such as Lenaerts (2006), who contends that the structure of taxonomic systems is not universal. What underpins many characteristics of the ethnobiological classificatory systems found in Amazonia, he adds, cannot be readily apprehended through the naturalist ontology of modern science. The main objective of Amazonian classification systems is not to achieve a complete and comparative description of animal and plant morphologies, but, rather, to class the forms of sociability established between humans and nonhuman species and to inventory the types of intentional behavior found among living beings. The systems Lenaerts studied in Peru and Brazil focus, we are told, on interspecies relations; this is why they are primarily orientated toward the inclusion of natural beings within the social sphere.

FIGURE 5. Young men running from tree to tree, 1981. Photo by John Wright.

FIGURE 6. Trekkers in their forest camp, July 2008.

FIGURE 7. Two brothers resting in the forest and telling myths, July 2008.

FIGURE 8. Going home with chonta palm fruit, 1981. Photo by John Wright.

FIGURE 9. Visit to a manioc and plantain garden, May 2007.

FIGURE 10. A well-known shaman (*meñera*), 1990.

FIGURE 11. Well-known leader preparing curare poison, April 2013.

Lenaerts' data, however, could be analyzed differently, taking into consideration that different and alternative ways of ordering the world may coexist within the same culture. Where Lenaerts identifies one single encompassing classificatory system, it may be possible to distinguish distinct contexts without having to deny the indigeneity of the logical context of ecological reasoning. As new ethnobotanical research shows, it is possible to identify the processes by which the cultural knowledge of ecological interactions between plants and animals gets encoded in the languages spoken by peoples who have inhabited the same ecosystems for many generations (Rival 2014).

Chapter 3, which was written especially for this collection, offers a detailed discussion of Balée's historical ecology approach to Amazonian forest landscapes. Balée's work on the Guajà and the Ka'apor has played an important role in shaping the debate about past human occupation of the Amazon Basin. It has also helped me illuminate certain aspects of Huaorani mobility. Through an in-depth discussion of Balée's main arguments, I defend the thesis that the Huaorani rejection of elaborate gardening corresponds to a specific historical experience and a particular type of social organization. I also argue that trekking, far from representing a necessary intermediary stage in the regression from horticulture to foraging, constitutes, in some cases, a sui generis solution to deep contradictory forces of a political, religious, and social nature. Such internal processes may have long predated the Conquest and the disruptions it caused. I conclude that reliance on resources created in the past may be a characteristic shared by various trekking and foraging groups of the Upper Amazon.

There are many unsolved tensions between materialist, scientific, and symbolist approaches within Amazonianist anthropology, all of which are linked to the difficulties anthropologists continue to meet in their attempts to undo nature/culture dualism. These three chapters do not offer a ready-made solution to these problems but point to ways of dealing with them. They open the door for a new kind of scholarship, which will allow for collaborative research with young Huaorani interested in cultural resilience, forest conservation, and territorial management.

1

DOMESTICATING THE LANDSCAPE, PRODUCING CROPS, AND REPRODUCING SOCIETY IN AMAZONIA

IN AN ARTICLE HE WROTE at the beginning of his anthropological career, Claude Lévi-Strauss (1950) noted that native Amazonians give preference to semiwild plant species over fully domesticated ones. Prior to later writings where he fully developed the concepts of *science of the concrete* and *untamed thinking*, and the theory of the Amerindian mythologizing mind, this seminal article inspired many researchers. Philippe Descola (1993, 1996) combined Lévi-Strauss's early insights with the more materialist approaches of André Haudricourt and Maurice Godelier to propose a new analysis of the symbolic domestication of nature by Amazonian Indians. In a more poststructuralist stance, Eduardo Viveiros de Castro (1998) argued that Amazonian conceptualizations of humanity are not more monistic than modern Euro-American ones. Their dualism is as radical as ours, but it sets human culture, not nature, as the prior given; nature is conceptualized as what is made or constructed by cultural subjects. Natural scientists, such as the botanist Charles Clement (1999), also rediscovered Lévi-Strauss's seminal hypothesis, which has since been strongly supported by the archaeological reconstruction of the origins and subsequent evolution of plant domestication in lowland South America (Piperno and Pearsall 1998; Bellwood 2005).[1]

My aim in this chapter is to review current debates about plant domestication in Amazonia and show how a more holistic and dynamic perspective on the interactions between Amazonian hunter-gatherers and agriculturalists requires the treatment of ecology and culture as interdependent variables. If the natural environment conditions cultural creativity, it is also true that cultural creativity sets new environmental possibilities. Ecological and biological factors determine what particular plant species are amenable to domestication and the rates at which plants may be selected for favorable traits, as well as the kind of changes in gene frequency occurring in the domesticated plant over time. However, a forest can be transformed through cultural creativity into a manicured manioc plantation, a multistory agroforestry system, or any other kind of cultural landscape. Similarly, a cultivator may choose to bring a plant under close control and propagate selected materials until the plant produces the desired characteristics; or one may prefer to manage the plant more indirectly by encouraging its development through minimal weeding and forest clearance.

I start the chapter by showing that the Huaorani share the Amazonian preference for semiwild forest plants as noted by Claude Lévi-Strauss. I continue with a section on research guided by the precept that plant domestication is an evolutionary question, before discussing the impact of conquest on the evolution of plant domestication in lowland South America. I then show that plant domestication cannot be properly understood without reference to identity politics and to contemporary interactions between foragers and cultivators. I conclude with a few remarks on the kind of holistic approach to human ecology that is needed to further our understanding of plant domestication and, more generally, interactions between nature and society. A holistic human ecology, which we could as well term an anthropology of life, should integrate and give equal weight to the cognitive, historical, and political dimensions of human nature.

HUAORANI TREKKING

To many Amazonian peoples, Huaorani included, subsistence is more than environmental adaptation. The economy often functions as a moral system; it is part of the cosmovision. Until not so long ago, and unlike their indigenous neighbors (all cultivating groups with a strong sense of identity as horticulturalists), the Huaorani chose to cultivate manioc and plantain only sporadically and mainly for the preparation of ceremonial drinks. Even today, many families prefer to secure their daily subsistence through hunting and gathering. Of course, like most native Amazonians, they cultivate some food crops as part of their subsistence economy. Yet, they tend to define themselves primarily in terms of what they hunt and collect in the forest. Through their cycles of residential mobility, foraging activities, and daily consumption of significant quantities of forest resources, men and women continue to concentrate on useful forest species, enriching their habitat through marginal modifications. For example, upon abandoning a hunting camp or a dwelling site, people often leave hips of fruit seeds behind. When someone decides to encourage the growth of a particular wild plant in the forest, she or he will clear the weeds around its base. The anthropogenic forests people have contributed to form through such activities are qualitatively different from those created through shifting cultivation. Experts in reading the signs of past human activity, the Huaorani selectively ascribe transformations in the forest to the deeds of a wide range of agents—ancestors, other indigenous groups, or supernatural forces. If the occurrence of *ayahuasca* vines (*Banisteriopsis muricata* or *B. caapi, mii* in Huaorani) is systematically attributed to the planting activities of long-dead Zaparo enemies, the presence of peach palm (*Bactris gasipaes*, *daguenkahue* in Huaorani) groves, by contrast, is invariably taken to be a form of ancestral legacy, that is, of Huaorani origin. The forest exists to the extent that humans in the past lived and worked in it, and by so doing produced it as it is today for the benefit and use of the living. In other words, people live their interactions with the forest as a kind of social relationship that extends across the generations. Trekking, thus, represents a fundamental way to reproduce society through time, rather than a mere mundane activity related to the pragmatics of day-to-day subsistence or to environmental and historical adaptation (Rival 2002).

According to oral history, the Huaorani, not unlike the Brazilian groups that Balée (1992) discussed, chose to flee away from coercive powers and to adopt a wandering way of life. Huaorani history is still poorly known. We will probably never know whether they are the descendants of more sedentary and sophisticated cultivators. But there is little doubt that their way of life has, for centuries, depended more on foraging activities than on agriculture. This explains why they invest considerable time and show great interest in hunting and gathering activities, why they prefer to rely on the incipient cultivation of fast-growing food plants, and why they largely subsist on resources that are the products of ongoing forest management activities.

We know that they have lived for a very long time in the interstices between the great Zaparo, Shuar, and Tukanoan nations of the Upper Marañon, where they appear to have constituted nomadic and autarchic enclaves. It is likely that

Huaorani groups lived in isolation for centuries, which would explain why their language is attached to no known phylum, and why their borrowing of non-Huaorani cultural traits was literally nil at the time of contact in the early 1960s. To the best of our knowledge, the core of their ancestral territory seems to have been the Tiputini River, from where they expanded east, west, and southward until they occupied most of the hinterlands between the Napo and the Curaray rivers in the aftermath of the rubber boom, which caused the disappearance of most Zaparo communities (Rival 1992). Of course, the fierce refusal of contact, trade, or exchange with powerful neighbors may have alternated with periods of rapprochement. However, it remains true that Huaorani isolationism, a key part of today's ethnic boundary maintenance tactics in the Ecuadorian Amazon, is likely to have prevailed over time.

The Huaorani are not only autarchic, but also highly endogamous (Rival 1992, 1993). Only the Huaorani, the speakers of *huao terero*—the Huaorani language—are truly humans; all other people are *cohuori*, strangers coming from the other side of the Napo River, or *quehueri*, cannibals feeding on Huaorani children. Their kinship system is flexible enough to accommodate demographic variations. The population is divided into dispersed networks of intermarrying longhouses separated by vast stretches of unoccupied forests. These intermarrying longhouses form regional groups, or *huaomoni* (literally "we-people"), who maintain relations of hostility with each other. A *huaomoni* group calls all other groups *huarani*, that is, "others" or "enemies." The core relation within a *huaomoni* group is the relation between a brother and a sister, who, once married in the same nexus, exchange their children in marriage. Marriage tends to be uxorilocal with men going to live with their wives' kin. Despite the prevalence of hostility and no contact, *huarani* groups are loosely linked by personal ties between individual relatives, who, for one reason or another, do not belong to the same *huaomoni* group. These privileged relations, mainly used in case of spouse scarcity within the endogamous nexus, secure the renewal of alliances without which the group could not socially reproduce.

The last group of uncontacted Huaorani, the Tagaeri, has chosen to remain in a complete state of isolation. The Tagaeri refuse all communication not only with *cohuori* outsiders, but also with former relatives who prefer to accept peaceful contacts and exchanges with non-Huaorani. The Tagaeri live in hiding with no cultivated crops and their fires burning only at night. They refuse marriage alliances outside their group. Despite the danger of being spotted by the oil crews that occupy their lands, they try each year to go back to their palm groves for the fruiting season.

MAKING THE FOREST ANTHROPOGENIC

The traditional system of social alliances, based on a strict closure of the Huaorani social world onto itself, as well as on the partial isolation and mutual avoidance of the regional groups, corresponds to a particular mode of subsistence and use of the forest. Lévi-Strauss (1950: 465, 467, 468) noted, more than forty years ago, that in South America "there are many intermediate stages between the utilization of plants in their wild state and their true cultivation" and that "farming always accompanies, and is never a substitute for, the exploitation of wild resources." This remark applies particularly well to the Huaorani context, where numerous plant species are encouraged to grow outside of cultivated areas as people engage in numerous daily actions (planting, selecting, transplanting, protecting, using, and discarding), which have a direct or indirect effect on the distribution of species, be they fully domesticated or not.[2]

Huaorani people consume daily a great number of cultigens that are not planted in gardens. They see in their forested land the historical record of the activities of past generations. They are quite explicit about the inseparability of people and the forest, which they describe as a succession of fallows. Most of the western part of Huaorani land is said to be *ahuene*, that is, secondary forest. Only in the Yasuní, they tell me, are *omëre* (pristine forests) with really high and old trees.[3] Secondary forests are further divided into *huiyencore* (four-to-ten-year old clearings characterized by the frequency of balsa trees), *huyenco* (ten-to-twenty-year old clearings), *huiñeme* (twenty-to-forty-year old clearings characterized by the high incidence of adult palms), and *durani ahuè* (forty-to-one-hundred-year old clearings, remarkable for their big trees). Before the arrival of missions, *huiñeme* forests were the preferred sites to establish main residences. However, all types of forest were—and still are—continuously visited and lived in for longer or shorter stays.

Cultivars are discovered throughout the forest. This further indicates an evident strategy of resource dispersion within specific regions. Fish poison vines are found along the creeks where people fish; semiwild fruit trees are found near hunting camps; and numerous useful palms (such as *Astrocaryum chambira*, in Huaorani, *oönempa*) are found along trails. The *huaomoni* groups are constantly moving through their vast and relatively stable territories. Hilltop longhouses are regularly left for hunting and foraging trips, during which forest management activities take place. Wherever a Huaorani is in the forest, they chance upon needed plants. Informants are vague on whether these strategic and handy resources were planted by someone or just happened to grow there.[4]

What matters to them is that their occurrence can be related either to individuals known for using a particular area regularly or to a house group who lived in the area, sometime in the past. For instance, when young Huaorani unexpectedly discover useful plants in a part of the forest they are not familiar with, they often attribute them, with noticeable pleasure, to the activities of past people. If they decide that these cultigens were left by dead forebears (usually great grandparents), they may see these plants as an invitation to move permanently and legitimately in this part of the forest and to create a new longhouse. When no certain link with past or present human activity is established, the wide occurrence of cultigens is linked to animal activity. For example, semiwild manioc is said to "belong" to the tapir.[5]

Many useful plants, however, are not connected to any human or animal activity even when their presence or absence affects human distribution. For instance, an informant who once said "we remain within the limits of the *oonta* (*Curarea tecunarum*) territory" was nevertheless adamant that the vine, which he gathered to prepare his hunting poison, just happened to be where we found it. However, given the cultural importance of curare poison, one wonders whether the *Curarea tecunarum* vine has not been subjected to human management. Although this cannot be solved before thorough botanical research is undertaken, the denial of plant management is interesting in itself. Another species, which does not seem to be managed in any intentional way, but whose spatial distribution greatly influences the Huaorani's movements and choice of residence, is the *ungurahua* palm (*Jessenia bataua*, in Huaorani *petohuè*). A number of informants have told me that one of the reasons why longhouses are built on hilltops is that this is where ungurahua palms grow. The ungurahua palm provides rich food, building materials, and raw materials for the making of a wide range of artifacts and remedies. Beside being an extremely useful plant resource, the ungurahua palm offers protection. Its wood makes good fire, even under the wettest conditions. The safest place to spend the night when lost in the forest is under an ungurahua palm. People say that ungurahua palms, which have deep roots and grow in fertile soils, can stop violent winds from felling emergent canopy trees. Finally, informants stress over and over again that those who flee from wars and spearing raids would not survive without the ungurahua fruit. It is rich in fats and proteins and ripens throughout the year. The fruit is also appreciated by woolly monkeys (*Lagothrix lagotricha*), a favored game animal. The ungurahua palm is never planted but grows along ridgetops where people collect the fruit during their gathering expeditions. They bring it back to a camp or longhouse hearth to simmer it. People are perfectly aware of the fact that these cooking activities encourage the germination of ungurahua pits, hence facilitating its propagation.

A large number of other food plants are propagated through human consumption rather than direct planting.[6] For example, the favored *daboca* (Solanum spp.) fruit grows where it has been discarded. As a very sour fruit, it is never completely eaten, and the seeds remain on the forest floor until the proper conditions of heat and light favor germination. There are numerous *daboca* bushes in manioc gardens, around houses, and along rivers, but according to my informants, none of them are planted. More generally, I would suggest that we should distinguish cultivation from domestication (Chase 1989; Yen 1989; Ellen 1994). Some plants, particularly trees, are cultivated without having been domesticated—that is without showing morphological and genetic modification. Cultivation, which refers to the human activity of encouraging the growth of a particular plant (i.e., protecting and weeding) does not imply any genetic response in plants. It is therefore perfectly conceivable to cultivate wild plants, as it is to manage domesticated species in the wild. And the Huaorani manage, rather than cultivate, two common Amazonian domesticates, the peach palm and sweet manioc (*Manihot esculenta*).

THE POLITICAL USE OF CULTIGENS

Clement (1988, 1992) has demonstrated that the peach palm is a fully domesticated palm. The Huaorani, like many Amazonian Indians, grow peach palm seedlings (usually from the stone, rarely from a basal sucker), which they replant later in the clearing surrounding the longhouse. It is likely that most peach palm groves start in this fashion. But, as forest regrowth would over-top the palms a few decades after the dwelling site has been abandoned, the groves would not endure without human intervention. Every year, at the beginning of the fruiting season (which generally starts in January and lasts until April), the intermarrying *huaomoni* groups converge toward their groves, generally at a two-to-three-days walking distance from their main residences. They spend the whole season collecting and preparing the fruit for their daily consumption and, more importantly, for drinking ceremonies and marriage celebrations. These groves are in fact old dwelling sites. They exhibit scattered potsherds and broken stone axes, which are proudly excavated and kept as the secure signs that "the grandparents lived there."[7]

As people prepare and consume vast quantities of fruit in season, new seedlings develop around the temporary hearths year after year. The peach palm fruit is not edible unless simmered in water for a few hours. Fruits at the top of the pot, which are not properly heated and, therefore, not completely freed from proteolytic enzyme inhibitors or calcium oxalate crystals, are discarded. Some of these fruits are eaten by animals, but a substantial number are left to germinate on site. Young saplings of *macahuè* are planted at the side of the thorny peach palm trunks to provide easier access to fruit bunches.[8] Old trees are felled for the quality of their *tehuè* (from *tey*, "hard" and *ahuè*, "wood"), which is used to make spears and a whole range of smaller piercing or cutting tools. In wartime, palm groves are destroyed to make spears. Enemy groups destroy each other's groves as a means not only to increase their stock of precious hard wood but also to suppress social memory. Without these landmarks, a group loses its sense of continuity and its claim to a particular part of the forest.

Although peach palm groves could not persist without human intervention, they are not properly speaking cultivated. Maintained through activities of consumption, they are the products of the activities of past generations of Huaorani and, more explicitly, of the deceased grandparents or great grandparents of those who come to feed on the trees. Peach palms and their seasonal harvests are taken to be gifts from deceased relatives. The house groups, who rarely see each other during the rest of the year, spend the fruiting season together on the sites where their forebears lived and died. Remembering them, they enjoy each other's company, chant to the bounty of the forest, and celebrate the marriage of those mature enough to have children of their own. The peach palm fruit, the fruit produced by past life activities, is food to the living who, through their present consumption activities, ensure the feeding of the generations to come. The peach palm materializes a crucial link between past, present, and future generations of endogamous *huaomoni* people. And when social dynamics lead to the disappearance of a particular *huaomoni* group, its peach palm grove, no longer maintained, disappears as well. Lasting longer than human lives, these groves are a source of pride, security, and rejoicing, the concrete and material sign of continuity.[9]

Huaorani manioc gardening (manioc has always been cultivated incipiently for marriage ceremonies) is not swidden horticulture any more than peach palm management is. Now living for the most part in not fully sedentary villages, Huaorani people grow manioc on a larger scale and use it for daily consumption. However, they are not, by any standard, horticulturists, especially when compared with the Shuar and Quichua Indians whose women are accomplished gardeners, and whose manioc beer is the symbol of gender complementarity and good living (Whitten 1985; Descola 1986). A few of the most striking differences can be cited for illustration. The Huaorani manioc gardens are small in size, poor in crop variety, and abandoned after only one harvest. The soil, hardly weeded, is not cleared of all its vegetation cover, nor is it burnt. There is no strict gender division of labor (gardening does not represent the secret domain of female knowledge) and no belief in the need to combine garden technology with magic.[10] Given a general lack of planning and concern for securing regular and continuous supplies of garden crops, households can spend months without any. Finally, manioc roots are not brewed into fermented beer. Quichua Indians, for whom manioc beer is not merely a staple food, but the sacred mark of social and cultural identity, profoundly despise the Huaorani way of growing and preparing manioc. They regard it as closer to animal than to human behavior. For example, they say that the Huaorani, who sometimes eat young and tender manioc roots raw in their gardens, behave like wild pigs—disregarding the fact that they always peel the skin off and clean the dirt off before eating.

Additional facts can be cited to support the contention that garden produce is primarily food for visitors rather than food for daily subsistence. Firstly, the level of gardening varies according to the degree of peace and the size of regional alliance networks. When a house group wants to renew its alliance with an enemy group, it uses manioc to prepare the feast drinks. In times of warfare and feuding, longhouses disperse in the forest and live without gardens for months. The wider the alliances, the more house groups visit each other, the more they organize feasts, and the more they plant manioc to prepare nonfermented manioc drinks, *têpê*. That planting manioc implies first and foremost hosting is further demonstrated by the expression used for rejoicing, *huatapè*, which literally means "give me another bowl of manioc drink," and elliptically entails "I laugh away with you, my visitor." It is also this main function of serving as food-drink for hosts that explains why gardens are basically monocultures. If forest products offer a rich and varied diet, gardens bring little more than manioc, plantains, or bananas. Finally, as planting manioc is an invitation to visit and feast, a house group never consumes the harvest of its garden alone. As soon as the manioc is ripe, formally invited visitors from allied longhouses or unexpected touring relatives join the hosts for a stay that can last until exhaustion.[11] Manioc gardens, therefore, form short-lived plantations that exist only through the labor of the living.

To sum up, both manioc and peach palm are domesticates used for ceremonial purposes. Both the cultivation of manioc gardens and the management of peach palm groves require little investment in time or energy. Manioc cultivation is extremely basic; it hardly transforms the forest cover. Peach palm groves are old dwelling sites managed to encourage the continuous growth of a certain palm species. Both plants produce food sufficient quantities to allow for the renewal of social ties between allied longhouses. The "amphytrionic" function of peach palm groves is in many ways similar to that of manioc gardens. But whereas peach palm fruit celebrates the seasonal encounters of endogamous regional house groups, manioc is used to forge new political alliances.

I would propose that this difference in use is related to the fact that manioc and peach palm grow at different rates. Manioc, like all garden crops, is a fast-growing, short-lived crop unfit for daily consumption. Peach palm, like most tree fruit, comes from a slow-growing plant whose bounty makes the forest into a giving environment.[12] The sweet varieties of manioc found in Huaorani territory grow so fast that the roots can be dug out as early as five months after planting. Full of vital energy, manioc fails to reproduce in situ. Never planted twice in the same place, it migrates throughout the forest, at the mercy of human alliances. Peach palm groves, on the other hand, grow very slowly and continue to give fruit in the same place year after year as long as house groups care for them. Manioc, a "migratory" fast-growing plant, is particularly fitted for the organization of "diplomatic" feasts. When a house group wants to renew its alliance with an enemy group, it uses manioc to prepare the feast drinks. Given that it is much more productive than the peach palm and that it can be cultivated at any time of the year, almost anywhere, manioc makes possible large feasts to which *huarani* guests can be invited. Whereas manioc is the ideal plant to feast with the "enemy," the peach palm, the slow-growing legacy from past generations, gives the perfect fruit to celebrate *entre nous*. The two plants, with their contrastive practical and symbolic qualities, enable the formation, or the renewal, of very different types of alliances.

PLANT DOMESTICATION AS AN EVOLUTIONARY QUESTION

The fact that Darwin dedicated the opening pages of *On the Origin of Species* to plant and animal domestication is an indication of how important the process of selection for desirable traits by humans has been, and still is, for our overall comprehension of the workings of natural selection (Diamond 1997: 130). Contemporary evolutionary biologists and botanists see plant domestication as a coevolutionary process resulting from the combined action of natural and human selection (Salick 1995; Elias, Rival, and McKey 2000). Consciously or inadvertently, people exercise selective pressure on cultivated plants through a number of sociocultural practices. They select and propagate some plants to the expense of others. Plant selection and propagation by humans are activities that result in genetic modification. Selection and propagation alter the mechanisms for seed dispersal. They also affect seed dormancy and encourage self-reproduction, either vegetatively or through self-pollination (Diamond 1997: 119–22). There is therefore no doubt that the question of why and how some prehistoric people transformed certain wild plants into crops is an evolutionary one.

However, scientific accounts of how evolutionary principles caused the transition from hunting and gathering to farming differ.[13] Whereas some authors stress the symbiotic mutualism that slowly and progressively developed between humans and the plants that coevolved with them (Rindos 1984), others prefer to restrict the process of domestication to conscious cultivation, which involves cycles of planting and harvesting in prepared fields clearly set apart from wild, natural habitats (Piperno and Pearsall 1998: 7).[14] Some authors put much emphasis on the fact that people were forced by environmental events or historical circumstances to embark on farming. Hancock (1992), for instance, wonders why the onset of agriculture took so long, given that prehistoric hunter-gatherers had the necessary knowledge and technology to farm long before farming was undertaken. He reasoned that "hunting and gathering was a very comfortable way of life, and humans had to have a very good reason to give it up" (Hancock 1992: 151). For Diamond (1997), that very good reason was the mass extermination of large mammals by early human hunters who migrated out of Africa and colonized Eurasia, Australasia, and the rest of the world. Left with no easily accessible source of wild food, they were forced to innovate (i.e., domesticate plant and animal species) or to conquer those who had invented new food production systems. For Winterhalder (1981) and Winterhalder and Goland (1993), decisions regarding the use of particular types of natural resources as food, as well as decisions to adopt new or different food sources, are both made on the basis of calculations of relative return rates. Thus for Winterhalder the very good reason that pushed past human ancestors to farm instead of hunting and gathering was either climate change or population growth.[15]

Either of these two causes would have demanded a change in subsistence decisions in order to maintain an energetically optimal level of resource use. According to the optimal diet model, resource intensification (i.e., the adoption of agriculture) is driven largely by changes in foraging efficiency and diet breadth. Piperno and Pearsall (1998: 11), who follow Winterhalder's particular brand of evolutionary ecology and flatly deny the importance of sociocultural factors, such as religious ideologies, feasting, or prestige in the birth of agriculture, explain that diet breadth expansion occurs in response to an increasing scarcity of highly ranked resources paralleled by a decrease in the foraging return rate.

In spite of these divergent opinions, there is broad agreement on two major aspects of the overall evolutionary explanation. On the one hand, protofarming started about forty thousand years ago (during the late Paleolithic); on the other hand, it did not give way to full-blown agriculture before about 12,000 years ago (during the transition between the end of the Pleistocene and the start of the Holocene). For Mithen (1996, 2006) the reason why protofarming could not develop before the late Paleolithic is that it involves actions and modes of thought that are exclusively characteristic of *Homo sapiens*. The reason why humans had managed and modified the natural environment since at least 35,000 BP but did not start depending on domesticated plants and animals until the last few thousands of years is that this major shift was triggered by climate change. The transition from foraging to farming was thus part and parcel of the profound environmental changes associated with the end of the last Ice Age—between 11,000 and 10,000 years ago. According to Mithen (2006), populations capable of modern human cognition and behavior, including forms of resource management similar to those found today among modern foragers and incipient farmers, evolved between 35,000 and 10,000 years ago. By accepting Mithen's position, we also accept the fact that previous glacial and interglacial environmental perturbations could not have led to conscious plant propagation by humans. In short, the factors necessary for the emergence of food production probably did not converge until the end of the Pleistocene (Piperno and Pearsall 1998). Piperno and Pearsall, who are the first authors to systematically examine the impact of the last Ice Age on the evolution of food production systems in the Americas are convinced that agriculture arose in various locations across the world independently, but for the same reason, beginning at about 12,000 years ago.[16] Its sudden, scattered appearance all across the globe was triggered by environmental change, which, in turn, led to an "important step in the evolving culture of human beings" (Hancock 1992: 151).

In their examination of the impact of the last Ice Age on the Amazon Basin, Piperno and Pearsall (1998: 53) note that there have been major natural and human disturbances of the American tropical forest during the late Pleistocene and Holocene periods (ca. 22,000 years ago to the present). They explain that these natural perturbations drastically changed wild resource density and distribution and probably called for significant subsistence adjustments by Native Americans, particularly during the transition period after the close of the Pleistocene between 11,000 and 10,000 years ago. During that period, large portions of Amazonia were covered with open, deciduous, and dry (seasonal) forest, not with the rain and wet forest as it is today. The forest environment was consequently richer in natural resources available to hunters-gatherers, and there were many plant species suitable for domestication. Many important crop plant ancestors were naturally distributed in tropical deciduous and semi-evergreen forests where the dry season is comparatively long and marked. It is also in these forests that large mammals, such as giant capybaras (*Neochoerus* spp.) and giant ground sloths (*Eremotherium* and *Megatherium* spp.), roamed and where human hunters lived. When the wet tropical forest reoccupied the open terrain that had expanded under the late glacial climate, the large mammals and open land plants disappeared. Holocene native Amazonians, who were then faced with expanding rain forests and diminishing foraging options, were forced to develop new food strategies; they started to domesticate available plant species (Piperno and Pearsall 1998: 90–107; see also Keyeux et al. 2002).

Piperno's and Pearsall's reconstruction of the Holocene transitional forest and the beginnings of plant domestication in lowland South America is convincing, and certainly more plausible than Diamond's geographical determinism and human over-predation thesis (see in particular Diamond 1997: 96, 103–7).[17] However, they too exhibit the same problematic tendency to reduce human affairs to naturalized ecological economics, presented as the domain of pure efficiency and rationality. Ironically, Diamond is more realistic than Piperno and Pearsall in his assessment of the political tensions caused by emerging inequalities between what he calls "history's haves and have-nots" (Diamond 1997: 87, 93–113). Although the latter recognize the past and present existence of complex and sophisticated agroforestry systems in Amazonia, they cannot easily reconcile this form of landscape management with their evolutionary continuum of types of food production. They concede that different food production systems may have coexisted after the adoption of agriculture but envisage this occurrence as a choice forced onto human societies by limiting local ecological conditions

(Piperno and Pearsall 1998: 7). The establishment and spread of what they call "food-producing behavior" (by which they mean agriculture, as if hunting and gathering were not forms of food-producing behavior) is envisaged as a purely unilinear progression. The challenge, however, is to differentiate what in human action is conditioned by our common biological makeup and what is the product of history. This is particularly important in the case of South America where human migrations are less well understood than they are on other continents (Diamond and Bellwood 2003; Schurr 2004; Bellwood 2005) and where contact with Europeans in the late fifteenth century caused human population losses and crops' genetic erosion of a magnitude so far unparalleled in human history (Clement 1999; Diamond and Bellwood 2003).

PLANT DOMESTICATION AS A HISTORICAL QUESTION

In a recent synthesis of all current information on Amazonian crop genetic biogeography, Charles Clement (1999: 188) notes—conservatively—that at least four to five million people lived in Amazonia at the time of conquest and that 90 to 95 percent died shortly after. He adds that by 1492 native Amazonians already cultivated or managed at least 138 plant species, of which a substantial number were in an advanced state of domestication. He classifies 52 plant species belonging to 27 families as already domesticated, and 41 plant species belonging to 23 families as cultivated and semidomesticated. More controversially, he inventories 45 species belonging to 17 families as incipiently domesticated. This survey leads him to conclude that 84 percent of the 138 crops cultivated or managed in lowland South America at contact most probably originated in the Amazon Basin and adjacent lowland regions, representing almost half (45 percent) of all the plants cultivated in the Americas (Clement 1999). Having classified Amazonian cultivated plants according to their degree of domestication (full domesticates, semidomesticates, and incipient domesticates) and their particular life history (annuals, semiannuals, and perennials), Clement distinguishes six plant categories. He then moves on to reconstruct the inter-related historical ecology of anthropogenic forest formations and crop genetic resources, and concludes that if a high percentage (68 percent) of Amazonian domesticates, semidomesticates, and incipient domesticates are trees and woody perennials, this is not to be attributed to the nature of the forest ecosystem but, rather, to the high dependence of domesticated annuals on human management. According to Clement, contact triggered two parallel processes: the physical disappearing of human populations and crop genetic erosion. This explains why diversity, especially the infraspecific diversity of cultivars, was reduced shortly after large indigenous Amazonian societies succumbed to world diseases and depopulation. Clement's comprehensive synthesis adds a new dimension to Balée's (1993) estimation that at least 12 percent of the Amazon rain forest is of anthropogenic origin; in other words, its present species distribution reflects some sort of human intervention. Recent archaeological studies of anthrosols (dark earth produced through repeated habitation and horticulture) and elaborate earthworks used as habitation mounds and designed to control water for food production (such as raised fields, mounds, and causeways, or tracts of reclaimed wetland savanna) point to the same long-term impact of human intervention on the Amazon's biotic and abiotic landscapes.[18]

Assessment and interpretation of the archaeological data from the Amazon Basin is not, however, without difficulties. The literature is full of debates fueled by disagreements between archaeologists on the existence and the form of pre-Columbian Amazonian chiefdoms, as well as the striking disparity between ethnographic and archaeological accounts. Archaeologists and anthropologists working in the cultural ecology tradition stress the social and cultural discontinuity between pre-Columbian and contemporary Amazonian societies with their basic social organization of small, politically independent and egalitarian local groups formed through cognatic ties. They treat high mobility and foraging as indicators of historical change. The nomadic, foraging way of life of interfluvial groups does not reflect, they argue, the pattern that predominated in pre-Columbian Amazonia where elaborate autochthonous chiefdoms developed and flourished. What is at stake in this debate is the nature of the changes that occurred before, during, and after conquest and how we are best able to understand the interactions between the natural history of the forest and the eventful, uneven, and violent history of human societies in this part of the world.

What kinds of society and what types of cultivation existed in the Amazon prior to 1492? I have summarized elsewhere the debates on Amazonian chiefdoms (Rival 2002) and have already commented on the theory of cultural devolution and agricultural regression, a theory which purports to explain the ecological, cultural, social, and political consequences of postcontact demographic collapse in Amazonia (Rival 2002, 2006).[19] I thus simply wish here to point to the problems of analyzing the link between large-scale field systems and more complex hierarchical polities or the relationship among domestication, sedentism, and social stratification from the premise that Amazonia was first and foremost a land of ancient chiefdoms and intensive agricultural systems. While I understand the desire of many contemporary archaeologists to acknowledge and accurately assess the level of agrobiodiversity and political complexity created by humans in the Amazon region between the late Pleistocene and European contact, as well as the extent of the erosion that ensued, I lament a tendency found in authors such as Roosevelt (1998) and Heckenberger (2005) to over generalize the power, stability, and importance of pre-Columbian chiefdoms. Given that the hinterlands were *simultaneously* used by indigenous populations living in sedentary, densely populated village settlements, and by small, mobile groups dispersed throughout the forest, I prefer to stress, like Denevan (1996: 659–61; 2001), that the—almost certainly conflictive—coexistence of various types of society and food production systems in fifteenth-century Amazonia. Renard-Casevitz (2002: 141) uses a similar approach when she cautiously warns that "there is no necessary connection [in the Bolivian Amazon] between the transformation of the landscape of the savanna and the existence of powerful chieftainships." She disagrees with the evolutionary reconstruction proposed by archaeologist Clark Erikson (2000), and refuses to interpret the Bolivian earthworks as a proof of the existence of hierarchically centralized polities in this region. In her view, these earthworks were produced by "sets of farmers settled in dispersed sites varying in size and formed by a reticular system of exchange" (Renard-Casevitz 2002: 141). Finally, we must acknowledge that not all people follow the typically western botanical classification of plants in two distinct categories: wild and domesticated (Clement 1999: 189; Rival 2006).

Errors as unfortunate as those in the 1950s–1970s will be perpetuated if the assumption that, if it had not been for conquest, Amazonia's native populations would have continued to develop intensive agriculture and would have become increasingly complex.[20] The consensual view that Europe's invasion of lowland South America caused not only the demographic collapse of native populations but also their massive cultural devolution fails to account fully for the dynamic interaction between history and ecology. Evolutionary/devolutionary processes, which, ultimately, always imply that agricultural intensification is inherently progressive, do not offer the best explanation of the link between the physical world and human societies. If we are to analyze human/environment interactions holistically, we need to take into consideration both the physical environment and the mental world of Amerindians.

Much more promising is an approach that recognizes that indigenous peoples actively manipulated the forest ecosystem, enriched the soils, managed and diversified a wide range of plant species, and, in the process, created the material and physical conditions to maintain different social formations. Only some of these were characterized by high-population density levels. Moreover, the crucial question of what motivated some groups to gather in large numbers and consume greater quantities of cultivated food crops must be addressed. If we accept Piperno's and Pearsall's thesis that food crops were progressively domesticated between 8,000 and 4,000 BP in southwestern Amazonia by small, fairly mobile family units in house gardens, we must recognize that the relatively sudden intensification of agriculture and the apparition of densely populated and stratified villages occurred only in some very specific areas.[21] Such areas have recently been identified with the Arawak cultural complex (Hill and Santos-Granero 2002a, 2002b; Hornborg 2005). I have argued in this section for a dynamic history of plant/human interaction in Amazonia, that is, a history where cultural choices matter. Foraging, incipient horticulture, and intensive, sedentary agriculture were not just alternative modes of subsistence. By choosing one mode of subsistence rather than another, people were also choosing a particular form of life, and a particular identity.

PLANT DOMESTICATION AS AN IDENTITY ISSUE

Native Amazonians, like all peoples, are active shapers of ecological, economic, and historical forces. Evans-Pritchard (1940), following in the steps of Beuchat and Mauss ([1906] 1979), showed a long time ago that the Nuer's deep sense of identity as pastoralists, although certainly shaped by environmental conditions, could not be reduced to resource economics or energy efficiency calculations. It is only by taking into consideration the autonomous dynamics and rhythms of social life that we are able to offer an explanation of why the Nuer valued cattle herding over all the other subsistence activities they engaged in. A similar argument was put forward by Moore and Vaughan (1994) in their historical reconstruction of Bemba life during the colonial period. Richards (1932) was right to point to the centrality of finger-millet cultivation and food production in Bemba life, but she did not see clearly enough how political the *citemene* agricultural complex was. A group's adoption of either hunting and gathering or intensive agriculture as main and valued subsistence strategy represents a collective choice. Integral to the identity formation process, this choice comes to form the basis for the development of historical consciousness. Although Diamond and Bellwood (2003) may disagree, much of the comparative data they present can, in my view, be read in this light. The shortcoming of both the evolutionary and the historical mode of explanation, as argued above, is that they leave no room at all for understanding the subsistence activities of trekkers and foragers in cultural terms, that is to say, for including in the analysis their own conceptualization of gathering and hunting in cultural landscapes or their own discourse about their subsistence practices. Archaeologists, such as Anna Roosevelt, historical ecologists, such as Bill Balée, and evolutionary biologists, such as Jared Diamond, assume that adaptation is best defined in terms of increasing sociocultural complexity built on increasing population density and sedentariness. These authors tend to think that where the land is arable, horticulture is to be expected. The absence of horticulture, therefore, requires an explanation which automatically locates hunter-gatherers at the lowest stage of cultural evolution and progress. However, we need to ask what indirect reliance on past agriculture, rather than on crops cultivated now, means *to the nonhorticulturalists*. What difference does it make, practically and symbolically, to hunt in a pristine, wild forest or to hunt in forests modified by previous human intervention and management?

Amazonian trekkers and foragers extract semidomesticates growing in ancient or old agricultural fallows. The issue is not so much whether trekkers and foragers develop their subsistence activities in pristine or culturally transformed forests. We know that humans have lived and survived without domesticates in rain forests (Bahuchet, McKey, and de Garine 1991; Hladik and Dounias 1993; Piperno and Pearsall 1998: 55–61). What matters, rather, is *how* they cultivate and *why*, that is, for which purposes. What we also need to know is the extent to which the answers to these questions differ for the two groups: those who rely primarily on hunting and gathering and those who produce and trade food crops. Most of the world's contemporary hunter-gatherers are directly or indirectly involved in other economic activities, such as marginal or sporadic farming activities and wage labor. What characterizes them is the way in which they engage in these economic activities, as well as the distinctive social relations they maintain among themselves and with outsiders. Hunting and gathering is as much a social and a cultural phenomenon as it is a form of ecological-economic adaptation (Rival 1999). If the regional context in which many Amazonian Indians live is hunter-horticulturalist, some are living according to the hunter-gatherer mode. We need to examine the social and cultural distinctiveness of the latter without starting from the dominant assumption that noncultivating behavior is attributable to cultural loss (Rival 2006).

Hunting and gathering is a way of life that human groups may choose to adopt and maintain. Said differently, hunting and gathering may be a form of adaptation to the environment, but it is before all a way of life that is a way of organizing society and thinking about the world. Evolutionary theory and history help us understand how human action has shaped nature, but to understand how nature has shaped human action, that is, how we have domesticated ourselves in the process of domesticating the environment, we need to envisage human intelligence as embodied, distributed, and social.

As mentioned at the beginning of this chapter, paleo-anthropologists think that the first humans colonized the far North, the Americas, and the islands of the Pacific either in the late Pleistocene or early Holocene when the last glacial maximum came to an end. It was only in the Holocene, beginning a mere 10,000 years ago, that agricultural economies developed (Mithen 1996, 2006; Diamond 1997) and that the emergence of genetic unity and cultural diversity really started to set in.[22] The early inhabitants of the Amazon Basin who first domesticated squash, maize, peach palm, and manioc roughly 8,000–4,000 years ago were fully adapted to, and cognizant of, an extraordinary diversity of environments, which they were able to observe, perceive, classify, understand, and discuss with as much sophistication as contemporary native Amazonians do. Moreover, they were as capable of symbolic behavior and "cognitive fluidity" (Mithen 1996; Carruthers 2002) as the latter. This is why the apprehension of natural history by either past or contemporary native Amazonians cannot be reduced to mere effective decision making about which resources to exploit in order to gain reproductive advantage. Amazonian environmental knowledge combines in complex ways intuitive biology, anthropomorphic belief, and ritual behavior (Rappaport 1999). The partial autonomy of sociocultural phenomena is directly related to cognitive fluidity and distributed intelligence. Together, they help us understand why the action of hunter-gatherers on the environment is complex, why hunter-gatherers transform nature even if they do not produce in the sense that farmers do, and why human choices and decisions are influenced by social considerations, political orientations, and cultural values.

The population bottlenecks that resulted in the twin emergence of genetic unity and cultural diversity cannot be divorced from the ways in which ecology, economy, and ethnic identity have become inter-related to form cultural wholes. Ethnic identity, that is, the recognition of a collective difference between "my group" and "your group" reflected or not by linguistic difference, is a form of historical self-consciousness, that is, the product of externally attributed and internally experienced qualities, including modes of subsistence, particular landscapes associated with one's mode of life, system of values, and political ethos (Leach 1954; Hornborg 2005). It is by examining the relationship between ecology, economy, and ethnic identity that we will really comprehend the dynamics of landscape and species domestication, as well as the impact of plant and animal domestication on human genetic evolution.

A vast body of ethnographic work suggests that despite clear differences in the intensity with which the Amazon forest is transformed, we find the cultural centrality of landscape domestication everywhere (Wilbert 1961; Denevan 2001). In all places, ecological affordances are matched by different subsistence options, and values are attached to economic activities that lead to specific environmental transformations while serving as foundations for ethnic identity construction. The many groups living in the upper Rio Negro left numerous petroglyphs and rock paintings, and the Wakuenai continue to create sacred landscapes through ceremonially chanting (Hill 1993). For some groups, such as the Huitoto (Griffiths 2001), the Achuar (Descola 1993), the Curripaco (Journet 1995), or the Makushi (Rival 2001), to name just a few, gardening epitomizes human work as a civilizing force, which is opposed to wilderness and savagery. While food made out of processed bitter manioc serves as a prime ethnic marker for many groups in northwestern Amazonia (Hugh-Jones and Hugh-Jones 1996), the production and consumption of sweet manioc beer is central to the Canelo Quichua's sense of identity (Guzman Gallegos 1997).[23] Alimentary choices (eating forest tubers or garden crops, hunted game or fish, and so forth) are used to draw the boundaries of differentiated moral economies based on, but not reducible to, subsistence activities. In Amazonia, you become what you eat, and the opposition between forest and garden food, or game and fish, is used to materialize a wide spectrum of identity positions or to articulate a range of more or less inclusive or exclusive definitions of humanity.

The association of civilized humanity and gardening commonly found in northwestern Amazonia is particularly striking, especially when compared with similar constructions opposing civilized gardeners to wild hunter-gatherers found in other regions of the world, particularly in central Africa. The patron-client relationship that unites Tukanoan communities of the Vaupés and the Río Negro with Makú bands is well documented. The Makú live deep in the forest and hunt, collect, and garden marginally. They periodically visit the sedentary, fishing, and manioc cultivating communities of their Tukanoan trading partners, where they receive garden produce, tobacco, and manufactured goods in exchange for their forest produce (especially game), labor, baskets, and blowguns. This relationship, which has economic, political, and symbolic dimensions (Ramos 1980; Jackson 1983), is almost identical to that described by Grinker (1994) for the Efe Pigmies and Lese Bantus. The Tukanoan Indians despise the forest-dwelling hunting Makú, whom they see as savages, incestuous and animal like (Ramos 1980: 166). This moral judgment clearly shows that foraging means more than simple adaptation to the physical environment. In some villages, the Makú are partially incorporated into Tukano society as second-class, marginal citizens and treated as dependent sons-in-law, even if a Tukano/Makú marriage alliance would be totally unthinkable. Treated as "owned" slaves, captives, or coresident clients, the Makú are seen as subhuman. In fact, their structural position is identical to that of adopted pets (Erikson 1984). For the Tukanos, the Makú do not simply "make a living," they live like savage animals. The Makú also perceive their way of life as more than simple adaptation to the forest environment. However, ethnographers tell us much less about Makú understandings of themselves and their relational order than they do about the Tukanos, their values, and their prejudices. Within their communities, the Makú emphasize egalitarianism and the collective appropriation of resources. With the Tukanos, they choose to be elusive. On the surface, they seem to comply with the commands of their nonforaging neighbors. However, as soon as they are back in their forest camps, the Makú make great fun of the Tukanos's airs of superiority. Moreover, no obligation ties them to the latter; they come and go to the gardeners' villages as they please. Only additional research will tell us whether the Makú have yielded control over some aspects of their material and spiritual life to their agricultural neighbors (Grinker 1994). There is, nevertheless, sufficient ethnographic evidence to support the thesis that subsistence and diet choices play a key role in shaping Makú and Tukano ethnic identities.

In other Amazonian societies, we find a positive correlation at the level of discourse between mobility and warfare on the one hand, and among peace, gardening, and village life on the other. Journet (1995) notes that the Curripaco, who identify horticulture with peace and the foundation of society, equate the nomadic style of the Makú, seen as antithetical to culture and anterior to civilization, with warfare, hunting, and autarky. Although the Curripaco were as ready to wage war as the neighboring groups they represented as warlike and fierce forest dwellers, they condemned violence morally, and saw themselves as being forced to resort to violence. Fausto's (2001) study of two Parakana groups who chose, after splitting, to live according to two divergent ways of life—nomadism and sedentism—illustrates the same association among pacific village life, horticulture, and sedentism on the one hand, and foraging, warfare, and nomadism on the other. However, the Parakana do not hold the same negative moral judgment on violence. The Tupí-Guaraní "mystical" wars, the more strategic violence practiced by Arawakan groups, and the forms of warfare and violence induced by colonial politics are profoundly different. To fight an enemy recognized as a complete other is not the same as to fight an enemy perceived as a recognizable other (Descola 1993). The volume edited by Hill and Santos-Granero (2002b) contains numerous references to the moral condemnation of violence as an important Arawakan ethnic marker. The prohibition of endowar, coupled with a strong ethnic prejudice against wild Indians, was central to the development of an Arawakan panethnic ethos. Moral barriers existed not among the lowlands and the highlands of Peru, Ecuador, and Bolivia as previously thought but, rather, between traders and warriors. As Lévi-Strauss (1943) pointed out some time ago, different visions of humanity are implicated in the "commerce or war" dialectics. What is at stake in the Amazon warfare complex is the definition of humanity. The human condition, as portrayed in Amazonian myths, is essentially a process of humanization or, in other words, of domestication. Today, the dual classification nomadic foragers/sedentary gardeners is no longer closely associated with the opposition between warmongering and peace but, instead, with the contrast between integrated indigenous communities and communities refusing all contact with outsiders.[24] There are today throughout the Amazon Basin individuals and communities who consider themselves "civilized." Not unlike their pre-Columbian Tukanoan predecessors, they appropriate the modern discourse of peace and civilization to force contact with nomadic groups and bring them to their villages to teach them "how to live as real humans." This usually involves educating them in the arts of sedentary village life and horticultural production. The ethnic antagonism of opposing societies who refuse to submit to the authority of chiefdoms and favor autarky over trade and interethnic exchange, and those who accept their incorporation and historical transformation is, as this most recent form of denigration shows, very old indeed.

AMAZONIAN LANDSCAPES: WILD, TAME, AND HUMANIZED FORESTS

I started this chapter by noting the continuing validity of Lévi-Strauss's perceptive remark on the Amazonian propensity to domesticate forested landscapes, rather than plant species. I then argued that if Clement is right to stress the enormous historical disruptions caused by conquest, reliance on semidomesticates should not be explained away as cultural loss. The intensification of plant domestication, far from being systematic, was highly localized and conditioned by cultural values. Some authors have attempted to identify historical continuities in the ethos and subsistence practices of socially stratified traders, such as those pertaining to the Arawakan Diaspora (Hornborg 2005). I have similarly argued that *some* Amazonian trekkers and foragers, far from being devolved agriculturalists, may be characterized by comparable historical continuities expressing values that stand in contrast to those held by their cultivating neighbors. By choosing to contribute to the transformation of the forest without intensifying the selection and the propagation of fully domesticated plant species, native Amazonians who choose to remain mobile and rely more on hunting and gathering than on cultivation also choose to transform human society in a way that is not conducive to the reproduction of political hierarchies or economic inequalities.

Ecology cannot be defined with sole reference to the natural environment. A biocultural phenomenon such as plant domestication needs to be replaced within its full historical and political context. In Amazonia, the interactions between foragers and cultivators, as well as the dynamics of social change, both historically and in the contemporary context, have involved contrastive and coexisting modes of sociality. As Winthrop (2001) puts it, patterns of economy and belief guide human action with regard to the environment.[25] Politics in Amazonia is characterized by undeveloped hierarchies, weak links between chiefs (hosts) and followers (guests), the importance of ceremonial life and feasting, and the prestige of having large quantities of food to offer. All these aspects have played a significant role in driving food crop domestication. They have also played a part in the use of foods—selected for their nutritional and symbolic importance—as ethnic markers. But it is also true that in many communities, indigenous ideas about space, time, the human condition, and wilderness as potentially transformable have been used to resist political pressures to develop and increase productivity. Adding to this play of contradictory forces, European influences after conquest and the needs of long-distance trade favored the evolution of subsistence systems in the direction of agricultural intensification, such as the extension of manioc or maize monocultures (Steward and Faron 1959: 293). These are precisely the trends that are rejected by those who choose to isolate themselves and to become "uncontacted" foragers. In short, there is more to landscape domestication than a linear move toward full agricultural development in a region where dual oppositions of the type fierce/tame abound, and where nature is constructed in terms of its ability to be domesticated, that is, its unrealized potential for civilization.

Plant domestication is an evolutionary, historical, and cultural process that needs to be viewed through the holistic lens of the new ecological anthropology paradigm. Its proper analysis requires the development of a unitary analytical framework that integrates relations among biology, ecology, economy, material culture, language, and identity. Whereas ecological studies are concerned with relations between living organisms that belong to different species and their environment, ecological anthropology focuses on the complex relations between ecosystems and social groups. As such, it directs our attention to the ways in which a particular group of people purposely or unintentionally shapes its environment, as well as to the ways in which relations with the environment shape a population's social, economic, and political life—in one word, its culture. Said differently, ecological anthropology explores the ways in which the environment is historically and culturally produced through human-nature interactions. Building on Roy Rappaport's (1999) interpretation of culture as a system regulating relations between people and their environments, the new ecological anthropology focuses on the interface between cultural and biophysical factors in terms of integrative, biocultural processes. Given that material factors, tools, technology, knowledge, and productive organization equally act as powerful mediators between the biophysical environment and human culture, ecological adaptations are never purely "natural." Biophysical factors, which are shaped by humans in a material sense, are also culturally perceived. As such, they form part of the ongoing relations of mutual adaptation between culture and material context. Given that the environment is always more than just a set of things to which people adapt, the influences of the biophysical factors on human behavior are never purely material.

It is now widely accepted that we all share the same biological intuitions (Atran, Medin, and Ross 2005; Mithen 2006). Mithen argues that if early humans such as *Homo habilis* had already evolved a capacity for ethnobiological knowledge, modern humans alone developed a capacity for language and general intelligence some 170,000 years ago. When *Homo sapiens* started to domesticate plants 15,000 years ago, their minds could process highly metaphoric knowledge, which complemented rather than replaced the previous intuitive physics, psychology, and biology that they had inherited from their predecessors. Therefore, the humans who first domesticated plants were capable of cognitive fluidity and creative imagination; they had religious beliefs and expressed their emotions through art forms. Domestication was, and still is, a conscious process. The actions of observing and experimenting, like those of selecting and propagating, are guided by cultural representations. The motivations underlying the actions involved in reproducing plants—or any other form of life for that matter—are neither purely pragmatic, nor simply aesthetic. Intellectual and scientific curiosity play a role as well.

Reproductive processes raise a host of questions that directly involve the perception of life. When it comes to plants, where the individual's functional unity is not as straightforward as it is in animals, the observation of morphological differences, the recognition of individual differences, and the capacity to recognize biological variation, whether based on genetic mutation or not, become very complex actions. It is much more difficult to understand the mechanics of heredity in plants than it is in animals.[26] It is perhaps this complexity that led Canguilhem to reflect that:

> It is too easily admitted that there exists a fundamental conflict between knowledge and life, and that their reciprocal aversion can only lead to the destruction of life by knowledge, or to the mocking of knowledge by life. But this fundamental conflict does not lie between thought and life within man; rather, it lies between man and the world within our human awareness of life. Intelligence can be applied to the living only if the originality of life is acknowledged. Thoughts about what lives must be formed from within life itself. (Canguilhem 1975: 4)

For Canguilhem, only a holistic approach to the unity of life will restitute the human shared apprehension of life as a biological fact. Anthropologists who wish to engage with evolutionary thinking accurately and without any reductionist agenda recognize themselves in Canguilhem's position. In a similar fashion, Piña-Cabral (2005) recently called for anthropology to re-encounter its universal claims and reaffirm its common ground.[27] To reclaim anthropology as metatradition, we need to start by recognizing the openness of social life. In addressing the challenges that face contemporary human societies, we need to acknowledge them as biocultural in part, without losing sight of the fact that they are moral challenges as well.

2
NAMING TREES

GIVEN THE UNPRECEDENTED LOSS OF BIOLOGICAL, linguistic and cultural diversity in the world today (Maffi 2001), the documentation of the biological and ecological knowledge of food collectors and crop planters has become a matter of urgency. Authors who have recognized the importance of documenting folk biology models in regions of high diversity (particularly in Amazonia) have called for a new approach to ethnobiology.[1] It is not enough to document how things are named and how named things are classified (Kohn 2002, Lenaerts 2004), although such activities are still considered to be central to how people come to know nature (Berlin 1992). Local people know much more about nature than their classifications reflect (Atran 1999). Another emerging debate concerns the relative ethnobiological knowledge of cultivators and noncultivators sharing the same biologically diverse ecosystem. For Berlin, who argues that systems of ethnobiological classifications "reflect not only the biological constraints of nature, but also the modifying processes of cultural history" (Berlin 1992: 268), there is a correlation between form of subsistence and type of ethnobiological nomenclature. Ellen (1999), however, has challenged the view that hunter-gatherers, whose taxonomic classifications appear to be less complex than those of agriculturalists, have a poorer knowledge of their environment than the latter.

After reviewing various explanations linking domestication to the growth of ethnobiological taxonomies, I present a brief summary of Huaorani ecological knowledge. I then turn to two recent ethnobotanical surveys conducted in Huaorani land and to some peculiarities of their plant naming system. What appears to characterize Huaorani plant taxonomy is not so much the shallowness of its nomenclature but the central importance given to ecological relations and phenological criteria. I end with a few general remarks on knowledge, language, and the environment in lowland South America.

THE ROLE OF DOMESTICATION IN THE EVOLUTION OF ETHNOBIOLOGICAL CATEGORIES

The development of agricultural systems is still considered today as one of the most significant moments of human evolution (Diamond 1997; Bellwood 2005). Bellwood's early farming dispersal hypothesis, which relies on a synthesis of data from archaeology, linguistics, and genetics, attempts to reconstruct the ways that farming developed when early agricultural populations spread through various regions of the world formerly occupied by hunter-gatherers— killing the latter off or converting them to the new food production system (Bellwood 2005: 273). In a similar vein, Berlin has long been interested in the impact of domestication and agricultural development on the evolution of ethnobiological categories (Berlin 1992: 260–90). In his summary of early research on hunter-gatherer taxonomies, Berlin (1992: 275–76) stresses what appears to be a common trait in these systems: the paucity—if not the absence—of taxa of specific rank.[2] These early studies seemed to suggest that the ethnobiological inventories of foragers contain significantly fewer named categories of plants and animals than those of cultivators. Given the predominance of evolutionary thinking and the paramount place accorded to the Neolithic Revolution in anthropology and archaeology, these studies were soon used to propose a new evolutionary typology. Brown (1985), for instance, compared the folk taxonomies of thirty-nine foraging societies and found that they differed from those of small-scale agriculturalists in two major respects. "While foragers possess sizable inventories of labeled biological classes, the inventories of small-scale agrarian groups tend to be much larger. In addition, binomial names are very common in folk taxonomies of cultivators but very rare in those of hunters and gatherers" (Brown 1985: 52). In a subsequent publication, Brown (1986) explored the evolutionary significance of the positive correlation between total number of taxa and form of subsistence, and concluded that the growth of ethnobiological nomenclature is driven by utilitarian needs linked to agricultural development. Because population density is much higher among small-scale cultivators, when crop failure occurs, he speculated, they must rely on wild plants and consequently be less selective than hunter-gatherers about what is edible or not. The exploitation of both domesticated and wild plants and animals by cultivators is far more intensive than the exploitation of wild plants and animals by hunter-gatherers. Consequently, cultivators develop greater interest in and knowledge of natural history than hunter-gatherers do.

Berlin (1992: 283) agrees with Brown that farmers' knowledge of plants and animals is vastly greater than that of noncultivators and that "domestication leads to the creation of folk specific taxa" (Berlin 1992: 286). However, his preference for a cognitive approach to environmental knowledge leaves him unconvinced by Brown's utilitarian argument.[3] Noncultivators are as good at observing as cultivators of the perceptually distinctive features of form and behavior in plant and animal species, but their curiosity is "passive," or at least not as "active" as that of observers ready to modify the species they observe and keen to create new varieties (Berlin 1992: 290). Furthermore, Berlin is well aware of the difficulties involved in relating the presence or absence of folk species to the form of subsistence (Berlin 1992: 98–99, 285–90). The first problem is that we know a great deal more about the ethnobiological classification systems of horticulturalists than we do about those of nonagricultural peoples (Berlin 1992: 274). The second problem is the degree of acculturation of the foraging societies included in these comparative studies. The third problem is the relative paucity of species in the environments of those that have been studied. To compare the classificatory systems of traditional subsistence horticulturalists living in areas of high biological diversity with those of acculturated hunter-gatherers living in regions where biodiversity is not as remarkable will not lead to conclusive results (Berlin 1992: 98–99). While maintaining the thesis that the knowledge of gardeners is more likely to be lexically encoded than that of foragers, Berlin thus acknowledges that his thesis can only be demonstrated through the comparative description of the ethnobiological knowledge of a noncultivating population occupying the same highly biodiverse habitat as a population of cultivators.

It is such a comparison that Balée (1994, 1996) undertook in his study of two Tupi-Guarani groups sharing the same forest environment in the Amazon region. He found that the horticultural Ka'apor, who create sizeable light gaps for their dwellings and gardens, exert greater influence on the forest than

TABLE 1. Comparison of Ka'apor and Guajá Names for Nine Species of the Inga Genus.

SPECIES	KA'APOR NAME	GUAJÁ NAME
Inga alba	iŋašiši'i	čičipe'i
I. auristellae	iŋaperëi'i	čičipe'i
I. capitata	iŋahu'i	čičipe'i
I. fagifolia	kaŋwaruhuina	čičipe'i
I. falcistipula	kaŋwaruhuina	čičipe'i
I. heterophylla	iŋaperëi'i	čičipe'i
I. marginata	iŋaperëi'i	čičipe'i
I. miriantha	iŋaperëi'i	čičipe'i
I. rubiginosa	tapi'irina'i	čičipe'i

their foraging neighbors, the Guajá.[4] The plant nomenclature of the Guajá, who exploit, use, and name fewer resources in their habitat than the Ka'apor do, is less sophisticated than the latter's. Let us examine three of the systematic comparisons offered by Balée in his various publications. Table 1 summarizes the comparison of Ka'apor and Guajá folk-specific names for nine nondomesticated species of Inga.[5] Whereas the Ka'apor linguistically differentiate five of the nine species, the Guajá use a single name for all of them.

Another major difference between the Ka'apor and Guajá plant nomenclature is that whereas the Ka'apor linguistically differentiate domesticates from phylogenetically related nondomesticates, the Guajá lump them together under the same generic name (Balée 1996: 480). For example, the Ka'apor use the terms *kaka'i* for domesticated cacaos and *kakaran'i* (literally "cacao-false") for nondomesticated ones, including *Theobroma speciosum*. By contrast, the Guajá use the same genetic term *ako'o'i* for all the cacaos.

More generally, the Ka'apor have nine times more folk-specific plant names than the Guajá (Balée 1996: 478), and the plant nomenclature of the former is closer to the Linnaean system than the plant nomenclature of the latter (Balée 1994: 333–62). These comparisons lead Balée to conclude that while the Guajá know their environment, "not all of this knowledge is so important as to be

TABLE 2. Comparison of Ka'apor and Guajá Names for Three Species of *Theobroma*.

SPECIES	KA'APOR NAME	GUAJÁ NAME
Theobroma grandiflorum	kipi-hu-ʔi	ako'o'ĩ
T. speciosum	kaka-ran-ʔi	ako'o'ĩ
T. cacao	kaka	ako'o'ĩ

compartmentalized in encyclopedic entries of that part of the lexicon concerning the plants" (Balée 1994: 206). Furthermore, he attributes the relative paucity of subgeneric data in the Guajá's plant nomenclature to historical factors that have influenced their mode of subsistence. Whereas the Ka'apor have continued to use the domesticated, semidomesticated, and wild plants of their proto-Tupí-Guaraní ancestors, the Guajá, who reverted to foraging, lost the use of many of these plant species, as well as the specific terms to name them.

For Balée, as for Brown (1986), "without horticulture, there is generally less need to know the specific properties, potential uses, or biological principles of a great range of plants, both domesticated and not" (Balée 1994: 222). Following Brown, Balée thus attempts to provide a model that correlates the rise of agriculture and the development of ethnobiological categories with the caveat that what is offered in the Amazonian context is a general typology of cultural devolution from cultivators to foragers, in which non-Tupí-Guaraní groups, such as the Huaorani, are included. Using Davis and Yost's (1983a, 1983b) brief description of Huaorani pharmacopoeia, which contains only 35 medicinal plants (many with magical, rather than chemical, properties), Balée argues that the Huaorani inventory is relatively poorer than the Ka'apor's, which contains at least 112 medicinal plants (Balée 1994: 113–15).[6] In his view, the Huaorani's relatively poor inventory validates the hypothesis that trekkers exhibit a truncated ethnobotany related to "a regression in knowledge due to the conquest and its many aftershocks" (Balée 1994: 112–15). As I shall argue in the next section, the actual breadth of Huaorani plant knowledge is lost in such comparisons.

The greatest challenge with any attempt to relate ethnobiological classifications and forms of subsistence in Amazonia is that, as some authors have observed long ago, plants that have not been fully domesticated remain important food sources, in fact, as important in some societies as domesticates

(Lévi-Strauss 1950). Moreover, there is great fluidity in this region of the world between horticulture and foraging (Leeds 1961). This has led recent commentators such as Bellwood, for instance, to concede that "the transitions through time and space between hunting and gathering and farming are rarely as sharp in the New World as in the Old" (Bellwood 2005: 146). Moreover, there is another explanation of why the knowledge of agricultural peoples in areas of high biodiversity is more likely to be lexically encoded than that of nonagricultural peoples, such as that proposed by Ellen (1999). Ellen agrees with Berlin, Brown, and Balée that subsistence specialization plays an important role in shaping a culture's folk biological knowledge. However, once formal (i.e., linguistic) knowledge is distinguished from substantive knowledge, it becomes clear that the knowledge required for effective low-intensity agriculture may actually be smaller than the knowledge required for hunting and gathering (Ellen 1999: 107). There is no necessary one-to-one correspondence between the way in which people label plants and codify knowledge, and the actual knowledge they deploy in subsistence activities. Rather than treating the ethnobiological knowledge of hunter-gatherers and horticulturalists diachronically, it might be more advisable to focus on social determinants, such as modes of communication and learning. Nonagricultural peoples living in smaller and less authoritarian groups than sedentary cultivators have fewer opportunities to share, organize, and label their collective knowledge of their biologically rich environments (Ellen 1999: 91–92). Ellen's solution, which avoids both utilitarian and cognitive premises, sheds new light on empirical evidence not easily fit into Berlin's nomenclature growth model. Morris (1976) and Gardner (1966), who worked among South Indian hunter-gatherers (the Hill Pandaram and the Paliyan), both remarked that their taxonomies of the natural world exhibit considerable variation. The knowledge these nomadic people have of their environment is at once utilitarian and idiosyncratic. Morris speaks of "individualistic cultures" relying "upon an idiosyncratic ordering of reality," and Gardner of "memorate knowledge" entirely gained through direct personal experience. The seven foraging cultures subsequently compared by Gardner share the same characteristics.[7] Their members are all skilled observers, whose environmental knowledge is, all at once, highly sophisticated, highly empirical, and highly personal. In all seven cultures, Gardner (2001: 14) found very little explicit verbal instruction. Direct individual observation, encouraged from an early age, is far more important. The cultivation by each individual of a large and reliable body of factual data is particularly valued, while expertise denied, and authority resented (Gardner 2001: 18). Finally, the absence of systematization and formalization does not preclude communication or common understanding, as individuals compensate for the high diversity of terms and concepts with intense interpersonal sharing. Individuals simply spend a great deal of time checking each other's personal knowledge and way of labeling. In the rest of this chapter, I propose to examine some aspects of Huaorani plant nomenclature that seem to share some characteristics with Gardner's findings.

TREKKING AND KNOWING THE FOREST

For hundreds of years, and until the mid-1960s, the Huaorani lived as forest hunters and gatherers in the heart of the Ecuadorian Amazon (Rival 2002). Residential mobility was high, albeit confined to particular areas. Small groups related through kinship and residence moved continuously between their main residences built on hilltops and smaller houses and shelters dispersed throughout their hunting territories. The overall population was divided into dispersed networks of intermarrying longhouses separated by vast stretches of unoccupied forest. For greater security and autonomy, house groups tended to isolate themselves from those with whom no marriage partners were exchanged. Using only blowpipes and spears, they primarily hunted monkeys, as well as some birds and white-lipped peccaries. Fishing, largely restricted to creeks, was a marginal activity that involved the use of fish poison and lances. Gathered fruit formed an important part of daily food intake.

Located between the Napo and the Curaray rivers, and extending from the Andean foothills to the Peruvian border, the Huaorani territory has no marked seasons. Annual precipitation averages 35 cm and is more or less evenly distributed throughout the year. Atmospheric humidity is constant and high (80 to 90 percent), and the soils, renowned as the least fertile in Ecuador, are permanently moist. On the western side of Huaorani territory, numerous streams and creeks cut across rugged terrain featuring sizeable hills (300 to 1,000 m above sea level) to form the Curaray's headwaters. On the eastern side, rivers, such as the Tiputini and the Yasuní, meander through more marshy lowlands at 280 m above sea level. But even there, 90 percent of the forest grows on well-drained *terra firme* (nonflooded upland). *Terra firme* consists mainly of heavily dissected terraces where differences in level may be as high as 40 m. The Huaorani live in one of the hot spots of biodiversity (Gentry 1988), and, as I shall argue below, it is clear that their extensive ethnobotanical inventory reflects the high number of species found in their territory. Throughout Huaorani territory, and within the Yasuní National Park, biodiversity is exceptionally high, although differences exist between lower eastern and higher western forests—the former being less biodiverse than the latter (Ter Steege et al. 2000).[8] Game is found in abundance as soon as one leaves the immediate vicinity of human settlements (Rival 2002).

No more than 600 at the time of contact in the 1950s, the population now counts around 1,850 people, of whom 60 percent are under 16. The increased presence of oil companies in Huaorani territory has, in recent years, led to dynamic and complex population movements, resulting in the creation of new communities near oil fields. Despite their recent riverine adaptation and accelerated process of sedentism, the Huaorani have remained highly mobile forest trekkers who continue to move among longhouses built on hilltops, secondary residences, and hunting shelters dispersed throughout their territory. Traditional foraging has been somewhat undermined by the introduction of garden crops, shotguns, dogs, and Western medicine, as well radio contacts. Petroleum development, the expansion of agriculture, tourism, and the creation of schools and airstrips for air transport have all had an impact on settlement patterns. Traditional longhouses are on the wane. However, despite changing settlement patterns and new hunting technology, hunting returns are still high. Collared peccaries (*Tayassu tajacu*) and rodents, such as agouti (*Agouti paca*) and capibara (*Hydrochaeris hydrochaeris*), are hunted much more often than monkeys. With increased sedentism and riverine adaptation, fishing has become as important as hunting. Fruits remain an essential part of the diet, particularly plantain, banana, and peach palm (*Bactris gasipaes* Kunth., Arecaceae). Other important palm fruits include ungurahua (*Oenocarpus bataua* C. Mart., Arecaceae) and morete (*Mauritia flexuosa* L. f., Arecaceae). The fruits of numerous species of palms, trees, or epiphytes are also regularly harvested and eaten. Although manioc cultivation has intensified, it largely retains its erratic character, with a few families cultivating fast-growing varieties that are widely shared upon harvest. In the twenty or so villages where the population has now agglomerated, families have added packaged food to their daily meals. Rarely purchased or individually owned, this food, like all trade goods, is widely circulated and subject to intense demand sharing (Rival 2002).

HUAORANI ECOLOGICAL KNOWLEDGE

As discussed in Clement, Rival, and Cole (2009), Huaorani people actively participate through cycles of residential mobility, foraging activities, and food consumption in the concentration of useful forest species. They are experts in reading signs of past human activity in the forest, and they are quick to ascribe forest alterations to the intervention of a wide range of actors. As they see it, the forest exists to the extent that humans in the past lived and worked there. By doing so, they have produced the forest as it is today for the benefit and use of the living. Trekking for the Huaorani is more than a mundane activity linked to the pragmatics of subsistence or to environmental and historical adaptation. Trekking constitutes their way of reproducing society across generations (Rival 2002).[9]

Notwithstanding their relatively restricted pharmacopoeia, the Huaorani demonstrate a remarkably accurate knowledge of pollination, dispersal, and animal behavior. Hunters can predict where animals are, which path they will take, or where they will spend the night. As Ellen (1999) has shown in the Southeast Asian context, the knowledge required for effective hunting and gathering has to be exceptionally extensive, even if it is not always formally codified. I have field diary entries filled with observations on the Huaorani's familiarity with the ecology of the forest's higher strata, which seems as developed as their understanding of what goes on at ground level. The Quichua, whose sisters or daughters have married Huaorani men and who often go hunting with their affines, and the Quichua teachers who live and work in Huaorani villages endlessly comment on the Huaorani's superior hunting skills, which they attribute to the latter's unique and intimate knowledge of the rain forest environment, as well as to their imputed magical connections with jaguars. The Huaorani's close identification with the forest world is thus constructed as much from without as it is experienced from within. Every researcher and tourist guide I know has remarked on their intense interest in and knowledge of the flowering and fruiting cycles of all edible forest plants, as well as of the preferred foods of most forest animals. Wade Davis also remarked in his collected souvenirs on the depth of Huaorani ecological knowledge (Davis 1997: 276–77).[10] Their extensive botanical knowledge confirms Ellen's thesis regarding the substantive ethnobiological knowledge of hunter-gatherers. Ellen, like Berlin and the other authors discussed earlier, thinks that foragers in biologically rich areas do not necessarily develop generic inventories of greater size than those of foragers living in biologically poorer regions (Ellen 1994). Whether this conclusion equally applies to the Huaorani remains to be examined.

HUAORANI PLANT CLASSIFICATION: A PRELIMINARY ANALYSIS

As a social anthropologist with no formal training in botany or ecology, what I know of Huaorani ethnobiological knowledge is based on observation, anecdotal evidence, and intuitive inference. It is therefore with some gratification that I refer here to two recent ethnobotanical studies that confirm my interpretation of Huaorani understandings of the natural world. Cerón and Montalvo (1998) surveyed 625 species in total, all of which have a Huaorani name and very often more than one (see below), as well as some use, although the use is sometimes marginal, such as "can be used as firewood" (414 species).[11] Of these, 402 species correspond to alluvial forest, 302 to primary high forest, 38 to garden plots, 27 to fallow forest, and 11 to riverbanks.[12] Mondragón and Smith's (1997) study is less scientific and less extensive (109 species registered), but in many ways more insightful, as their research goal was to inventory plants that the Huaorani define as the most useful in their daily lives.[13] The plants in the collection have 66 uses relating to artifact making and 51 relating to healing and health. Thirty are used for food, 16 for ornamental purposes, and 11 for ritual or ceremonial purposes.[14] Both Cerón and Montalvo and Mondragón and Smith remark on the Huaorani's ability to locate flowering and fruiting trees. Cerón and Montalvo mention the Huaorani's great ability to climb trees and inspect treetops. Despite obvious methodological shortcomings, these authors collected ethnobotanical data in the most "natural" conditions, that is, walking in the forest with Huaorani collaborators. All remarked on the depth and salience of Huaorani ecological knowledge. All were equally struck by their collaborators' unique ways of identifying plants. Despite the constraints and limitations of narrow questioning, Huaorani informants could not bring themselves to name a plant without placing it back within its ecological context. Cerón, Mondragón, and various other botanists told me that one of the most frustrating aspects of these ethnobotanical surveys was to have to record simply plant names, when so much else was being explained by indigenous collaborators. Cerón and Montalvo, who studied the ethnobotany of several other Amazonian societies, noted that the number of wild species used

TABLE 3. Huaorani and Quichua Names for Twenty-one Species of the Inga Genus.

SPECIES	HUAORANI NAME	QUICHUA NAME
Inga acreana Harms	*anganahue, ebenbahue, mimontan*	chuna pacai
I. acuminata Bentham	*mimuntan, mimuntahue*	pilingas, nina pacai
I. alba (Swartz) Willdenow	*anganahue, ebenbahue*	sacha pacai
I. auristellae Harms	*mimoncahue, mimontan*	pilingas, quina pacai
I. bourgonii Aublet (DC)	*ebenbahue, behuetempoye*	sacha pacai
I. capitata	*mimontun, tuica aun, huehuetenpuyo, aahue, auñabo*	poroto capsi, rumi pacai
I. chartacea Poeppig	*mimontan, hueibahue, mimuntahue*	sacha pacai
I. coruscans H. B. ex Willdenow,	*ebenban*	sacha pacai
I. densiflora Bentham	*nomonebe, ehueban*	machetona pacai
I. edulis C. Martius (introduced)	*ago, sampi* (Shuar generic term for Inga)	coto pacai, turo pacai
I. leiocalycina	*goihwagahue, noyhuagahue*	sacha pacai
I. oerstediana Bentham ex Seemann	*gontocan, contacahue*	barizo pacai
I. punctata Willdenow	*noyhuagahue, oohue*	canashi pacai
I. ruiziana G. Don	*viriquiu*	vaca pacai
I. sertulifera DC. sp. aff.	*au*	sacha pacai
I. spectabilis	*paven, anawenta*	castella pacai, machetona pacai
I. tessmanni Harms sp. aff.	*huamuncahue*	sacha pacai
I. thibaudiana DC.	*tecanamue*	bariza pacai
I. umbellifera (Vahl) Steudel	*ñuygüahue, tuhuicahue*	pilingas
I. vismiifolia Peoppig	*igüabahue*	sacha pacai
I. sp.	*begoguetempoe, ihua,* and *ahue* (Cerón and Montalvo collection) *iwaao, ewemaowenemengo* and *hauwae* (Davis and Yost collection), *huerekeonhue, ahuatanghue* and *ahuatahue* (Mondragón and Smith collection)	quillu pacai

TABLE 4. Huaorani and Quichua Names for Seven Species of the Theobroma Genus.*

	HUAORANI NAMES	QUICHUA NAMES
SPECIES OF WILD CACAOS		
Herrania nitida	*bonguinca*	*cambig, cambia*
H. nycterodendron R. E. Schult.	*buikahue*	*cambig, cambia*
Sterculia apeibophylla Ducke	*bukahue*	*yacu puscula*
S. colombiana Sprague	*bukayahue*	*puscalan, acatuyo yura*
SPECIES OF SEMIDOMESTICATED AND DOMESTICATED CACAOS		
Theobroma glauca Karst.	*tuveraca, tuverancahue*	*sacha cacao* (literally "wild cacao")
Theobroma sp.	*tëpëña*	*sacha cacao*
T. subincanum Martius	*tepenca, tepencahue, pepencahue*	*puca cacao*
T. bicolor Bonpl (introduced by missionaries)	*cupehuenca, cupemuenca*	*patas*
T. cacao L. (introduced by missionaries)	*cupehuenca, cupemuenca*	*sacha cacao*

*Data provided by Rocío Alarcón, pers. comm., 2000.

by the Huaorani as plant food is the highest recorded for the Amazon Basin.[15] Furthermore, they indicate that although name variation is surprisingly high, all their informants used the same nomenclature parameters to name plants.

Although the comparative material, which would allow us to draw a systematic comparison of the plant nomenclature of the Huaorani and that of their closest horticulturalist neighbors, the Napo Runa Quichua, is not yet available. The existing data, no matter how patchy, indicate that the Huaorani use many folk-specific names, at least as many as the Ka'apor do.[16]

For the genus *Theobroma*, we can see that the Huaorani differentiate nondomesticated species from domesticated ones.

A distinctive aspect of the Huaorani plant-naming system as it emerges from the studies of Cerón and Montalvo (1998) and Mandragón and Smith (1997) is that different names are often given for the same tree species (see Table 4 and Table 5, respectively). Most often, once synonyms are eliminated, a tree will have only two names: one generic and one specific. For instance, many tree species with removable bark belong to the family Annonaceae and are used in the fabrication of bark cloth called *oñetahue* (also spelled *oñatahue* or *uñetahue* from *oñe*, "bark," and *ahue*, "trunk" or "tree"), and something more specific. *Crematosperma gracilipes* R. E Fries, for instance, is called *oñetahue* and *muncabatahue* (or *muncapata*). Similarly, a number of species belonging to the family Lauraceae are named *ocatoe* (also spelled *ocatohue*, *ocatahue*, or *ocatue*, from *ocata* "calabash" and *ahue* "trunk," or "tree"), and something else.[17] Another example is *Pouteria bangii*, called *ontogamo* or *meñimo*. In some cases, it appears that names encode habitat specifications. For instance, in the family Chrysobalanaceae, species from the genus *Hirtella* and the genus *Licania* appear to be named according to whether they grow in alluvial or high (i.e., hill top) forest. This also appears to be the case for the genus *Xylopia* and the genus *Guattaria* in the

TABLE 5. Huaorani Names for Plants Growing in Alluvial and High Forests.

SPECIES	HUAORANI NAME (HIGH FOREST)	HUAORANI NAME (ALLUVIAL FOREST)
Hirtella triendra	guiñamuncahue	Ayamuñihue, amungagive, amungabecamo
H. excelsa and *Licania gracilipes*	meñingohue	—
Xylopia sericea	yimatue	uñetahue
Guatteria multivenia	guinogohue	uñetahue, numatahue, ihuamagueme, begoe

To recapitulate, many tree species are known by at least two different vernacular names (six names for a single species is not uncommon), particularly in the families Burseraceae and Myristicaceae. This clearly needs further investigation. At this stage, there is no evidence to support the hypothesis that the number of names increases with either the use made of a particular species, or its area of distribution. The only strong correlation I could establish on the basis of the data Cerón and Montalvo collected is that species with more names tend to be species found in either alluvial or *both* high and alluvial forests. Tree species exclusively found in high forests tend to receive only one name.

A final characteristic, the encoding of ecological information, while being fairly common, applies most especially to culturally significant species, such as *B. gasipaes* or *Oenocarpus bataua*. Plants are named contextually in relation to the state of regrowth of the forest patch in which they are found, or in relation to their own growth and maturation status. For Rocio Alarcón, an Ecuadorian ethnobotanist who has worked with various indigenous populations, it is clear that the Huaorani classificatory system is unusual in specifying the plant's current developmental state, such as whether the plant is immature, adult and flowering, adult and fruiting, or adult but sterile, and so forth. The plant name may also indicate whether the fruit are ripe or not. Each part of the plant (and each phase of growth and fructification) receives a distinct name. The more the plant is used, the more complete the set of names. For example, an ungurahua palm encountered in the forest will be named *petohue* if it is an adult palm not currently bearing fruit. If it bears fruit, it will be referred to as *petomo*. If the palm is just about to start the fructification cycle, it will be called *petoyepo*. If it is a young, immature palm, it will be called *petoyo*. If the leaves are just coming out and opening up, it will be called *petocagi*.[18]

These examples illustrate the fact that an individual plant is not considered simply as the mere, abstract representative of a particular species.[19] Rather, it is treated as an individual member of a class belonging to a specific environment, and as a specific living organism undergoing a continuous process of change. This is why phenology is so important in Huaorani folk biology. Going back to the contrast between the classification systems of sedentary horticulturalists and those of hunter-gatherers, it is now possible to argue that the Huaorani, although much more mobile and far less interested in agriculture than the Ka'apor, have developed an ethnobotanical knowledge of equal richness. Unlike the Guajá, they have not lost specific terms for different species in the same genus, nor are they prone to indulge in taxonomic and nomenclatural lumping. Their botanical nomenclature formally expresses phenological states and ecological relations, and exhibits significant interpersonal variation (Gardner 2001). Such variation in a small, highly mobile population inhabiting a highly diverse environment requires further reflection and further investigation. We need to ask why some species seem to be known by different names, while others do not. Is there a relationship between name variation and morphology? For instance, are morphospecies lumped together? Is name variation a function of the difficulty of differentiating species on the basis of visual cues? Is there a relationship between name variation and dialectical differences, or unevenness in knowledge distribution or use?

This preliminary analysis has been offered for discussion on the understanding that it is highly provisional. Further research is needed to provide a systematic account of Huaorani ethnobotany, in particular, to establish whether name variation is more often caused by dialectal differences, substantial ecological differences between the various regions making up Huaorani land, the phenological state of the plant, or other factors. It would also be interesting to examine the density and distribution of key tree species across all the forest types between the Napo and Tigre rivers to see whether their shared properties have led to the selection of one single name for the different and substitutable species encountered by mobile communities passing through a highly diverse environment at regular intervals. Furthermore, we need to know more about the mechanisms by which native Amazonians and Western scientists experience and cope with the complexities of tropical ecosystems.

MOBILE PEOPLE AND MEGADIVERSE PLANT COMMUNITIES

I provided in this chapter a precursory examination of a domain of Huaorani cultural knowledge—ethnobotany—which I could not properly analyze previously for lack of sufficient data. Such data is now partly available thanks to the work of several Ecuadorian botanists and biologists. Much more research is needed to produce a full account of Huaorani ethnobiology, but the information currently available is sufficient to highlight various features that may be shared by other Northwest Amazonian cultures. I offered some evidence to support the hypothesis that the Huaorani system of plant classification exhibits a linguistically codified knowledge that gives precedence to ecological relations over purely taxonomic or classificatory relations. This hypothesis requires, as I argued in the first section of this chapter, a new way of understanding the correlation between agricultural development and the growth of plant nomenclature in a region of the world characterized by high biological diversity and lack of clear boundaries between foraging and horticulture. After a brief ethnographic summary, I mentioned some of the most obvious methodological problems relating to the analysis of ethnobotanical data (i.e., Huaorani tree names) recorded by botanists and ecologists during biological surveys directed at the study of the dominance and distribution of tree species in upper Amazonian forests. The two studies on which I mainly based this preliminary analysis stress the existence of a cross-cultural agreement in folk taxonomic systems and recognize the importance of knowledge specialization, particularly knowledge specialization in the context of subsistence activities. In continuation, I discussed various features of Huaorani tree taxonomy and showed the cultural significance of ecological and biocultural interactions. This approach allowed me to suggest that the psychological salience of ecological properties, for instance the contrast between high and alluvial forests, or the importance given to phenological states, is formally expressed at the level of the lexicon.

There has been considerable debate in the literature concerning the relationship between living kinds and the terms existing in a language to refer to them. Authors have disagreed on the principles that underlie naming systems and determine whether a species receives a distinct name or not. Whereas some authors have privileged perceptual discontinuities, others have prioritized utility. And whereas some interpret the striking similarities existing between most folk taxonomic systems as a result of the structural properties within the natural world, others interpret them in terms of universal properties of the human mind (Medin and Atran 1999). For authors such as Berlin, Medin, and Atran, our perceptual system has evolved in adaptation to the biological world. Berlin, however, argues for a direct correlation between plant domestication and the growth and complexity of lexical encoding. The more a population intervenes in the reproduction of plants, the more its ethnobotanical inventory will expand, for both wild and domesticated plants, as well as for plants and animals. Brown chose to explain this causal link with reference to the need to secure a subsistence buffer in case of crop failure. However, one may equally propose, like Ellen, that a sound knowledge of ecological properties is essential for using a forest environment appropriately, or that successful hunting entails a deep knowledge of natural history. Moreover, it is far from unreasonable to propose that ecology may also be considered as a domain of intellectual interest in its own right, an argument that Lévi-Strauss (1966) made with force over forty years ago. Totemic thinking,[20] however, has not been found in many foraging societies.[21] Moreover, animistic thinking often supersedes totemism in

Amazonia (Descola 1996). For Bird-David (1999), the prevalence of animism in egalitarian foraging societies relates to a strong sharing ethos and a cultural preference for interpersonal relationships. For Lenaerts (2004), animistic beliefs, that is, the inclusion of natural beings in the social sphere, underpin many characteristics of the ethnobiological classificatory systems found in Amazonia, in particular their context dependence and their focus on interspecies relations.[22]

What is so interesting in the Huaorani plant-naming system as it is partly sketched here is that conceptual ordering seems to result from recognizing an order that exists in nature (Berlin 1992), as well as from the cultural priority given to ecological relations over taxonomic ones.[23] As I have tried to show in this chapter, Huaorani knowledge of plant phenology is not only an implicit part of their extensive substantive knowledge of the rain forest's biological diversity, but that it also gets expressed at the level of the lexicon. In other words, it is formally codified, at least in part. The formalized expression of substantial ethnobiological knowledge about the environment in Huaorani plant taxonomy is puzzling. We need to know the extent to which their naming system results from cultural choices. As Atran (1999) has shown in his study of the Itzaj Maya's preference for causally based ecological reasoning, classificatory systems can include cultural preferences without these being necessarily interpreted as a result of arbitrary impositions. A thorough understanding of the cognitive and cultural processes at work in the Huaorani plant-naming system will require a comprehensive study of the folk biology of both the Huaorani and their agriculturalist neighbors, particularly the Quichua speakers with whom they now intermarry. We already know that Huaorani culture does not fit the cultivator/trekker/forager typology used by Balée to classify Tupí-Guaraní groups according to their specific historical ecology. As I have suggested elsewhere (Rival 2006), Northwest Amazon trekkers and foragers, who are not easily classifiable as devolved agriculturalists, may have had a historical trajectory different from that of the Tupí-Guaraní. Although there is no comprehensive Runa Quichua ethnobotany presently available, we know from partial studies that the Huaorani, who possess a vast botanical knowledge, are as generalist as their cultivating neighbors, if not more.[24] By combining taxonomic description (of the structure of folk biological categories) with an examination of how these categories are used in inductive reasoning (following the methodology developed by Atran and his collaborators), further studies will hopefully shed light on the dynamic interaction between plant classification and horticulture in the Upper Amazon. Future studies will need to address two central questions. What knowledge transmission occurred between the warring tribes of horticulturists and trekkers in Upper Amazonia? And how has the kind of ethnobotanical knowledge outlined here, with its rich encoding of complex ecological data in various dialects, been passed from generation to generation within a society marked by intense warfare?

3

HISTORICAL ECOLOGY IN AMAZONIA

THE AMAZON REGION has been described as containing the largest contiguous expanse of tropical rainforest in the world, a forest that has for centuries captivated the Western mind as pristine or untouched wilderness. Many scientists have dedicated their working lives to the documentation of the extraordinary biological and cultural diversity that Amazonia contains, including anthropologists interested in the parameters of nature and culture as analytical categories. This body of scholarship has helped raise awareness about the power of human activities to create and change the landscape in interaction with natural processes. It is no wonder, therefore, that current debates about human environmental interactions in the Anthropocene have renewed interest in these Amazonian studies. One particular contribution stands out: that made by Bill Balée, who attempted to capture the spatio-temporal dimensions of human environmental interactions at a time when the nature/culture dualism was still largely unquestioned. He has argued, for instance, that "the presence of the forest would not be explained without including people from the past, and the people of the present who lived there would not be there without that forest" (Balée 2013: 19). A distinctive aspect of his contribution has been to suggest that landscape creation over time is a process that can either enhance or degrade natural processes. His work has inspired many archaeologists to engage ecological science, as well as many conservationists bent on imagining different landscape futures through restoration ecology, "rewilding," and other management strategies.

In this chapter I discuss the main components of Balée's historical ecology approach and show how his ideas have shaped my analysis of Huaorani culture. I end with a reflection on the continuing difficulties that Amazonianist anthropologists face in their efforts to overcome nature/culture dualisms, and I propose a number of leads for future research.

WILLIAM BALÉE'S APPROACH TO AMAZONIA'S FORESTED LANDSCAPES

Balée's work, which spans over thirty years, has played an important role in changing the way we look at the Amazon rainforest (e.g., Balée 2013).[1] Like most specialists (and the public at large), he started his career thinking that the Amazon was the last remaining great wilderness on earth. While conservation biologists tended to see wild nature as areas devoid of human presence and influence, environmental anthropologists and archaeologists tended to think about nature in terms of limits and constraints to which humans were forced to adapt. Ethnographic work with the Ka'apor, followed by various field research projects with other groups who spoke Tupí-Guaraní, convinced Balée otherwise. His approach has been to find out how the forests growing in the Amazon Basin, where humans have lived for at least 11,000 years, have changed over time. Understanding this past, in his mind, is only meaningful if it is intrinsically linked to a search for ways to maintain Amazonian forests as resilient and evolving legacies of both nature and culture for the future.

DOCUMENTING PAST HUMAN ACTIVITIES IN FORESTS THOUGHT TO BE PRISTINE

After a period of intensive postdoctoral fieldwork (1984–88), during which he studied the species contents and distributions of different kinds of forests within Ka'apor territory, Balée formed the conviction that human influences shaped the natural environment over long periods of time. The study of various indigenous agroforestry systems in Maranhão, Brazil, for example, alerted him to the presence of surface pottery and charcoal in the soil. By systematically mapping the differences between old fallows and patches of undisturbed forest, he came to realize that he could treat forests (and their heterogeneity) as objective records of past human interactions with plants, even if local inhabitants appeared not to have any social memory of such history or any means of differentiating between different types of high or ancient forest.

Over the years, and through careful examination of botanical and ethnobotanical data, Balée has marshaled new empirical evidence that challenges earlier claims that Amazonia lacks in resource potential, or that human activity in this part of the world has done no more than marginally disturb natural processes. His initial focus was on differentiating old fallows (forests he alternatively termed *artificial*, *cultural*, or *anthropogenic*) from high forests, presumed by scientists to have remained beyond human influence. Despite their apparent similarity, these forests can be differentiated in terms of species distribution, trunk sizes, soil types, and signs of ancient settlements, the latter signaled by the presence of potsherds on the ground's surface. He also established that native classifications of forest and swidden types, as well as oral histories, converge more often than not with the observable physical differences he saw in the material record. This led him to argue that a corpus of evidence (the documentation of indigenous and traditional environmental knowledge, observations of contemporary gardening activities, and the study of archaeological sites) can be combined, correlated, and used to reason more inductively about the long-lasting effects of past human interference on forested landscapes.

Building on his comparison of forest types within Ka'apor territory, followed by a sustained comparison of Ka'apor and Guajá ethnobotanies, Balée proceeded to look at various historical trajectories and patterns of change within the Tupí-Guaraní linguistic family. This led him to argue that Amazonian nomadic bands have not wandered at random but have moved their camps from cultural forest to cultural forest, such as palm forests, bamboo forests, or Brazil nut forests, which do not grow in undisturbed parts of the forest but on ancient dwelling sites. It follows that foraging bands, such as the Guajá, the Kaingang, or the Sirionó, are best understood as having progressively lost village life and cultivation abilities in the aftermath of conquest, with, in the process, most of their domesticated crops. In other words, wandering native Amazonians are able to subsist in the rainforest without cultivated crops thanks to a few essential "wild" resources (palms, fruit trees, or bamboo), which are, in fact, the products of the activities of ancient populations, whether their direct ancestors or Arawakan enemies (Balée 2013: ix).

More recently, Balée has refined his forest inventory methodology to apply it to newly discovered archaeological sites where he has found, according to his predictions, anthropogenic forests characterized by a greater concentration of palms, vines, lianas, fruit trees, and other heavily used forest resources, as well as the wide occurrence of charcoal and numerous potsherds in the soil (e.g., Balée et al. 2014). His important discovery that local concentrations of specific plant species can be viewed as good indicators of past human activity and as reliable empirical records of environmental and social history is now used to convince ecologists, such as McMichael (McMichael et al. 2012, 2014), that past human activity has shaped species diversity much more deeply and more extensively than they are prepared to acknowledge (Balée 2013: Chapter 11). For Balée, then, humans have influenced the structure of the Amazon forest not only at local levels (alpha diversity) but also at much wider scales (beta diversity).

This succinct summary highlights Balée's scientific approach to the historical ecology of peoples and forests in the Amazon region. This approach has given precedence to the following: (a) directly observable data derived from field research on livelihoods and environmental management; (b) ethnobiological inquiries focused on naming and vocabulary items; and (c) botanical surveys realized by teams of indigenous consultants working with Western natural scientists. His initial focus on the ways in which particular Tupí-Guaraní groups perceive, categorize, utilize, and manage the plants and animals present in their forests (and reason about the impact of human action on the forest ecosystem) has shifted over time toward a systematic questioning of scientific assumptions about the nature of forest ecology. Ecologists, who privilege evolutionary explanations of speciation and spatial heterogeneity, do not, according to Balée, pay sufficient attention to temporal processes or to the ways in which anthropogenic factors may dramatically alter the interplay of pattern and process on which ecosystem functions depend.

Given the relevance of Balée's work for current debates about Amazonia's past, present, and future, and given the influence his formative ideas have had on my approach to Huaorani society and culture, I propose to examine some aspects at greater length below. I start with his continued interest in long-term change, including the characteristics of pattern-process relationships over broad spatial extents. I then move to his theorization of human and human-mediated influence on the forested landscape. Finally, I examine his approach to post-contact "attrition."

THEORIZING LONG-TERM CHANGE

What makes Balée's work so compelling in the context of today's numerous academic discussions of the Anthropocene is that he is one of the few authors who, over the last three decades, has systematically concerned himself with the general question of how human populations—in successive generations—have affected not only the patterns of distribution and abundance of plant species in Amazonia, but also the evolutionary process that has shaped these patterns. Anthropocene researchers bent on pushing anthropogenesis back into human history (i.e., prior to industrialization) tend to think of human impact as a uniform and global phenomenon. Balée, by contrast, carefully and systematically records the changes that have occurred in a region long thought to be primeval. Humans, who first arrived in the Amazon Basin as hunter-gatherers, progressively domesticated some of the world's major crops in the Basin. In the process, they underwent a series of sociocultural formations but continued to maintain, if not enrich, the region's biological diversity. The time frames Balée envisages, therefore, are human, rather than ecological, which brings him to consider evolution as a kind of history (Balée 2014: 22).

To grasp fully Balée's overall thesis that current patterns of species abundance and distribution cannot be properly understood without reference to human history, even in the Amazon rainforest, we need, I wish to contend, to appreciate the profound influence that Carl Sauer's work has had on him. For Carl Sauer, who thought about human ecology in terms of *cultural morphology*, studying culture necessarily implies analyzing cultural change in the light of a culture's history. In other words, the study of culture is the study of how people live in places and of how, by so doing, they end up shaping these places. Seen from a different angle, by looking for signs of human culture in particular places, a student of culture is in fact studying landscapes, an undertaking which requires a long-view approach to land use and much direct field experience. This is why Carl Sauer proposed that the landscape should be geography's unifying object of study. In Sauer's formulation, and for the many scholars he has influenced and inspired, the landscape is never merely a spatial phenomenon. Being the living (and hence changing) scene on which "the activity of man unfolds itself" (Sauer 1925: 25), it is always already cultural and temporal (Sauer 1925: 36–37). Best apprehended as a functioning, interdependent, and patterned system, and best grasped as the organic unit of land and life (Sauer 1925: 26), a landscape is thus a valued habitat shaped by people in thought and in action. Given that culture is the agentive or shaping force through which humans shape nature (Sauer 1925: 46), the landscape necessarily bears the material signs of subjective and aesthetic expressions (Sauer 1925: 48), signs that, moreover, reveal the extent to which people, far from adapting passively to given environmental conditions, continuously work at transforming them (Sauer 1925: 52). Often accused of antimodernism, Sauer defended *ethnopluralism* in the face of Eurocentrism (Denevan and Mathewson 2009). He dedicated much of his research to the landscapes created by rural folk and indigenous peoples, both in the past and in the present, for he saw in their land ethic and ingenuity valuable historical alternatives to the destructive nature of both colonial and modernist patterns and processes.[2]

Although he has never explicitly engaged Sauer's ideas and concepts, Balée has clearly made the concept of landscape central not only to his work but also to the historical ecology approach he has championed. Historical ecology, which in many ways can be taken as a synonym of landscape history, charts landscape changes over time. The landscape, seen as made up of both people and the environment, is treated as visual evidence of the interactions of culture and environment through time. In the case that concerns us, the landscape, formed in the ancient past from the dynamic interactions between forests and native Amazonian communities, unfolds in the present as the material manifestation of these relations, thus allowing for a more empirically grounded—and more holistic—analysis of human ecology (Balée 1998a: 1).

Like Sauer (1950), who argued that broadcast fires can create niches for new species in the landscape (while simple deforestation drastically decreases their numbers), Balée stresses that the human impact on the Amazon landscape has been as varied as the languages, political systems, and societies present in Amazonia. Humans can either increase or decrease the biological diversity found in nature, and the influence of prehistoric and pre-Columbian peoples on the primeval Amazon forest can be demonstrated to have enriched its biological diversity, unlike mechanized modern practices, which are destroying it at an alarming rate (Balée 2013). Many of his conclusions, therefore, converge with those of geographers who have applied Sauer's cultural geography to the Americas, especially those of William Denevan, whose critical essay on the "pristine myth" (Denevan 1992) and study of traditional indigenous agricultural systems (Denevan 2001) are essential readings on past human-environment relations in South America.

Faithfully applying Sauer's premise that change is inevitable and continuous, and that neither plant nor human communities remain static (Tansley 1935; Sauer 1950), Balée has systematically argued that a landscape necessarily undergoes distinct successional regimes. Humans will change their environment, indirectly and directly, inadvertently and purposefully. A landscape can never be returned to a former state—let alone a pristine one. To apprehend its historical contingency (i.e., history as a process of continuous change), one needs to measure and evaluate the spatial and temporal dynamism of inhabited ecosystems. Amazonia's forests were first peopled thousands of years ago by humans who hunted, gathered, and used fire, and who, over millennia, increased heterogeneity through cultivation and domestication. Such changes can only be grasped diachronically by looking for material signs of the reciprocal interactions between human and ecological dynamics over long periods of time. Balée's historical ecology, not unlike Marvin Harris's cultural materialism, takes scientific knowledge to be of a different nature from other kinds of knowledge, in that it seeks to explain the material causes that condition human life (e.g., Harris 1968: 655–74). This explains why he has systematically looked for material signs of culture in order to understand how human culture shapes the environment. However, unlike Marvin Harris (and in this he may be closer to Julian Steward and to Carl Sauer), Balée does not discard the significance of ideological and aesthetic motivations, as long as material traces of these motivations can be found and identified.

The focus of Balée's work is on forest succession and on how this phenomenon may have been influenced by human habitation of the landscape long before human communities began intensifying plant domestication and before they extended their agricultural systems. Having empirically researched and analyzed the anthropogenic origins of cultural forests, Balée has finally reached the conclusion that human-mediated disturbances have played a key role in shaping primary and secondary forest successions in the Amazon.[3] His major contribution to Amazonianist anthropology, archaeology, and ecology is to have consistently argued that what ecologists take to be successions (referring to species turnovers in specific areas) must in fact be understood as landscape *transformations*. The science of nonequilibrium systems ecology uses a terminology that continues to promote the idea of primary and secondary successions as purely ecological phenomena, while it is known that *successions* are often initiated by human action (Balée 2006). The anthropologist thus prefers to talk about transformations instead of successions in order to recognize more fully the fact that natural environments are shaped by human-mediated disturbances. To better reflect the fact that human activity apprehended in the long term necessarily alters the biomass, Balée thus advocates that we should rename primary and secondary successions *primary* and *secondary landscape transformations* (Balée 2013: 159–81).

CONCEPTUALIZING HUMAN INFLUENCE

Having taken a long-term approach to Amazonia's environmental and human history to show that indigenous knowledge and traditional technology developed over thousands of years can profoundly alter the distribution of tree species and even the chemical composition of soils, Balée has also been centrally concerned with the nature of human influence. How direct or conscious were the transformative actions of past humans? How aware were they of the anthropogenic nature of their landscape transformations?

For Balée, human adaptation to the environment is a dynamic process involving the management of altered landscapes. Landscapes, which are by definition the products of human alterations, are therefore artificial, or, in other words, caused to some extent by human behavior.[4] He cautions that analyses of human behavior in terms of intentionality will be useful only to the extent that purposefulness is understood to vary in degree and in intensity, and only if scientific means of measuring anthropogenic interference in terms of gradation and variability are readily available. His relative indifference to human agency looked at in terms of intentionality may be due to the kind of human signature he has been looking for in the forested landscapes of the Amazon Basin. His primary interest has never been the concerted determination and willed cooperation that crop domestication and the full formation of agricultural systems have undoubtedly required in this region as in others, but, rather, the more diffuse type of intentionality that seems to have characterized the activities of prehistoric hunter-gatherers and horticulturalists, and which can be shown to have caused gradual landscape transformations over thousands of years.

The Ka'apor, with whom he first studied the phenomenon of historical landscape transformation, can differentiate fallows from high forests but not the intermediary stages between the two. Moreover, they can differentiate themselves as people with crops from the Guajá, who do not cultivate; this difference, however, is perceived in terms of ethnic identity and food habits. Although they have bred plants for centuries and are decisively proud of it, the Ka'apor do not appear to do so by conscious design. They have no terms for semidomesticated species, even though on occasion they plant nondomesticated tree species. The presence of ecologically important tree species in their fallows is attributed to animal dispersal behavior and the presence of stone axe heads in the high forest to spiritual forces. Gradual change, Balée (2013: 60–69) concludes, is not perceived or memorized locally; it has to be reconstructed analytically by the scientist. The Kayapó, by contrast, appear to intentionally plant "forest islands" (*apêtê* [literally, "made," from the verb *apêt*, "to work, to make"]) in transition zones between savannas and high forests with the intention of benefitting their future descendants (Posey 1985).[5] For Balée, the cultural contrast between the

Kayapó, for whom the production of beauty and of new generations of beautiful people is a central value, and the Ka'apor, who prefer to represent their fallows as "one of the unintended (yet expected) results of human/animal interactions" (Balée 2013: 69), could not be starker.

Balée has maintained a sustained interest in these two contrastive indigenous discourses on forest management practices, not least because many of the species planted by the Kayapó in *apêtê* are also present in Ka'apor fallows, although, as already mentioned, not planted by them (Balée 2013: 69). Interestingly, today he offers a slightly different interpretation of this difference. The Kayapó encourage a primary turnover of species by encouraging trees to grow where there had only been grasses. Their forest islands thus correspond to a primary landscape formation not unlike the prehistoric mounds found on the large island of Marajó in the delta of the Amazon River or on the Ibibate mound and in the forest of the Bolivian Amazon (Balée 2013: 177–78). The Ka'por cultural forests derive instead from secondary landscape formation. This implies that the influence of the Ka'apor, who alter the distribution of species primarily through their subsistence activities, is much more indirect and intermediate than that of the Kayapó. Because these activities take place in a forest that has been gradually transformed over long periods of time by similar previous activities, the Ka'apor are best apprehended as part of a long chain of human intervention, which has gradually caused changes in the structural composition of the forest. To them (and to the ecologist), however, the forest continues to look primeval.

The cultural difference between the Ka'apor and the Kayapó, which was analyzed in the early 1990s in terms of intentional planting versus protective management (or direct versus indirect manipulation, see Balée [2013: 66–70]), is now thought to involve two different time frames: primary landscape formation versus secondary landscape formation (Balée 2013: 2). This new way of presenting the data confirms Balée's continued preference for a descriptive acceptation of the landscape in marked contrast with Posey's approach. It is worth noting that before his untimely death Posey was increasingly moving toward an interpretive acceptation of landscape formation among the Kayapó.[6] In Balée's explanatory framework, cultural difference arises from the fact that the slow and progressive transformation involved in forest successions over many generations cannot be cognized in the same way as genetic changes occurring in short-lived organisms can. The myth of wilderness may blind natural scientists to the human signature, but native Amazonians have simply no means of recording successional transformations. *Cultural Forests of the Amazon* (Balée 2013) ends with an unambiguous statement about human consciousness in relation to primary and secondary landscape transformations. Only in the former case is it possible to ascertain that the landscape results from conscious human intentions.[7]

RETHINKING POST-COLUMBIAN HISTORY

One of Balée's main interests while conducting comparative research on Tupí-Guaraní groups was *agricultural regression*. Today, he prefers to speak of a gradual process of *attrition*, that is, the cultural effects of the unwilled and historically contingent abandonment of agriculture. Broadly in agreement with early challenges to the then dominant thesis that the Amazon's biophysical characteristics impeded the full development and expansion of agricultural civilizations, Balée has never engaged directly with discussions of what archaeologist David Harris calls intermediate subsistence systems (Harris 2012: 21). Perhaps it was obvious to Balée at the time, given his Sauerian outlook on processes of change, that the emergence and establishment of agricultural systems had been a very slow, uneven, and gradual process. That the transition from hunting and gathering to intensive agriculture occurred in Amazonia is to him both undeniable and relatively unimportant. What matters is that the transition was historically curtailed (Clement 1999), and even reversed. In this he fully agrees with archaeologists such as Donald Lathrap, Robert Carneiro, and Anna Roosevelt. This explains why Balée's concern has been with the dramatic effects of the post-Columbian demographic collapse on the historical trajectory of Tupí-Guaraní groups. Not only were they forced to abandon sedentary village life bit-by-bit, but they also lost in the process the agricultural food production systems, as well as their trade networks, they inherited from their ancestors. As with any process involving human environmental interactions, this loss of social, political, and techno-economic complexity had to be a gradual process. It is this gradual transition that Balée set out to empirically trace. Much of the methodology he developed in the 1990s, and to which I referred earlier, aimed to demonstrate how a number of Tupí-Guaraní groups progressively transitioned from agricultural sedentism through trekking to complete nomadism, a process of regression involving in some cases, such as the Sirionó, the loss of fire-making technology, the most basic of all environmental management tools (Balée 2013: 102).[8]

A striking aspect of the argumentation is that it involves the same logic of reasoning as the one used in demonstrating the mechanisms of change at work in primary and secondary types of landscape transformation. Historical change is conceptualized as a slow, continuous, and gradual process even when it is triggered by dramatic events. The argumentation also starts from a similar postulate, according to which humans continuously affect their environments in ways that concentrate useful resources and sustain incremental productivity increases. The conviction that no society will willingly live without agriculture, once it has been mastered, structures the demonstration. In other words, people do not give up civilized arts once they have acquired them. Such abandonment, which has to be gradual, cannot result from free choice; it is best understood as change forced on people by death, conquest, or warfare (Balée 2013: 73–74).[9] Balée thus refutes Scott's (2009: 188) argument that trekkers and foragers may deliberately give up sedentary lifestyles in their wish not to be governed (Balée 2013: 73). His account of meetings with "wandering Indians" Aurê and Aurá, who he describes as orphaned "feral children" (Balée 2013: 17), dramatically illustrates his vision of contemporary hunting and gathering as the result of accidental human crises. Such life trajectories cannot be seen as the outcome of a willed cultural or political option.

To demonstrate that post-Columbian trekking and foraging are not pristine modes of adaptation but successive forms of historical regression, Balée set out to demonstrate that the forests to which trekking and foraging groups migrated and adapted are anthropogenic landscapes, that is, enriched biotic niches created in the past through agriculture. As mentioned earlier, the study started with a systematic comparison of Guajá and Ka'apor ethnobotanical classifications, which allowed Balée to document the dynamics of language retention and change through attrition. The Guajá and the Ka'apor both inhabit the same habitat and speak related Tupí-Guaraní languages. However, they use the forest according to two different subsistence economies—the Guajá as nomadic foragers, and the Ka'apor as semisedentary horticulturalists (Balée 2013: 99). Subsequently, a comparative examination of the plant vocabularies and ethnobiological classifications of other Tupí-Guaraní trekkers and foragers enabled Balée to substantiate his thesis regarding the gradual loss of agricultural knowledge through contact, displacement, and attrition. This led him to the conclusion that foraging Tupí-Guaraní societies, such as the Guajá, Hetá, and Aché, had undergone a "parallel historical regression from prior agricultural societies to exclusively foraging ones" (Balée 2013: 85).

Incidentally, the more Balée has analyzed plant vocabularies (both plants "grown by people" and plants that "thrive on their own in the forest") as historical records of cultural changes "embedded in subconscious linguistic processes" (Balée 2013: 21), the more he has tended to use forest inventories to provide material evidence of past *agricultural* activities and neglected other types of human signatures linked to, for instance, hunting and gathering activities (Rival 2006). It is not surprising, therefore, that his work has been influential in terms of establishing a new standard model in archaeology. According to this model, contemporary groups of foragers, trekkers, and shifting cultivators who live in marginal isolation in seemingly pristine forest environments are best analyzed as the descendants of larger, more sedentary social formations that were destroyed by the European conquest (e.g., Stahl 2008).[10] There is hardly any consideration in this new narrative of intermediate subsistence systems or of their historical resilience (Harris 2012). Moreover, there is even less attention paid to the particular forms of cultural consciousness that may have driven collective choices toward landscape retention and/or transformation. As I discuss further below, to assume that agro-ecosystems were created or adopted purely in terms of inevitable temporal dynamics and built-in incremental productivity, or that historical contingency is sufficient as an explanation for temporal reversals and productivity decreases, is not satisfactory.

SEEING THE HUAORANI THROUGH A HISTORICAL ECOLOGY LENS

Following in Balée's steps, I started my career as an anthropologist with the conviction that culture does not mechanically respond to predetermined environmental conditions. With the aim to find better theoretical approaches to human adaptation, I looked at Huaorani culture through the lens of hunting and gathering studies. While trekking, gathering, and hunting with Huaorani friends of all ages during fieldwork, it became obvious to me that we were not responding to perceived limitations in the natural environment. I also became aware of the fact that the men, women, and children with whom I *omëre gobopa* (forest trekked) saw their activities as part of a wider set of actions, which altogether resulted in improved food productivity and species richness. Huaorani were fully conscious of the fact that their activities prolonged that of past people (whether direct forebears or not), animals, and other kinds of humans present in the forest. They knew that all these activities, taken together, resulted in altering the distribution of plant and animal species in ways that made the forest abundant in useful resources. Moreover, they seemed to understand this overall enrichment as a kind of generative power, which I termed *natural abundance* for lack of a better term (Rival 2002: 88–92). Clement (2014) calls this ongoing modification of the floral structure *landscape domestication*.[11] By trying to understand landscape domestication as integral to the Huaorani hunter-gatherer worldview, I have also sought to identify specificities in their environmental knowledge, economic preferences, sociopolitical values, and more broadly, cultural choices and priorities. The Huaorani bountiful landscape corresponds to a coherent set of relational qualities, which resonate with what have been described in the literature as characteristics of hunter-gatherers: high mobility, a general lack of interest in property and accumulation, egalitarianism and food sharing, and a present-oriented attitude to life (Rival 1999).

REFUTING ENVIRONMENTAL AND HISTORICAL DETERMINISMS

The category of hunter-gatherers, with its assumptions regarding political evolution and economic development in historical societies, has deep roots in European thought. It is therefore not surprising that when the study of hunter-gatherer societies became an international academic field in the mid-twentieth century, the main purpose was to deconstruct the constitutive assumptions (both evolutionary and anthropological) behind the nineteenth-century reworkings of this particular "stage" of human evolution. The project of undoing this unworkable (nonunitary) category through critical engagement was so successful that hunter-gatherer studies is today mainly the concern of archaeologists researching Paleolithic livelihoods and Neolithic transitions. In anthropology, the livelihoods of contemporary communities once described as living chiefly through hunting and gathering are today described as indigenous or even "peasant" ways of life. As discussed earlier, Balée has used the term hunter-gatherers to refer to the descendants of Tupí-Guaraní groups who trek through ancient cultural forests, which they understand to be the creations of pre-Columbian agricultural societies. Decimated by diseases and wars during the sixteenth and seventeenth centuries, they survived to the present day with no, or few, domesticates thanks to past landscape transformations.[12] My use of the term, by contrast, has been guided by an interest in delineating the cultural orientation of highly mobile groups who are prone to abandon horticulture as easily as they are to take up crop cultivation.

A split after a series of political conflicts in the densely populated community where my doctoral fieldwork started (Dayuno) deeply influenced the course of my research. I followed the largest faction to a distant part of the forest, which had remained inhabited for at least five or six generations. To my surprise, my host family happily lived for months in hunting camps with no garden products. Sharing their lives during these months of intense mobility confirmed what I had already suspected from traveling to many hunting camps and to remote communities all over Huaorani territory. Rather than being essential to their diet, crops were seen to be mainly useful for ceremonial and political purposes. The initial faction went through a series of fluctuations (with additional splits and the incorporation of newcomers in various waves) before finally stabilizing around a number of allied family groups. This led me to fully appreciate the dynamism of Huaorani social life; it also gave me many opportunities to observe the multiple impacts the process had on the forest environment. In just a few years, a new village with a school, cultivated plots, and an airstrip (QuehueireOno) was gradually reconstituted at the site of the main hunting camp (Rival 2002). In the twenty years that have elapsed since, QuehueireOno has moved location several times; it is also now the name of a river association that comprises four different communities and operates a thriving ecotourist business. As for Dayuno, it was used by Huaorani and non-Huaorani alike for years as a large fishing and hunting reserve, until a couple who had been married there in their youth (and had lived for a while in QuehueireOno) returned with some of their married children to create a small community. They have now built their houses where the school and the health center once stood, and they named the site New Dayuno.

I used my research findings to contribute to a body of scholarship that has established that hunting and gathering is a viable way of life, even in the Amazon rainforest, where it is perfectly possible to survive without horticulture. Like other authors (e.g., Zent and Zent 2004; Politis 2007, 2014: 1041), I have argued against explanations of foraging in terms of optimization and rational choice, and stressed instead that, over time, human living necessarily transforms pristine nature into anthropogenic landscapes. Applying Balée's thesis about species enrichment to the Huaorani landscape and combining it with the insights of evolutionary biology (e.g., Rival and McKey 2008; Clement, Rival, and Cole 2009; McKey et al. 2012), I have defended the thesis that hunting and gathering is much more central to the subsistence economy of trekking people like the Huaorani than crop cultivation. Whereas they will readily give up the latter, they will not easily renounce the former. Huaorani trekking, I have thus concluded, is ill understood as "agricultural regression" or "secondary adaptation." It is through mobility that hunter-gatherers make landscapes out of their natural environments. Hunting and gathering, a way of life with its own logic and its own dynamic, has too often been defined by what it lacks, rather than in terms of its distinctive features, in particular its propensity to represent a collective desire to maintain a certain type of relationship with others (Bird-David 1990, 1992b). The idea that being on the move reinvigorates people and plants and, as such, contributes to the renewal of abundance, is central to the Huaorani trekking orientation.

According to Huaorani ethnohistory, their forebears have moved great distances along ridges parallel to rivers flowing into the Amazon, mainly *yarëcape*, or "moving up," the rivers along which *cowodi*, "the enemy" lived.[13] Traditionally established on hilltops where the vegetation and the soil contained signs of having been previously inhabited by past people with whom genealogical connections could be reactivated, longhouse groups were closely associated with palm groves and other culturally modified forest patches. When judged to be politically propitious, inter-longhouse alliances were fostered through invitations to drinking festivals. Organization of such festivals required the intensification of crop cultivation and, in particular, the expansion of plantain and sweet manioc monocultures on the hill slopes down from the hosting longhouse and onto neighboring hills. Longhouse members would also embark on shorter, more frequent treks as part of their hunting and gathering activities, managing their trails and often protecting or propagating useful plants wherever they went, including at their temporary hunting shelters and stopovers (Rival 1998b; Zurita 2014: 240, 251). Trekking, as a way of life, involved a continuous search for unoccupied lands; what nomadic Huaorani bands looked for were abandoned forest patches. Seen in this light, trekking results not so much from a will to escape the violence of more powerful others, but the strategic use of interstices between the ethnic territories of more sedentary enemies. Huaorani trekkers chose at times to transport with them planting materials over great distances. At other times, the decision was to abandon everything and to leave. In either case, people would not depart without having burnt houses and plantations first. Used as an endpoint (to destroy dwellings and cultivated fields), rather than as a starting point (swiddens were established through slash-and-mulch, not through slash-and-burn), fire was more than an environmental management technique. Upon settling in a new territory, people would slowly reconstitute a domain composed of a longhouse and of dispersed hunting camps, each surrounded with plants obtained from various sources: old fallows and ancient settlements, the gardens of enemies, or the high forest. I came to understand through field observations and conversations that cultivation, a process that was often interrupted and started up again, was anything but cumulative.[14] To my friends and informants, to be a Huaorani meant to be a hinterland trekker, a type of being very different from their riverine enemy. Trekkers made the forest by moving through it.

I have, over the years, developed a deeper understanding of the complexities and nonlinear interactions between hunting and gathering and farming in the early part of the Holocene (e.g., Harris 2012) and have come to appreciate the importance of agriculture as a bearer of collective identities (see Chapter 1). This has increasingly led me to question the continuing assumptions in Americanist archaeology regarding the "nonprimeval" and post-Columbian nature of contemporary hunting and gathering in lowland South America. Of course, essentialist uses of the label *hunter-gatherer* must be analyzed critically (e.g., Bessire 2014; Gordillo 2014). It is equally true, however, that challenging evolutionary models on the basis that historical trajectories are not necessarily determined by ecological adaptations (Politis 2014) requires that we acknowledge the resilience of livelihoods centered on hunting and gathering activities (Politis 2007: 342). The purpose of anthropological analysis is to go beyond apparently obvious factual statements. The issue is not whether the Huaorani cultivate plants or not, but how and why they cultivate them, and why trekking, hunting, and gathering were subjectively and symbolically so important before the advent of "civilization" (Rival 1992, 2002).

HUAORANI HISTORICAL AND CULTURAL DYNAMISM

When writing my doctoral dissertation, I felt caught, as many young ethnographers do, between a drive to explain the present and a need to reconstruct the past. The advancing oil frontier and the dramatic changes it had brought in its wake made the task particularly challenging and arduous. In the early nineties, the Huaorani ethnic territory was legally constituted in terms dictated by the opening of new oil fields south of the Napo River. In every community I visited, people told me that the Huaorani had now decided to become "civilized"

(Rival 1992, see also Chapter 8). On more than one occasion, I irritated young men who visited their families between work contracts with the oil companies. They would put their radios full blast or strike up a popular tune at the top of their lungs upon hearing their elders chant or recite myths for me. Civilized people had no time to waste with stupid traditions. Twenty-five years on, the distinctive shape taken by the Ecuadorian oil industry and its geopolitical and economic specificities appear to me much more clearly, as do the unique meanings of "civilization" in Huaorani land. Regular visits to Huaorani friends and stays within the communities where I had initially sojourned have helped me grasp the multiple microscales at which the collective desire for civilization has unfolded spatially and temporally intertwined with the oil industry. There are many different ways of living a Huaorani life today, but this internal heterogeneity is still shaped by collective, rather than individual—choices. Moreover, internal diversity has not come at the expense of panethnic solidarity, even if the shape and purpose of "Huaorani nationality" often remains incomprehensible to outsiders, especially Ecuadorian officials and tourists who need to believe, for slightly different reasons, in the pristine myth of wild forests and uncivilized, savage peoples.

Today, the Huaorani landscape is shaped by many more human-mediated influences than the trekking and dwelling activities evoked above, and it is hard to imagine what their overall long-term effects will be. One thing is certain, however. These influences are as heterogeneous as the collective choices represented by the forty-eight currently existing communities, not to mention the bands in voluntary isolation (see Chapter 9) or the families who spend more time in their hunting camps than in the villages to which they supposedly belong, at least according to their identity cards.[15] Interestingly, the Huaorani continue to understand their choice of living close to oil companies and missions as a desire to become "civilized," a desire they contrast with that of the Taromenani, which is to continue to live *durani bai*, that is, as life was lived in the ancient times (see Chapter 9). Another interesting fact is the way in which plant cultivation, though no longer an essential mediator in intergroup relationships, continues to organize the spectrum of possibilities. Communities in the vicinity of oil pumping stations where villagers now subsist with no cultivation at all constitute one end of the spectrum. Small and relatively isolated hinterland villages organized around subsistence farming (Zurita 2014) constitute the other end.

Zurita's doctoral thesis, which examines the cultivation practices of families with whom I lived (Dayuno) and worked (Zapino) twenty-five years ago, explores how people moved their dwellings and fields from hilltops to alluvial plains along the Nushiño River as part of their project of civilization.[16] Her remarkably detailed study of new forms of Huaorani landscape formation in the villages of New Dayuno and Tepapare empirically establishes that mobility has not decreased with the intensification of agriculture.[17] Cultivated plots valued for the food security they afford to households are not only part and parcel of everyday existence, but also, once fallowed, temporal and spatial markers of family life and history. Family estates centered on cultivated forests, which villagers intend to pass on down the generations as inalienable property, have been intentionally and gradually developed. Planted or appropriated by senior household members, individual trees (palms, domesticated or semidomesticated fruit trees, or even old canopy trees) mark out family lands; they are also used as material symbols and proofs of a family's collective property rights over a particular forest domain.

Zurita's account powerfully conveys the overall coherence of the new agro-ecological system. Efforts to isolate management activities or to privilege some over others are illusory, and, as she shows, it would be equally self-defeating to separate activities and forms of management in terms of "tradition" or of "novel adaptation." According to her understanding of what New Dayuno and Tepapare cultivators told her, the agro-ecological system starts with the building of a new house and the opening of fields to feed the house dwellers (Zurita 2014: 170). Once installed through radical intervention (such as stripping the forest soil bare), the family estate is maintained through careful and more indirect overall management activities (such as selective weeding, protecting certain plants, or encouraging the growth of others). If we were to apply Balée's terminology to the activities described by Zurita, we could say that the installation of the family estate corresponds to a primary landscape transformation, while the ensuing overall management constitutes a form of secondary landscape transformation. The fact that old villages and settlement sites are used both as seed banks and as hunting grounds by families in the process of constituting their common landed estate (Zurita 2014: 287) justifies this interpretation. This is also the case with many other observations made in the thesis, which show that people do not distinguish between wild and nonwild species. For instance, a survey of cultivated species found in various swiddens indicates that these contained as many species obtained during trips to jungle towns as species obtained from the high forest (Zurita 2014: 156). Choice, which is much more significant than provenance or origin, blurs boundaries between "hunting," "gathering," "cultivating," and "fishing." As Zurita rightly insists, landscape formation corresponds to the self-conscious assembling of many different kinds of beings.

The agro-ecological system Zurita describes is valued by her informants as a consciously chosen and coherent set of techniques and activities. The gardeners she worked with explained with pride why they prefer monocultures to polycultures; why they choose to broadcast corn, but sow peanuts; and why their fields, unlike those of Shuar or Quichua cultivators, are mulched, rather than burnt (Zurita 2014: 162–70). Furthermore, if they expressed nostalgia while evoking the natural abundance of places they no longer inhabit (hilltops), or of *durani bai* (times long gone), the gardeners preferred to emphasize the transformations they and their landscape had undergone with civilization; they stress that it transforms everything at once: the wild and the domesticated, food habits and houses, and the use of plants or animals (Zurita 2014: 308). For instance, the consumption of palm grubs has dramatically increased with civilization, as people no longer restrict themselves to the palm grubs that feed all year long on *ñemebo* (*Jacaratia digitata*). Instead, they now fell other palms as well, such as *nantohue* (*Mauritia flexuosa*), *tepa* (*Iriartea deltoidea*), or *petöhue* (*Oenocarpus bataua*), with the purpose of encouraging their colonization by a wider range of Coleoptera, even out of season (Zurita 2014: 256).[18] Finally, the fact that curare poison is still widely manufactured by men who no longer use it in hunting (Zurita 2014: 194) can also be explained in terms of its continuing symbolic importance for those who have chosen to become "civilized Huaorani."

In Tepapare, New Dayuno, and other Huaorani villages, new forms of mobility have reorganized trekking activities so that they may continue to afford independence and autonomy while sheltering people from the exigencies of market exchange. Tentatively generalizing her findings, Zurita argues that the reimagining of cultivated forests as inalienable family estates constitutes a modern response to the sequencing of time and the institutionalization of trade. The ways in which villagers in different communities couple social and ecological time through dynamic forms of resistance and accommodation to diverse markets (bushmeat trade, logging, handicrafts, community development, tourism, oil industry, and more) remain to be fully documented. These processes are important to an overall understanding of the heterogeneity of landscape formation in the Ecuadorian Amazon today, as similar human-mediated influences also shape the ethnic territories of other indigenous groups and, no doubt, the strategies of settlers as well. Forest inventories of the type promoted by Bill Balée would be very useful in establishing the ecological value of the heterogeneous diversity so created (Balée 2006).

CONCLUSION

As I have tried to show in this chapter, the term *landscape* is a polysemant that has been increasingly used in the Amazon context to capture different aspects of the many interactions between humans and their living environments. Landscapes become cultural artifacts indirectly as the products of the irreversible passage of time. Their historical production is a gradual and slow process, which bears and retains the material manifestations of human activities. A landscape lens thus unsettles functionalist or neofunctionalist concerns with environmental adaptation on the one hand, and assumptions by natural scientists about ecological processes on the other. A science of ecology that ignores or belittles the role of humans in shaping natural environments or the antiquity of human action on the environment leads to a misperception of history, of the present, and, indeed, of reality. Indigenous systems respond to elements in the structure and the function of the tropical rainforest, and to specific selective pressures. The design of sound forest conservation policies, therefore, requires an accurate scientific understanding of forest *transformations*, rather than forest successions.

Although aesthetic properties and subjective values have not been completely ignored by authors such as Balée, the prime place granted to the diachronic perspective tends to overshadow the role played by human memories, self-conscious designs, and historical agency. As I have argued in this chapter, human signatures need to be considered in terms of articulated collective projects and local systems of knowledge that reveal shared experiences of environmental modifications. Inspired by Balée's interest in human-mediated influences on the forest, I have tried to delineate the contours of the Huaorani landscape, pointing to the specificities of Huaorani ways of trekking, foraging, and inhabiting forest gaps, which people maintain over time, and to which they return periodically. The management and use of two different domesticated crops, manioc and peach palm, which, as I have argued, are associated with alternative social forms and contrastive social times, are key to the ongoing formation of the Huaorani landscape (Rival 1998b, 2002). We have known for a long time that there is a continuum between the forest at one end of the spectrum and cultivated fields at the other, with various management practices in between (Wilbert 1961). In the Huaorani case, a greater reliance on peach palm has traditionally corresponded with high mobility, trekking, and a certain social closure. A greater reliance on manioc, by contrast, has corresponded to an increase in intercommunity feasting, the expansion of marriage alliances, and larger longhouses.

As I have argued in Chapters 1 and 2, cultural differences between communities associating themselves more with foraging or with farming become apparent through close examination of cosmological ideas, rituals, values, and modes of relationality. The recent study by Zurita (2014) shows that at least some Huaorani communities have shifted their position along the spectrum between foraging and farming. These communities are in the process of composing family estates where manioc and peach palm (as well as many other wild and cultivated plants) are being rearticulated into agroforestry systems thought of as patrimonial legacies to be inherited by direct descendants, while also offering food security and autonomy in the present. Moreover, and as discussed earlier, Zurita shows that a new indigenous mode of temporality based on modern chronological categories acquired through state schooling accompanies the subtle differences in botanical knowledge, cultural preferences, and individual and collective decisions around the management of plants that she documents in her thesis. This, to my mind, indicates that the communities in which Zurita has worked are actively reworking the symbolic power of time gaps in the landscape.

The historical consciousness I was trying to capture in my work was rooted in emotions and memories that could only be aroused through forest exploration. Trekking through a landscape full of signs of the presence of others (present and past, human and nonhuman) involves apprehending the passing of time in terms of a multispecies history, which I took to be a form of "living in the present" (see Chapter 7). I understood that temporal gaps produce wealth and abundance, and that the Huaorani disposition to suddenly leave everything behind constitutes a powerful means of creating temporal and spatial gaps. The dialectics of identity that I saw in Huaorani forest trekking (*ömere gobopa*, or "I go on a walk through the forest") involves forms of abandonment and going away that form an intrinsic part of what gives value to the past. The Huaorani dialectics of identity do not rely on the authoritative transmission of similarity, or on the appropriation of difference. Instead, the past is valued in terms of experiences linked to acts of abandonment. Beyond creating discontinuity, abandonment offers a promise of reencounter, albeit under a new guise. Meanwhile, the landscape continues to age until it gets regenerated through some catastrophic event (Rival 2005). As growth, energy, aging, and other irruptive issues trace or reshape the contours of the penetrating oil frontier and its affordances (see Chapter 9), I am no longer certain that living in the present captures all the facets of the love for trekking.

Balée has argued that past human activity has created heterogeneity over time, enriching the entire forest biome in species (Balée 2013: 159) and resulting in at least 12 percent of the Amazon region becoming anthropogenic while, in a sense, remaining primeval (Balée 2013: 3). Native Amazonians have gradually transformed the places they lived and visited into landscapes that do not reach climax states of diversity and complexity but "continue to unfold with no specific destination or endpoint" (Balée 2013: 181). The Huaorani landscape represents one of these "unclimaxing" cultural spaces, where the composition of forests was changed without domesticating species, and where a multitude of semidomesticated, fruit-bearing tree species were allowed to thrive. Constituted through a logic of abandonment, which is also a key to personal autonomy and freedom, this landscape irradiates with indigenous understandings of change and transformation, vital energy and growth, intensity and depletion, and decay and renewal. Some of these understandings are discussed more fully in the rest of this book, some others remain to be fully engaged with.

PART II

IN THE LONGHOUSE

OVERVIEW

THE THREE CHAPTERS IN PART II address a number of questions that have shaped the growth and theoretical relevance of Amazonianist anthropology over the years. Though far from being a unified, homogeneous field of research, Amazonianist anthropology has renewed, through its debates and diversity, our thinking on society, individuals, and the state; history, historiography, and historicity; regional ethnology and cross-cultural comparative models; and research ethics. In lowland South America, social structures tend to relate to the construction of the individual and the fabrication of the body rather than to the definition of groups and the transmission of goods, as, for instance, in Africa. In many contexts, the circulation of symbols and substances guarantees social continuity and reproduction more effectively than the lineal transmission of physical substances would. Numerous nonhuman persons people the social worlds that make up Amazonia, a region where invisible dimensions always lurk behind visible ones. In no known Amazonian language are the categories *person* and *human* established as equivalent, or even as overlapping. Apart from being dualistic, reality is also in constant flux. In this highly transformable, double-sided world, identities are continuously recycled and essential human qualities re-embodied and reconfigured. Yet, ethnographic evidence also points to contexts within which high fluidity and instability get "frozen" into lasting patterns of "essence" and "process," thus providing rich materials to rethink the nature of the social.

Unsurprisingly, poststructuralists and postmodern analysts have used Amazonian ethnographic materials along Melanesian ones to redefine society in terms of sociality and social reproduction in terms of embodiment and personhood. The centrality of Melanesia and Amazonia in contemporary anthropological theorizing is largely due to the twin efforts of two authors, Marilyn Strathern and Eduardo Viveiros de Castro, and their followers. Eduardo Viveiros de Castro has called into question the very idea of society as a Western theoretical construct based on a series of dualisms (individual and society; society and culture; society and nature; or primitive society and modern society) that distort and misrepresent the reality of Amazonian social worlds. In a parallel argument to Strathern's deconstructions of the fixity (and biologization) of human social nature in the Melanesian context, he has stressed the prevalence in the Amazonian context of cosmic distinctions between human and nonhuman entities. Strathern's reconceptualization of gender from an attribute of individuals to a modality of relations was aimed at destabilizing the dualism of biological determinism and cultural conditioning that underpins modern Western feminist politics. Viveiros de Castro's *perspectivism* and *multinaturalism* have similarly recasted the nature/culture dualism that pervades Western views of humanity and animality. Sympathetic to the argument that the cosmological categories of Melanesian and Amazonian societies need to be fully taken into consideration if we are to avoid ethnocentric interpretations, I nevertheless remain unconvinced by the claims that an interest in political and economic considerations necessarily imposes a misleading sociocentric or structural-functionalist cast onto indigenous categories and relational modes. Said differently, whereas recent poststructuralist interpretations have tended to privilege the analysis of indigenous ontologies (most often taken to mean modes of identifying the types of beings existing in the world) accessed through the study of myths, I have consistently maintained that our analyses must continue to pay attention to the ways in which people relate to each other and come to form lasting social institutions.

The three chapters in Part II discuss the quality and nature of relations between *nanicabo* (residents of a longhouse). As I illustrate, the polarization between hypersociality and hyperalterity, as well as the strategies put in place to overcome the dual opposition between real humans (i.e., insiders, coresidents, or consanguineal kin) and enemies (outsiders, affines, or predatory nonhumans) can be examined fruitfully through a sociological treatment of *nanicabo* residential sociality. Together, these three chapters offer an understanding of the dialectical relations between cosmological schemas and forms of social organization that highlight Huaorani specificities, which are ill understood, I argue, through the lens of "perspectivism." They also shed light on how Huaorani people value processes of maturation, growth, and self-regeneration, while apprehending the natural bounty of the forest as resulting from the interlocking of animal, plant, and human life cycles.

Chapter 4 focuses on the uxorial condition of Huaorani fathers. I show how husband and wife, by observing the couvade ritual restrictions, get *reborn* as mother and father. This leads me to discuss the ways in which childbirth materializes the conjugal tie and, in a sense, *creates* marriage. In contrast to a perspectivist treatment of couvade rituals, which stresses the need to protect infants from acquiring the bodily characteristics of game animals (e.g., Vilaça 2002), I emphasize the sociological relevance of placing and attachment in the creation of the parent/child bond, as well as the jural and physical nature of Amazonian fatherhood.

Chapter 5 offers a rich discussion of the notion of shared substance that underpins *nanicabo* sociality. It is commonly said that Amazonian societies offer the best examples of *nurture kinship*, by which it is meant that kinship is constituted on the basis of emotional attachments and memories of being related through caring and feeding rather than through blood (i.e., pre-given) or genetic (i.e., fixed) ties. In the Huaorani case, I argue, it is the fact of dwelling together over time, rather than food sharing, that underpins the indigenous notion of shared substance. To apprehend the Huaorani *community of substance* in all its dimensions, we need to understand relatedness as a biosocial phenomenon. The sharing of substance between Huaorani coresidents is not constituted by linguistic practices (such as the correspondences between food and sex famously commented upon by Edmund Leach in his introduction to structuralism) or by the remembrance of nurturing acts; rather, it builds up gradually from the intimate routines and sensual processes that tie together people whose project it is to live together well.

The central role played by the gradual incorporation of external creative and generative powers in the making and sustaining of social links is taken up in

FIGURE 12. Giving birth today, July 2007.

FIGURE 13. Mother and daughter resting in a hammock, June 2005.

FIGURE 14. The good life, the Huaorani way, July 2008.

FIGURE 15. Girl sharing her sweet with her pet monkey, August 2008.

FIGURE 16. Little girl in a forest camp with her pet monkey, July 2008.

FIGURE 17. Tamed deer, Damointaro, July 2008.

FIGURE 18. Guests resting at a festival (*ëëmë*), Miwaguno, April 2013.

Chapter 6, which examines the gendering of kinship in the light of the prey/predator dialectic. I argue that consanguinity and affinity give shape to quasi-social structures materialized as two gendered perspectives on the social whole. I also argue that "femininity" and "masculinity" need to be analyzed in terms of a complex dialectic between body and soul. Through their bodies, humans (as well as animals and plants) are either male or female. Gender parity reflects the symmetric complementarity of sexed bodily dispositions. This parity permeates all social activities, including marriage alliances and feasting. The differential attachment of the soul to the body in men and women leads to subtle asymmetries that give meaning, shape, and value to uxorilocal residence. By cultivating their particular attachment to cosmic forces, men become warriors and shamans who develop the ability to cumulate human and nonhuman identities. Women ceaselessly work at grounding and taming the longhouse's hearths, gaining, in the process, a collective power that suffuses the production of the longhouse as a politically autonomous and economically self-sufficient unit. Gender relations are therefore deeply implicated in the constitution of the cultural forests examined in Part II.

4

HUMAN BIRTH

Hosting a New Life

IN HUAORANI SOCIETY, as in many others, the birth of a child represents an important act of social creation. Undoubtedly, the observances that surround childbirth are meant to protect the health of the newborn. As I shall show in this chapter, their procreative force goes far beyond. Huaorani birth rites, I argue, are embedded within a larger ritual framework through which life is transferred, intimate relationships formed, and coparenthood institutionalized.

"TWO MAKING" SEX: SEXUAL COMPLEMENTARITY

Upon arriving in July 1996, in the Huaorani community where I carried out most of my fieldwork, I was closely and relentlessly questioned by my women "kin" about my reproductive state. This was because on a previous visit seven months earlier I had plainly lied to them in the hope of getting more accurate and detailed information on procreation, pregnancy, and birth, and said that I was pregnant. Now trapped in the lie, I tried to elude their questions by saying that this early pregnancy had ended with a miscarriage. At this point, my classificatory sister and close informant Hueica made an appearance. She was slowly approaching, holding her third son born just a few hours before my arrival, and showing the signs of fatigue and physical strain that delivery leaves on a woman's face. Had I really been pregnant on that previous visit, I would have given birth more or less at the same time as Hueica. Noticing my growing infatuation for her baby, and acknowledging my childlessness, she often gave me the newborn to carry around. This of course did not go unnoticed, and it raised a series of speculations in people's minds. One late afternoon, as I was sitting in Hueica's house with the baby on my lap, visitors poured in for an impromptu drinking party. There was an unusual tension in the air, and a word I had never heard before, *tapey*, got repeated several times amid loud laughs and ribald comments. Broad jokes flew faster and faster, and the men's shaking with laughter started to make me feel vaguely uncomfortable. It all became unbearable when two of my male classificatory cross-cousins, who were more or less my age, directed their *gauloiseries* (bawdy remarks) openly at me: if I so wished for a baby, I only had to ask them. Their behavior was most unusual. Huaorani men had never treated me as a desirable female, and I had so far enjoyed the freedom and peace that being a kinswoman gives. I received no dirty looks, no ambiguous comments, or provocative gestures, just amusing requests concerning my own female relatives, such as "if you live with us, your daughter will have to stay and marry one of our sons," or "bring me your younger sister, I am bored with just one wife." I swiftly went to find refuge near Hueica by the hearth, and shouted back that I would not listen to their bad words. Hueica added angrily that they would all have to leave the house if they kept misbehaving, and "normal" conversation resumed. This is how I came across the word *tapey*, the only "obscene" expression to be found in the Huaorani language. It is obscene because unless used between a woman and her husband, it causes considerable embarrassment and discomfort. *Tapey* is what women say to men when they want to copulate. It means "let's make another child." Ironically enough, missionaries of the Summer Institute of Linguistics (SIL) have used this word to translate the honorable, male-centered biblical term *to beget*.

In Huaorani culture, sexuality is the reproductive activity by which heterosexual pairs (men and women who are not siblings, belong to the same generation, and are of approximately the same chronological age) are *mina pa*, or "two making," or *arome mö*, "sleep as one," and consequently, *nincopa*, "multiply through copulation." The expressions *hua ñoô imba*, "it is a good thing that they should sleep together in the same hammock" and *mö*, "to sleep," "sleep together," "to sleep as one," and "to be married" are also frequently used to speak about conjugal lovemaking. *Niñe* is what all sexed animals do to reproduce, from crocodiles, to birds, jaguars, monkeys, and dogs. Making love involves two persons in one hammock, and only two; so if a man has several wives, he goes in turns from one hammock to the next. Husbands and wives sleep together as part of growing into an organic unit that will eventually produce children. Sexual intercourse is overtly geared toward reproduction. Having babies is not seen as a by-product of sexual pleasure but as a reward in itself, for adulthood is about pairing and giving birth to children. The few unmarried men I know live with their married sisters, and act as second husbands in terms of the division of labor. The single mothers I know live with their mothers and married sisters. Their children have *no father*, for, as I shall explain in greater detail below, no man has shared substance with them through repeated intercourse, and no man has performed the couvade for them. There is "no good reason" (*ononqui*), it is said, for the birth of these children.

Sensuality, which a Huaorani would translate as "we live well" (*huaponi quehuemonipa*), is not centered on genitalia, nor is genital pleasure the exclusive realm of adult heterosexuality (see Chapter 5). Sensuality is best seen as one of the ways in which the longhouse sharing economy is materialized, or as a form of promiscuous well-being. People living in the same longhouse gradually become *aroboqui baön anobain* (of the same substance, literally "of one same flesh"). The physical reality of living together, that is, of continuously feeding each other, eating the same food, and sleeping together, develops into a common physicality, which is far more real than genealogical ties. Children actively seek sensual pleasure, which does not require sexual maturity. Whereas reproductive sexuality—the conscious and focused action of making a child—is goal-oriented, sensuality, like all forms of bodily pleasures, is amorphous and diffuse.

As I have discussed elsewhere (Rival 1992, 1996a), ongoing common residence in the longhouse forms the sociological basis of the sharing economy. Sharing practices express and continuously reassert togetherness, and the repeated and undifferentiated *action* of sharing that goes on within the longhouse turns coresidents into a single, indistinct substance. Even if living together turns people into the same substance, the process is not irreversible. The sharing of a common substance lasts only as long as it is sustained through continuous sharing practices. It is not permanent and can be discontinued. However, reversing the process is a serious matter. Individuals who leave one group for another undergo a change of identity, which is usually marked by the adoption of a different personal name. They have become "other" and cannot go back to the longhouse they left, where they would be taken for malevolent spirits, who have returned only to kill and devour their former kin associates.

The principle by which people become related through common living applies to diet restrictions as well. When a *nanicabo*, "member of the longhouse residential group," is sick, all residents must respect the same food prohibitions to help him or her recover. By contrast, cognatic relatives living elsewhere have no such restrictions. Relatedness may result from consuming together or avoiding food together.[1] Everyone in the *nanicabo* partakes in everyone else's care and well-being, and the more people spend time together, the more they become alike. Persons and communities are processes that unfold in time, through the cumulative experience of living side-by-side, day-after-day. *Nanicabo* members share illnesses, parasites, a common dwelling, and a common territory. Sensual bonding, as diffuse as food sharing, unfolds as one aspect of the pleasure of living in each other's company. Sensuality is practiced not as the realization of private fantasies but as the bodily expression of sharing. This implies that the need for comfort and physical contact is not necessarily eroticized. The wish for contact is not construed as sexual, nor the desire for affection taken to be a desire for sex (see also Liedloff [1975] 1986: 151, 152). It is therefore not surprising that the evangelical missionaries who translated part of the Bible into Huaorani had great difficulty in finding the right term for adultery. They finally settled for *nano tohue nono* (literally, "someone who's having fun"), and resorted to the made-up expression "someone who's repeatedly having fun" (*èè quète ante nè tohuenga*) to translate the word *prostitute*. But Huaorani sexuality is not predicated on the repression of sexual desire. Moreover, as orgasm is not considered the ultimate, most pleasurable bodily experience, its attainment does not constitute the main channel for the building up and the release of sexual energy. In my view, the almost "anti-orgasmic" character of Huaorani sexuality is not caused by the fear of losing vital substances and life force; rather, it results from the diffuse, unfocused nature of sensuous pleasure.

Huaorani culture does not represent men and women as classes of people constituted by and through sexual desire, except, perhaps, in myths about the lethal sexual attraction between humans and animals. A great number of myths involve women who copulate with animals (anacondas, monkeys, tapirs, and so forth), become pregnant, have their insides devoured by the monstrous fetuses they carry, and then die (see Chapter 5). The brother-sister incest myth, in which a brother transforms himself into a mosquito and seduces his sister by getting into her throat, could also be interpreted as a form of animal-human intercourse, but it does not have the erotic charge found in the other myths (Rival 1996b). As I understand them (on the basis of conversations with informants and of ethnographic observations), these myths express the antisocial nature of excessive sexual desire and unreasonable attraction. They also, albeit more indirectly, suggest that sexuality is really about child making, and that this activity, which should only occur within the same species, starts as *tapey* and ends up as *baromipa*, (literally, "creating the child"). The suffix ending *tapey* derives from—or at least is related to—the expression *tey*, which indicates force and vitality. The same suffix is found in *maney*, the action of inserting manioc stalks into the holes hastily created with the digging stick into the forest ground before tree felling. The expression *tey* is used by hunters when blowing a dart through the blowpipe. *Baromipa*, on the other hand, is also used to talk about the making of a blowpipe or spear by a man and the making of a pot by a woman. I am not sure whether the term *baromipa* is also used with reference to the conjoint making of a hammock by the conjugal pair. However, and revealingly, *baromipa* has been used by the SIL missionaries to translate "God's creation." Taken together, these notions shed light on the belief that a child cannot form and remain in the mother's womb unless semen accumulates through repeated intercourse and, in some cases, through intercourse with more than one man. The same belief is found in many Amazonian societies where the couvade is often found in association with uxorilocality, if not matrifocality (Munroe, Munroe, and Whiting 1973; Rival 1998a).

MEN'S PARTICIPATION IN THE BIRTH PROCESS

Multiple biological fatherhood (or *partible paternity*) is widespread in Amazonia (e.g., Beckerman and Valentine 2002). Among the Huaorani, whereas it is the official father (the man who lives uxorilocally with the pregnant woman and forms an economic partnership with her) who cuts the umbilical cord, receives the newborn, and buries the placenta, any man who has contributed semen may observe the taboos associated with the couvade by which he publicly acknowledges his creative contribution to the making of the child.[2] Although there is no native term for *couvade*, the institution exists among the Huaorani in ways very similar to those described in Amazonian ethnology.[3] As elsewhere in Amazonia, Huaorani birth observances fundamentally consist in perinatal dietary and activity restrictions for both parents. Sometime toward the end of the pregnancy, the expectant couple stops eating fish and most types of meat. They are only allowed *yahuè* (toucan, *Ramphastos cuvieri*) and *barè* (curassow, Cracidae) meat.[4] In case of polygyny (men often marry two or three [classificatory] sisters), the other wife or wives eat, work, and sleep as usual, and so do all the siblings of the baby-to-come. From the time the mother enters labor to some days following the birth, the father restricts his food intake to boiled plantain or manioc broth. He avoids hunting and stays at home as much as possible, preferably lying in his hammock, where he spends the night alone (rather than with his younger children and wife, as usual).

When asked why they restrict their diet and daily occupations before and after childbirth, men invariably answer that, firstly, they do it because their wives do; and that, secondly, the newborn, who "is one flesh" with its mother and father, must be protected from wasting away. The couvade is not a male rite, but the rite of a couple. Parents are anxious to protect infants from diarrhea and weight loss, which are perceived as a form of bodily "liquefaction." Food taboos are aimed at "hardening" the body, that is, at reinforcing its intrinsic energy. The goal is to make the baby vigorous and strong, so it can grow fast and develop into an independent member of the longhouse. Men I interviewed insisted that *both* parents were protecting the infant's vigor and assisting its fast growth through fasting. This fact seemed to be far more significant to them than the precise details of what particular food should be avoided and why. What mattered also was that dieting parents behaved differently from fellow coresidents. Only parents-to-be avoided walking in the forest to protect themselves and the child from animal attacks. During conversations with informants, I also realized that these protective measures and restrictions were not different from those observed by the sick. In either case, the endangered vital force of particular individuals was restored through collective effort and the strict limitation of imports from outside the longhouse.

Individual behavior, however, seems to vary a great deal within these general guidelines. Couvade restrictions may last from a period of six months (three months before and three months after birth) to just one week. If few informants observe the most stringent diet (manioc broth), almost all report some kind of fasting in connection with their wives' pregnancies. The biggest change in food intake I have detected is the radical shift from a mainly meat, to a mostly vegetable diet. It is also worth mentioning that if not all young fathers observe the couvade today, those who do not are not acting differently from their wives. In other words, there are no cases of women dieting and giving up ordinary activities while their husbands do not or, for that matter, of husbands respecting couvade rites when their wives do not. When Hueica was expecting her second child, for example, she accepted from a North American missionary nurse vitamin and mineral pills, which although explicitly prescribed for her, she shared with her husband Ñame. Many young parents find perinatal observances bothersome and impractical. Ñame, currently the Health Coordinator of ONHAE (Organización Huaorani de la Amazonía Ecuatoriana), spends much time visiting indigenous communities and meeting officials in the provincial and national capitals. Just before taking on this responsibility, he and his wife left the house of his parents-in-law (where they had resided since their wedding) to live in his parents' village. As Ñame's duties prevented him from coming back home for the birth of his third son (briefly alluded to at the beginning of the previous section), Hueica's mother trekked all the way from her home to be with her daughter during childbirth and help her look after the two older sons. This time, as her husband was away, Hueica did not observe couvade restrictions, and I am almost certain that Ñame did not restrict his food intake or activities either; but he did radio his wife from the organization headquarters at least once a day. And, although both have great faith in modern medicine, had anything gone wrong during the delivery, or had the newborn been unwell, they would have immediately started couvade restrictions, and Ñame would have come back home right away no matter what.

Huaorani men do not imitate childbirth but take an active part in it and often act as midwives. Except for the cases when labor starts during the night and when the mother has no time to reach the kitchen area, births still take place near the hearth, which is now located away from the sleeping quarters. Huaorani women give birth in an old hammock especially hung near the hearth for this purpose. The middle cord is pulled out when labor pains finally appear. The hammock, now split in two halves in the middle, allows the newborn to pass right through the hole onto large leaves on the ground. The expectant father helps his wife during labor by massaging her back. He applies *huento* (stinging nettles, a common analgesic) on her tummy, back, and temples. He may reach into his wife's body if there is a difficulty, such as when the umbilical cord is wrapped around the baby's neck. He also knows how to assist her in breech deliveries. The father cuts the umbilical cord with a sharp instrument (usually a knife-shaped piece of bamboo), wraps the placenta in the large leaves on which the baby was born, and buries the bundle with the afterbirth in the nearby forest at the foot of a slow-growing tree. Traditionally, the placenta was placed in a *caanta* (a special clay bowl) also used by a girl to drink when she menstruates for the first time. This bowl is still used by men to prepare and store curare poison (see Chapter 6).

A young husband is aided in all these tasks by his mother-in-law (he usually resides uxorilocally), at least until he acquires sufficient knowledge and experience. He might in fact do no more than observe her during the birth of his first child. But by the third or fourth delivery, roles are reversed. The prospective father is in charge, and his wife's mother might not even be present. The other men of the longhouse, especially the father, unmarried brothers, and brothers-in-law of the mother-to-be, if they have not deserted the communal dwelling, keep aloof from other coresidents and move about inconspicuously. Today, few Huaorani still live in longhouses, but births have remained communal events in which a woman's close female kin (her grandmother, mother, classificatory mothers, and sisters) actively participate along with her husband and the young children who are commonly associated with her household. Even when she lives virilocally, a woman seeks to involve her mother in the birth process. It is not uncommon for her husband's mother and father to leave the common residence just before labor pains start, and come back when the infant is several weeks old.

Whereas it is the official father (the man who lives uxorilocally with the pregnant woman and forms an economic partnership with her) who cuts the umbilical cord, receives the newborn, and buries the placenta, and as mentioned earlier, any man who has had intercourse with the mother-to-be may observe the taboos associated with the couvade. It took me a long time to understand that when an informant mentioned several names in answer to my question about who their father was, or when people were arguing about who exactly was the father of a person whose genealogy I was trying to chart, they were not fooling me, confusing genealogical and classificatory fatherhood, or making bad jokes. Alleged or claimed fatherhood can be translated into a multiplicity of more or less official links that blur distinctions between cognatic and affinal kin, and between the biological and social aspects of kinship. The fact that more than one father can be socially recognized is not without consequences. Children (particularly male children) who would have been potential affines had cofatherhood not been claimed, are now half-siblings. Cofatherhood does not seem to have much impact on marriage alliances; most alliances are considered acceptable as long as the rule emically expressed as "if the mothers are different—not sisters—the children can marry" is respected. It multiplies links and reinforces solidarity among men both inter- and intragenerationally. However, given that inseminators give up their routine activities and restrict their diet, but are not involved in the delivery of the child they have helped create, and given that the newborn's maternal grandmother helps in the birth of her grandchild but does not observe couvade restrictions, only the official father fully participates alongside the mother in the birth process.

All men (but only two women) I interviewed about couvade restrictions mentioned a popular myth about a time when babies were raised by their fathers. Because women did not know the muscular movements to expel babies out of their bodies, men were obliged to cut their wives open, extract the babies, and feed them until they were old enough to fend for themselves. As women never survived the operation, and as there were not enough women available to remarry, men could have only one child. The myth can be summarized as follows.

> It was a tragic, terrible period of our history, for married men could only have one child, whom they delivered by killing their wives. Women had a birth canal and a hole, but it was too narrow to let the child out, so men had to cut their pregnant wives open to get the baby out.
>
> "One day, *wegönhuè* observed an expectant couple from a distance. The woman was close to giving birth, so her husband went to the forest to prepare the spears for the caesarean section.[5] He was in grief at the thought of having to kill and bury his wife, and raise the baby on *kapamo* juice.[6] But while he was busy making his spears, the little rodent came near the pregnant woman, held her in the back, and taught her muscular movements to dilate the birth canal. The baby was born just before its father's return. He was absolutely stunned and delighted. The word spread around, and pregnant women from the vicinity came to learn from the woman who had given birth without losing her life. From then on, the Huaorani race grew and multiplied."

When telling this myth, men put the stress on how terrible it is *for the husband* to lose his wife. The new father has no problem coping with, caring for, or feeding the child. But he is now spouseless, and left with a single child. The primary concern here, which is with what happens to the wife/mother, represents the almost exact reversal of the concern expressed in the couvade.

HOSTING THE NEWBORN

There is only one term in Huaorani, *tèquè eñaringa*, that translates to fetus, newborn, and infant; it literally means "in the process of being born." As in other parts of Amazonia, the child is said to result from the coagulation of female blood and male semen (Rival 1998a: 638). I felt during conversations with informants (observing the movement of their scooped hands) that they were trying to impress on me that there should be an equal proportion of semen and blood, and hence repetitive sexual intercourse. As the clot forms, it is activated—energized—by the Creator's soul matter and becomes a child. So the child is all formed from the start; there is no process of transformation or metamorphosis, only a process of growth.[7] Likewise, delivery is not sufficient to give birth to the child, who is definitively born only when the father and the mother have ended the couvade restrictions and when a classificatory grandparent (a grandmother for a girl, a grandfather for a boy) has given him or her at least one personal name. Going a step further, I would say that the moment of birth is not the beginning of life per se but, rather, the transfer from one dwelling (the womb) to another (the longhouse). The word *ne eñaca*, or "guest," is actually "the one who is born." The word *ne ocöinga*, or "host," is "the one who is at home." And the word *huiñègäncoo*, or "womb," is "the place where children multiply." All this suggests that birth is part of a wider process of gradual incorporation by which children, who start their lives in the mother's womb, are progressively integrated within the longhouse sharing economy. This requires a period of transition during which they are exclusively fed by their biological parents.

According to Huaorani etiquette, hosts must give to their guests unilaterally and upon request. Guests are considered to be pure consumers, just like newborns, at least when they first arrive. Outside formal attendance to drinking ceremonies or feasts, visiting, which is always surrounded with an aura of tension and uneasiness, is fairly restricted. Visiting connects close kin who, having ceased to live together, now partake in the sharing economy of different longhouses. Therefore, the connection is never between the visitor and *all* the members of the visited longhouse. The visitor is the guest of one or, at most, two or three longhouse members. A married man living uxorilocally who goes back to spend some time with his mother and sisters represents the typical visitor. If he comes accompanied by his wife or another member of their longhouse, these stay outside. He alone, the authorized guest, sits inside the longhouse. The wife partakes in the commensality of the visited longhouse from outside and converses with the hosts through the palm wall. When food is served, she receives a share indirectly from the hands of the official visitor. Another reason why visiting creates uneasiness is that guests are suspected of wanting to prolong their visit with the intention of shifting allegiance from one longhouse to another or to find refuge there after a raid. Because guests may potentially cease to be exogenous to the *nanicabo* they visit, and turn into new coresidents, visiting is always on the verge of leading to a process of incorporation and, as such, is intrinsically ambiguous.

With the birth of each child, parents are like hosts to newcomers, their guest-children, whose attachment to the longhouse is at first tenuous. Parents are involved in the business of creating a new life, that is, of adding new members to the *nanicabo*, and they protect the fragile connection between the child and the *nanicabo* by respecting couvade restrictions which entail the alteration of their sharing patterns within the longhouse. From this perspective, parents, whose productive activities have diminished almost to nothing, have very little to give away to coresidents from whom they receive much less than they normally would because of the stringent food prohibitions they are following. In other words, parents undergoing the couvade while directing most of their giving-away practices to the newborn, the privileged center of their sharing relations, *share less* with their fellow coresidents.

The child exists as a person from the first conscious parental acts of feeding, which denote, at the same time, the parents' partial exclusion from the *nanicabo*. Moreover, their fasting and inactivity strongly identifies them with the newborn with whom they form a community of substance. When both parents observe the couvade restrictions, the child is publicly linked to caretakers; it is a welcome guest. The parental ritual behavior signifies that the child's existence is unconditionally accepted. An undesired child cannot become a person; it is killed and buried with the afterbirth. A woman pregnant against her wishes does not abort but, having gone through the pregnancy without observing any couvade restrictions, buries the newborn with the placenta right after delivery. It is extremely difficult for orphans to survive, even when they have been adopted or when they are under someone's protection. Social bonding starts before birth and develops and grows after birth as the child's needs are satisfied and its expectations fulfilled. Well-being is a prime concern of social life and so is caretaking. Parents, through their repeated acts of unilateral giving away (i.e., sharing), transfer life substance onto a separate individual, who is no more linked to the mother than it is to the father and who is made to feel just as at home in the external world as it was in the womb.

The couvade, therefore, also relates to a certain conception of children as inherently social, of child development as the natural development of self-reliance, and of individuals as their own proprietors. A child's inferior strength and dependence upon adults neither implies that its motives are not social nor that it should be treated with less respect than an adult. There is no trace here of the view that childhood is an antisocial, animal-like stage in the individual's life cycle. Absent as well is the view that childhood is the painful and conflictive process by which children grow up only if their needs are frustrated, or the view that the relationship between "owning" parents and "owned" children is necessarily adversary. There are no wild instincts to tame or domesticate through socialization. If the newborn demonstrates its willingness to live by performing successfully during delivery and by actively breast-feeding and if its *genitrix* and genitor(s) show their intention to welcome and host its new life through performing the couvade, then the newborn is considered human, hence social, that is, as social and human as it can be at this early stage. The implication is, therefore, that the child's process of becoming a person fully immersed in a developed web of sharing relations is inseparable from the process by which its parents become parents, that is, a married, reproductive couple fully inserted within a matrifocal house group. As we shall see below, this is particularly crucial for the child's father.

In addition to the couvade, two important ritual practices denote the great importance of becoming a father. The ritual recognition of paternity finds full expression in the sacrifice of a young child on the grave of its dying father. It was not before the summer of 1996, when I had my most trusting informants role-play a killing raid and the burial of a dying warrior, that I could fully appreciate the nature and importance of what I call a child sacrifice, for lack of a better term. When a warrior is found in agony, left with spears run through his body and no chance of surviving, his male relatives dig a shallow grave to which he is carried by his female relatives. His wife puts their youngest child in the grave with him, and the two die by suffocation. When questioned on this issue, informants unanimously answered that this was done "so the father would not leave the land alone, so he would not feel lonely in the afterworld."

In the second ritual marking the social significance of fatherhood, a man of mature age, whose children are already married, and fully incorporated into his wife's house group acquires the ability to establish consanguineous ties of a more personal and mystical nature. He becomes a shaman when the spirit of a jaguar adopts him as his father and comes to visit him at night in the longhouse. The jaguar spirit first appears in dreams. If welcome and encouraged to come back, he makes the man "die" temporarily and takes the place of his soul. He speaks and chants, and he refers to the unconscious man whose body he possesses as "my father," addresses the man's wife as "mother," and the man's children as "siblings." The term *meñera*, or "shaman," may derive etymologically from *miñe*, "jaguar," and *bara*, "mother." Furthermore, dead shamans are said to transform into female jaguar cubs who eventually possess other mature men, who in turn become shamans. Contrary to the common practice in Northwest Amazonia, however, a shaman is never called to purify the newborn and its parents before their reintegration within the longhouse. Is the father adopting a jaguar son conceptualized as a female-like agent with the capacity to engender a child? Or is it, rather, that the male body can, after having begotten human children, host a spiritual, animal force? I do not know. But whatever the answer, what remains significant in this form of incorporation is that it takes the form of a father-son relationship.

PARENTING IN NATIVE AMAZONIA

Although found in other parts of the world, the couvade is first and foremost an Amazonian rite.[8] When analyzed in its proper regional context, with no pretention of developing a general theory to explain its origin and institutional development, the couvade appears clearly for what it is, a rite of coparenthood.

The term *couvade* covers a wide range of behaviors and symptoms found in many cultures, all suggesting active male participation in pregnancy. Anthropologists have offered different interpretations of culturally imposed restrictions on the daily routines of expectant fathers, as well as of the various physiological and/or psychosomatic manifestations that often accompany them. Couvade or *human brooding* is a strange old French term that literally means "poultry breeding;" it is widely found on the World Wide Web and is still sometimes used in anthropology. There are many internet sites where expectant fathers swap stories about their weight gain, swollen bellies, hot flushes, exhaustion, or even morning sickness. On other sites, symptoms associated with the "couvade syndrome" are discussed by male health practitioners who advise anxious fathers-to-be on how to cope with the physiological and psychosomatic side effects of living with pregnant partners. Such modern anxieties, found almost exclusively in Western industrialized societies, are often discussed in the context of paternal instincts supposedly characteristic of all humans and other mating animals, especially birds.

Anthropologists, who have stressed the need to differentiate couvade as a psychosomatic complaint from couvade as a ritual, claim expertise on the latter rather than on the former. However, the identification of the behavioral regularities with an aim to create typologies or engage in cross-cultural comparative analysis has proven a continuous challenge. In its broadest sense, the couvade involves the father giving up his normal routine activity around childbirth for a range of ritualized practices either before, during, or just after the child is born. Uneven data quality has hampered the scope of anthropological generalizations. Empirically, couvade practices can be very elusive, varying in force and intensity not only between cultures, but also between regions, historical moments, and individuals. Furthermore, the reporting of such practices by avid collectors of exotica or keen evolutionists has not been immune to biases. Taking these caveats into account, we are left with solid evidence for a few regions of the world, especially lowland South America, rural Europe, and Southeast Asia.

As with other key anthropological terms such as *totem*, *taboo*, *hau*, or *mana*, shifts in the interpretation of the couvade reflect changes in dominant explanatory modes over time while revealing continuing tensions in anthropological theory. For nineteenth-century cultural evolutionists, couvade rites indicate a transition from mother right (matriarchy) to father right (patriarchy). For early twentieth-century structural-functionalists these rites point to sociological imperatives. For instance, in societies where the marriage institution is weak or insecure, couvade rites have been found to correspond to public assertions by the father of his physiological and moral bond to the child. In other words, such rites constitute paternity claims. For late twentieth-century kinship specialists, by contrast, issues of symbolic signification get the upper hand, and the couvade is no longer seen primarily as a social institution. Rather, it is studied in terms of abstract substance categories, which people use to make sense of the ways in which they come to relate to each other and through which they end becoming who they are.

The richness of lowland South American ethnographic descriptions of the couvade allows us to understand more fully the diversity of means through which cultures symbolically rework the biological processes involved in human procreation and reproduction. Even more importantly, it illustrates the extent to which ideas about relatedness and shared substance may depart from Western notions rooted in biology and genetics. Métraux's short article on the couvade written for the *Handbook of South American Indians* (1946–50) was the first synthetic and comparative analysis of this custom in the Amazon region. In it, Métraux emphatically stressed that the Amazonian couvade was not motivated by a male desire to imitate childbirth, and that perinatal food and activity restrictions applied to *both* parents. While following Tylor (1865), Frazer (1910), and Crawley ([1902] 1927) in interpreting these restrictions as a form of sympathetic magic, he also noted that food prohibitions were primarily aimed at the temporary elimination of animal flesh from the parents' diet. Métraux (1946–50: 374) then concluded that, for those who practiced it, the couvade was the "expression of the close bond between the father and the infant's clinging soul."

The challenge of explaining the couvade as both a rite of parenthood and the expression of a strong spiritual connection between a father and his child has been taken up more recently by Rivière (1974) in an influential contribution to the debate. His solution to the conundrum is that the couvade, not unlike Christian baptism or *compadrazco* in Latin America, is a rite of spiritual creation. Rivière thus interprets the couvade as primarily concerned with the creation of a complete person, composed of a body and a mind—or soul. The new individual's physical part is delivered (i.e., born), but the spiritual part must be created, and if the father participates in the former, his primary responsibility is in the latter. In the same line of reasoning, Menget interprets the process by which a new human person is brought to life and new relationships are created in terms of the "universal system of elementary symbolics" (Menget 1979: 257). One element of this system is the representation of vital fluids, which structures the constitution of the person, her or his relationship to society, and the creation of new individuals. Menget, following Héritier (1979), and perhaps more in tune with lowland South American social philosophies (Seeger, da Matta, and de Castro 1987), and as Rivière would himself contend today (pers. comm., 1997), locates the phenomenon of spiritual creation within a more general theory of substances, which also encompasses incest prohibitions. He finds that the classification of food into forbidden and recommended categories, which underlines diet restrictions and incest taboos and codifies the fundamental opposition between weak substances (water, milk, sperm, white flour, and lean meat) and strong substances (fermented foods and foods rich in blood and fat), works to ensure that the progressive separation of parental substance, divided by the couvade, does not get reunited through incestuous union.

If we now turn to more ethnographic materials, we note that most Amazonian anthropologists have insisted, like Métraux, that couvade restrictions are observed by both parents. And like him, they have been primarily concerned with the active participation of the father in the birth process, as if the mother's ritual restrictions were natural and matter-of-fact. Such oversight may be due to the fact that pregnant and breast-feeding women in Western societies are also subjected to all sorts of behavioral and dietary change. Like Métraux, most ethnographers have paid more attention to food restrictions than to behavioral ones. But unlike him, they have stressed that couvade restrictions are essentially similar to those observed on many other liminal occasions, such as a girl's first menses, illness, death, or shamanic initiation. A comparison of their accounts shows that in addition to widely practicing birth observances and explaining them in quite similar terms, Amazonian Indians also usually do the following: (1) conceive of the child as the product of paternal and maternal influences (in other words, the child results from the complementarity of shape and substance or of two substances, such as blood and semen); (2) believe that repeated sexual intercourse before and throughout pregnancy is necessary for the fetus to develop and grow; (3) grant a special role to the mother's mother during delivery, sometimes in partnership with her son-in-law; (4) equate the end of the couvade with the naming (with or without ceremony) of the child; (5) prefer to space and limit the number of their children; and (6), try to achieve (and use infanticide if necessary) an equal number of male and female children. Beside these common features, which should form an essential part of any proper analysis of childbirth ritual restrictions, there is some variation in the duration and severity of the couvade. These are some of the most salient: (1) the intervention of a shaman to reintegrate the couple and the newborn within the communal dwelling; (2) the preferred location for, and the participation of the father in, the delivery; and (3) the exclusivity of physiological paternity (whether several genitors are recognized or not).

The six common features identified above equally apply to the Huaorani couvade. They highlight two important characteristics of Amazonian birth practices. The first one is that childbirth does not constitute a radical break (it is not an event) but, rather, is the process by which a new human life is gradually incorporated within the longhouse. The second characteristic is that childbirth is at once child centered and parent focused. Perinatal restrictions protect the child and create new relationships among, on the one hand, the child, the child's father, and the child's mother and, on the other hand, the parents and the house group. They also emphasize, along with native theories of procreation and sexuality, that the creation of a new human life requires the same involvement from the two sexes, even if equal participation in child making affects men and women differently.

It seems to me that Rivière's (1974: 432) exclusive focus on the transcending effect of culture, which works at ordering and transforming raw biological matter (he sums it up with the formula birth:couvade : nature:culture), risks the danger of overlooking the two central characteristics mentioned above. In the Amazonian context, the individuation of the child does not depend only on its getting a soul, as well as a body, but also on its being placed within a field of social relations ultimately leading to its successful incorporation within a specific social group. By giving priority to a hierarchical symbolic ordering that makes the spiritual creation of the child not only necessary to its welfare, but also socially more significant than its biological birth, Rivière could be read as ignoring such placement. Furthermore, given the father's special role in creating the child spiritually, his interpretation implicitly leads one to infer that fatherhood is more social than motherhood. This is in some ways the conclusion also reached by Bloch and Guggenheim (1981) in their study of Christian baptism and by most Melanesianists interested in male initiation rituals (see in particular Godelier [1973] 1982). I am not denying that some Amazonian male initiation rites (Hugh-Jones 1979), like their Melanesian counterparts, promote the symbolic appropriation of female reproductive powers by men. But to equate the couvade with ritual rebirth during male initiation would distort the ethnographic data and mislead the reader.

The couvade is not a rite of fatherhood but a rite of coparenthood with special implications for men given the uxorilocal nature of Amazonian societies. Menget's interpretation is similar to Rivière's in that both look for the signification of the couvade, not within the institution itself but within the structural and abstract properties of dualist categories of substance, which, ultimately, determine the social order. Menget's structuralist theory is attractive in that it draws no distinction between bodily substances and food substances (food substances are processed by, and in, bodily substances). His view is now shared by anthropologists who understand kinship processually (see e.g., Carsten 1995). However, the problem with Menget's theory, as with many structuralist theories, is that it tries to derive marriage rules from incest prohibitions. I do not take issue with Menget on his well-taken point that Amazonian parents understand the protection of their newborns in terms of the substances that make up the person but, rather, that he overlooks the sociological significance of the father's recognition that he and his newborn share the same substance. Ritual abstinence by a man on the birth of a child corresponds to his public notification that he is connected to this child and to its mother, quite independently from marriage and residence. Through observing the couvade restrictions, a man claims to be a father. If he lives uxorilocally with the child's mother, his claim furthers his incorporation within his wife's *nanicabo* as kin, while at the same time he makes his relation to his sisters (potentially the future mothers-in-law of the child) more affinal. Menget's global representational system ultimately articulates the categories of "same" and "different." Among the Huaorani, identity and alterity do not overlap neatly with gender categories. Within the category "true human beings," that is, Huaorani people as opposed to all other kinds of people and spirits, the gender category "woman" includes the most alike and the most different. Whereas mothers and daughters (i.e., sisters) are most identical, *mengui*, or "female cross-cousins," are most "other." If men's relationships—even that between male cross-cousins of either sex—are always "consanguinisable," it is absolutely impossible to consanguinise relationships between *mengui*. This is why women are both a source of identity and of difference.

Sperber's (1996) critique of Menget entirely misses the sociological significance of the couvade, for his interest in the end is not to understand the couvade in its Amazonian context but to explain a sociocultural phenomenon, which leads him to criticize what he sees as the arbitrary nature of most anthropological interpretation. For Sperber, Menget should have described the individual mental states of the Txikáo men he discusses at the beginning of his article and then should have tried to answer two questions. How did this ritual first appear? And in which sense can it be said to be beneficial? The latter question ultimately raises the more fundamental question of why a particular representation is more contagious and more frequently implanted in a particular population. Sperber's hypothesis is that the *man* undergoing the rite believes that the precautions *he* takes do prevent the dangers and risks associated with the transmission of life. His starting point, therefore, is Frazerian; it is sympathetic magic he seeks to explain. For this, he focuses on the cognitive mechanisms by which such a potentially harmful fasting ritual as the couvade is selected and transmitted over generations. He identifies four psycho-social reasons underpinning the magical belief: (1) all misfortunes call for explanation; (2) authority holders are entrusted with the responsibility of determining the cause(s) of misfortune and of prescribing preventive remedies, as well as with the task of transmitting the group's customs and lore; (3) when misfortune strikes, those who were supposed to have behaved in a certain way and have not are held responsible. They, therefore, abide by the custom as a means for personal protection; and (4) because the couvade has no real efficacy, its persistence must be explained in terms of the fact that actors make inadequate inferences on the basis of observed facts. One could well say that Sperber's thesis does little more than reexamine Homans's (1941) synthesis of Malinowski's ([1948] 1954) and Radcliffe-Brown's (1965) positions on ritual and anxiety from the viewpoint of evolutionary psychology.

There are several problems with Sperber's hypothesis. The first one is that he naturalizes the mother-child bond by thinking of the couvade as primarily the father's concern and by taking the reasons for the mother's precautionary observations before, during, and just after childbirth to be obvious (Sperber 1996: 54). Then, there is the problem that by seeing the couvade as a defense mechanism against the risks of childbirth, he does not explain why beliefs structured around sympathetic magic and contagion are so widespread in Amazonia, particularly when it comes to the ritual association or pairing of closely related entities such as begetter/begotten, killer/victim, or predator/prey (Taylor 1950: 349). In each of these cases, the individuation of "self" and "other" is at stake. Finally, Sperber's hypothesis in no way addresses the fact that the newborn's welfare depends on its insertion within a web of relationships. All the available ethnographic evidence supports the contention that this is as profound and transmittable a motivation as the concern with protecting the baby's health. As I have tried to show, the Huaorani's understanding of the couvade is inseparable from the notion that people who live together come to share the same substance and that the good health of longhouse coresidents largely depends on sharing practices, including that of fasting together. The incidence of perinatal risk is not higher in Amazonian societies, and newborns are not perceived as fragile and weak individuals any more than in other, noncouvade-practicing societies. Like many birth rituals, couvade restrictions are at least as much parent centered as they are child centered (Bloch 1992). I therefore argue against Sperber that the couvade is profoundly Amazonian, and its existence is intrinsically linked to the structural position of fathers, be they uxorilocally incorporated or not.

Ethnographies from lowland South America, where couvade rites have been widely reported and are still practiced, well illustrate the tensions that are constitutive of anthropology as a discipline beyond theoretical fashions. Native Amazonian societies are famous for the puzzles they present to the Western mind, especially for what appears as a lack of institutional complexity combined with material simplicity, both found to be at odds with the richness of mythological elaboration. With their many recalcitrant meanings and forms, the cultural models of procreation and parenting have been equally found confusing, if not baffling. The notion that babies get formed by accumulation of semen from successive copulations with one or more men are very common in

Amazonia; so is the idea that a successful birth entails a spiritual as well as a physical creation. The co-procreation ideal is often confirmed by kinship terminologies, and sexual permissiveness often gets institutionalized in various forms of ceremonial friendship and/or ceremonial extramarital sex. Moreover, plural paternity and extramarital sex are commonly justified on the ground that men and women have a moral duty to respond to the sexual advances of opposite sex cross-cousins (real or classified); keeping for oneself is a sign of stinginess. Social fathers differentiate themselves from biological fathers by claiming the bonds they wish to forge with their children and their children's mothers. Finally, many different parent-child relationships are considered possible and valued, not least those arising from adoption and fostering.

As the Huaorani example illustrates, couvade rites and restrictions may thus make sociological sense, but they also articulate cosmological principles. To analyze and interpret these rites correctly, it is necessary to look beyond the patterning of parent-child bonds at various sociological levels (the nuclear family, the longhouse, community networks, etc.). If biological connections through birth play a role in structuring mutual obligations, so do nongenealogical ones (the sharing of food and other substances through common living) and nonbiological ones (name sharing in particular). It is through the body, ultimately, that persons are produced, social groups made, and differences created. Embodied relatedness takes root in the care that one exercises in carving the human out of the nonhuman through conscious and repeated intervention. There is a danger that if its father hunts or if its mother eats game, the unborn child or infant will take on the characteristics of an offended animal spirit or even lose its weak spiritual force to the nonhuman world. This explains why parents, who are responsible for the physical and spiritual well-being of their offspring, drastically restrict their contact with the nonhuman world around childbirth and interrupt their subsistence activities by eliminating dangerous foods from their diet. Aimed at preventing illness or death, couvade prohibitions thus also express the uncertain and transitory nature of the native Amazonian person, caught up in a continuous process of "other-becoming."

CONCLUSION: THE VALUE OF REPRODUCTIVE SEXUALITY

I have so far discussed the role Huaorani people attribute to sexuality and childbirth in the creation of parenthood and the formation of intimate relationships.

I have critically reviewed past anthropological interpretations of the couvade and suggested that their greatest failure has been to overlook the fact that procreative life giving involves the complementary participation of the two sexes and often implies the constitution of some kind of androgynous agency. I now summarize my argument on the birth process in many Amazonian societies and conclude that it should be analyzed from the viewpoint of its transformative effect on the procreative couple and, in particular, on the father. This leads me to reassess today's dominant thesis in Amazonian anthropology that warfare, predation, and devouring are the necessary means for the constitution of collective identities and for their social reproduction. Finally, I will go back to the feminist and postfeminist quandaries with which I started this paper to argue that subjective identity cannot be properly analyzed without reference to the beginning and perpetuation of life.

As I have tried to show in this chapter, the newborn child is a key element in the reproduction of Huaorani social life. The birth process—of which couvade rites form an intrinsic part—represents a state of inception, as well as the incorporation of a new life at several levels. First, there is "the social placing of the newborn" (James 1997), that is, the recognition of the child before its full social integration, which in Amazonia occurs with the naming ceremony. In other words, the inception of life is socially marked prior to the social recognition of hereditary transmission. Then there is the fact that couvade restrictions are meant to secure the child's initial attachment to life. Life, far from taken-for-granted, is seen as dependent as much on the attention and care it gets from the sharing community as on the child's will to live—and to live with a particular set of parents (see Wagley 1977: 135). The parents do not give life to the child, but foster its introduction within the longhouse community of substance. It is because newborn babies are guests of their parents on whom they exercise exclusive demand sharing rights as part of their progressive incorporation within the sharing community that Huaorani couvade restrictions, I have argued, temporarily reorder the longhouse sharing economy. Finally, the father and the mother have worked and made the baby together; they have shared the capacity to produce kin. So the child can also be said to create an enduring couple out of its coresiding parents. The couvade, in this light, represents a "second marriage," and not a "second birth" primarily concerned with spiritual creation (Rivière 1974: 431). It does not replace the creativity of biological parents with that of spiritual parents but celebrates reproductive sexuality, that is, women's and men's power to create new social beings (bodies and souls). The fact that in many Amazonian societies marriage is not the object of any ceremony, and that it is publicly acknowledged only after a couple has one or two healthy, thriving babies (Kensinger 1984) confirms that childbirth materializes the conjugal tie and *creates* marriage. So the wife and the husband are in a sense "reborn" as mother and father during the birth process.[9] This seems to be confirmed by the nature of couvade restrictions, which as Guss (1989: 135) has so rightly stressed, make the parents of a newborn child follow the diet of an infant throughout the fasting period the first years of a child.

If the birth of a child irrevocably transforms sexually mature men and women into parents, it remains nevertheless true that fatherhood and motherhood constitute two nonequivalent forms of parenthood under the uxorilocal regime prevailing in many parts of Amazonia. I am aware that my structural-functionalist argument focused on the uxorial condition of Huaorani fathers does not adequately explain the role of the couvade in societies with a strong patrilocal ideology. A truly pan-Amazonian explanation of the couvade may require that we transcend the sociological level of unilocal marriage rules to define the jural and physical nature of Amazonian fatherhood following Houseman's (1988) structural thesis regarding the nonempirical and universal character of the differences between male and female parenthood within the framework of their hierarchical integration. A number of authors have stressed the fact that the couvade makes the social unit of parents-and-child visible (notably Fock 1963; da Matta 1982; Seeger 1981). This in no way implies their allegiance to a Malinowskian functionalist interpretation of the nuclear family with its universal function of nurturing children, for it is the fact that mothers undergo couvade restrictions as native members of the longhouse, while fathers do so as incomers, which is socially significant. By dramatizing men's equal participation in procreation and by making it visible, perinatal observances have the catalytic effect of furthering the absorption of in-marrying men into their wives' houses. The rule of uxorilocal postmarital residence, and the critical importance of fathering children in men's social careers, are two closely related social facts. Men start their married lives as affinal guests, almost as visitors, but progressively lose their affinal guest status through fathering, that is, cohosting children guests. By increasingly participating in their wives' *nanicabo* through living, sharing food, and bringing children to life, married men end up belonging to the groups among which they reside with their wives. When their daughters reach puberty, they take them on a ritual hunt, as if the incipient sexual maturity of their female offspring represents the promise of more consanguinity—more kinship. When some of their sons and daughters have married and born them grandchildren, they let the jaguar spirits visit them and adopt them as sons. And they meet death, their bodies marred and riddled with the spears of the enemy, along with their last child, buried by their wives and wives' female kin as fully incorporated, consubstantial kin.

What about cogenitors who participate in the making of the child and respect couvade restrictions without actually being uxorial fathers, that is, living with the child and its mother? Cofatherhood, I would argue, is identical to wife swapping (Viveiros de Castro 1992: 168–72), in the sense that these two very Amazonian practices equally render kinship categories elusive and ambiguous. This is particularly clear in the Huaorani case where a single term, *nanoongue*, is used for "wife," "husband," "wife's (classificatory) sisters," and "husband's (classificatory) brothers." As such, in-marrying men develop conjugal ties with one or two of their first wives' younger sisters (therefore strengthening their evolving position as insiders and fathers), and men, who are occasionally permitted to have sex with their classificatory wives, "cosire" the children of their classificatory brothers. True, Huaorani *nanicaboiri*, or "house groups," are unusual in their extreme preference for limiting the number of incoming sons-in-law, their high percentage of double cross-cousin marriages (i.e., alliances between two longhouses united through cross-sex siblingship), and their "filial adoptive" relationship to the supernatural world. Huaorani society may be extreme in its treatment of the wife-husband relationship as the axis of consanguinity and of the brother-sister one as the axis of affinity. It nevertheless remains the case that the widespread character of shared biological paternity throughout Amazonia must be accounted for. Paradigmatic consanguinity is neither purely female, nor paradigmatic affinity purely male everywhere (Viveiros de Castro 1992, 1995; Descola 1993: 175).

Finally, I have briefly alluded to the fact that sexual isomorphism (i.e., the reproductive power of husband-wife or brother-sister cross-sex pairs) equally underpins Huaorani representations of procreation, social reproduction, and fertility—as either "natural abundance" or "increase through gestation." The Huaorani's cultural insistence that they can reproduce themselves without the intervention of external creators may well be exceptional. However, their "victims of predation" syndrome nonetheless requires serious consideration. Amazonian anthropologists need to exercise caution when claiming that killing, cannibalism, and predation are the primary means of social reproduction throughout Amazonia (Menget 1985; Viveiros de Castro 1992, 1995). Whether homicide and warfare (in opposition to biological processes such as birth which are not specific to humans) are the products of consciousness and intentionality, the real sources of a group's fertility and procreative power (Taylor 1996) remain to be seen. My endeavor in this chapter has been to demonstrate that the birth process is a rich cultural domain, at least in societies practicing the couvade, and that life giving may involve as much consciousness and intentionality as, and be politically as significant as, life taking.

5

LIVING WELL

Huaorani Sensuality and Happiness

MANY COMMENTATORS have pondered over contemporary Euro-American obsession with erotic pleasure. Some of them have also reflected on the puzzling gap that usually separates erotic fantasies from the actual experience of sexual pleasure. Their conclusions as to the meanings of everyday sexuality have more than often been contradictory. For sexologists, good sex is eminently physical and practical—all it needs is getting the mechanics of stimuli right in order to climax into orgasm. Psychoanalysts, by contrast, focus on the unconscious mind and the socially rebellious way in which humans often organize their sexual drives (Bristow 1997: 61). Freudian thinkers start from the premise that all social bonds are ultimately sexual (Erikson 2005) and human beings fundamentally incestuous (Héritier, Cyrulnick, and Nouri 2000). Law and morals, reinforced by the fear of castration, universally ensure that unconscious wishes for sexual encounters with parents or siblings are kept at bay (Freud [1950] 1983). The celebrated poet and writer Octavio Paz defined love as the discovery of the mysterious unity of life (Paz 1993: 105). Like all animals, humans copulate and reproduce sexually; but unlike any other biological species, the human species alone can transform the sex act into both voluptuous attraction and deep attachment through a wide range of practices, institutions, rites, and representations (Paz 1993: 106). A master deconstructionist, such as Michel Foucault, deplored our current obsession with erotic pleasure, and said with dark skepticism that sex "has become more important than our soul, more important almost than our life" (Foucault 1978: 156, quoted in Bristow 1997: 10). He did not believe that eroticism and love could be universally fused into the "double flame" celebrated by Paz. Many thinkers today, like Foucault, analyze sexuality as a distinctly modern and historically specific construction, which cannot be readily applied to sexual arrangements found in the past and non-Western societies (Weeks 1995). What about the neo-Darwinian accounts of human sexuality proposed by evolutionary biologists and psychologists? These focus on the genetic basis of different male and female psychosexual behavior. Natural and sexual selection are believed to explain, for instance, the fact that men prefer pornographic magazines, while women get more pleasure out of romance novels (Symons 1979: 170–80). Faced with such a bewildering array of positions what, the anthropologist may ask, makes sex erotic? What kind of sex makes people happy?

Indigenous views are often revealed in clashes between differing practices. If I ask myself what kind of sex makes my Huaorani friends happy, I immediately think of an incident, vividly remembered and confined to field notes. It occurred approximately halfway through my first period of fieldwork, and it alerted me to the highly contextual reality of erotic thought and behavior. I had followed "my" *nanicabo* down river to an important meeting that Shuar and Quichua organizations had convened with the oil companies. The meeting was followed by a big party celebrating Elf Aquitaine's donation of a school and a health center to a Shuar settlement. Oversized speakers blasted trendy tunes of *musica tropical*, or "tropical music," to which a mixed crowd of indigenous settlers and "nationals" (mestizo colonists), oil workers, soldiers, prostitutes, and farmers danced energetically. I saw two prostitutes approach Mengatohue, an old Huaorani shaman. They invited him to an erotic dance. Mengatohue seemed to respond favorably to their advances, smiling back and joking. Apparently willing to be initiated in the art of brothel dancing, he started to imitate the prostitutes' arm and hip movements with gusto. But nothing in his derisive gesturing betrayed any sign of arousal. The dance lasted some time as the old man mocked the two young women, and the women responded with indulgent superiority. When they grew tired at their lack of success, they turned their attention to a more receptive man, a Shuar who had worked for years on the oil frontier. When the party finally ended in the early hours of the morning, the improvised dance hall became increasingly quiet. It had gradually turned into a dormitory for the Huaorani guests, and everyone was now asleep. The following day, the party was commented upon endlessly. Jokes and excitement are normal fare in the aftermath of such occasions. But this time, my travel companions also assailed me with questions about *cohuori* customs: Do the *cohuori* always pay for sex, as they do to get food in shops and restaurants? Do the women who sleep with men for "laughing sex" have babies? Is it because they eat the body of Christ and drink his blood (i.e., Catholic) that *cohuori* behave like this? Their puzzlement at the sexual behavior encountered on the oil road was caused not only by its contrast with their own ways, but also by its departure from what they had learned from exposure to evangelical Protestantism and strict Christian ethics. My own puzzlement was that even if the two very attractive prostitutes had—undoubtedly—made Mengatohue laugh, their erotic dance did not turn him on; he was not seduced.

My attempt in this chapter is to ethnographically describe what kind of sex makes a Huaorani man or woman happy and, by comparing their ideas about sex and love with those found in other Amazonian societies, as well as in ours, to explain why their way of behaving sexually, as opposed to their way of fantasizing about sex, is best described as *diffuse sensuality*. After having outlined the main characteristics of the Huaorani longhouse and the sex practices that take place under its roof, I discuss some of the fantastic representations of human sexuality contained in myths. I then briefly compare Huaorani sexuality with that of two other Amazonian societies, on which two well-known ethnographies of sexuality have been written. I end with a few remarks on the challenges of studying the general and the particular in the human condition.

SENSUALITY, WELL-BEING, AND SEXUAL PLEASURE IN THE HUAORANI LONGHOUSE

Living well is the central ambition of the Huaorani women, men and children who have so freely shared their daily lives and values with me during fieldwork. The Huaorani justify many of their ways of doing things and the decisions they make with a simple phrase: "because we want to live well" (*manomaï huaponi quehuemonipa*).[1] *Huaponi quehuemonipa*, often shortened to *huaponi*, an expression continuously used in conversations (as a form of acquiescence) or during visits (as salutation), refers to the pleasure of sharing life together. People who belong to the same longhouse care for each other and attend to each other's bodily needs.[2]

The longhouse is the material embodiment of the diffuse mix of intimacy, relaxed sensuality, and warm physical contact that characterizes *huaponi* relations between coresidents. It consists of a vast rectangular roof that extends to the ground where neither the hard sun nor the cold rain can penetrate, where the warmth of each woman's hearth can be felt, where there is always something to drink or eat, where one can relax in a hammock in total comfort, and where each one can be at ease. It is the domain of domestic peace, stability, and mutual compatibility erected by the *huaorani* (true humans) against outside threats and hostilities. Sex and age differences are played down, and a great deal of equality and freedom ensues. Because individuals of either sex show a high degree of self-sufficiency in providing for their own needs, togetherness is not lived as a source of dependency. Men and women, and adults and children, freely move in and out of the longhouse to trek in the forest or to visit relatives. Yet they firmly belong to their collective residence, which acquires its own identity, both in the eyes of insiders and those of outsiders. House groups come to be *united in life*. The expression *ayeromonque quehuemoni* (we live together as one) implies that coresidents are the ones who matter. By continuously feeding each other, eating the same food, and sleeping together, coresidents often develop a shared physicality of greater import than that resulting from genealogical bonds. People actually say that by living together side-by-side they gradually become *aroboqui baön anobain* (of one and the same flesh).

The longhouse is built in a joyful atmosphere (*totequehue*, or "living laughing"). While senior men erect the central poles, mature men prepare the wooden frame, and younger men and boys collect the palm leaves that will make the outer roof. Women led by the oldest woman of the house clean the forest floor and level it, while they look for potsherds and other signs of previous human occupation. Another group of women and girls go into the forest to collect the special palm leaves used for the inner roof.[3] Each married woman has her own hearth on which her husband and children may cook. Each couple has its own conjugal hammock, which is shared by their youngest children. A man married to two or three sisters takes turns sleeping in his various conjugal hammocks. Sex and births occur in a hammock by a woman's hearth inside the longhouse. And it is there as well that a woman takes pleasure with a lover; she is the host, and he the visitor.[4] Old couples with adult children tend to sleep side-by-side, each in a separate, individual hammock. Bachelors sleep apart in the back of the longhouse, or, sometimes, in an adjunct shelter, and so do very old widows and widowers. Not only is the longhouse strongly associated with a founding grandmother figure, but it also—literally—becomes the tomb of a woman too old to go on living (Rival 2005). In short, the longhouse objectifies important symbolic and organizational aspects of kinship, in particular the identity of women with uninterrupted consanguinity, men with domesticated affinity, and coresidency with sensual intimacy.[5]

Each *nanicabo* is known to other house groups under a collective identity derived from its corporeity and communal existence (Rival 2002). Yet, these corporeal units are composed of highly self-sufficient, autonomous persons, whose unique, individual characteristics are publicly acknowledged and greatly appreciated. *Huaocä* (the individual person), has great value in this society, and full development is nurtured by all possible means. Like in most highly mobile societies, pregnancies are spaced. Gaps of five to seven years between full siblings are common. Only *wanted* babies survive and are cared for. Breast-feeding is prolonged, and women breast-feed their sisters' children and sometimes their grandchildren in addition to their own. When I visited Bebantoque in the summer of 1989, she often had her sister Nemo's one-year-old daughter at one breast and her own six-month-old son the other. On August 25, I noted in my diary that she breast-fed both a baby monkey and Nemo's daughter. Nemo had gone upriver with her husband and older children. The baby monkey had survived a hunt, and Bebantoque was raising it as a pet for her children. When I asked the old Guiketa to tell me his life story, he started by saying that his father had been killed in a raid while his mother was pregnant with him. A few months after he was born, his older brother died of a snake bite, at which point his mother decided not to look after him any longer. "My mother said, 'why should you live when my dear older son is dead?' From then on, I was cared for by my sister. She saved me, she gave me a happy childhood."

Infinite care is taken of infants, and great attention is given to young children. Although the mother has prime responsibility for childcare, especially in the first year, the father takes an active role as well, and so do all the longhouse members. Their dedication to the new member is very physical, as one might expect given the vulnerability and needs of a young life. But there is something more to it. People really enjoy the presence of young children; they are a source of marvel, laughter, and happiness. Babies are associated with what is new and beautiful. Men, women, and children simply enjoy spending a great deal of time playing and interacting with babies and toddlers. Such playful interactions are exactly what *huaponi quehuemonipa* is all about. Things do not change much when children grow up and learn to walk and talk. Education is based on an ethos of pleasure and care and of full respect for bodily needs, including emotional needs. Children are encouraged to grow fast and become autonomous. As they get older, they learn to value independence and self-sufficiency through a nonauthoritarian education that respects them as individuals. Like their adult kin, they spend much time in the forest. They hunt small game and gather in bands, the younger learning from the older. Although the ethos of personal autonomy is pan-Amazonian, as it is found among the Huaorani, whose historical past is marked by violent conflicts and the constant fear of raiding parties, it is particularly developed. Children are taught to survive and look after themselves from a very young age.[6]

In Huaorani land, no one can be coerced in any way. No one can force or order another person to do something. It is also understood that one should not force oneself either. Learning and execution occur through voluntary (rather than willful) participation. Coercion brings about illness, danger, or evil spirits. To accomplish anything well, one must be in harmony with oneself and with one's surroundings. Personal autonomy, freedom of movement, and mobility are closely related, and often expressed through poetic imagery involving flying birds. Cobari sang a beautiful song about *maeñe* (a type of blue parrot) in Quihuaro on January 24, 1990, which ended with the lines, "when a drinking party is announced, we swiftly run to it, run, run through the forest. . . .When there are conflicts and disagreements, we decamp in no time, like the *maeñe* bird."

Individuals who made one's autonomy possible are vividly remembered. Yohue from Zapino sang a love song in memory of his mother the day I visited him in 1990. In this song, Yohue started by comparing himself as a baby with the *chahua mango* fledgling cracking its shell open while in the nest. "Like this bird," sang Yohue, "I was born in a large nested leaf" (i.e., hammock). He then went on to remember all the things his mother did for him.

> She allowed me to grow and develop through her care. She did so many things for me, helpless creature, so I could grow. I could not even get the food to my mouth, but she fed me, she gave me everything, and this is why I will never forget her. When I was a toddler, she kept the ground clean so that I would not harm myself or fall in the mud. Thanks to her, I have grown into a strong youthful man, and I can sing today, with pleasure and delight. Full of joy, health, and strength as I am today. I shall never forget her. My memory is sharp, and I am a fantastic singer.

The song was at once very personal and totally generic. Yohue undoubtedly did remember *bara* (mother) as he sang, but he was also fully aware of the fact that he was singing a traditional Huaorani song. Moreover, Yohue did not simply sing the song as he learned it; he sang it as his uncle Omayèbè used to sing it. He also added that Omayèbè learned the song from Meñèbè. When people remember kin, either dead or absent, they do so in this very concrete, vivid way. What they remember are the individual idiosyncrasies of the person being remembered, such as the unique way the person walks (or walked), talks (or talked), or sings (or sang). In addition to an infinite number of physionogmic details, what is remembered are the characteristic expressions, tone of voice, and demeanor of a particular individual. Individuals are much valued for the diversity they create (Rival 2002: 100–2). Creativity and innovation result from such unique bodily expressions, and there are as many ways of being embodied as there are individuals.

The well-being of individuals does not conflict with the well-being of the *nanicabo*, for one implies the other. Social values do not generally conflict with personal experience.[7] Togetherness is expressed and continuously reasserted through sharing practices. When a *nanicabo* member is sick, all residents respect the same food prohibitions. It is this shared collective curing effort that helps the patient to recover his or her good health. Longhouse members share illnesses, parasites, a common dwelling, and a common territory. Love and care are social relations that create solidarity through intimate and sensual bodily practices. True individuals are never alone (Rival 2005). *Huaponi*, glossed here as sensual happiness, is inseparable from love, *huaarete pone* (think the good, the beautiful).

Children are central to this ethos of personal autonomy and communal sharing. They seek sensual pleasure as actively as adults do, for sensuality, which does not require sexual maturity, is an essential part of belonging to the longhouse. Jules Henry's (1941: 19) remark that "the basis for man's loyalty to man [among the Kaigáng] has roots in the many warm bodily contacts between them" equally applies to the Huaorani among whom too "children [lie] like cats absorbing the delicious stroking of adults" (Henry 1941:18). I witnessed much caressing going from adults to children, and children to adults. Caressing is not simply a way of finding human warmth and comfort; it is also a way of learning about a new body and a new person. Looking at someone is not enough; body peculiarities need to be discovered through touch.

The mixture of bodily closeness, physical proximity, and sensual intelligence described here is characteristic of daily life, which unfolds in the comfort of proximity and the intimacy that goes with holding and touching familiar bodies. Such human contact and bonding occur between spouses, cross-sex siblings, and male cross-cousins. Men who are warming up around the campfire after a day's walk in the forest sit close to each other. They hold hands or crouch against each other forming a human chain. Young men love to stand around the fire or sleep together, arms around one another, legs slung across bodies, caressing in little knots of three or four. I have not seen young women do so with the same frequency. This mixture of holding and caressing is very different from the overt sexual gestures we have grown accustomed to in our society.[8] To caress allows one to know intimately the shape and the texture of a foreign body, and begin to understand how it works. What one is curious about is the extent to which another person's body is similar or dissimilar to one's own body.

If the longhouse epitomizes the sensual nature of physical comforting, sex, thought as heterosexual and reproductive, relates to the lovemaking activities of pairs of men and women who are not siblings, belong to the same generation, and are of approximately the same chronological age. Lovemaking in this sense is hardly differentiated from the state of being married (see Chapter 4). When a man and a woman marry, they become *nanoongue* (spouse). The husband's brothers and classificatory brothers (i.e., parallel cousins) become *nanoongue* to the wife, and the wife's sisters and classificatory sisters become *nanoongue* to the husband. A Huaorani may have sex with any of their *nanoongue*: that is, if a man, with any of his wife's sisters or female parallel cousins, and, if a woman, with any of her husband's brothers and male parallel cousins. Such extramarital liaisons do not cause sexual jealousy or conflict, so long as they are discrete and sporadic. Brother-sister incest is disapproved of, but does occur. Brother-sister incest is morally less upsetting than a sexual affair between affines belonging to different age groups, such as, for instance, an actual or potential son-in-law and his mother-in-law, a man and his father's sister, or a woman and her mother's brother.

I do not have full or firsthand knowledge of Huaorani love and sexual life, but I slept near men and women often enough to know that the lovemaking that goes on in the hammocks when the night sets in is not what we would call erotic passion. Lovemaking is not generally focused on penetration, or sexual activity centered on ejaculation. As copulation lasts for an unusually long time, it seems that lovers aim to achieve diffuse bodily pleasure. I once visited a distant *nanicabo* with one of my "brothers," who had awoken the desire of one of the young female residents. Although they had never met before, or heard of each other's existence, they spent the night making love together in her hammock. This, however, did not stop them from continuing to participate in the *nanicabo*'s nocturnal conversations or from exchanging jokes with other visitors and coresidents. For a woman, "fun sex" is sex with an unexpected male visitor, especially if he is *huaca* (nonrelated). Such visits by unrelated Huaorani men often turn into revelry and sexual teasing, as girls and women spray their male guests with manioc drink or other fluids, including breast milk. A one-night stand with a *huaca* lover is referred to as *ononqui niñi imba* (copulate with no good reason). Such sexual encounters are always initiated by the woman; she is the one who proposes, the one who invites, the one who solicits sex.[9] On April 19, 1990, in anticipation of such an adventure, Meñemo sang the following song:

> How happy I am, two boys
> Came for a visit, the Cononaco[10]
> Men are boring,
> Come in my hammock to
> Chat with me.

The word most commonly used to convey the feelings that exist between spouses, *huarique* (love), is not exclusive to the conjugal relation; it equally applies to other intimate relations pertaining to the longhouse. Sexual intercourse is *niye* (for both animals and people) or *nimoi* (only for people). When the male partner ejaculates, said my young friend Cahuitipe, it feels very, very good: *totequehuenga wenguengä* (ejaculation resulting in a feeling of great joy). Cahuitipe did not know whether there is an equivalent term for the female partner, nor did he know whether the expression used by women who wish to copulate, and which literally means "let's make another child" (Rival 1998a), could be used to mean "female orgasm" as well.[11]

My general impression is that Huaorani culture does not eroticize sensuality. Genital pleasure is not treated as the most pleasurable of all pleasures, nor is it clearly distinguishable from other bodily pleasures. Straight sex may be fun, but so are many other types of bodily contacts. Bodily pleasures, such as the pleasure and contentment felt during sexual intercourse, the pleasure and contentment of a three-year-old caressing the breast of the woman from whom she or he is feeding, the merry feeling of someone stroking gently the body of a caressing companion, the gratification caused by the action of delousing someone's head, or the pleasure of being deloused by someone's expert hands, are not differentiated and ranked on a scale. The interest in developing an intimate knowledge of bodies leads to a form of sensuality that merges physical proximity and well-being. Everyone in the longhouse partakes in everyone else's care and well-being. This represents an enormous investment in sustaining life and happiness within a specific group of persons—matched by a parallel and similarly striking disengagement from material possessions.[12] Passionate, exclusive lovemaking might be happening in secret places known only to lovers, but such possibility was never mentioned to me. I asked many times whether couples would go to the forest to make love. Each time, my question was met with surprise, then puzzlement, and each time the answer was that no, this really was not something the Huaorani would do. Another indication that marital sex is akin to the general *nanicabo* sensuality described in the previous section is that men do not have to abstain from sleeping with their wives before hunting or making curare poison.[13]

FANTASY SEX: MYTHS, DREAMS, AND WARFARE

Octavio Paz (1993), who defines romantic love in the West as one of our highest civilized achievements, links the capacity for love and erotic pleasure with art and poetry.[14] In his recent theory of the evolved mind, Geoffrey Miller (2001) similarly proposes that art is linked to sexual courtship. Going beyond Donald Symons's (1979) focus on our dual-sexed nature, he argues that music, language, and culture are largely the by-products of the sex drive that has pushed male and female humans to communicate and compete with each other over thousands of generations. Although Paz and Miller use radically different arguments and analytical frameworks, they both recognize the central role played by sexual fantasies in human cultures, as well as the inseparability of anatomy and fantasy in human sexuality.

For the Huaorani, imagined sex is very different from lived sexual experiences. Most remarkably, their myths and dreams tend to elaborate one single theme: the lethal sexual attraction between humans and animals. Huaorani sexual obsessions do not concern the nature of sexual desire or the way in which sexual desire constitutes gendered subjects. Rather, they depict sexual desire and sexual pleasure as something that takes a life of its own in monstrous encounters, as if the sexual organs had detached themselves from the bodies to which they belong and had become autonomous. Numerous myths tell the stories of Huaorani women who copulate with male animals (anacondas, monkeys, tapirs, and so forth).[15] The liaison is usually initiated by the animal partner. However, the sexual attraction is mutual. In some stories, the female human (often already married) continues to live with her human kin while having an affair with her animal lover. In others, she goes to live with him in his land, sometimes among his people. In all these stories, the women eventually become pregnant and die in due course (see Chapter 4). The most popular of these myths involves a young woman who becomes fatally attracted to a giant earthworm (*cuica*).[16]

There are many different versions of this popular myth. Women and girls giggle with delight whenever the myth is told. When the giant worm is inadvertently met in the forest, its sight provokes a similar excitement, in fact, mild arousal. With about five times the diameter of a human penis, and approximately ten times the length, the *cuica* worm has a peculiar—shall we say suggestive—way of progressing on the forest floor. In most versions of the myth, the worm resides underground beneath his lover's house, next to the hearth. In other versions, the worm lives in the manioc plantation next to the house, underneath a log. In some versions, the human lover is a young, unmarried girl. In others, she already has a husband. In all of the versions I heard, the worm inserts itself in the human body he wishes to seduce sub rosa. The girl or woman is sleeping, for instance, or she is cooking. She does not know why, but she suddenly feels unfathomably well and incredibly happy. After several encounters, she realizes that it is *cuica* who gives her such awesome pleasure, and she starts participating more actively in the liaison, actually taking the initiative of going where *cuica* hides and calling him to come out. In some versions, she ends up dying while pregnant. In most versions, a mother or grandmother (if a girl) or a husband (if a married woman) discovers her secret and kills the worm. The girl or woman falls into a deep melancholy and, in some versions, ends up dying of sorrow.[17]

On the basis of numerous conversations with informants, as well as ethnographic observations, I have come to understand these myths as expressing the antisocial nature of excessive sexual desire and unreasonable attraction. Too much sexual pleasure kills. Pure sexual pleasure is lethal, for it expresses the autonomous desire of the sexual organs themselves. By becoming detached from the bodies to which they belong, they become uncontrollable, and drive their owners to incomparable sensual pleasure, but also to their death, unless the conscious realization of the danger is incurred or some human intervention allows the pleasure victims to regain sufficient control to end the voluptuous and deadly encounter. People's erotic dreams involve nonhuman lovers (*huine* [animal seducers and cannibalistic spirits]) who pretend to be loving humans to better trick their victims. Myths speak of fantastic associations, in which uncontrolled sexual excitement, loss of self, and death are irremediably linked. That such myths involve a seduced human and a seducing animal is unsurprising given the particular importance of animals as significant others in Amazonian societies.[18] The awesome animal sex matches the fetishized human one—this is the thrill. But the animal can overwhelm and destroy its human sexual partner—this is the danger. The myths articulate common Amazonian anxieties about lack of control and self-control, excess and balance. Numerous Amazonian anthropologists, including, of course, Lévi-Strauss, have noted the central importance of self-restraint and self-discipline in Amazonian myths. They are moral values that must continuously be reaffirmed against forces that weaken human checks on physical appetites. Crocker, among others, beautifully exposes the Amazonian desire to "master the world of organic form," which, for the Bororo, involves "the necessity of rules governing the control of organic process, especially that of sexuality" (Crocker 1985: 289). Moderation and the rejection of invading powers, as well as domineering behavior, are absolutely central to the Amazonian political project of personal autonomy.

In the Huaorani case, fantasy sex may also be linked to affinity and warfare, although the ritual connection involved here is far more difficult to interpret than that between sex, dream, and myth.[19] On April 15, 1990, as I left a distant house in the Yasuní with Inihua who was going to be my guide for the next six weeks or so, I heard him shouting his last au-revoir to his kin from the canoe. "*Cuñado menqui huati bito hermana huati huati menqui.*"[20] The joke was accompanied by the familiar obscene gesture of a right-hand finger sliding to and fro within the left hand folded into a tube. As Inihua was leaving his *nanicabo*, he was reminding them (his wife included) that visitors may always be treated as potential affines and invited to stay. He was also indicating that nonrelated men (including non-Huaorani men) can always be treated as virtual affines, a relationship potentially or effectively sealed by the sexual union of one man with a sister of the other. In June 1997, I heard the expression *huati huati* in an entirely different context. I was involved in the filming of a mock raid when a shout made me jump. The film crew had brought a large doll made of rugs to be used in role-play as the victim of a spear-killing attack. As Yehua and his brother thrust their spears into the dummy, they shouted "*huati huati*" with force. The barbed ends of their spears were pushed back and forth with astonishing force and determination in the rugs that filled the doll's "entrails." The extreme rapidity of the slashing movements frightened me. I had never seen these two normally pacific men break loose in such a way. The contrast between their sudden outburst of fury and their usually gentle, controlled behavior could not have been greater. Although not a culture of the erect penis, Huaorani culture does contain associations between warfare and sexual violence. Such associations, however, are not of conquering men or victorious warriors abducting and raping the women of the conquered. Huaorani men do not use their phallic power to abuse or humiliate the defeated, and certainly not to violently inseminate unwilling female bodies. Yet, in the corps-à-corps encounters of war, men thrush their spears in a way that mystically fertilizes their bodies and the bodies they are destroying.[21] But is the action of spear killing really that of men? As I have argued elsewhere (Rival 2005), killers overwhelmed by rage are not considered to be fully human.

The young men who have worked for the oil companies are aware of the existence of all kinds of sexual behaviors that are morally condemnable. These practices are called generically "to annoy" (*molestar* in Spanish), "to do something that irritates" (*buyo aquequi*), or "to do something that is sinful" (*huihua aquequi*). Such transgressive behaviors do not occur within Huaorani society, and people are generally horrified by the idea of rape (*huihua mahaca*), for instance. In July 2005, a hundred Huaorani women marched on Ecuador's capital city to protest against alcoholism and the sexual abuses plaguing the villages close to oil fields. The *huihua aquequi* behaviors recognized within Huaorani society are brother-sister incest and adulterous sex, the latter being identified as sinful by those most committed to evangelical Christianity. Brother-sister incest was always disapproved of, but never considered a perversion. The most important rule in Huaorani ethical code is that sex cannot be used for political domination, which is what *huihua aquequi* sex strives to achieve according to my informants. It is therefore not surprising that sexual fantasies do not contain violent images. Of course, *huine* spirits are inherently violent (they are cannibals). However, they do not violate their victims sexually; they devour them.

SEX, CULTURE, AND MYTH IN THREE AMAZONIAN SOCIETIES

To what extent are Huaorani views of human sexuality similar to those found in other Amazonian cultures? I summarize here what we know of Amazonian ordinary and fantasized sexual activities, focusing more specifically on Gregor's (1985) and Murphy and Murphy's (1974) ethnographies, the only two lowland South American ethnographies dedicated to the study of sexuality. What interests me most particularly in Gregor's and the Murphys' work is their special focus on mythology and ritual, or, as I call it here, "fantasized sex." Both the Mehinaku and the Mundurucú share the "Yurupari complex," with its association of men's houses, myths of archaic female dominance, and uses of sacred ancestral flutes forbidden to women in male initiation rituals. The Yurupari complex, which shows remarkable parallels with the secret men's cults found in Melanesia, has been extensively documented and discussed in the Amazonian anthropology literature.

There are differences between the Mehinaku and Mundurucú kinship systems, marriage rules and rules of exogamy, which I have no room to discuss in detail here. However, when compared to the Huaorani, the Mehinaku and the Mundurucú appear to share numerous sociological characteristics and to depart from Huaorani ways of organizing society in broadly similar terms. Like many Amazonian societies depending on bitter manioc, the Mundurucú and the Mehinaku show a relatively well-developed gender division of labor, with women working harder than men. Gender roles are further segregated due to the existence of men's houses. Both cultures equally stress the polluting nature of female genitalia, the need to respect a wide range of sexual prohibitions, and the ritual importance of sexual avoidance. Menstruating and birth-giving women are secluded. Women fear pregnancy and worry about having unwanted children. The Mehinaku and the Mundurucú are particularly extreme, and unusual according to Amazonian standards, in their ideological assertion of ritual male dominance. In both societies, men traditionally reside in the men's house, which is surrounded by family houses strongly identified with groups of women related through consanguinity (Murphy and Murphy 1974: 116, 133; Gregor 1985: 110). Men proclaim their superiority over women by virtue of possessing erect penises full of semen. Men alone have the fertilizing power of procreation. Women do no more than cooking and feeding the fetuses inserted in their wombs. In both societies, however, women normally ignore men's proclamations and in no way see themselves as inferior. The stress on sexual difference and gender antagonism is mainly expressed in the ritual context. It is in myth rather than in reality that women are dangerous to men and that men must control them. Women's exclusion, intimidation, and threats of gang rape relate almost exclusively to the rituals surrounding the sacred flutes.

Social institutions based on an ideology of patrilineal descent are too weak to secure any real political power to men. It is precisely the lack of hierarchy and power asymmetry which exacerbates male ritual aggression toward women and explains sexual antagonism (Murphy and Murphy 1974).

Although Gregory and the Murphys are far more interested in the representation of sexuality in myth, ritual and dream than in people's actual sexual practices and love experiences, their books contain sufficient ethnographic data on the latter to support the view that the Mehinaku, Mundurucú and Huaorani ordinary sex lives have much in common. In the three societies, having sex is characterized by the same relaxed freedom, as well as the same lack of technical savoir faire or imagination. Gregor (1985: 9, 34) speaks of the lack of variation in positions, and Murphy and Murphy (1974: 152) of "an active preoccupation with sex, but little of a colorful nature."[22] The straightforwardness of heterosexual sex and the horror manifested at positions or actions other than straight vaginal penetration, including foreplay and clitoris stimulation, parallel strong moral views on what constitutes legitimate sexual relations. For example, the Mehinaku, like many other Amazonian people, hold that "the only proper sexual object is a cross-cousin of the opposite sex" (Gregor 1985: 9). They see proper human sexuality as what distinguishes humans from animals and civilized tribes from savage forest-dwelling groups (Gregor 1985: 52).

The three authors equally view part of child socialization as the reinforcement of the absence of any sense of guilt and lack of sexual repression. Sexual encounters are not considered secret or shameful. They form an integral, and quite public, part of human life. Murphy and Murphy (1974: 151) note that "the Mundurucú do not have the acute sense of embarrassment about sex that is characteristic of our own society, and they do not insist on total privacy." Sexual freedom is simply a part of the general freedom from interference that governs egalitarian societies. I would add that in many Amazonian societies, marriage is a gradual affair that starts with a young man visiting his sweetheart at night in her hammock in her communal house. Such visits are subjected to the same gossip that surrounds extramarital affairs, but no action is taken to legalize the union until the birth of the first child.

Gregor and the Murphys also report the muted character of sexual jealousy, both for men and women, but especially for men.[23] As sexual freedom continues pretty much unabated after marriage—as long as it is discrete—extramarital affairs are very common. Gregor (1985: 37) adds that sexual liaisons give way to long-lasting, affectionate relationships. This explains why extramarital affairs, far from being a source of conflict, bring cohesion to village life. To this we can add the mention of more institutionalized forms of extramarital sex in some Amazonian societies. The Araweté, for example, practice *sexual mutuality*, as they say, by which two couples spouse share over a given period of time and become ritual friends (Viveiros de Castro 1992: 168). That adultery, far from being a source of shame or humiliation, contributes to social solidarity partly explains why sexual banter is not only well developed but also a source of constant entertainment in Amazonian communities. The muted character of sexual jealousy is also probably related to the right granted to women to have lovers and to enjoy sex. Murphy and Murphy (1974: 150) stress that "women maintain a strong degree of control over their sexuality, despite male ideology." Gregor (1985: 33) mentions that it is usually Mehinaku women who choose which of the four culturally acceptable positions the couple adopts during a sexual encounter. Finally, it is clear that native theories of procreation, embryology, and multiple paternity militate against strong sexual jealousy (see Chapter 4).

To recapitulate, like many postcolonial Amazonian societies, the Huaorani, Mehinaku, and Mundurucú are remarkably egalitarian. Amazonian political institutions and ideologies are not generally conducive to domination, coercion, or oppression. Historical change is denied, ignored, or rearticulated in mythic terms referring to a primordial era, a time when animals and humans were not differentiated. Or, when it is wholeheartedly embraced, it is not accepted with nostalgic reference to ancestral traditions but, rather, as the process through which kinship is created anew in each generation. Personal autonomy is not only highly valued, it is also central to the organization and continuity of social groups (Rivière 1984). Endogamous kindred-based residential groups represent the social ideal of identity, sameness, and nondifferentiation. The incorporation of "others," considered necessary for social reproduction and cultural continuity, is a source of both danger and creativity. Reciprocity is difficult to achieve and exchange a source of ambivalence.

Compared to Mehinaku and Mundurucú society, Huaorani society is more extreme in its endogamous and autarkic tendencies. Warfare and predation are, beyond the units of sharing or reciprocal exchange, essential components of social reproduction (Rival 2002, 2005). Another aspect of Huaorani "particularism" is the total absence of rape and domestic violence from social relations. The only form of physical violence, which consists in spearing "enemies" during a killing raid, is most often exercised by men against men. Ongoing residence, founded on a unique combination of individuality and togetherness, allows persons and communities to unfold in time through the cumulative experience of living side-by-side, day-after-day. Such absorption in domesticity may seem dull and boring, but it makes people incredibly happy; the Huaorani are gregarious fun lovers. Sensual bonding, as diffuse as food sharing, unfolds as one aspect of the pleasure of living in each other's company. Love and care are social relations that create solidarity through bodily practices. These sensual practices constitute, manifest, and reproduce love as a form of collective well-being and happiness or the value of living as one content body. Sensuality is neither centered on genitalia, nor is it the exclusive domain of adult heterosexuality.

When it comes to fantasized sex, the Mehinaku (Gregor 1985: 55, 150), like the Huaorani, find lovemaking with animals "better than human intercourse." However, here too animal sex constitutes "a threat to normal sexual relationships," and expresses a similar anxiety regarding orgasmic pleasure and the loss of self-control it entails. However, the Huaorani would not interpret what Gregor calls (wrongly in my view) *bestiality* in Freudian terms. Huaorani men are not locked in a continuous struggle "with the problems of masculine self-definition and separation from women" (Gregor 1985: 10). To them, loss of self-control is not linked with loss of male identity. In fact, mentions of animal sex in Huaorani mythology concern women far more often than men. The myths express more of a concern with the monstrous child that may result from the sexual union of a female human and a male animal than they do with orgasm as a source of boundary loss, although the two are closely interrelated.

According to their ethnographers, masculine identity among the Mehinaku and the Mundurucú is particularly fragile and vulnerable, certainly more than it appears to be for the Huaorani, at least at first sight. Gregor (1985: 9–10) notes that sex brings ambiguity to Mehinaku social life, which, from the male point of view, becomes divided between sentiments of warmth and connectedness with women on the one hand and a great deal of anxiety, fear, antagonism, and insecurity on the other. Murphy and Murphy (1974: 226–31) talk of a Mundurucú masculine personality structured by anxiety, chronic sexual frustration, and high levels of dissatisfaction leading to high levels of sexual antagonism. Moreover, the three authors identify fundamental similarities between the "battle of the sexes" and male psychosexual identity in both Euro-American and Amazonian cultural settings. They argue that Euro-American and Amazonian men equally view women as alluring, emasculating, and arousing primitive fears of dependence and loss of male identity. Following Freud, they explain the presence of identical psychodynamics in the Amazon Basin and Euro-America with reference to universal anxieties brought on by the separation from the mother, which similarly structure male individual personalities all around the world. The contribution of social anthropology, therefore, is to show how social arrangements and institutions interact with these psychosexual proclivities. Whereas the ongoing battle of the sexes and the pervasiveness of sexual ideas is blunted in Euro-American societies (divided by class, education, religion, race, vocation, and so forth), it is manifest in Amazonian villages. This is particularly so in those organized around men's houses, where "the intensity of the men's house pattern is directly related to the structural features that unify the men in opposition to the women" (Gregor 1985: 209).

This all-too-brief comparative discussion allows us to see that what is at work here may be less universal than what Gregor and the Murphys claim. More than the universality of masculine psychology, it is the contrast between sexuality as lived in ordinary social life and as represented in myth and ritual that their ethnographies make so plain. The masculine vulnerability they find expressed in dream, myth, and ritual is also present in Huaorani society, but in a different realm, that of warfare. Huaorani men do not feel threatened by women and sex, but they are subject to fits of homicidal rage, which cause them to lose their humanity temporarily. As I have argued elsewhere (Rival 2005), to retain or regain their humanity, Huaorani men must belong to affinal matrifocal networks. This brief comparative sketch highlights fundamental aspects of Amazonian gender and personhood that require further comparative analysis and further theorizing. To accomplish this task adequately, ethnologists need to address the striking contrast found between Amazonian sexual practices and the sexual world painted in myths. Myths, rituals, and ideological statements constitute only one source of cultural knowledge about sexuality and human nature. The challenge of understanding human sexual behavior remains that of reconciling everyday ordinary sex with ritualized sex, animated as it is by the fantastical possibilities of the human imagination.

LOVE, EROTICISM, AND THE HUMAN CONDITION

I have so far established that the diffuse sensuality found in the Huaorani longhouse, far from being exceptional, is typical of the free and relaxed attitude to sex found in Amazonia, including in groups characterized as living particularly anxious or tense sexual lives, such as the Mehinaku or the Mundurucú. But to what extent can we say that Amazonian ways of loving and having sex are comparable to ours? This is obviously a very difficult question to answer, given the peculiarly Western objectification of sexuality alluded to earlier. Bloch (2000), who follows Malinowski in his endeavor to explain cultural variability with reference to universal human needs, cautions us to study invariant human nature in a way that describes accurately the modes of symbolic communication found in human societies. The challenge, as always, is to differentiate what in human action is conditioned by our common biological makeup from what is the product of history. The shift in dominant representations of sex that has taken place during the twentieth century, from Victorian hyper-repression to present-day commodification of erotic desire and normalization of transgressive behavior in the name of individual freedom and choice, could not have been more extreme. Moreover, the multicultural societies that make up contemporary Euro-America exhibit a bewildering range of attitudes, behaviors, values, and beliefs. However, there is ground to argue that the sensual activities I have described in this chapter are not as distant from our own everyday practices as it may appear.

We too long for physical expressions of sex that are not dissimilar from the infantile need for physical contact. As Malinowski (1927: 246–50) contended, such need is not sexual, even if it has often been construed to be so, at least since Freud's Oedipus complex. Even in our culture, which increasingly represents sexuality as an abstracted domain of transgressive potentialities, erotic behavior is firmly embedded within mundane sociality (Rival, Slater, and Miller 1998) and gets muted within households. Working couples with children lose libido through sheer physical exhaustion. To enjoy lovemaking in the way envisaged by Paz, and cultivate it as passionate and exclusive erotic love, requires time and a certain detachment from the constraints of reproduction and the burdens of childrearing. It is terribly hard to imagine Tristan and Iseult, or Dante and Beatrice, as parents. Another important cause for "the relative hyposexuality of the married state" (Symons 1979: 112) has to do with the fact that individuals forming a family unit undergo complex changes of emotions. A child's birth creates new relations of intimacy within the family. Parents intuitively feel that *the same kind* of love should apply to all individuals belonging to the household. Family love, they feel, should be nonexclusionary.[24] There is also the fear in parents, which easily translates into shame and loss of sexual stamina, that their children might catch them in the act.[25] Of course, these facts are gendered in complex ways, and whether men and women love and desire sex in the same way is hotly debated in Euro-America as it most likely is in most societies.

As I have tried to show in this chapter, there are greater cultural variations between representations and ritualizations of sex than there are between conjugal experiences of sex. We do not find in Amazonian societies Paz's notion of love as the purifying movement from sex (low and animal-like), via eroticism (the cultural and refined pleasure of the flesh), to love (the noble and synthesizing sentiment), which fuses body, mind, and soul into one single and exclusive passion for the beloved. Nor is sex thought of as the necessary hygienic release of biological energy envisaged by Wilhelm Reich. Marquis De Sade's erotic art of seduction and domination and Bataille's aesthetics of morbid transcendence are equally absent. Eroticism developed historically within courts peopled by divinized humans and anthropomorphic deities who used their sublimate arts to enliven daily routines structured by racial, class, and gender divisions (Paz 1993), all things of which Amazonian social worlds are entirely devoid. Twenty-first century Euro-American representations are unique in their utopian definitions of sexuality as sexual desire and will to identity. By contrast, Amazonian constructions tend to build on the ordinary pleasures of embedded sexuality. The health of bodies and minds is maintained through the nurture and care of individuals longing for physical comforting. Happiness is cultivated as a birthright, and life sustained as peace and contentment. The need for affection, especially in children whose condition of vulnerability reminds us all of the precariousness of human existence, gets gratified on demand. Love and sex consist of a set of practices that are deeply embedded in relational contexts. They are not divorced from mundane domesticity or from reproduction taken in the broader sense. In short, what seems to be most at variance in human sexuality is not domestic sex within family units and the corollary "familiarity [that] dulls the edge of lust" (Symons 1979: 110) but, rather, mythical, mystical, or ritualized sex. Such imagined sexuality, I have argued, involves others who are, more often than not, unequal others.[26]

Symons's (1979: 127) thesis that sexual activity tends to be reduced by marriage and that the emotional attachment of long-married couples changes from the orgasmic to the affectionate calls us to revisit Westermarck's theory of incest avoidance, monogamous marriage, and exogamy. No one has done more than sinologist Arthur Wolf (1993) to show the continuing relevance of Westermarck's understanding of the human aversion to marrying housemates or to revive the anthropological interest in "the incest taboo." By looking at the connections between sexuality and parenthood, Wolf and Durham (2005) have established three important facts. Firstly, they have compiled new scientific evidence that confirms Westermarck's Darwinian induction that inbreeding is dangerous (Wolf and Durham 2005: 25–27, 134–35). Secondly, and on the basis of detailed empirical research, they have proven that early association inhibits sexual attraction (Wolf 1993). Moreover, they have shown that humans are not alone in avoiding sexual intercourse with consanguineous kin. Incest avoidance is found among primates, as well as in a number of other animal species (Wolf and Durham 2005: 62–67, 162–63). Thirdly, by looking at human sexuality in terms of its biological and psychological aspects, they have shed new light on its cultural meanings and social functions. Having rejected both Lévi-Strauss's emphasis on gift exchange and exogamy and Freud's perpetual struggle between selfish sexual drive and repressive social order, they propose a range of nonfunctionalist explanations of the link between biology (inbreeding avoidance) and social institution (the incest taboo). The nonfunctionalist explanation of the incest taboo proposed by Wolf is based on a new evolutionary understanding of developmental psychology that reconciles Melanie Klein's psychoanalytical tradition with Konrad Lorenz's ethology. For Wolf and his colleagues, sexual bonds must be differentiated from asexual bonds, and sexual imprinting from asexual imprinting. "The bonds an infant forms with the mother and other caretakers are fundamentally different from those formed between adult sexual partners. Infant/caretaker bonds are inherently contrasexual.... Attachment and aversion are two aspects of the bonds formed in infancy and early childhood.... What natural selection selected for is a universal disposition to form contrasexual attachments to those persons by whom and with whom one is reared" (Wolf 2005: 14). Erikson, a contributor to the volume edited by Wolf and Durham (2005), uses a slightly different terminology. He contrasts two types of bonding that are biologically and psychologically distinct, each adaptive within a different social context: *familial bonding* (also described as the familial type of social affiliation) and *sexual affiliation*. Erikson adds that "the propensity for sexual affiliation develops much later than that for familial bonding" (Erikson 2005: 175–77).[27]

The data presented in this chapter certainly supports the thesis that not all human bonding is of a libidinous nature—as affirmed by Freud. Much of what I have described as everyday, lived sexuality among the Huaorani, other Amazonian peoples, and, for that matter, among ourselves seems to fit Erikson's category of familial type of social affiliation. However, to argue as Wolf does that "attachment is inherently contrasexual" (Wolf 1993: 167) requires deeper thinking about the meanings of "sexual" and "erotic." As I have tried to argue here, we need to understand much better the nature of sexual arousal on the one hand, and the nature of enduring attachments between spouses on the other. Rather than erect a tight wall between sexual and familial affiliation, as Erikson does, or contrast marriages that involve association before the age of three and marriages in which the couples are not brought together until later (Wolf 1993: 161) as Wolf does, we need to return to the questions Durkheim (1898) raised in his critique of the Westermarck's effect. As Lévi-Strauss (1983) has argued, promiscuity and conjugality do not exclude, but imply each other. The institutionalized coexistence of monogamy and promiscuity has given rise to different social arrangements and cultural representations. The sex that makes people happy in everyday family contexts is quite unlike the fantasized sex that excites and arouses them. For example, the Muria, who represent erotic freedom and marriage as incompatible, have instituted the bachelor's house where young unmarried men and women are left to learn and experience the arts of sexual pleasure before stepping into conjugal monogamy, economic partnership, and parenthood. Unmarried and married lives are based on very different, yet complementary, principles, and social solidarity equally depends on both (Elwin 1947; Gell 1992). Among the Mehinaku and the Mundurucú, the men's house also creates a form of social solidarity different from, and complementary to, that of the extended uxori-matrilocal household. However, the conflicted masculinity that ensues does not allow for the same neat partition in the life cycle between erotic sensuality and family love. In their attempt to escape the institutionalized tensions pervasive in Amazonia between affinity and consanguinity, the Huaorani have created a longhouse where diffuse sensuality leaves very little room for erotic expression, and a society where exogamy cannot be fully realized.

6

FEMININITY AND MASCULINITY IN HUAORANI LAND

I ARGUED IN CHAPTER 4 that the Huaorani couvade, far from being a father's rite, should be understood as a rite of coparenthood through which both parents actively involve themselves in the protection of their newborn to ensure the baby's fast and vigorous growth. Ritual abstinence by a man on the birth of his child corresponds to his public announcement that he is connected to the infant, quite independently from marriage and residence. Through observing couvade restrictions, a man claims to be a father. I further argued that if the creation of a new human life requires the same involvement from the two sexes, equal participation in child making affects men and women differently given that postmarital residence is uxorilocal. The birth of a child represents an essential moment of the life transfer process by which the in-marrying husband becomes a kinsman to his wife and to her *nanicabo*. In other words, the gradual incorporation of the infant in the longhouse furthers the husband's incorporation in his wife's house group, progressively turning him into consanguine kin. My argument stressed the fact that while mothers undergo couvade restrictions as *native members of the longhouse*, fathers do so as incomers. The claim of paternity, while furthering the uxorilocal husband's incorporation within his wife's *nanicabo*, also affects the way he relates to his sisters. More than his siblings, they become the potential future mothers-in-law of the child he has chosen to father. This led me to conclude that the joint effort through which the husband-wife pair transfers life onto a new human person remodels the configuration of both affinal and consanguineous ties within the longhouse where a child is born, as well as between allied longhouses. This then led me to surmise that gender asymmetry is located neither in the husband-wife relationship, nor in age hierarchies among siblings. Rather, it is a consequence of uxorilocality, a condition affecting *all* sibling relationships.

In this chapter, I further develop this argument by examining how uxorilocality relates to the various types of marriage exchange found in Huaorani society. I show that the structural properties of the marriage system are in fact intrinsically linked to the conceptualization of male and female agency within a universe animated by transcendental and predatory violence. Huaorani uxorilocality, as both an institutionalized social form and a social ethos, is dialectically shaped by political opposition to predatory biopolitics, which are eminently gendered. The male person, particularly susceptible to the ideological force of predation, has a tendency to split, a process that female agency continuously works at containing and restraining. I end with a discussion on the composition of the Huaorani male and female person, which I offer as a partial answer to the vexed question of the relationship between sex, body, and soul in the Amazonian context.

THE HUAORANI ENDOGAMOUS MARRIAGE: AN IDEAL AND ITS LIMITS

The Huaorani are nomadic, autarkic, and highly endogamous hunter-gatherers, who by tradition cultivate manioc and plantain sporadically for the preparation of ceremonial drinks and live in *nanicabo oncoiri* (multifamily dwellings) on hilltops away from rivers. On a north-south axis, their territory stretches between the Napo and the Curaray rivers; on a west-east axis, from the Andean foothills to the border with Peru. Huaorani political economy is structured according to three spheres of exchange that form an essential backdrop to the marriage system: (1) the undifferentiated sharing of substance within the longhouse; (2) the parity of male and female contributions within the endogamous realm; and (3) the overpowering unilateralism of cosmic predation.

Transactions occurring within the longhouse residential group, which constitutes the basic social unit of Huaorani society, are characteristically of the "demand-sharing" type, as first identified by Peterson (1993) for egalitarian hunter-gatherers. The remarkable features of the longhouse sharing economy, with its unique combination of communality and personal autonomy, have been described at length elsewhere (see Chapter 5 in Rival 2002). The repeated and undifferentiated action of sharing that goes on within the longhouse turns coresidents into a single, indistinct substance, so that people living in the same longhouse gradually become "of the same flesh."[1] Longhouse members, who procure alone and consume together, develop a maximal sense of individuality and autonomy. At the same time, they constitute an homogeneous living body, the *nanicabo*, which perfectly illustrates the nature of Amazonian social units, at once "body-sharing" and "body-producing" (Viveiros de Castro 2001: 43). The *nanicabo* represents an interesting elaboration of one particular aspect of Amazonian biopolitics, the daily fusion of physiological production and biological reproduction. Social reproduction is thus represented, practiced, and materialized as the continuous production of the body through feeding, sensual pleasure, and other expressions of material and emotional care. These processes are intimately related to the body-making practices associated with procreation and birth.

The *nanicabo* political economy of shared substance, through which individual persons can be recognized as equally unique, leads to a general playing down of status differences based on age and gender. However, gender becomes sociologically significant in marriage affairs when the risk of potential asymmetry and hierarchy between husband and wife, and/or between their respective natal houses, is high. Consequently, the structuring role of gender is best understood in relation to specific combinations of individual uniqueness and particular instances of togetherness. Strict reciprocity, the hallmark of daily transactions between husbands and wives, as well as of marriage alliances between sets of brothers and sisters (or between their children), traces the contours of endogamy and defines the second sphere of exchange.[2] The third system of exchange, characterized by the unilateral cannibalistic threat that *cohuori* endlessly inflict on *huaorani*, maps out the symbolic order through which powerful neighboring tribes and evil spirits seek to appropriate *huaorani* human force and vital energy. Predation, which does not concern marriage exchange directly but provides an emic explanation of why extreme political, social, and economic closure is necessary, is dealt with in a later part of this essay.

No clear marriage rule is ever stated, except under the implicit form: "If the mothers are different (i.e., not sisters) the children can marry," which is the most common definition of a good marriage. However, it is obvious to any Huaorani that the bride and the bridegroom must come from different longhouses, but marriage with someone too distant is highly dangerous and should be avoided at all cost. As for the possibility of marrying a non-Huaorani (defined until recently as dangerous cannibals), it is hardly thinkable. In other words, we are dealing with a highly endogamous and autarkic society, composed of unambiguously exogamic longhouses. In this context, there is no marriage prescription but a gradation of strongly prohibited to strongly approved marriage alliances, which equally apply to men and women. A woman cannot marry her younger or older brother, nor a man of her parents' generation. Her marriage with an unrelated man or a cross-cousin living in a different regional group is neither prohibited nor approved of; it is simply extremely dangerous. Moreover, such an alliance almost always means that she would have to leave her native house group; marriage with distant kin tends to be virilocal. The intermarriage of sets of same-sex or cross-sex siblings is frequent and commended. Marriage between bilateral cross-cousins is highly praised.

Although marriages between a *huaorani* and a *cohuori* may have happened on rare occasions in the past, they were caused almost certainly by extreme and desperate situations.[3] Literally, *huaorani* and *cohuori* are like two different species, two different kinds of beings; *cohuori* are predators and *huaorani* prey. *Cohuori* steal *huaorani* to eat them exactly like game; they enslave children, and occasionally abduct women, although both Huaorani children and women would let themselves starve to death rather than live with *cohuori* and become one of them. Frustrated Huaorani warriors may have at times abducted *cohuori* women, but they would be forced to eke out a miserable existence at the margins of society, as no Huaorani woman, even those accepting—always reluctantly and temporarily—virilocal residence would ever accept to cohabit with a non-Huaorani woman. Similarly disparaging cases are known whereby a brother and a sister end up marrying each other, hence committing incest. This aberrant situation (but never as abhorrent as a *huaorani-cohuori* marriage) is the subject of various myths.[4] Disapproved of, incestuous marriages occur in very isolated longhouses cut off from regional endogamous alliance networks.

The ideal and most common marriage alliance involves spouses exchanging longhouses linked through affinal brother-sister ties. Kinship being cognatic, the preferred residence is ambilocal, and the preferred marriage is a tie established within the group rather than between two groups. The perfect marriage involves two brother-sister pairs who have intermarried, live close to one another, and marry together at least one of their maturing children.[5] In the early

1990s, I spent some months with such a kindred distributed in two contiguous longhouses. Conta and her brother Yehua had married Mengatohue and his sister Dabe years before. I could not establish with certainty how many children each couple had produced, for there were married daughters and sons living in distant villages, children who had died at various points in time, and children born to other fathers than Yehua and Mengatohue (but whom the two men had contributed to creating by having sex with their pregnant mothers). What seemed to matter to my hosts, rather, was that Ontogamo and Nenqueri, the two sons of Conta and Mengatohue, had married two of Yehua's and Dabe's daughters, Huaane and Menganita, and that the two couples had produced seven grandchildren. Yehua and Dabe lived with an older daughter (Huiña), her husband and their eight children, and a younger son, who was still a bachelor. They were often visited by a married son (Dagaipe), who lived uxorilocally with his wife and their two children. It took me some time to work out who belonged to which longhouse group, as people were continuously passing from one house to another or eating at different hearths, and the children seemed to have no fixed residence at all. Besides, small groups variously composed of residents from either house would leave together to trek and camp in the forest. They would not always return with the same party. After a week or two, however, I could distinguish passing visitors from residents. I could also identify the men with specific hearths, where they would invariably sit to make curare poison or repair a tool. In short, there were, despite the apparent fluidity of house membership, fixed associations between a particular hearth, a set of individuals, and a longhouse. The preference for a form of endogamy centered on affinal brothers and sisters was further confirmed when I surveyed 114 marriages in 5 different settlements in 1991. The data showed that 43 percent of the total number of marriages were between bilateral cross-cousins, 26 percent between sibling sets, 22 percent between apparently unrelated Huaorani men and women, and 8 percent between a Huaorani and a non-Huaorani (Rival 2002: 120).[6] However, the survey also highlighted a fact that I had already observed in Conta's and Dabe's longhouses but to which I had not given full attention: the structural importance of uxorilocality. Even in the most endogamous "neighborhoods," not all resident married men were "paired" with a sister. There were in every *nanicabo* in-marrying men whose sisters and mothers lived far away, such as in the case under discussion: Cuhue, who married Dabe's daughter, Huiña. Endogamy is achieved first and foremost by marrying close, which, whatever the form, entails the direct, reciprocal exchange of marriage partners between people who live close-by (the ideal type being a sister and a brother marrying two of their children together). But not all marriage exchanges can take this form, and more distant in-marrying spouses must be incorporated, which is perfectly acceptable as long as young adults belonging to distant groups are circulated fairly, that is, as long as an initial marriage exchange is both reciprocated and leads to subsequent exchanges. However, the politically sensitive issue of postmarital residence remains to be solved. For reasons detailed below, it is considered more acceptable for a man to take up residence after marriage with his wife and his wife's kin in her natal *nanicabo* than the other way around. Or, said differently, the ideal norm of reciprocal spouse exchange is skewed in practice because uxorilocality is preferred over virilocality.

This situation echoes Peter Rivière's thesis that uxorilocality is structurally and functionally necessary in Amazonian societies where reciprocity can only be ensured through immediate exchange (Rivière 1984: 104–8). Guiana society, he explains, is distinctive in according central importance to the allocation of people in marriage, particularly women.[7] In an unpublished paper, he remarks further that there is no clear-cut rule of postmarital residence in Guiana, although the expressed preference is for settlement endogamy. Because this is not feasible, men must go out and seek a wife. It follows that "uxorilocal residence is the aggregate outcome of individual negotiations in which the wife's parents have the advantage" (Rivière, n.d., 16). He contrasts this situation with that prevailing in Northwest Amazonia where virilocality is made possible in two types of society. Virilocality occurs in two ways: (1) among Tukanoan peoples whose residence groups are defined by patrilocal descent, which allows for affinal ties formed in this generation to be carried over into the next; and (2) among the Yanomami, where a man either captures his wife, if he has no woman to reciprocate (i.e., abduction), or receives a wife from his affines if he has a woman to give in exchange (i.e., immediate, balanced exchange). Inspired by Meillassoux's (1981) view that gynecostatism represents a peaceful solution to matrimonial circulation in groups lacking the political capacity to negotiate reciprocal marriage exchange, Rivière 1(984: 107) concludes that the contrasting rules of (Northwest Amazonian) virilocal residence and (Guianese) uxorilocal residence are ultimately caused by the same variable: "the degree of control that each society exercises over its women." Virilocality, in other words, implies either greater control of men over women, or endemic warfare.[8] In Huaorani society, where marriage exchanges mainly involve individuals (rather than descent groups), and where it is men (rather than women) who move, one finds the same direct link between uxorilocality and the politics of immediate (i.e., reciprocal) exchange.

I have outlined here some of the properties of Huaorani endogamy and marriage exchange, and I have shown how uxorilocality becomes a necessary sociological component of ideal propinquity. The longhouse, this undifferentiated social whole made up of autonomous individuals, which articulates the sharing of all with strict parity between complementary pairs of male and female actors, operates a skewed politic of placing in its struggle for humane survival. Enough has already been said to show that matters are not reducible to earthly marriage politics in a social universe with no clear or permanent exchange groups, and with no obvious wife takers or declared wife givers. Uxorilocality goes beyond the economics of bride service to address matters of value and worthiness, that is, the human person and the person's constitution. The question we need to ask next is whether the female person and the male person are constitutionally equivalent and what role uxorilocality plays in gendering personhood.

THE MALE AND THE FEMALE PERSON: IDENTICAL, EQUIVALENT, COMPLEMENTARY, AND YET, DIFFERENT

Upon completing fieldwork among the Huaorani, I really felt that I had the privilege of documenting one of the few truly gender-equal societies on earth. One of my teachers soon took me to task, and asked me to demonstrate how, and in what ways, the sexes were equal among the Huaorani. One of my first assignments was to work on Collier and Rosaldo's (1981) bride-service model.[9] I immediately felt admiration and sympathy for Collier and Rosaldo's tremendous theoretical achievement but was compelled to argue against their premise that political power and social hierarchy is founded on sexual politics. Yes, marriage is a political institution, but it is not about sexual politics as understood by twentieth-century feminists.[10] Ethnographic evidence led me to argue that conjugality is used, not to foster the political and economic dominance of men over women, but to enforce the strict equivalence of gender (Rival 2002: 122–24). In Huaorani society, as my argument unfolds, sex is not the paramount source of sensual pleasure and political domination. Sex is an intrinsic part of living and parenting, and wives, even when mothers, are not seen as less attractive than young unmarried women. Here marriage is not about men regulating and controlling the sexuality of women. Rather, it represents the political moment when older generations coerce younger generations into conjugality and parenting, by which they reproduce the social order that produced them. If gender differences are created and sustained in the process, they are neutralized by the play of cross-sex sibling political alliances.

Sexual differences are embodied in a way that suggests both equivalence and complementarity. The word for *onquiyè* (girl) is very similar to the word *onguiyè* for (boy). These two words are also used to mean *female* and *male*, whenever sexual differences are recognized in plant and animal species. Similarly, the words *onguè* (male sexual parts), *onguènca* (testicle), and *onguèngö* (penis) mirror the words *öñè* (vulva) and *öñèngä* (female sexual parts). Again, these terms are applied to humans and animals indifferently, and sometimes to dimorphous plants as well. However, female internal sexual parts, such as *möwoyatacuu* ([vagina] literally "the windy canal" or "envelope where to sleep"), *huiñègancuu* ([uterus] literally "the womb, envelope, skin where children multiply"), and *wepèncuu* ([ovary] literally "the envelope, skin producing blood") do not have male equivalents. This difference is further elaborated in the sociological explanation of womanhood as potential motherhood. Whereas a female person is identified to a male person before and after marriage, she is distinguished as "nonmale" during her childbearing years. Sterile women, women who do not wish to engage in sex (and live without a husband or a lover), and menopaused women are all said to be like men. No stigma whatsoever is attached to their "status." Motherhood is taken plainly to be a natural fact of womanhood, and female persons who do not wish to be, or are no longer, fecund are simply *onguiyè anobain* (like men). When a wife and her husband are no longer producing children, they stop sleeping in the same hammock. Each weaves a separate, single-place hammock to be tended side-by-side, and each makes an individual hearth on which to cook separate meals to be shared with each other as with all other coresidents.[11] Finally, the kinship terminology contains at least as many non-gendered kin terms as gendered ones.[12] There is no term for the hearth group, but there is the term *tè huè* for the mother and her offspring, which refers to the clump formed by the first palm to grow from a planted chonta (*Bactris gasipaes*) seed and its shoots. This botanical image expresses the fact that there are as many hearths as there are married women in the longhouse, where at least one fire is kept going at any given time of the day or the night.

With Collier and Rosaldo's model still in mind, I have shown (Rival 2002) that ordinary Huaorani social life accords little importance to gender difference. Conception, birth, childcare, and upbringing, either in representation or in practice, are very similar for boys and girls. Parents undergo the couvade for boys and girls, and rapid growth and autonomy are encouraged in both (Rival 1993). Boys and girls receive names from their grandparents, which are bestowed onto them by their mothers. Both start wearing the *cumi* (cotton hip cord) when they are around three and thought old enough to walk in the forest on their own to collect food for their own consumption or as gifts for their mothers and grandmothers. Boys and girls both get their ears pierced with a needle of chonta palm wood at the start of their adolescence, and both wear balsa wood earplugs, the distinctive mark of their ethnic identity (Rival 1996a: 128–29). Both spend an equal amount of time exploring the forest with other children, the younger learning from the older, or helping their mothers with childcare (Rival 1996a: 325–27). Both hunt birds with small blowguns made by male coresidents, fish with nets made by women, and work in their parents' gardens. Both chant the *amotamini* songs characteristic of Huaorani lore (Rival 2002: 100–1), and both actively participate in the lively storytelling sessions that mark *nanicabo* togetherness at the end of the day before the night sets in. Adult men and women wear no additional clothing on top of their hip cord, which men use slightly differently than women, as they need to tuck their penises upright. Apart from the fact that women keep their hair longer in the back, men's and women's hairstyles are identical. Both men and women pluck their facial and pubic hair, and both use similar body paint designs. And when their elders have decided to marry them, a young man and a young woman are equally seized and brutally forced to sit side-by-side in a hammock, each with one leg swiftly tied to the other's matching leg.[13] Finally, both have the same right to refuse or to accept an arranged marriage.

    I have discussed elsewhere how the ritual creation of gender groups in festivals and wedding ceremonies can also be interpreted as a means to erase all other social differences. With men and women losing their individual identities as kin, affines, friends or enemies, or old or young in ritual, the feasting group gets constituted as simply sexually dimorphic (Rival 2002: 133–40). The transformative force that fuses all celebrants into one large group creates the right conditions for marriage. Individual producer-consumers are transformed into two sets of gendered reproducers who complement each other in their reciprocal work exchange while remaining primarily consumers of naturally abundant food. Huaorani gender symbolism, far from expressing hostility between the sexes, is used ritually as a means to overcome potential conflict and to transform social division into necessary complementarity. Furthermore, if Huaorani cosmology and rituals are saturated with sexual and other bodily images, these are not used to symbolize male supremacy, but the importance of organic life, fertility, and biological reproduction, which are bisexual by nature and androgynous by definition (Rival 2002).

However, notable gender differences do exist, which are all the more striking when examined against the general backdrop of minimal sex-role differentiation discussed above. Although they keep performing essentially undifferentiated or overlapping tasks in their daily lives, boys and girls also acquire gender-specific techniques as they grow and mature. When five or six years old, boys, who may have been playing with clay or even making pots with their sisters, mothers, and aunts, gradually stop doing so. They also stop digging out clay from shallow riverbeds while fishing, and stop offering it to their female kin to whom they now simply communicate the resource location. When a few years older, they also stop fishing and spend more and more time hunting and learning the use of full-length blowguns and spears. Just before reaching adolescence, boys also start learning to make curare poison, as well as their own weapons. They learn to attack peccaries frontally, spear in hand, like their older male kin. Girls, who are ritually taken by their fathers on a hunt when they menstruate for the first time, continue to pursue their "childlike hunting" activities throughout their youth. Female participation in "adult hunting" does occur, but it is not as publicly valued as male hunting. Girls and widows may hunt with their male kin's blowguns as do married women when their husbands happen to be away.[14] However, women never make (or hunt with) weapons or curare.[15] The growing complementarity between adolescent boys and girls is publicly formalized with the economic pairing of a pubescent brother and one of his sisters. This special bond and cooperation continues until marriage (and often beyond), even when the brother, now a bachelor, starts spending less and less time within his natal *nanicabo*.

Nothing in Huaorani ethnography could lead me to accept Collier's and Rosaldo's thesis that marriage produces conjugal obligations and economic transactions which invariably undermine the political position of women.[16] Transactions between husbands and wives, unlike those practiced with other *nanicabo* coresidents, are strictly reciprocal; one gives in response to what one receives and vice versa. Whereas coresidents tend to obtain food independently to then share it out, married couples seem to engage in complementary activities; each reciprocates with goods and services of a different kind. Reciprocal exchange is closely related to complementary production. Men and women know how to do, and can do, almost every item belonging to their society's cultural repertoire. However, when married, they tend to specialize in certain activities. A married woman will not go hunting on her own on a regular basis while her husband stays home. A married man rarely prepares fruit drinks (he is more likely to cook meat or foreign food) or harvests a garden, unless his wife is ill or absent. Many activities become the regular task of one member of the conjugal pair, although this implicit division of labor may vary from couple to couple or from one longhouse to the next. However, in all cases, the time spent on shared tasks more or less equals the time spent on complementary tasks. Furthermore, conjugality does not affect the autonomy of individual producers; husband and wife have equal rights on the products of their common, shared labor. Whereas conjugal pairs form productive units, each spouse remains an independent food sharer within the longhouse. Conjugality affects production patterns but not *nanicabo* sharing or visiting patterns. Marriage organizes the production of goods not their circulation. Conjugal complementarity introduces a certain degree of division of labor, but it is not converted into a rigid code of conduct, and different domestic and productive tasks remain equally valued.

Finally, I came to realize that the reciprocal nature of marital life is directly correlated to its reproductive function. The marital relationship demands the rigorous respect of mutual obligations because conjugality is before all joint parenting. Marriage is about producing children, that is, increasing the number of *nanicabo* residents. Whereas the association of autonomous and self-sufficient producers sharing their products forms a suitable base for *nanicabo* sociality, it is not sufficient to bring new members into the world. For this, married couples must turn into productive units and *work harder*, a fact continuously stressed throughout the wedding ceremony. Balanced reciprocity between husbands and wives ensures a real increase in work output. Moreover, it ensures that fathers and mothers share equally in the procreation process and the growth of children. Couvade rituals illustrate this aspect of gender symmetry in so far as the child is thought to contain an equal quantity of blood and semen, hence the equal participation of the father and the mother in the child's ritual protection. The fact that the strict division of labor between husband and wife and the reciprocal exchange of goods and services are relaxed once a couple's children have all married further confirms the reproductive function of conjugal parity. Now equal and independent longhouse residents, the old spouses no longer form an economic partnership differentiated from the longhouse sharing economy.

Sororal polygyny is also thought in terms of joint capacity for hard work in marriage. Sororal polygyny is usually initiated by the wife's younger sister who refuses to marry out and leave her native *nanicabo*.[17] To be married to only one woman or to her sister(s) as well makes little difference from the man's point of view, except that he must work harder and produce more—hence he demonstrates his industriousness, strength, and generosity. As the sisters divide up the wifely tasks among themselves (each has her own hearth, and the husband goes in turns from one hammock and one hearth, to the next), their productive output also increases. The division of labor now shifts significantly from that of between husband and wife, to that of between the "sedentary" and the "foraging" wives. The determination of a young sister to marry her older sister's husband, directly linked to the notion that marriage implies the absorption of one spouse into the other's family, reinforces the uxorious nature of the marital bond. The choice of young women who prefer to replicate the marriage bond of an older sibling rather than introduce additional men in the longhouse is fully supported by their house group, who is always anxious to limit the number of outsiders who join it. Sororal polygyny thus results from the high value women attach to living with their mothers and sisters. They value their native *nanicabo* above all and would do everything in their power not to leave it. Like these demand-sharing younger sisters, unmarried brothers and brothers-in-law all agree, albeit for different reasons, with limiting the inclusion of in-marrying men to no more than one or two (three at the most, in the largest *nanicaboiri*). Everyone considers male accretions as politically deleterious, and everyone expects the incorporated few to work relatively harder than their native coresidents. In-marrying men have no reason to dissent, as working harder and marrying several times in the same house reinforces their political position. It could be said that sororal polygyny and uxorilocality makes sisters structurally equivalent. This is perhaps why children of sisters are considered to be "more the same" than children of brothers. Although both are, in technical terms, classificatory siblings, children of brothers are not as similar as children of sisters because "they grow in separate houses and their mothers are different" (Rival 2002: 124).

We have a clear indication here that the perfect symmetry between husband and wife, which mirror the balanced reciprocity of brother-sister marriage exchange and, more generally, the ideal equivalence of male and female, deviates into asymmetrical positions. Uxorilocality, a condition that affects *all* sibling relationships, results in a certain gender asymmetry, which cannot be attributed to the conjugal tie per se or to age hierarchies among siblings. Uxorilocality implies that women are by definition "of the house" (host), while men *become* hosts. The term *ne eñaca* ([guest] literally "the one who is born") and the term *ne ocöinga* ([host] literally, "the one who is at home") shed some light on the political meanings of visiting and belonging. Hosts are in the house, or of the house and, as such, are required to give to their guests, unilaterally and upon request. A host, by giving away to the guest without expecting anything in return, is like a reproductive couple, a nurturing parent, or a tree. A guest, on the other hand, is a pure consumer, just like a newborn baby (Rival 2002: 144–47). Uxorilocality, or the successful taming and integration of in-marrying male spouses, needs to be understood within the more general deployment of strategies aimed at controlling outside imports. In order to limit the power asymmetry built into the host-guest relationship, the Huaorani highly restrict visiting. The situation of orphans and war refugees are, for the same reasons, precarious. Their welfare and *nanicabo* membership entirely depend on the protection they receive from the individual who has taken them under his or her wing. The tie between protector (a full member of the longhouse) and *protégé* (who rarely achieves full-member status), more tenuous than the tie of adoption, is akin to pet keeping. A protégé is considered to be the entire responsibility of the protector, who if disappeared would leave the protégé without any legitimacy and membership status. Uxorilocality thus expresses a wider political concern with who lives where, rather than with who is exchanged for whom. Huaorani body politics, I would argue, is a politics of *placing*.

I would further argue that women play a direct and active role in uxorial politics. Huaorani residential society maintains the integrity of a core of related females at the heart of extended families. It does not provide men with a separate corporate men's house (such as amongst the Kayapo, for instance) or with the ritual possibility of transforming the longhouse into a male-only ceremonial center (such as among the Barasana).[18] Men's physical distancing from their birth group is considered essential to the male maturing process and necessary for their successful and gradual incorporation within the group where they marry and procreate. Men, who start their married lives as affinal guests, almost as visitors, are progressively transformed into insiders, or hosts. It is because their *nanicabo* membership goes without saying, as it were, that women control to a large extent the process by which outsiders are incorporated within the longhouse. Men, who cannot easily reconcile being a son and being a married father, experience a tension between past belonging (to the natal house group) and future destination (their belonging to the *nanicabo* in which they marry and father children). They need affinal women to foster their passage from one type of membership (and identity) to the other. Men living uxorilocally have more diffuse social networks and more extensive visiting rights than women. A clear-cut boundary, both physical and social, is maintained through stringent restrictions on female visiting and feeding between groups of consanguineous women, who are close and mutually dependent, and affinal women, who are considered *hua* (totally others). There is no mechanism by which female cross-cousins can become blood kin or coresidents, and maximal social distance exists between potential or real sisters-in-law. Whereas mothers and daughters and groups of sisters are closely identified, female cross-cousins are most different. It is not surprising, therefore, that women are in charge of incorporating outsiders and visitors or of naming their kin by transmitting personal names from the old generation to the new one. In a society that seems to define affinity as the domain of potential rapprochement and similarity, one may even wonder whether affinity is the right term to qualify the lack of relationship between these totally unrelated female alters.[19] Without the links men maintain with their sisters and mothers, self-sufficient residential units formed around consanguineous women would stand as unconnected forest islands.[20]

In this section, my attempt has been to demonstrate that although the male and the female person are to a large extent constituted as identical, the uxorial condition of male adulthood entails a clear existential disjunction between female continuity of belonging and male sequential adherence. In the next section, I go a step further to show that men's survival depends on being embedded through uxorilocal residence within a matrix of domestic life, which offers their souls the most secure form of earthly attachment.

ASYMMETRIC ATTACHMENT OF THE BODY TO THE SOUL

Murphy (1960: 189) said of the Mundurucú that they see the enemy as given in the nature of things and beyond the control of the members of their society. This remark applies equally well to the Huaorani. As mentioned at the beginning of this chapter, the Huaorani's extreme political, social, and economic closure corresponds to their perception that they, the true human beings, are under constant threat of being captured and eaten by non-Huaorani cannibals. Intratribal warfare is explained by invoking *pïï* (a form of anger). Common answers to why people killed each other in the past are: "when they were angry, they killed"; "their disagreeing about a matter made them so angry that they would get their spears out and kill"; or "if someone in the longhouse became sick and died, the men would get angry to the point of being driven to cause someone to die, anyone." Men have to be under the influence of *pïï*, a mixture of courage, fearlessness, anger, and force—both moral and physical—to make spears and to use them in killing true people (i.e., Huaorani).[21] *Pïï* as raw energy or vitality dwells within men's and women's bodies alike. But only men become *pïï inte*, the "fit of rage itself" (rather than just feeling its presence in the body), which is a transformation that if sustained long enough, drives them to *tapaca hueni* (spear kill) one or more victims. Once *pïï* takes over the killer's body, he no longer listens and kills blindly; it does not matter who the victims are, for the goal is to bring death forth. The victims may be either *huarani* (unrelated others) or *guirinani* (kin by blood or by residence), for *pïï* turns the killer temporarily into a being with no relatives.

Death is always interpreted as directly or indirectly caused by some human or human-like agency, which in turn, triggers the homicidal emotion. Only deaths in old age (discussed below), or voluntary deaths, are not conceptualized as murders. The *daicahuo ähuente hueni* ([unwanted death] literally "dying of fever") receives very little elaboration in comparison with the *hueno tenongui* ([willed death] literally "causing someone to die by spearing"), as if the meaning was created by *pïï* and conceptualized as pure physical sensation or raw desire. *Pïï* or homicidal furor is represented as something natural or the emotional response of an individual man to a particular change in his social environment, more precisely, to the death of a relative. The rage which, located within the killer, transforms a male kin into an external aggressor who kills indiscriminately is what is culturally meaningful. I witnessed men becoming *pïï* on several occasions. Each time, the first manifestation of rage was directed against the man's young children. His wife (-ves) and other coresidents had to contain him, stop him from seizing his spears and killing in his own house. Once I heard a man infuriated by the death of his son who had drowned in the Curaray River sing "I want to kill, as a result you are to die. My becoming angry drives me to want to kill, resulting in your dying." Today, while *pïï inte* men seize their shotguns and shoot aimlessly above their heads, women prevent tragic accidents by fleeing to the forest with their youngest children. Older children run away and hide in the forest or take refuge in an allied longhouse. They do not come back before the rage has deserted their father's body. After the first fit of rage, men usually channel their *pïï* energy by planning a killing raid. Their rage and determination to kill, which they sustain through chanting, may spread contagiously to other men in the longhouse. They need to remain in a state of rage throughout, from the fashioning and decorating of spears, to the finding of, and spying on, victims. Victims are ambushed and killed when they are most vulnerable or least suspicious. More often than not, war parties are aborted, as men cease to feel *pii* while looking for, or spying on, the enemy. The feeling may even wane before while men are, for instance, sharpening their spears.

A *cohuori* predator killing his *huaorani* prey is seen as committing a predictable act similar to those found within the animal kingdom. Non-Huaorani exert predation on Huaorani in the same way as jaguars or harpy eagles predate on monkeys and birds. Huaorani are killed as prey and consumed as food, and their bodies used to feed other bodies, whose nature it is to kill and eat. By contrast, a Huaorani killing another Huaorani is not driven by some kind of "instinct," even if the embodied drive to kill is considered to be a natural male disposition or susceptibility beyond rational control. A Huaorani killing another Huaorani does not consume his victim but exchanges an unwanted death with a death he causes. Men possessed by *pii* turn into alienated killers who temporarily become as wild as jaguars, and as nonhuman *cohuori*. *Pii* causes men to become *huaca* (other) and to destroy the intimate social order of the house groups to which they belong. An old warrior told me once "when I am angry, I am like a jaguar, I can go on my own and live alone in the forest, like a jaguar. Not even the jaguar can threaten me or harm me, for I am so angry." Most of the time, the state of homicidal furor is temporary, and restructured *nanicaboiri* soon resume their ordinary life of sharing and unity. Some pathological killers, however, are collectively remembered as half-mythical antiheroes. They are represented as fierce, perfectly autonomous, and dreadfully lonely individuals who live kinless and without society, alone with the trees and drinking their own urine. All are said to have been orphans, and to have spent their lives under the influence of *pii*, wild, uncontrolled, and fully disembodied from the shared substance of their *nanicaboiri*. They killed so many Huaorani and non-Huaorani, the tales go, that they have ceased to be real humans. When such killers are eventually eliminated, there is no one to avenge their death; their death is an end in itself.

Homicide, therefore, is not presented as an exploit, an act of bravery, or the source of mystical vitality but, rather, as an uncontrollable drive, the unfortunate outcome of *pii*. *Pii*, which is beyond human control, explains why violence, a necessary part of human interaction with the nonhuman world, is inevitable between real people despite the moral anxiety it causes. Homicidal rage comes from without, and society must work at containing it and at mitigating its effects. The enemy is not incorporated but expelled. If the mad killer, the insider turned outsider, represents otherness created from within, the end result is that he is eventually expelled without, and permanently so. The victim of internal warfare is typically a dying warrior, and it is the killed, not the killer, who is culturally and socially valued. Dying warriors belong to their kin, who remember and keep the tale of the circumstances in which they died alive (Rival 2002, Chapter 3).[22] Tales of warfare are tales about men who, buried alive by kin, die as kin now fully transformed into cognatic members of their wives' groups and attached forever to their wives' homeland. Such tales focus on the suffering inflicted on the speared body, which culminates in the excruciating pain and slow death of moribund victims unless they are found by compassionate relatives who dig a fairly large and deep grave, and bury them alive. When the victim is male, as it is most often the case, female kin line the grave with bamboo mats on which they lay the dying body to hasten his death and put an end to his suffering. There are many stories of dying fathers buried alive with one of their children, usually the last one, so that, I was told, "the father does not leave the land alone," and so that "he does not feel lonely in the afterworld."[23] The rite by which a dying brother or husband is buried with his child by female kin recalls the somewhat reversed situation described in a myth about birth in which men had to cut their wives open to give birth to their children whom they nursed and raised on their own until a small rodent taught a pregnant woman how to give birth naturally (see Chapter 4). The burial place, with its trapped *onohuoca* (body soul), becomes a place vividly remembered. To be killed is culturally more significant than to kill. If being killed is the most human death, it is because one dies as a victim and a kin, in short, as an insider. To conclude, the Huaorani warfare complex, with its focus on the killed and the fate of the killed, represents a fascinating reversal of the Amazonian theme of incorporation of externality and otherness. Far from incorporating outsiders who are then gradually turned into insiders, it turns insiders into temporary or permanent outsiders (Rival 2002: 66–67).

Huaorani ambivalence toward dreams and hallucinogenic drugs can also be understood with reference to the belief that if otherworldliness cannot be suppressed entirely, it must be contained. People do not grow the powerful hallucinogenic vine locally known as *ayahuasca* (*Banisteriopsis muricata*), which they say "belongs to the *cohuori*" (i.e., Zaparoan and lowland Quichua groups), but they may collect it from old fallows along riverbanks to prepare a decoction used for extreme emergencies, such as when a sickly child is struggling between life and death. If the child survives, especially a male, he becomes susceptible to dream visits by mystical jaguars and then may lead a shamanic career in mature age. Shamans are thus survivors of serious childhood illnesses, and their relatives do everything in their power to prevent them from dreaming about jaguars or from ingesting *ayahuasca*. When possessed by the spirit of a jaguar, a shaman is always surrounded by relatives, who control the mystical presence through their jokes, mockery, and laughter.

I also interpret the preference for blowpipe hunting as part of this continuous exercise in containment. As I have explained elsewhere (Rival 1996b), the blowpipe, a powerful instrument for monitoring social closeness, puts uxorious men in a position of control as defenders of endogamous relationships. The *oömena* ([blowpipe] literally "two halves that blow") is incorporated into mythical discourse to express the correspondence between the symbiotic relationship existing between a longhouse and the monkeys it consumes, and the privileged alliance of restricted exchange between a brother and a sister. But for such an alliance to be possible, one brother (the oldest, incestuous one) must be expelled from society. Out of reach and incommunicable, he becomes the son whose loss the mother grieves bitterly. The idea that the uxorial man who is successfully incorporated within his wife's longhouse and securely allied to his affinal sister cannot be a good son for his mother is further developed in another myth that tells the story of an old woman abandoned without food by her living son and his family but rescued by a long-dead son (Rival 1996a: 84–86).

Men need protection from the predatory forces that shape the universe, and in addition to the precautions mentioned above, they rely above all on the life-giving powers of their wives. It is significant that it is imagined that the great Creator figure, Huègöngui, lives at the end of the world in a big house with his wife and grandchildren.[24] In a myth that focuses on the murderous intentions of three grandchildren and on the resuscitating skills of the wife (she "rebirths" her husband each time his vengeful grandchildren put him to death), we find, I wish to contend, the idea that gender complementarity in reproduction naturally corresponds to the human potential to assert sociality against the inhumanity of predation and violent death. The following excerpt illustrates my point.

> The river otters [one of the grandchildren's bodily appearance] went back to their grandparents' house, and lied to their grandmother, saying that Huègöngui was

bathing in the river. But in actual fact, they had thrown him in a blazing fire. Night was falling, her husband had still not returned, and *Ñëñë* started to worry. She worried that the mosquitoes would bite him, then she worried that he may have died, but then she thought that he would live again. In the morning, she collected *mö* leaves in the forest, before making her way to the fire site, where she gathered her husband's ashes. She prepared a funnel (*ontabepo*) with the *mö* leaves and filled it with the ashes. She cautiously poured water into the funnel after having placed a small clay pot (*caanta*) underneath. The dripping water made a noise; it sounded like words uttered by a human voice. The voice said, "Now more than ever, we are thinking of killing." When the pot was filled, she covered it with a lid, and thought to herself that her husband would be alive again the following day. In the morning, she discovered a four-month-old baby in the clay pot. "Huègöngui, God the Creator!" she exclaimed. She went with her grandchildren to the river to bathe Huègöngui. *Ñëñë* sat in the river holding her baby husband. The grandchildren transformed themselves into a swarm of blood-sucking insects (*mento*), and hovered thick as a blanket over the baby and his carer. The poor *Ñëñë* could not help it, she dropped the baby in the water. The grandchildren, transforming themselves back into river otters, jumped in the river and devoured the baby. One got his right arm, the other a leg. A fish called *queremene* caught the rest of the baby's body, cooked it, and ate it. They all thought that God would be reborn the following day.

In the morning, *Ñëñë* collected the remains of the baby's body and the ashes from the fire that the *queremene* fish had prepared and repeated the same procedure with the funnel of *mö* leaves, ordering her grandchildren to bring her a pot full of water. As they trickled through the funnel down into the *caanta* clay pot, the drops spoke again: "The trees will burst and you will live a better life. New trees will grow, balsa, palms, and many other plants." *Ñëñë* was delighted. She covered the pot with a lid thinking that God would be reborn the following day. This time, a ten month old baby came out of the pot, walking. *Ñëñë* carefully avoided the river; she was not going to take any risk this time. She warmed some water and bathed the baby inside the longhouse. The river otters went fishing and brought a large catch of catfish for their grandmother, telling her that this food would help her get plenty breast milk. The baby grew big and strong. As her grandchildren continued to behave well, *Ñëñë* told them they could stay around. This is why there are still river otters today, and why we still live well.

Without overinterpreting the myth, I feel confident in viewing it as the cosmological elaboration of a muted representation of society with the taming, creative, and reproductive wife at its core. The true movers in this story, it seems, are the grandchildren, who, acting under the guise of woodpeckers, river otters, and mosquitoes, transform themselves in order to destroy their grandfather's body. Huègöngui is, of course, the master Creator; new forms of life (both vegetal and animal) are generated from his sacrificed body. However, none of this could effectively happen without the agency of Ñëñë—Huègöngui's wife and the river otters' grandmother. Moreover, it is as surrogate mother to her husband that she reveals her creative power. Ñëñë begets Huègöngui through a filtering operation that reverses the (over) cooking process that destroyed his life in the first place. Moreover, her human conduct, manifest in her homely and caring ways, encourages the river otters to finally behave as proper humans. Ñëñë is the center of the longhouse, she propagates life, nurtures it, and transforms her descendants into real people. As I see it, the myth, which clearly emphasizes the wife/grandmother's creative capacity to make kin, articulates "the uterine logic of the house" (Lea 1995: 218).

As such, the myth reiterates the message that if men are potential hostages to the predatory souls of others, women are fundamentally associated with the mother's life place, the source of all regeneration. The very same image is found in the representation of a woman's good death. Whereas a man dies of a good death when speared by his enemy and buried alive by his kin, a woman in old age should ideally let herself starve to death and perish within a deserted, decaying longhouse. Women are thought to live longer lives than their husbands, whom they survive in widowhood for many years until their senses are so diminished that they lose the elementary capacity of feeding themselves. Ancient widows become delirious. As they start imagining that long-dead kin are feeding them, they keep refusing the food offered to them by living kin, who eventually move out and build a new longhouse in a distant forest clearing.[25] The sons of the defunct widow come back a few months later to burn the dilapidated dwelling down.[26] Once cleansed by fire in this fashion, the former dwelling site becomes a fertile burial place, a grove to which new generations seasonally trek in search of natural abundance. Its origin blurs with that of similar ancient dwelling sites now used as palm groves where *huaomoni*, or endogamous neighborhoods, converge every year during the fruiting season. For several weeks, palm fruit are collected and prepared into drinks, both for ordinary and ceremonial consumption (Rival 1993). Women proudly collect potsherds and broken stone axes from shallow digs, which they preciously keep as evidence that "our grandmothers lived in this place." I cannot help but find in this tale of female endurance in the face of death and immortality "the telluric permanence of the female body" (Guillaumin 1996: 100).

DISCUSSION

On the basis of the ethnographic evidence so far discussed, I wish to argue that it is because men are particularly receptive to the inhumanity of predatory death that society works to embed them within matrifocal networks. Huaorani survival fundamentally depends on uxorilocality, which in addition to the sociological properties explored in the previous section, provides society with the means to ensure that men remain fully human. Men's humanity entirely depends on their successful incorporation as in-married husbands within matrifocal house groups structured through inchoate, yet real, lines of reproducing mothers and daughters. Their daily social work implicitly counters the powerful forces that dictate that lives must be lost for life to be perpetuated. To give full sociocosmic significance and value to the reproductive work of familiarizing and kin making is difficult. Killing and destruction fare much higher in people's memory than growth and peace. People are by far more expansive on the subject of war than on the subject of peace, as if peace was meant to be experienced rather than discoursed upon. It is as if people, while having a lucid understanding of how their destruction is productive for their enemies, were unable to grasp their own sustained reproductive power with the same explicitness. People take their inner force and power for granted, for I wish to suggest they naturalize social relations according to two contrastive models of nature. People's creative power, which derives both from production and from consumption, is neither denied nor devalued. On the contrary, it is seen to prolong its effects beyond death. For the forest, far from being a pristine environment external to society, exists as the product of the productive and consumptive activities of past peoples. Both the forest and society are regenerated through the business of ordinary life without need for accumulation, surplus, stealing, or the transfer of life energy from one sphere to another. The Huaorani vision of life is not limited fertility but natural abundance (Rival 2002). Identity is not naturalized or essentialized with reference to a narrative of origin that hides power differentials (Yanagisako and Delaney 1995). Rather, we find the naturalization of social relations.

Social relations are modeled after two distinct natural processes. At the most exclusive level, the absolute lack of sociality between *cohuori* and *huaorani* is naturalized as the animal-like relation between predator and prey. At the most inclusive level of social interaction, that between *nanicabo* coresidents, the system of representations focuses on common living (from food sharing to substance sharing) as an organic process. In this sense, the notion of shared substance constitutes a type of biologisation of social bonds; *nanicabo* sociality is in part biotic. It is prolonged with the naturalization of the diachronic relation between past and present people, which consists of making the dead a source of plant food freely tapped by the living. As I have shown in my analysis of drinking ceremonies and manioc festivals, the ritual association between guests and hosts, or birds and fruiting trees, develops the same imagery (Rival 2002, Chapter 6). The life-sustaining relationship between people and forest plants, particularly fruiting trees (as well as the impersonal agencies perceived as fulfilling a similar function), is characterized by great generosity. It is in the nature of trees and other food plants of the forest to give continuously to humans without asking anything in return. The power to generate vitality is thus associated with spontaneous vegetal growth. Social reproduction and continuity do not depend on the violent acquisition of external political or religious powers. For instance, Sun sends his son "the true people" in a pure act of "natural" generosity to share civilization with them.[27] By contrast, the aggressive relationship between prey and predator, characteristic of the top of the trophic chain, leads to extreme hostility and separation. It is in the nature of the powerful *cohuori* to reproduce themselves by continuously snatching the creativity, vitality, and life force of *huaorani* people, who can do no more than elude contact with their violent attackers.

In "predatory mode," the non-Huaorani predator robs the life of its Huaorani victim. In "natural-abundance mode," Huaorani guests become rejoicing birds feeding with great gusto on a large fruiting tree. At once gregarious and cacophonous, the atmosphere is peaceful and conducive to marriage celebration. In one context, powerless prey are condemned to death and *huaorani* humans devoured; in the other, humans belong with the vegetarian bird species that color the world with their songs and bright feathers and, like them, live, rejoice, and multiply. Let us examine in greater detail the ecological relations underpinning these two modes of naturalization. The prey-predator relation found in parts of the animal kingdom is a unilateral relationship of feeding; individuals from one species feed on individuals of a less powerful species. The Huaorani represent themselves as the less powerful species. Large sections of the natural world, however, depend on feeding relations that are devoid of aggression. Huaorani thought selects and particularly values symbiotic relations between fruiting plants and vegetarian animal species that are mutually beneficial to each other. Such associations across the fauna/flora divide create the right conditions for the biological reproduction of varied forms of life.[28] Rather than imagining the trophic chain as continuous, ranked, and hierarchically encompassing with mankind and other great predators competing at the top, Huaorani thought seems to have selected two entirely different and opposed modes of interspecies feeding. And, as true humans, they have decided to replenish themselves in particular association with trees and a few tree-dwelling species in a forest environment that gives in profusion without asking anything in return. The slow biological process that leads to maturation and fruiting relies on telluric energy to create fertility. Telluric energy endures, for it uses itself over and over again. Through time release, it is able to make life out of the dying. In the same way it is in the nature of trees and other forest plants to give food continuously to animals and humans without asking anything in return, past people also "did" this and "lived" in the forest (i.e., through their subsistence and ceremonial activities) "made it grow." The forest, which stands as the historical record of past human activities, is inseparable from the people who have lived in it and with it. If the predatory mode potentially leads to *huaorani* extermination, naturally abundant plant life secures *huaomoni* reproductive power.[29]

Although these two modes of naturalization cannot be interpreted to correspond to a male and a female perspective on society (Hugh-Jones 1995), they do overlap with "natural" differences between the sexes.[30] Sharing the same cultural identity, men and women are equally vulnerable to predation, but men can turn into enemies of their own people in ways that are not available to women. And if men and women jointly partake in the forest's natural abundance, it is first and foremost through a woman's death, which involves her willed assimilation to the telluric process of decay and plant growth, and which mirrors her will to procreate (Rival 1998), that the long-term, interspecific continuity of society is secured. Crocker (1969: 50) said a long time ago that the Bororo universe expresses two principles of organization: the inequality of like items related asymmetrically and the equality of unlike items related symmetrically. Later in the article, he added that "the idiom of Bororo social organization goes beyond the social facts of descent and affinity. The units involved are not groups of persons contrasted on the basis of differential descent, but rather categories of social states of being opposed through differences in kind." The Huaorani likewise express the contradictory nature of their social models in terms of the complementary opposition between femaleness as more "plant like" than maleness and maleness as more "animal like" than femaleness.

In reanalyzing this ethnographic material in terms of the construction of the male and the female person in uxori-matrilocal societies for the purpose of writing this chapter, I became increasingly convinced that a direct link exists between Amazonian uxorilocality and body-soul constructions. Amazonian sociology is incomprehensible unless we examine it in the context of the cosmological principles in which it is embedded. In a previous publication, Viveiros de Castro (2001: 33) argues that "the soul is the eminently alienable, because eminently alien, part of the Amazonian person." I now see an obvious convergence between Viveiros de Castro's argument and Rivière's (1974) understanding of the couvade. Rivière (1974: 431), focused on one aspect of the rite, the close bond existing between the parents and the infant's clinging soul, analyzes the couvade as a "second birth" primarily concerned with spiritual creation. If we replace "spiritual creation," or a concern for increasing the attachment of spiritual energy to the infant (Rivière 1974: 429), with "soul attachment," or a concern for placing the soul within the body, we see that the two explanations largely overlap. Primarily concerned as I was with the position of the husband/father in my own analysis of the couvade (Rival 1998), I somewhat neglected the importance of the spiritual bond between parents and child and, more generally, the fate of the soul matter. Perhaps analyzing the situation from the wife's perspective, I stressed the fact that the Huaorani couvade activates the attachment of the in-marrying husband to the wife's house group. As I saw it at the time, the most salient aspect of the ritual is its celebration of the parents' real procreative powers, which makes it almost an antithesis to the Christian spiritual sponsorship or *compadrazgo* so famously discussed by Gudeman (1971). This is why, I continued, marriage, which is not the object of a specific ceremony in many Amazonian societies, is not socially meaningful until the couple has given life to at least one thriving baby. Childbirth materializes the conjugal tie and, in a sense, *creates* marriage. In observing the couvade ritual restrictions, I added, husband and wife are "reborn" as mother and father.

As I see it today, the "missing" link between a focus on placing and attachment, and one on the parent-child bond is the nature of the body-soul dualism. This is why Viveiros de Castro's (2001: 33) comment that "the Amazonian construction of kinship concerns essentially the fabrication (and destruction) of *bodies*, while 'souls' are not made but *given*" is compelling. But when Viveiros de Castro says that the Amazonian soul is a "given" dimension of the person in the sense that it is neither created nor the product of transformation (at least not in the same sense that the body is), and that, therefore, it can be taken away from the person, he does not differentiate between the male and the female person. For this author, humanity is purely defined in contradistinction to animality. I have presented sufficient evidence in this essay to point to the limits of an anthropological analysis of humanity, even in the Amazonian context, which would obliterate the difference between femaleness and maleness. Among the Huaorani, as I hope to have shown, the mother/child bond is not exactly the same as the father/child bond, and the political consequences of life giving are not similar to those of life taking, even if both actions require the same amount of consciousness and intentionality. We need to recognize with Marilyn Strathern (2001) that social categorization invariably draws on sexual imagery, and that sexual imagery is also drawn upon when conceptualizing the nature of social relationships. Gender may not be an immutable attribute of whole persons, but sexual difference is, and it is from this basic difference that more abstract and vague principles (femaleness and maleness) are extrapolated to articulate what in society divides and unites or what separates and connects. Amazonian cultures, like many cultures around the world, conceptualize souls/spirits and bodies as partly independent modes of being that occupy different ontological planes. While bodies are made nonmysteriously by androgynous couples engaged in reciprocal exchange, souls proceed from supernatural forces and get secretly inserted in fetuses during pregnancy. This results in Huaorani men being different from Huaorani women, even if the source of this difference is unclear. Are men different from women because their bodies are different or because their souls are different? Or is the difference located in the way their souls are attached to their bodies? We know too little about the nature of the Amazonian soul matter or spiritual energy to answer these questions conclusively. What follows is therefore somewhat conjectural.

Huaorani uxorilocality, which strengthens women's control of reproduction and social relationships, corresponds to the fact that the process by which women who live together and are consanguineously related obtain and exercise their biopolitical force and transformative power in a way that men can never fully experience. Following the same reasoning, the parent-child bond is modeled after the mother-child bond, which is given as the most powerful, intense, and enduring of social bonds. It is only when defined as a kind of mothering that fathering is recognized as established and expressed bonds of kinship. Fathering, however, also implies a more spiritual connection to cosmic forces, when, for instance, men become shamans or when the violent death of a kin puts them under the direct influence of a powerful emotion like *pïï*, which, as explained earlier, links them to a mystical level of reality. Temporarily dehumanized when possessed by homicidal fury, men become dangerous killers whose complete predatory transformation is prevented thanks to their uxorial condition. Affinal women thus play a crucial role in embedding men within communities of life and in facilitating male participation within the human society of the here and now. Death undoubtedly represents a major transformation affecting the relationship between bodies that grow together and soul matter, which exists in finite quantity and flows from body to body. Men communicate more easily than women with the land of the dead, and death suspends the process of male domestication by matri-uxorilocal house groups. When women die, they continue to contribute to the formation of life for the living. Whereas the Huaorani male person, split as he is, seems to be particularly susceptible to the contrary pull of the two kinds of energy, the female person, at once one and multiple, seems to be far more rooted in the telluric vitality of her body than she is receptive to the cosmic pull. The contrastive, gendered representation of death I have discussed in this chapter provides a clear indication of the fact that Huaorani men and women are not human in exactly the same way. Interestingly, Huaorani social thought seeks to theorize this particular form of dualism with reference not only to the human body, but also to the ecology of life. Femaleness, consanguinity, and symbiotic relations pertaining to the plant world are contrasted to maleness, affinity, and predatory relations prevailing in some parts of the animal kingdom. Yes, bodies are made, but the aptitude of one's body to make bodies is as given as the soul matter is, particularly in women. It is therefore time we admit that the body-soul duality prevalent in Amazonia cannot be accurately grasped without reference to sexual dimorphism. However predatory the male cosmic energy from which the soul matter seems to originate, it can never entirely subvert the body's energy, female in its roots and androgynous in its manifestations.

It follows that if we are to accept with Viveiros de Castro (1998) that Amazonian affinity is a cosmological principle closely linked to religious ideas about otherness and group identity, we must also recognize in the "uxorilocal inflection" of Amazonian society a cosmic dimension. In the same way as affinity must be understood beyond the pure economic and political facts of labor control and marriage rule, uxorilocality, I wish to argue, plays a role in creating society and the cosmos. The myth about Huègöngui and his wife illustrates this perfectly. Whereas affinity represents the outer movement of asymmetric relations with the cosmos and enemy societies, uxorilocality represents the inner construction of cognatic kinship and sociality. Consequently, affinity and consanguinity cannot be opposed as the purely given to the entirely constructed (Viveiros de Castro 2001). Affinity and consanguinity are dialectically related. The former cannot exist without the latter. Both are partly given and partly constructed through uxorilocality, a process that is eminently gendered. Cosmic affinity is linked not only to animality but also to maleness. Uxorilocality relates to the vegetal world and to femaleness, both in its mundane and in its cosmic dimension. Women's alliance with biological life runs from birth to death, as does their close association with the domesticating forces of the hearth and the physical structure of the longhouse. More than a simple rule of residence, uxorilocality as practiced and thought of by the Huaorani structures society and regulates gender relations. Uxorilocality allows men and women to achieve a great deal of gender equality, both materially (economically) and politically. However, because men are "extractable from their natal kin," and feel a contradictory attachment to their natal families and to their families of procreation, new asymmetries arise.[31] Men's spiritual connection to cosmic energy makes their attachment to either family all the more difficult.[32] Because men can *be pïï* rather than just feel the fit of rage in them, they need to immerse their bodies and the soul matter they contain within their conjugal families, where corporal strength derives from unbroken attachments between mothers and daughters to whom they are initially related through affinity. A man's mother and sisters cannot protect him from mystically connecting with predatory cosmic forces as efficiently as his affinal cross-sex kin. As I have argued elsewhere (Rival 2002), Huaorani perspectivism must be understood from the viewpoint of the prey, not of the predator. Ecological awareness is shifted to a different level of energy flow and biological organization, resulting in subaltern resistance to the call of imperious supernature. It is because the Huaorani do not abstract human beings from the matrix of their relations with other living organisms (Feely-Harnick 2002: 217) that their understanding of life processes is profoundly gendered.

PART III

IN THE MIDST OF ENEMIES

OVERVIEW

WHO ARE THE HUAORANI? What has their trek been in the course of time? How many ridges have they walked over; how many hills have they inhabited with their chants? How many fights have they fought in dreams, curing sessions, dances, or tales? How many warriors lost their earthly lives in elusive combats? And how many lives did they snatch in return? Who were the enemies they fought against? How many chose to abandon the fight and live peaceful, settled lives with riverine neighbors instead, and for how long? Is the trek finally over? I have attempted to offer partial answers to these questions by arguing that Huaorani people do not constitute a single nation—or "nationality" to use the term in vogue in Ecuadorian indigenous politics. Their society is not a neat constellation of institutions, and their ethnic union is sealed in no sacred text setting the parameters of their agreed congregation. They have no state to sacrifice their lives for, no common cause to abide by, and no paramount chiefs. In other words, they do not form a polity in the Euro-American sense of the term. What binds them together is a joint commitment to freedom and to personal autonomy, and a common passion to resist the forces of predation, which they identify with coercion, exploitation, alienation, and hierarchy.

In Part II, I presented trekking as a political strategy aimed at protecting longhouse sociability against the stratified chiefdoms and capturing societies that have occupied Upper Amazonia for centuries. What is distinctive about the Huaorani, I have argued, is their determination to cultivate their quality of "prey" as a source of humanity; thus, they refuse to become like their powerful neighbors who, as they see it, produce and reproduce themselves socially through the predatory incorporation of others. Such an orientation has forced the Huaorani to radicalize many of the cultural traits that characterize Amazonian societies. Fiercely egalitarian and impervious to coercion or to any form of command, Huaorani people learn from a very young age that real human beings must have full control over themselves; one needs to know how to survive without others, as much as to live in togetherness. They also learn the benefits of following great and generous leaders and attune their productive activities to the beautiful ways of the latter without ever letting intensification or amplification turn into domination or hierarchy. Shamanic protection is not always efficacious; cannibal enemies cannot be kept at bay permanently. Their constant attacks wound individuals, if not entire groups, sometimes mortally, and leave survivors with no other resort than to hide deeper in the forest or to flee farther away. In times of destruction and dispersion, greatness turns into fierceness, and war takes over hunting. Frontiers that had barely existed become the focus of assiduous patrolling. Killing the external enemy has a ripple effect on intraethnic relations and destabilizes peace until a new equilibrium is found.

In Part III, I revisit previous analyses of Huaorani culture and society in the light of recent evolutions and transformations. My goal is not to come up with new theorizations, or to propose a better historicization of contemporary processes. It is, rather, to offer new layers of rich ethnographic data that illustrate the contemporaneity of Huaorani cultural forms. Far from blending away within a regional cultural system shaped by the dynamics of interculturality, Huaorani culture brings a new vital intensity to Ecuadorian culture by participating in it from a position of radical difference. Chapter 7 offers a contextualized reflection on the giving environment thesis. The Huaorani's unique way of knowing nature and of understanding the ecosystem of which they are a part is rooted in a subsistence economy that, depending chiefly on hunting and gathering, restricts the use of cultivated products to festive and ceremonial occasions. The forest, far from being a pristine environment external to society,

FIGURE 19. Bameno villagers getting ready to present their traditions at the Amazon State University, Puyo, April 2015.

FIGURE 20. Young men at a school festival, QuehueireOno, May 2015.

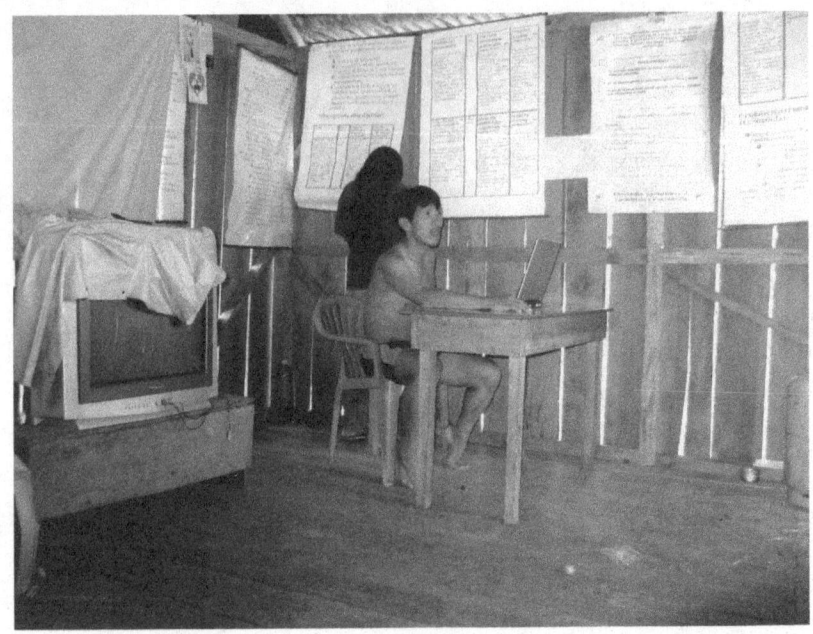

FIGURE 21. Leader preparing a conservation management plan for his community, Damointaro, July 2006.

FIGURE 22. Use of the tribal leader's picture by government officials, May 2013.

FIGURE 23. Housing along an oil road, 2010.

FIGURE 24. Author in a conversation with secondary school pupils, Quehueire Ono, May 2013. Photo by Felipe Mincaye.

FIGURE 25. Participatory workshop, Puyo, May 2013.

results from the productive and consumptive activities of past people. Forest and society are regenerated through the business of ordinary life, rather than through accumulated surplus, stealing, or the transfer of life energy from one sphere to another. I show that although circumstances have changed, Huaorani people continue to find ways of countering the timeless transformational whirlpool that engulfs their predatory enemies by anchoring their society within the forest ecosystem and its cycles of growth, decay, and regeneration.

Chapter 8 offers a diachronic overview of Huaorani interactions with the oil companies that have, over the years, blanketed their territory with roads, wells, pumping stations, and other infrastructural developments. As such, it purports to illustrate the varied ways in which the values of natural abundance have been transposed and adapted to the oil frontier. Through the use of new ethnographic data, as well as new readings of past data, I show that the economy of procurement, which constitutes the forest as *natural abundance*, tends today to be relegated—or at least confined—to hinterland communities. With the expansion of the oil frontier, I argue, it is the logic of "obtainability" that structures the claims of communities settled along the oil roads.

Chapter 9, which is based on entirely new fieldwork carried out between 2013 and 2015, is to a large extent experimental and exploratory. I use rich ethnographic vignettes to illuminate Huaorani engagements with the state and to reflect on the project of President Correa and his government to transform Huaorani people into Ecuadorian citizens. I show the subtle inclusions and exclusions through which citizenship is wrought and open new paths for further reflection and further research.

7

FORESTS OF ABUNDANCE

"*NATURALEZA* (NATURE)? It's *durani bai* (like in the old times) in Huaorani." This impromptu translation cropped up casually in a conversation I had with Nihua in his home village of Damointaro in August, 2008. Prompted by the presence of a group of Peace Corps volunteers, the conversation was about the advantages and disadvantages of different types of *cohuori* toilets. They had come to replace some of the flush toilets installed by an evangelical mission with compost toilets (*inodoros secos* in Spanish, which literally translates as "waterless, odorless toilets"). "If you stay too long in the same place, pathogens build up." This is why, Nihua said, *durani bai* people moved around a lot. A family would arrive in a place they liked in the forest, plant a chonta palm, build a shelter, and live there until their manioc was ready to harvest.While living in the place they liked, he continued, the family would already be preparing other places where it would be good to live one day. He was talking about camps built along hunting trails. This is where people most enjoyed spending time hunting, gathering, making objects, planting—in short, living. He then added something that appeared unrelated at first. "It is not when a young couple gets married that the biggest *ëëmë* (drinking festival) is organized. It's when they are mature enough to head their *nanicabo*, when, for the first time, it is their turn to be *ahuene* (leaders, hosts)." Now full hosts, the couple were no longer juvenile; their parents lived with them, rather than the other way around. By saying that the largest and most significant *ëëmëiri* were organized in celebration of transgenerational links within the longhouse, Nihua was not denying the importance of affinal relations between longhouses but simply stressing the existence of another, perhaps less obvious, perspective. As family groups move through the forest, they also move through time.

In April 2006, on a visit to Toñampari (a community three hours away by foot from Damointaro), I came across a thriving chonta palm grove that was no longer used for *ëëmë* festivals.[1] It belonged to Paa and his children. When Paa was away in a remote part of Huaorani land on a visit to one of his daughters, Amo, the youngest of his married sons, took me around. He had just finished his diploma in tourism and relished the opportunity to practice his guiding skills. The chonta palm grove was about halfway up a hill on the family's hunting trail. There were about thirty adult chonta palms. They were mixed with chambira palms and all planted approximately twenty years prior.[2] More talkative than his father, Amo was a pleasant and attentive guide. Like Paa would have done, he told me about *durani bai* traditions, putting, perhaps, more emphasis on how things have changed since. Unlike his father though, he wasted no opportunity to compare ethnic preferences and to contrast Huaorani and Quichua ways. *Why*, I wondered, this insistent pointing out of what was characteristically and uniquely Huaorani?[3] "*Durani bai* groves were much larger" he remarked. "They were located—like this one, halfway to the top of the hill, to protect the trees from storms and wind damage. They lived forever." He also mentioned woodpeckers.[4] Amo explained that Huaorani never built their houses or planted their chonta palms on the flat lands along rivers where woodpeckers live, as these birds damage trees by piercing them through and through. We had reached the grove's upper limit. The sun had broken through the clouds, glaring onto our faces. "Do you see the sun ray striking the palm over there? Do you see how the erect chonta is glaring at us, bathed in sunlight? This is what awakens a man's burning desire. This light rushes through him; he feels the urge to make his spears. He wants to make them." Amo then reminded me that men go to chonta palm groves in secret; no one is to know how many spears a man has made or where he has hidden them. As we went downhill and slowly returned toward Toñampari, Amo switched to other topics. He described the grove as their hunting ground and showed me how it was managed to ensure its continuous enrichment. Due to his father's and brothers' careful management (they never felled their chonta or their chambira palms and never harvested all the fruit), there was always an abundance of fruits to attract animals.[5] Then he proceeded to go into great detail about the preferences of various animal species: which ate the chonta palm fruit up in the tree, which ate it on the floor, which preferred the flesh, which preferred the nut inside the seed, which knew how to crack the seed open, which discarded it instead, and so forth. He spoke at length about how each animal species would come at a different time and use parts of the fruit that another species had left behind, and also about the great distances over which the seeds were dispersed. Only a few rodent species (he mentioned the Quichua name of one of them: *changsha*) would actually bury the seeds, an action indispensable for the growth of palm seedlings. Finally, Amo mentioned that his *guirinani* (relatives and friends) were allowed to harvest from his forest whatever they needed as long as they respected the rule of not felling the palms.[6] No one organized *ëëmë* anymore; collectors simply returned to their homes and eat "cada uno por su cuenta" (Spanish expression meaning *for themselves*).

Two months later in June 2006, I went to Bameno (at the other end of the ethnic territory), where chonta palms fruit almost all year long.[7] The fruit start ripening in the first week of January and go on ripening until the end of May. They "come out" again in September and can be harvested until late November. In Bameno, therefore, the peach palm fruit season (*daguenka tëre*, "February to April") not only extends into *gata tèquè guèpempa tëre* (the "season of fat monkeys," May to August), but also overlaps with the "season of wild cotton" (*bobeca tëre*, September to early December) when kapok, an essential part of the hunting gear, becomes available in large quantities. Hueica and her son Tepeña, who came from a community not far from Damointaro, accompanied me to Bameno. They had not visited Penti and Daboto (Bameno's *ahuene* couple) for a long while. We counted fifty chonta palms (four yellow, twenty-three bright orange, and twenty-three yellowish orange) along the airstrip and in the gardens closest to the houses. Some were already developing new fruit bunches that would be ready to be harvest by the end of August. Daboto showed Hueica the ancient grove that her great grandfather had planted in the 1930s. His group had been forced out of the Yasuní where rubber traders were active. Some of her forebears had been captured and sent to Iquitos. They managed to escape and, having found their lost kin, had trekked back upriver. By then, however, a war between Ecuador and Peru had broken out, the international border had moved, and Daboto's forebears had feared again for their lives.[8] The trekkers thus spent many months hiding in the forest with nothing else but their blowguns, quivers, and fire-making kits. They lived well nevertheless, thanks to the abundance of forest fruits and to the legacy of chonta palms. It is possible that Bameno's more Amazonian climate (lower elevation, higher temperatures, and dryer climate) favors the chonta palm. Its present-day abundance, however, is also a result of the cultural preferences and historical circumstances of Daboto's forebears. Penti had a complementary explanation to offer. Bameno's chonta palms fruit much longer than those found in the Western part of the ethnic territory because they are *durani bai* palms; in other words, they are stronger palms. In the other villages, he told us, people plant chonta varieties that were introduced by missionaries and colonists. These palms are weak; they easily get damaged and rot in no time. Worms get into them and kill them. We found out during our visit that Daboto's mother, sisters, and brothers would trek to the grove whenever they needed planting materials for their new gardens. Located at a fair distance from the village's current location, the ancient palm grove seemed to have been mainly used as a seed bank. The fruit were not harvested for human consumption but left for birds, monkeys, and rodents to feed on. The day I went to the ancient grove with Hueica, Daboto, and one of Daboto's sisters, we found half-eaten chonta palm fruit lying on the floor. "You see?" Daboto remarked. "A bird ate it yesterday or perhaps the day before; but it has not rotted; look, there is not a worm; the flesh is healthy." We also saw *guiyitehue-ayè* (small chonta palms), whose fruit are almost white under the skin. Were they classed as a different species or a different variety? I was anxious to know whether they were considered to be feral or wild, and my questions became tiresome. The only thing that seemed to matter is that people would not collect the fruit of these palms to obtain seeds to replant. They were simply edible, like so many other forest fruits. As we were leaving the grove, Daboto's sister gave Hueica ten large, overripe, and half-eaten chonta palm fruit to replant in her own garden. Before reaching the village, we stopped in one of Daboto's sister's manioc plantations. She showed us a little palm growing in its midst. "*Boyëgo* (green agouti) planted this chonta palm, and I am looking after it now.⁹ One day, it will be tall and strong like the palms you saw in Penti's garden. The fruits will be as large as daboca (*Solanum sessiflorum*), rich, oily, and bright red. Come back then, and we will organize an *eëmë*!"

Hueica told me that night that she intended to plant the seeds she had received from Daboto's sister in her father's chonta palm grove. He had started this grove a long time ago with seedlings he had brought back from the high forest, when she was still a little girl. These seedlings, she added, had grown out of seeds buried by *boyëgo* in a forest clearing. Without *boyëgo* (*huatun* in Spanish), the *omëre daguencahue* (*chonta del monte* in Spanish) would not grow, and Huaorani people would not have strong, long-lasting palms in their gardens. Fond memories of Dabo, her father, came to me as I watched her speak with such animation. He had told me years before that the chonta palms planted by *boyëgo* last much longer, at least twenty-five years. *Boyëgo* lives in bamboo forests, and its *omëre daguencahue* forms clumps that last forever.[10] When hunters come across these clumps, they associate them with *memeiri* (ancestors). People do not eat the fruit of these chonta palm groves, but use the seeds, which are very strong. Like her father all those years ago, Hueica told me that the best way to prepare the seeds before planting them is to paint them with the blood of a freshly hunted monkey. Alternatively, the seeds can be bathed for a day in a small *ohueta* (gourd container) containing the collected blood.[11]

NATURAL ABUNDANCE

It is through such visits and conversations that I learned to pay attention to Huaorani representations of the environment. I could find no vernacular term or phrase to translate literally what I came to call the Huaorani vision of *natural abundance*. However, as I have argued (e.g., Rival 2000), this term goes some way to capturing indigenous constructions of the relationship between humans and the forest over time. A first and obvious aspect of natural abundance relates to the multitude of indirect actions that take place when people on a trek manipulate in one way, or another, cultigens they find useful, beautiful, or interesting. As illustrated above, these indirect actions are often intended to encourage the continuous growth of certain fruit trees and palms in old dwelling sites and to facilitate the propagation of certain plant species. And as discussed in Part I, it is with such indirect actions (I used to call them "more or less intentional management practices") that people domesticate the forest landscape. These actions, I am keen to stress, reveal a deep and extensive knowledge of ecological relations between plant and animal species. A second aspect of natural abundance is the cultural preference for forest foods that are "found" in great quantities rather than purposefully cultivated. *Abundance*, in other words, relates to "encountering" rather than "producing" large amounts of things; it is their quality as unexpected finds that makes them exciting, strong, and powerful—in one word, abundant.

A number of superlatives, emphatic suffix markers, adverbial forms, and, above all, speech diacritics (tone of voice, wordless exclamations, and gestures) are used to convey the ravishing pleasure associated with the sight or the recollection of an abundance of useful resources or foodstuff. The awesomeness of abundance is expressed through the expression *baacuuuu waaaponi!* (literally, "so many, this is awesome!"). This is an expression that would mean little without the lengthening of the vowels, the bodily gestures, and the facial expressions that go along with it. A stretch of forest full of ripening fruits will provoke enthusiastic exclamations, as will the sight of congregated birds and monkeys or the sound of an approaching herd of peccaries. When I put seventy-five bush knives to dry on a platform one summer (they had gotten very wet during the river journey), I was not thanked for the gifts but greeted with expressions of marvel, such as "there are so many of them, so, so many.... We cannot count them!" Demonstrations of excitement and enthusiasm at the sight of abundant resources were so overt that for a long time I considered the task of identifying the social values they signaled to be simple and straightforward. Abundance is what occurs *naturally* without direct planning or targeted intentionality, or in other words, without labor.

This conclusion irked those among my contemporaries bent on rereading Amazonian ethnographies in the light of Marilyn Strathern's passionate rejection of Maurice Godelier's Marxism (e.g., Godelier and Strathern 1991) and feminist materialism (e.g., Strathern 1988). The new intellectual fashion was to demonstrate that kinship and the economy are necessarily constitutive of each other. A generation of Amazonianist anthropologists trained in Great Britain and led by Peter Gow (1991) and Joana Overing (1991) began to write ethnographies that illustrated the many ways in which native Amazonians produce beautiful and moral persons. Over the years, a new theory of mindful production has emerged. For its proponents, Amazonian humanity results from a process at once aesthetic and moral, which requires hard work, endurance, and the mastery of cosmic energy. Work, both a human virtue and a social value, produces enhanced conviviality, the ultimate social goal. Working hard, therefore, is considered to be a central part of what people understand as living well (e.g., Overing and Passes 2000; McCallum 2001; Londoño Sulkin 2012; Ewart 2013).

This Amazonian *Homo Faber* thesis did not seem to capture the essence of Huaorani work ethics. I could not, therefore, embrace it wholeheartedly. Regardless of their size or quantity, products of human labor did not awaken the admiration and the enthusiasm of my friends and hosts in the way that naturally occurring resources did. For example, none of the aforementioned superlatives seemed to apply to a large manioc garden under production, a hip of hunted game, or a basket full of collected nuts. As mentioned already, a peccary herd passing by may cause much excitement: "there were so many, many, many of them!" But no one would think of exclaiming this at the sight of twenty dead peccaries lying on the floor awaiting to be butchered and cooked. Similarly, a palm grove in February will cause people to exclaim, "there is so much fruit. The fruit is ripe!" But no one would marvel at five or six big jars of fruit drink lining the longhouse wall. These observations have led me to conclude that a resource created through hard work is not perceived as abundant (e.g., Rival 1998b). In order to understand the special qualities of natural abundance, I have thus turned to the modes of engagement that transform nature into a giving environment: (1) the relationships that make forest resources bountiful; (2) the shamanic practices that increase game availability; and (3) the ritual celebration of abundance (Rival 2002).

INTERPRETING THE GIVING ENVIRONMENT

Bird-David's (1990: 189) thesis that hunter-gatherers view their environment as unilaterally giving was extremely useful for theorizing Huaorani natural abundance. Bird-David shows that the Mbuti pygmies, for example, perceive the forest as an "ever-providing parent" rather than as "reciprocating ancestor" (as their neighbors do). Part of my early work consisted of establishing similarities between the modes of distribution and property relations, which characterize the Huaorani economic system, and those of the groups Bird-David compares (e.g., Rival 1998c). Gatherer-hunters, as she calls them, give without expecting an equivalent return on the basis of a particular view of themselves and of their natural environment. This in turn explains why their economy is constructed in terms of giving and sharing (as within a family), rather than in terms of reciprocity (as between kin). Over the years, as I discuss below, these ideas have been enriched with reflections on Marx's labor theory of value (e.g., Balbus 1982), Lévi-Strauss's critique of Western productivism (e.g., Lévi-Strauss 2001), and discussions within French anthropological circles of Haudricourt's approach to technical efficacy (e.g., Ferret 2012).

As with other anthropologists contributing to the field of hunter-gatherer studies (e.g., Ingold 1988; Bird-David 1992a, 1992b), my objective was to theorize foraging as a productive—hence social—activity. Instead of rejecting Marxian approaches to the materiality of life, however, I had hoped that the critical use of Marxist concepts (labor, productive consumption, social metabolism, and so forth) would have allowed me to have come closer to indigenous representations of the labor process and to shed light on the Huaorani construction of the forest as a giving environment. Of course, what Marx actually intended with notions such as "the primordial character of labor" and the "primacy of production in all societies" is far from clear or consistent. Moreover, and although the conception of human labor is multilayered, the meanings deposited by Greek philosophy, Christianity, Hegel (with his principle of domination and objectification), and Marx himself (in particular his theory of increasing socialization through the intentional transformation of nature) have crystalized and merged into one overall dominant representation of labor in the West as the quintessential expression of human nature. My interest was to salvage in Marx ideas about labor as the most social and most powerful means for self-realization that would not dehumanize Huaorani forest practices. As Balbus (1982: 16) points out, Marx sometimes conceived of production as a transhistorical, universally applicable theoretical category, which allowed him to equate production with the human condition. At other times, he was careful to stress that the category of production is only relevant to characterize some historical periods, especially the rise of capitalism. The ambiguity of Marx's formulation originated in his stubborn tendency to equate the process of production, as a whole with, on the one hand, social relations of production and, on the other, productive activities (Balbus 1982: 30). This tendency is highly problematic when it comes to analyzing noncapitalist societies where the determination exercised by the mode of production ends up meaning something radically different in practice.

A short text by Lévi-Strauss (2001) helped me engage the anthropological uses of Marx's ideas on labor further. Motivated by a wish to convince Japanese industrialists that the notion of productivity is necessarily relative, intrinsically linked to the development of capitalism, and only partially a matter of economic theory, this text offers a remarkable synthesis of some of the ideas that had become dear to Lévi-Strauss since he wrote *The Savage Mind* (1966). These include an evaluation of the achievements of the Neolithic Revolution (when compared with those of the Industrial Revolution); the ethics, aesthetics, and cultural patterning of various (often coexisting) modes of production; and the primacy of nonutilitarian, noneconomic concerns in driving productivity. Examples used in this short piece range from ancient agrarian societies to contemporary foraging ones. They all show that productivity (or the why and the how of wealth creation), far from being a historical or a technical necessity, is embedded in social norms and moral values. This led Lévi-Strauss to conclude that each form of productivity has its own value. A wise society, instead of destroying its past, he suggested, knows how to capitalize on it. Two additional arguments are worth commenting upon in greater detail.

The first one deals with the heterogeneous evolution of productivity, which, far from being gradual or progressive, should be envisaged as a compromise of a whole range of possible choices, each with its own costs and benefits. These alternative forms of productivity represent different but equally valuable forms of "know how" (savoir faire), which should be allowed to continue to exist, as they embody forms of knowledge worthy of maintenance. Examples of plant and animal domestication are used to show the contemporaneity of forms of foraging and farming. They also illustrate the central place granted by Neolithic science to cultural choice, values, and nonutilitarian concerns. The balanced nature of Neolithic wisdom is then contrasted with the modern predicament (if you do not move forward, you go backward), which forces us to behave as predators when it comes to the exploitation of natural resources.

The second one offers a subversive understanding of the internal necessity for productivity as self-expression and creative achievement. The example given concerns manual workers who "divert" tools and materials from the factory—as well as time—in order to fulfil a need for playfulness, subjectivity and identity through the making of things ("*le goût de produire*").[12] Rendered illicit by a system that reduces labor to its economic function, *bricolage* undoes alienation, while generating social networks and new levels of solidarity. Lived as a ritualistic artistic engagement, bricolage embodies the universal desire to produce value and beauty. It expresses the human drive to leave a personal mark on the world through objective and material projects, which, once realized, constitute visible expressions of one's inner self. To me, this sociologically suggestive example shows us a Claude Lévi-Strauss ready to side with "inferior others" in a way that sheds a clearer light on the science of the concrete presented and discussed in *The Savage Mind*. By contrasting the productivity of manual workers inside and outside the factory, the author successfully eludes normative beliefs about what constitutes higher and lower forms of thinking, making, or being. Instead of counterpoising science's abstract, conceptual thought with the intuitive, sensory-based concreteness of mythic thought, or of unwillingly opposing common sense to scientific knowledge, he simply shows that industrial consciousness and scarcity economics are transitory forms of knowing the world. As mentalities change, historical moments of heightened productivity (or productivism) are necessarily followed by phases where other logics are allowed to prevail.

I have used these analyses as a source of inspiration in my quest for the distinctive and essential characteristics of Huaorani natural abundance and have not attempted to contribute to their theoretical development. Fully aware of the conceptual and terminological limitations of my various attempts, and largely unsatisfied by them, I am nevertheless intuitively convinced that I have managed to capture some of the most important aspects of Huaorani thinking about the link between work and the humanized forest landscape. I summarize these findings below.

There is no word in Huaorani to talk about work as an abstract category. Many specific terms are used to describe the making of particular objects or the doing of specific tasks. However, three conceptual terms (*baromipa*, *quëqui*, and *huentey*) hint, when analyzed together, at what could be described as a Huaorani work ethic. *Baromipa*, ([procreate] literally, "child making") is sometimes used to refer to the making of artifacts and weapons. The Summer Institute of Linguistics selected this term in its translation of the Bible to talk about the creation of the world by God. That the term *baromipa* is used in everyday life to refer to many forms of doing and making may be indicative of the fact that these activities are considered to be creative. The term *quëqui*, however, is used much more frequently. For example, Huaorani say *omëre quëqui* (doing in the bush) when clearing the forest to plant crops; it is also a term used by men who open seismic trails for the oil companies operating in Huaorani territory. The most common expression for this kind of work, though, is *omëre gomonipa* (work journeys), which links working for the oil companies with hunting-and-gathering activities. Another is *omëre äante gobopa* (I visit the forest to bring something back). *Huentey*, a term wrongly translated by schoolteachers and missionaries as "lazy," refers to the state of perfect stillness and tranquility felt by someone lying in a hammock while chanting softly. To be *huentey* is to be in a state of perfect inaction and contentment, a feeling that flows over from the singer to all those present in the longhouse. The opposite of activity and movement, *huentey* is best understood as therapeutic action. It is a form of "social work" that prevents the buildup of tensions and helps restore harmony. There would be much more to say about *huentey*, but I have said enough to show how essential it is to notions of personal balance and group unity. Activities described under the labels *quëqui* or *baromipa* should be undertaken freely and with pleasure, a state of mind that *huentey* helps achieve. There is a strong sense among the Huaorani that to oblige someone or to force oneself to do something leads to disharmony, unbalance, and, ultimately, disaster. When it comes to past human activities that "have made the forest grow," the terms *quë* (work) and *huè* (live) merge seamlessly to suggest that the natural growth of the forest is encouraged by subsistence and ceremonial activities.[13]

What makes Huaorani thinking about human labor so different from our own is that the forest is represented as a combination of elements that are direct manifestations and concrete objectifications of past human actions, including the work activities of unknown human others. Said differently, the presence in the forest of abundant resources is thought to result from the daily consumptive and productive activities performed by people who died a long time ago. A hilltop is covered with producing palms because "the grandparents used to live there. This is where they built their longhouse, where they lived together without splitting up, and where they made gardens to feast with the enemy. . . . Do you see this poison vine, right there? My grandmother must have caused it to grow. . . . Look, there used to be a creek down that way, she must have fished in it." Those are remarks I heard over and over again while walking through the forest with Huaorani companions. In the course of living, a residential group hunts, gathers, and manages a whole range of useful plants along hunting trails and streams. People cook and eat, discard fruit seeds, throw away roots, and cut down trees to light for other tree species to grow (see Chapter 1). People are ecologically aware of these processes, just as they are of the intimate, symbiotic connections between their being alive (i.e., producing and consuming) and the state of the forest. The long-dead people of the past are not treated as exchange partners; they do not ask for anything (as African ancestors would), and the living do not feel they owe them anything. What they give to the living is not really a gift but, rather, a by-product or, one might say, an outcome of the fact that they spent their lives giving to and receiving from each other. Moreover, if people today are invariably able to detect in the landscape the activities of people who are no longer alive, they can never be sure of their identity. What matters, instead, is that past human activities can be differentiated from the activities of animals and other nonhuman beings.

Explained in terms of past human work activities, the concept of natural abundance has allowed me to make better sense of the Huaorani's sharing economy. The *nanicabo*, which shows no age or sex segregation and which may number between ten and thirty-five members, constitutes the basic unit of Huaorani society. Most *nanicabo* members hunt and gather every day, generally alone. The goal of each procurer is to obtain enough food to feed the self and to share with coresidents. Even young children make sure they have at hand enough foodstuff, not just for their own consumption, but also to give away, especially to their grandmothers, mothers, and elder sisters. Personal autonomy, a core value, is best expressed as the individual's ability to extract from the forest fairly large quantities of food, which are carried back to the longhouse. As most productive activities are carried out alone, social life is organized around the collective sharing of individually procured food. In other words, whereas the longhouse economy is structured by the sharing of forest food individually obtained by each member, the *nanicabo* is reproduced as a collectivity based on nonreciprocal relations, in which givers do not become creditors, and receivers are not debtors.

Drinking ceremonies or dance and song festivals are organized whenever there is an abundance of fruit. In their songs, feast goers identify with birds gorging themselves on seasonal fruits. The chants, endlessly repeated throughout the night, tell of birds gathered on a tree covered with ripening fruit. The vivid lyrics describe the colors, noises, and movements of the flying creatures, as well as the sweetness and abundance of the juices that compel them to congregate. When no fruit is left, they all leave and fly away, each bird going back to its own business.

Tomëmo behuenqui ponga abi
Tomëmo behuenque bamenenga abi
Ëëmo amina bamenguina amina
Amotamini

In this collective representation of the feasting group, the emphasis is on individual freedom and independence. Rather than mutual obligations or rights, what binds feast goers together is the pleasure of consuming abundant and delicious food. If food is abundant, congregation and sharing ensue. Manioc drinking ceremonies make for an interesting variant, which I have called *created abundance*, for lack of a better term. The preparation of manioc into a ceremonial drink entails the symbolic transformation of manioc into fruit, and of the "owners of the feast" into *ahuene* (literally, "of the tree").[14] Ceremonial consumption, particularly in the case of manioc drinking celebrations, points to the structuring significance of the host-guest relationship, which is constituted by unilateral giving within a social field comprising not only human actors, but also living organisms and artifacts. Hosts are in the house, or of the house, and as such are required to give to their guests, unilaterally and upon request.[15] As noted earlier, a host, by giving away to the guest without expecting anything in return, is like a reproductive couple, a nurturing parent, or a fruiting tree. Guests, on the other hand, are pure consumers, just like newborn babies.

Past human work, identified as a primary source of abundance for the living, allows real people to defend their humanity as "prey at the center" against the predatory attacks of *cohuori*, as alluded to in Chapter 6. I will have more to say on the unbreachable rift between *huaorani* and *cohuori* in the following chapters. As *cohuori* are exterminators who unilaterally prey on their victims, *huaorani* have had to protect themselves by choosing to live in nomadic enclaves in the interstices between larger and more powerful ethnic groups, fiercely refusing contact, trade, and exchange. Inserted within the cosmic economy of predation of their enemies, the Huaorani attribute their survival to their forest-based sharing economy and to their isolationist politics.

The above summary shows that Huaorani culture does not separate "first nature" from "second nature," for the forest is—and has always been—a patchwork of ancient dwelling sites or forest groves. The forest is where generations of people have dwelled, married, and died, making the world as it is through continued interactions with other forms of life. Through the life cycles of their house groups and the deaths of their women, Huaorani people tap into an enduring form of energy that uses itself over and over again to make life out of what dies. What does not grow, decays; the forest has always already been lived in.

Readers familiar with recent debates in Amazonianist anthropology may find my approach to natural abundance lacking in discussions of cosmological ideas and ontological categories. Bird-David's (1990, 1992a, 1992b) giving environment, after all, is largely a thesis about correspondences between social relations and cosmology. My objection to this criticism is multifold. I wish to start by stressing that I would have incorporated the analysis of myths much more extensively, if our knowledge of Huaorani linguistics were sufficiently advanced, a point I have already stressed in the introduction. Moreover, and as illustrated by the myth evoked earlier on Tocari, Huaorani mythology has been extensively reworked by Dayuma and the missionaries she worked with, rendering their interpretation even more challenging.[16] In any case, I have never been convinced by the structuralist argument that myths represent a synthesis of indigenous representations, and hence a master key to culture. Keeping in mind the above caveat, research on a notion such as *huentey* would certainly benefit from a closer examination of the cosmos in relation to personhood. However, in my view, much work remains to be done on the interplay of ontological categories, place, and practice, as well as on the complex and dynamic interactions between cultural values and political and economic contexts.[17] The confusions between anthropocentrism and anthropomorphism, as well as a tendency to equate the human point of view with morality, are two additional weaknesses of mainstream approaches to Amazonianist anthropology. For all these reasons, I remain quite critical of the ways in which cosmological ideas have been deployed in perspectivist and structuralist approaches.[18] Fortunately, new analytical frameworks that promise to break more fundamentally with the nature/culture dualism are now emerging (e.g., Kohn 2013; Tsing 2013, 2014). Future ethnographers will have better analytical tools to understand the *nanicabo onco* (longhouse) as an entity through which human and nonhuman participants form places and nurture landscapes that endure over time. Whether there will be competing approaches—no doubt—to analyze the socioecological relational practices that I have described in my work, which will best convey to readers Huaorani ideas about vegetation and social growth, as well as other non-Western conceptualizations of forest and society, remains to be seen.

ENVIRONMENTAL GIVENS

Natural abundance depends on the creation of gaps in time and in space; today, it requires new dispositions. With *civilization*, a term the Huaorani often use to encapsulate the changes that have transformed them in the course of four generations, the logic of abandonment (burn the longhouse, leave everything behind, and move to another part of the forest) is no longer an easy option. Conversations with Nihua, Amo, and Penti reveal how social time and ecological time are being interlocked in their communities today.

Nihua and his wife Queñe no longer form a juvenile couple. After some years spent away from Damointaro, they are now back as trained professionals. Queñe is a qualified nurse, and Nihua an "expert" specialized in *proyectos y tramites* (projects and paperwork). Nihua, who wants Damointaro to become a foundation (Fundación Damointaro), hopes I can help him with this project. As we walk the streets of Puyo, he fires question after question about my time with the Ñameiri in QuehueireOno. How did I help Moi make "international contacts" (*contactos internacionales*)? I laugh. "Moi does not need my help; he can fly with his own wings." Nihua slows down as he speaks to himself as much as to me. "I need some more feathers on my wings." Spending time in Damointaro with Nihua's *nanicabo* makes me understand what the project will achieve for the villagers. As a close-knit *huaomoni* group regularly visited by evangelical missionaries, they do not worry about internal cohesion or evil influences, such as *trago* (alcohol), *ayahuasca* (Quichua hallucinogenic drug), or *ají* (chili pepper), which is another dangerous substance used by non-Huaorani.[19] (These Spanish terms were used in the conversation, which was, otherwise, in Huaorani.) Their connection to the invisible world is healthy; it protects the community's welfare, well-being, and harmony. Although Damointaro villagers have relatives in all other Huaorani communities, Nihua thinks that new organizational forms and property rights are needed to ensure harmony and balance in connections with other settlements. There is a continual threat that the Huaorani may kill each other off ("*se pueden acabar, matandose entre ellos*"). Moreover, tensions over hunting territories, resources, and access rights granted by some Huaorani families to their Quichua affines have increased throughout the ethnic territory. Finally, in Nihua's view, efforts to control outside influences and to secure village autonomy require the close presence of *durani bai*.

The rearticulation of *durani bai* by Damointaro villagers as both ancestral tradition and nature is fascinating. It led to many conversations during my stay in 2008. "Look at the pet animals that come and go freely around here. They help us make our village *durani bai*," I was told.[20] The desire to keep animals close ("even pumas" said someone) by creating an environment amenable to animal visits intersected with many aspects of Damointaro's *huaponi quehuemonipa* (good life project). I heard, for example, that Shuar teachers had been admonished for having brought *chicha fuerte* (strongly fermented manioc beer). Their loud parties and brawls frightened animals away, and this was wrong. For Menga (Nihua's father), hearing pumas at night on the hills around the village was a good thing, especially between February and May, the mating season. He imitated the cry of a puma looking for a mate. "These animals just want to make love and fabricate babies" he remarked; "they must be left alone to enjoy life." He then launched into a long speech mixing mythical tales and stories from his *memeiri* (forebears). He interspersed them with ecological observations and contrasted, for instance, the birds that sing when a puma crosses the forest with those that sing when a jaguar passes by. Menga was known to spend hours listening to the voices of the forest and to observe interspecies relationships on end. One day, he told me all he knew about the different bird species that live together and the monkey species that mate together successfully. He added with a wink that offspring of crossed species are real molesters, not unlike Toñampari villagers.[21] To conclude, in Damointaro, the wish to keep animals close-by has redrawn boundaries around inhabited spaces, species, forests, and people. Pets are normally confined to the longhouse, and deer, a tabooed game in the past, were never the target of taming practices. Damointaro was the first Huaorani community to benefit from the government payment for ecosystem services program known as Sociobosque. This state conservation program opens up new ways of reimagining the forest at a time when anthropogenic groves are no longer maintained as such. Finally, the reimagined forest allows Damointaro villagers to attract tourists, anthropologists, and, more generally, foreigners who love "nature," while keeping at bay dangerous *cohuori* such as Shuar teachers and Quichua affines.

Amo is not nostalgic about the demise of the traditional *durani bai daguenkahue ëëmë* (chonta palm drinking festivals). Toñampari, the largest community in Huaorani land, celebrates its foundation day every year during the third week in January with at least eight hundred participants in attendance. The costly celebration, which lasts nearly a week, is financed by a range of provincial authorities and national institutions.[22] In many Huaorani communities, *durani bai* drinking festivals are no longer organized as activators of the differential potentiality between short-lived and slow-growing food crops (Rival 1998b). If village celebrations are still based on the articulation of different types of allies and affines, their politics are overshadowed by the pull of otherness, like in Toñampari. *Cohuori* sponsorship, participation, values, sports, food, drinks, and, more generally, material goods are central to the success of a modern *ëëmë* (see Chapter 9). Paa's enriched forest grove is less geared toward expanding his *nanicabo*'s alliances than it is toward strengthening its autonomy and continuity over time. Amo does not simply attract tourists to his *nanicabo*'s domain, he also goes there with his children and with youth who want to learn *durani bai* facts: the leaves used for dyes, the fibers for weaving, the herbs that cure, and so forth. The domain is not as extensive as a *durani bai* hunting territory, yet it contains as much richness and diversity. While close to the village and its amenities, it is nevertheless a land where animals and plants thrive; visitors would not dare violate Paa's conservation rules. Like the families studied by Zurita

(2014), Paa and his sons have constituted a patrimony. Family domains (*monito omë*, "our land") such as these signify both autonomy and abundance.

Bameno is, by choice, the most "isolated" of the three communities discussed in this chapter. In fact, Penti grew up in Toñampari and moved to remote Bameno to take up a position as a primary school teacher. After a few years, he married Daboto, his double cross-cousin. They now have eight children and several grandchildren. When people talk about Bameno as isolated, what they really mean is that it is *guubè imba* (far away) from other human settlements.[23] Visiting Bameno is mainly done during the annual drinking festival, which takes place two months after Toñampari's and a few weeks before Mihuaguno's. It became clear to me during a recent visit in the spring of 2013 that the popularity of Bameno's annual drinking festival involves more than the usual reasons: meeting friends and distant relatives; finding romance; participating in sports; or enjoying life with people one sees only occasionally. Those who choose to travel that far are usually seeking more than a festival ambiance. A couple of years ago, I was traveling with a group of youths who had just returned from Bameno and were heading to a community on the oil road that had invited them to participate in a football tournament. Listening to their conversations, I understood that their stay in Bameno had meant experiencing the proximity of a life that no longer exists elsewhere. What young and old equally appreciate in Bameno is the *durani bai* feel of the place. For many people, like for these youths, *durani bai* continues to matter. Ironically, in our globalized world, the "isolation" of Bameno attracts rich Westerners seeking wilderness and authenticity. Almost all the documentaries, photographic albums, and TV reality shows that depict the Huaorani are done in "authentic" settings around Bameno, the most sought-after tourist destination.[24] What makes Bameno more exotic than other Huaorani communities is the relative absence of signs of "civilization" and "mixing." The village is located in the heart of the Yasuní National Park. Villagers, who apart from Penti, do not speak Spanish fluently, avoid contact with oil companies, loggers, or nationals, and with all external influences that threaten to break what they see as their life of freedom, independence, and peaceful tranquility. Many of the practices and bodies of knowledge documented and discussed in Part 1 and Part 2 are commonplace in Bameno. In addition to its impressive chonta palm heritage, the village keeps a harpy eagle and many pets that roam free in and about the longhouses. Quemperi's jaguars watch over the well-being of the community. Traditional hunting and fishing techniques are still commonly used, and game abounds.[25] Bameno's forest society is intact.[26] Consequently, Penti and his *nanicabo* do not have to construct their domain, as Paa's *nanicabo* has had to, or to work out complex rights and rules with the government, as Nihua's *nanicabo* is doing. They simply need to continue to live with it and to defend it from encroachment, predation, and decay. This requires special skills: in particular, the art of articulating *durani bai* as the twin force of nature and tradition for both *huaorani* and *cohuori* publics.

Huaorani people have mastered over centuries the art of harnessing the spontaneous productivity of their forest environment. Produced by delayed returns, natural abundance ties forest beings within cycles of mutuality. As such, it is seen as a result of a multiplicity of indirect human actions delicately inserted within a wider web of past and nonhuman activities. Powerful cosmological forces may have brought the forest landscape that people inhabit today into existence (see Chapter 6). However, it is the cumulative, gradual, and indirect action of transforming the forest through living that turns it into a rich and life-sustaining environment for humans and other species alike. As I have shown in this chapter, Penti's, Nihua's and Paa's *nanicaboiri* face different pressures, constraints, and circumstances yet share the same values. Autonomy is secured by carving out domains in which the evolving maintenance of interlocked ecological and social processes is protected as the source of natural abundance.

8

PREY AT WAR

THE APPREHENSION OF THE FOREST as natural abundance, which I have analyzed as a particular way of constructing the environment (see Chapter 7), has allowed Huaorani people to maintain a high degree of personal and collective autonomy in a world where they have experienced themselves as prey to powerful, predatory neighbors. It is because *huaorani* are under constant threat of being captured and devoured by *cohuori* that social relations are modeled after two distinct natural processes, natural abundance and ontological predation. *Huaorani* and *cohuori* are like two different species—two different kinds of being. The aggressive relation between prey and predator is marked by extreme hostility and separation. It is in the nature of *cohuori* to reproduce themselves by continuously snatching the creativity, vitality, and life force of *huaorani*, who can do little more than elude contact with their cannibal attackers and constitute themselves as prey at the center by building a life-sustaining relation with the forest. It is in the nature of forest trees and food plants to give continuously to humans without asking anything in return. It should be no surprise, therefore, that Huaorani prey-predator mythology, which is extensive, articulates the Amazonian metaphysics of predation in quite unique ways.

In this chapter, I revisit the correlation I established in past publications between the natural abundance of the forest and the perception of foreign organizations as sharing agents that give unilaterally, like fruiting trees in the forest (e.g., Rival 1998c, 2000). The opportunities I have had over the years to observe strategic deployments of the logic of natural abundance have guarded me against facile interpretations of the fast-changing political economy in which ontological predation has been dynamically applied. I am therefore in a position today to convey more fully the creative richness of indigenous responses to Ecuador's oil development and forest conservation policies. Whereas my previous work focused on the host-guest relationship (and its function in structuring exchanges polarized between unilateral giving and demand sharing), I see today that there is more to Huaorani reactions to corporate outsiders than the tensions between created and naturally occurring abundance, which take center stage during ceremonial feasting.[1] More importantly, emphasis may now be given to the fact that indigenous responses evolve over time. In the first and the second sections, I discuss the evolving work and exchange relations that Huaorani people have had with oil companies and, in the third section, interactions with the "green economy" and the conservation industry. The conclusion briefly outlines the changes that have followed from the current government's *citizen revolution* (*revolución ciudadana*) and then goes back to evolving Huaorani dealings with *cohuori* otherness.

WORK ENCOUNTERS WITH THE OIL INDUSTRY

Petróleo, Lanzas y Sangre (Viteri 2008), the memoirs of an Ecuadorian oil camp administrator, is a remarkable book on more than one count. The book, which covers the entire working life of Jorge Viteri (from the late 1960s to the mid-1990s), contains invaluable data on encounters between indigenous men and women and the moving oil frontier. The early days of oil exploration on the lower course and south bank of the Napo River are described vividly, and reading Jorge Viteri's memoirs brought back many memories for me. As a young anthropologist in training, I had little time for the social structures and cultural forms of the frontier. My ethnographic eyes were riveted on the people the oil workers and settlers feared, despised, and called *los aucas* (the savages), or with undisguised sarcasm, *los amigos* (the friends). Jorge Viteri was an exceptional human being, a man of unlimited generosity and kindness, who did everything in his power to better the life conditions of the workers under his supervision and to solve equitably the ceaseless conflicts occasioned by the seismic activities the companies he worked for undertook. I met him on several occasions during fieldwork, as well as in the years after he had retired. I loved visiting him to chat about the Amazon and its people whenever I was in Quito. Jorge's capacity to care for even the most humble soul was exceptional, as were his attempts to recover corpses of workers, who had died from injuries or had disappeared, and his efforts to ensure that even the most remote forest camps would be sufficiently provisioned with fresh food, regardless of the additional costs to the company.

Jorge's lively account offers readers a chance to glimpse the harsh reality behind oil development, deforestation, and land colonization in the Oriente (as the Amazon region is known in Ecuador). Depopulated by the 1941 war with Peru, the region was progressively reconnected with the rest of the country when Jorge began his career in the oil industry. To a region left with very few farms and a handful of military posts, the budding industry gradually added air transport, more military check points, some unpaved roads, and a number of well-connected entrepreneurial traders followed by waves of migrants who arrived from diverse poverty-struck regions. Mixed-blood pioneers from the Andes and Black farmers from the coast soon created settlements along rivers and newly opened roads. Then came Quichua and Shuar families in search of virgin lands. All took advantage of government policies that promoted the "productive occupation" of *tierras baldías* (empty lands). Jorge's descriptions of Coca (officially named Francisco de Orellana) resonate with my memories of the town, which I first visited in 1988. Until the late 1990s, Coca still looked and felt like the hastily built base camp described in *Petróleo, Lanzas y Sangre*. Not yet a proper town, it did not have the buzz of places north of the Napo River, such as Lago Agrio, or even Shushufindi where oil had been extracted on a large scale for almost twenty years. Coca's sole purpose was to supply teams of workers who moved back and forth between the forest, to the east, and civilization, to the west.

The alternation of buzz and quietness, characteristic of the progressive development of the oil frontier in Ecuador, encapsulates on a smaller scale much of what one reads about booming and busting extractive frontiers in Latin America (e.g., Santos-Granero and Barclay 2000; Little 2001). Extractive frontiers are sometimes celebrated as places of exceptional creativity and times of freedom where wealth and privilege get subjected to democratic redistribution or where risk taking, gambling, and the invention of new forms of life are rewarded (e.g., Cleary 1993). However, Jorge's account stresses the exploitative and destructive nature of the frantic activities through which oil wealth has been constituted in the Oriente. Workers, who are not allowed to unionize, are employed on short-term contracts and receive lower wages than expected. Having no employment security, they combine their short-term contracts with numerous other economic occupations, some more legal than others. Skilled workers, with better wages and more permanent contracts, fly back and forth by plane between their hometown and their workplace every few weeks. They see their job as a temporary outpost placement. Unskilled laborers, by contrast, have no choice but to live permanently in the region to which they migrated where they have to make a living in one way or another. They occupy land around oil camps or in burgeoning urban settlements, and those who have retained links to their places of origin cannot afford to travel back. Whereas skilled workers build their middle-class lives in wealthy, developed parts of the country, unskilled workers raise their families on the pioneer front, which often lacks basic services. Moreover, and as Jorge's book makes clear, the service economy that has developed around the oil camps is structured by gender relations that are extremely exploitative of women. His account painfully illustrates the destructive nature of the frontier; not only are many human lives lost to accidents and illnesses or wasted away in alcohol or prostitution, but the forest is also destroyed through a combination of ill-conceived and badly implemented agricultural policies complemented with reckless, hasty practices inspired by a "do-fast-and-cheap" mentality. Reading this account, one is left to wonder what the frontier would have looked like if the educated, middle-class workers had settled permanently with their families along the Napo River instead of living double lives. Finally, Jorge's memoirs make countless references to his dealings with indigenous communities, whose fight to retain territorial rights and to defend their cultural traditions he fully empathized with.

Although the manners and demands of *los aucas* were, for the most part, incomprehensible to him, Jorge, through kindness and empathy, learned how to manage situations in ways that would minimize, if not entirely eliminate, violent conflict. His pragmatic approach to the Huaorani's visits, requests, and robberies did more to illuminate the specificities of the oil frontier than entire political economic treatises. Incidents are reported and described in detail for the years 1976, 1977, 1983, 1984, and 1986–1988. Some involved house groups who, for various reasons, had not joined the Summer Institute of Linguistics (SIL) missionaries to the west. Others involved workers and their families who had accepted life in missions, but whose behavior in the oil camps was as menacing as that of those who had not. Several cases relate to clashes with fierce Huaorani who stubbornly refused contact, systematically attacked camps, and sometimes killed workers with their spears.[2]

The first incident reported in the book occurred in July 1976.

> In the early days of July, we heard through the radio the frightened voice of the cook of one of the trailblazing brigades. He informed us that *the friends* had arrived; there were two men, two women, one with a baby, all entirely naked. The worse was that these Huaorani were extremely curious. They began to touch the workers all over their bodies, inquisitively, taking off their shirts and even their trousers, in order to establish their gender. They also grabbed the torches, and every object that caught their attention. The women were the most annoying, and when they tasted the food they discovered salt for the first time. I had to go in and calm the workers, and replace all the objects that the Huaorani had taken from them. The list was long, from underwear, shorts, and trousers, to shoes, and so forth.
>
> This is when One-Eye came on the scene. The cook of a perforation brigade (these were the most visited of our workers) informed me that a new group of *friends* had just arrived. They had probably found them by following the sound made by the drill and the water pump when perforating. The cook was frightened: "The *friend* carries a spear; he is one-eyed, and seems to be the chief. He's arrived with women and small children; they must be a family." Later on, through Father Labaca, we would learn that One-Eye's name was Ompure. On that day, he and his family ate what they wanted, and pried into everything. One of the women left with a big metallic cooking pot, the others with the sugar and the biscuits. One-Eye became famous from that day on, because he simply took everything he found in his way. Our workers quickly learned that to avoid being robbed of their personal belongings—watches, mirrors, torches, batteries, and so forth—they had to hide them in the forest. The situation became increasingly critical for the workers and the company as a whole. There was nothing we could do to avoid these visits from *the friends*. They did not harm our workers, but the workers were so afraid of them that, according to the foremen, many wanted to get their pay and clear off. (Viteri 2008: 149, my translation)
>
> At the end of July, *the friends* showed up again. First they came in groups of three or four, but little by little they would arrive in larger groups at the tents of our workers. It is as if they had organized their looting campaign according to a planned schedule of daily visits. They no longer made any effort to ask; they would

simply grab what they could, and leave. But no other family frightened our workers more than that of One-Eye. He would arrive with his women and all their small children, and they would take whatever they wanted. The cooks and their helpers began to fear staying alone in the tents. (Viteri 2008: 154, my translation)

By mid-August, visitors to the oil camps had grown in boldness, subjecting frightened workers to more systematic and more intimate body inspections. Nothing was left behind; hammocks, mosquito nets, blankets, and tents were now an integral part of the booty. Workers, forced to spend the night in the forest with no shelter, clothes or food, had to wait for the delivery by helicopter of new camp supplies and equipment in replacement of what had been lost to the foragers. Jorge adds that the situation had now reached the limits of the tolerable. "It seemed like One-Eye had declared war on us." (Viteri 2008: 156, my translation)

By December, the Huaorani had understood the connection between radio contact and helicopter delivery.

At that point it was no longer necessary for the cook or his helper to inform us by radio that *the friends* had arrived. All of a sudden, at the least expected hour, whether in the morning or in the afternoon, we could hear the voices of different *friends* who would take turns to call: "Pañacocha, Pañacocha, over." *The friends* had fast learned the purpose of radio communication. (Viteri [2008: 168] italics in original, my translation)

The war on oil wealth continued to evolve in the course of time, especially after the decision made by Jorge's company to employ Huaorani men. Now working as *macheteros* (bush cutters), these men began to plan the looting of camps with relatives from their home communities. To Jorge's horror, the targeted objects were no longer clothes or coca cola bottles, but explosives, engines, and chainsaws (Viteri 2008: 256–59). Brought back to the villages, dynamite was used for fishing, a practice learned in the oil camps from other workers. There were also rumors that angry men threatened to use dynamite to destroy the homes of those who had aggrieved them. Jorge's depiction of Huaorani harassment as some kind of warfare may appear far-fetched. Yet, that demands for clothes, food, and other objects are best understood as a form of war is confirmed by historical information in Cipolletti (2002).

In 1941, a house group allied to that of the great warrior Moipa attacked a Napo Quichua family (Yumbos as they were called at the time), killed a couple, and kidnapped a prepubescent girl, Joaquina Grefa.[3] She lived in captivity for fourteen months in a longhouse of thirty-four, that included six children (a remarkably low number when compared with present-day demographics!) and two abducted Quichua women, who had married Huaorani men. Joaquina was physically transformed into a Huaorani person who wore no more than the traditional cotton hip cord and the typical *dicago* (enlarged earplugs). She had no social contacts other than with her housemates and, sporadically, with members of Moipa's house group, who lived several hours away. Coerced into living a Huaorani life, Joaquina observed and participated in her captors' daily activities almost like an immersed ethnographer, assessing her new social and cultural experience from the perspective of her Quichua persona. Although she had no sympathy for her captors (she escaped before they had a chance to marry her to one of them), she was old enough to appreciate Huaorani ways against Quichua stereotypes, especially their respectful and egalitarian treatment of women and the joyful tranquility of their domestic arrangements. Countless times, she was brought by the women with whom she resided to the outskirts of Shell Mera to observe, from a safe hiding place, the traffic around the airport. Although she knew perfectly well that planes were machines that transported people and merchandise, she would not dissuade her housemates from believing that planes were men-birds. Once wounded with spears, these creatures dropped their guts full of precious metal tools near Huaorani houses. What missionaries and other "gift droppers" intended as peaceful and generous acts was interpreted by her companions as the spoils of war and magical hunts. Joaquina noted the multiplication of raids followed by victory festivals during her time in Huaorani land. During these festivals and the weddings that ensued, men and women would dance adorned with items of clothing stolen from the camps set up by small groups of pioneers or mineral and oil prospectors. Used exclusively for ritual purposes, these precious items were carefully kept in special boxes until the next festival. For Cipolletti, this is a clear sign that Huaorani warriors intended to kill off the foreigners, whose every movement their wives had studied so keenly but had not realized that the foreigners were so numerous that they could never be eradicated. Ironically, then, whereas oil workers and settlers moved in slowly, imagining the aucas to be not only fierce but also numerous, the Huaorani multiplied their attacks in the hope of putting an end to the invasion of their lands either by killing the enemy off or by permanently driving it away.

Many of the observations I made during my first period of fieldwork (1989–91) recall or complement those of Jorge Viteri. Between 1985 and 1992, close to 90 percent of Huaorani adult men had worked for *La Compañía* (The Company) as unskilled, short-contract laborers in one of the two companies that carried out most of the seismic surveys south of the Napo River, the French CGG (Compagnie Générale de Géophysique) and the North American corporation Geosource. By 1997, when I carried a census with the CGG, less than 10 percent of the men worked for wages in the oil sector. Although the period of full employment was short and has long ended, it reveals key features of Huaorani responses to the oil frontier, which, as I detail later on, still structure current monetary arrangements between their communities and the oil companies who operated in their territory.

Men would be notified of the start of a new seismic program by radio, both in Spanish and in Huaorani. They would discuss the matter among themselves, evaluating each other's intentions of enrolling. Although the final decision was always left to the individual, a clear—albeit diffuse and informal—consensus always arose as to who would leave and who would stay in the community. What made particular men decide to enroll on a particular contract was not so much a need for cash, but the timing, location, and composition of the work team. Before deciding whether to enroll or not, men would check whether close relatives from whom they had been separated by mission life and who now lived in a distant community were going to be among the crew. The CGG workers' files revealed a common pattern: groups of agnatic kin tended to work in areas once occupied by their direct ascendants. In other words, related men would enroll with the CGG to work in a stretch of forest identified as former hunting territories, which they or their parents abandoned when the SIL invited them to relocate westward in the Protectorate (see Maps 1A and 1B in the introduction and Rival 1996a). Informal conversations with workers both in the oil camps and in their homes confirmed my hypothesis that by opening seismic trails in a particular area, men felt they were reclaiming stretches of the forest and securing their group's territorial rights against potential encroachments or counterclaims. Finally, even though they would rarely enroll for contracts longer than eight weeks, married men would leave their community only if their houses were in good condition and if their wives had sufficient food supplies. The work that men were asked to perform (clearing the forest with machetes and axes) was harder than, but not different from, garden clearing work, and *omëre quëqui* (doing in the bush) was used for both. When referring to their work journeys for CGG or Geosource, men would literally say they were "busy land doing in the company," using terms and expressions referring to trekking and the carrying of heavy loads, not unlike when hunting in preparation for a great *ëëmë* festival.[4]

Huaorani men had employment priority for all the exploration programs that took place in Huaorani land and in the Yasuní National Park. This measure was suggested to the CGG and to Geosource by the Capuchin mission after its regional head, Archbishop Labaca, was murdered by a group of fierce red feet. Moreover, men were allowed to terminate their contracts whenever they wished, and, according to my calculations, around 30 percent opted for the early termination of their contracts. My queries at the time suggested that men, who treated their *machetero* jobs as extended hunting trips, were anxious to move on and to return to their home villages. More often than not, men would also shorten their work contract under pressure from their wives, who had heard rumors of unfaithfulness or prolonged visits in communities neighboring the oil camps. It was also brought to my attention that women, in addition to pressuring their men and demanding their return, would also put pressure on CGG and Geosource. I discovered that, for instance, helicopters were sent to villages with food supplies, a minimal compensation, as the women saw it, for the temporary loss of their men's workforce. Thus, CGG and Geosource began to include Huaorani villages in their work schedule as additional camps to supply and service, a decision unwelcomed by other companies, who feared a recrudescence in camp looting. Some villages requested that they deliver the supplies in the form of clearly labeled, individual parcels—one for each family.[5]

In the camps, while socializing with non-Huaorani workers, men tended to stick together; they bathed, ate, and slept together at a safe distance from the rest of the crew. What they seemed to enjoy the most about their work experience was the access it gave them to parts of the forest they had not visited before. Camps moved along the seismic lines every two or three days. By the end of a contract, a *machetero* had easily covered 1,200 km of forest tracks. Upon return to the longhouse, these tracks were the subjects of lively conversations with older relatives. Men also enjoyed flying in helicopters and having their meals prepared by the cook. Transport between camps was almost always by helicopter unless the proximity of a navigable river allowed for a cheaper solution. Given the prohibitive transport costs, pieces of heavy equipment (containers, camping gear, electric wire, tubes, iron sheets, and more) were usually left behind in the forest. These discarded objects and materials were subsequently retrieved by trekking bands, and brought back to settlements, sometimes over great distances.

Huaorani workers were often visited by relatives, who smoothly blended camp visits with foraging activities and treks. I dreaded these acquisitive visits and the uneasy situation it created for me; I never knew in advance when a hunting or gathering trip would include a visit to an oil camp. Visitors were not welcome but nevertheless stayed on for some time fascinated by the camp's organization, the vast supplies of food brought by helicopter, and the activities surrounding the preparation of food. The cooks who prepared daily meals for the workers were under intense pressure to share out the food supplies with visiting Huaorani. They knew it was pointless to refuse; visitors would simply raid the kitchen and take everything away, very much as Jorge describes in his memoirs. On more than one occasion, telling me not to worry, my trekking companions laughed at my disapproving face. A radio message would be sent to the headquarters, and a helicopter full of replacement stock was soon dispatched.

Old seismic trails were systematically used for hunting. On more than one occasion, I helped Huaorani companions plant manioc and plantain in helicopter landing pads, which soon transformed them into impromptu garden clearings. Land doing for the company was always more than a means to obtain cash; it provided new sources of food and raw materials. I never heard anyone question La Compañía's queer obsession with explosives and trail cutting. On the contrary, its efficacy and material wealth were considered awesome. The Company had chainsaws, outboard motors, trucks, helicopters, good kitchens, plenty food, and clothes. It worked fast and moved about swiftly. La Compañía had strength and power, which was manifest in its high performance and superior technology.

Over time, however, this mutual accommodation went somewhat awry. The drilling of the first exploratory wells had none of the good-natured character of seismic prospection. Before a well is drilled, service companies work on the site for several months to clear it. The site buzzes with noise and activity, the sky is crisscrossed with helicopter flights, and the ground is cluttered with heavy machinery. Exploratory well sites become the centers of intense village disputes. When the platform for PetroCanada's exploratory well was built in the spring of 1989, about one hundred men from four different villages (Dayuno, Huamono, Zapino, and Golondrina) were employed for two months. People understood that food, clothes, tools, outboard motors, and chainsaws would be distributed in exchange for the right to work without disturbance or disruption. Although there were enough goods for everyone, fierce competition ensued, for each village was determined to claim exclusive rights over the well site and to everything it contained. None of the four villages was prepared to let the others share access to the new source of abundance. Similar disputes multiplied throughout the 1990s, as the last chapter of Jorge's book, which covers the years 1993–1996, indicates.

LIVING WITH OIL EXTRACTION

Whereas Huaorani people successfully fit the prospection phase of petroleum development in their procurement economy, on the whole, the commercial extraction phase is best described as epoch making. When a twenty-year agreement was signed on August 13, 1993, between the Dallas-based company Maxus and ONHAE (Organización Huaorani de la Amazonía Ecuatoriana), the focus was on Block 16 (Maxus's operation block) where major wells were about to come under full production. Exploratory drilling, the most labor-intensive phase of oil development, was almost over. What made the Maxus-ONHAE agreement of "friendship, respect, and mutual support" a game changer, however, was the fact that Maxus took over the responsibility for organizing community-company relations throughout the ethnic territory, which included the blocks operated by other companies.[6] The agreement bound the oil company to liaise with various government ministries to fund and to organize the provision of education, health, and community development assistance to all existing communities. The document specified that "nondependency-creating actions that will enhance the Huaorani's capacity for self-management" would be programmed until 2013.[7] It also stipulated that Maxus, in addition to providing the goods and services requested by the Huaorani people, would also offer vocational training and give Huaorani men employment priority in its operation block. In addition, it would coordinate all the scientific research to be carried out on the Huaorani population, its ethnic territory, and the Yasuní National Park.[8] This encompassing agreement was signed during an official ceremony that took place in Quihuaro with the participation of hundreds of Huaorani. The signature was legally witnessed by the president of Ecuador, the minister of energy and mines, the minister of national defense, and PetroEcuador's chief executive (Maxus 1994). The Maxus-ONHAE agreement, comparable in more than one respect to treaties signed in the course of history between Native Americans and Euro-American commercial institutions, is by far the most ambitious social corporate responsibility (SCR) program ever implemented in Ecuador.[9] When Maxus merged with Repsol in 1995, the agreement was simply carried over with additional infrastructure and commercial activities added to the program of "economic improvement." It continued to be executed by the same team of Ecuadorian social developers.[10]

A number of authors have discussed the impact Maxus and its activities have had on the Huaorani people and often have included in their discussions the companies that preceded Maxus (such as Conoco) or followed it (YPF [Yacimientos Petrolíferos Fiscales], Repsol, and PetroBras). These studies show that contracts were more often than not to the advantage of the foreign companies, rather than that of the Ecuadorian government or the Huaorani people (e.g., Nárvaez 1996), and that on-the-ground practices were far from the SCR rhetoric (e.g., Kimerling 2012, 2013). They also document the shifting ties between Huaorani people and the oil industry, as well as the ambiguous politics of their leaders (Gondecki 2006, 2015; Ziegler-Otero 2004; Colleoni in progress). Gondecki (2015) highlights the wider and contradictory discursive context in which Maxus inserted its community and environmental policies. His account illustrates the political ingenuity with which Huaorani people have confronted large-scale encroachment on their homeland.[11] However, a proper study of Huaorani understandings of how they have been affected by the industrial deployment of oil has yet to be written, as well as the story of their copartnering with Maxus, YPF, and Repsol.

Rival (2000) represents a first attempt to capture the Huaorani experience of the oil industry in general, and of Maxus in particular. However, my focus on the ambiguous character of Maxus's wealth (resulting from the overlap between natural and created abundance) and on the ways in which Huaorani people attempted to channel it through the creative deployment of the host-guest relationship did not go far enough in highlighting the specificities of the presence of oil in Huaorani experiences, practices, and discursive representations.[12] It is only after many visits over the years to communities settled along the oil roads that I came to appreciate that the logic of "obtainability" had surreptitiously replaced the logic of procurement. My initial analysis stressed cultural strategies deployed in an effort to naturalize Maxus and to treat the entire oil industry as a bountiful oil camp or harvestable forest grove offering itself to foraging humans. However, by moving next to operating wells or along the roads that began to blanket their lands, Huaorani people soon experienced the industry's organizational structure, policies, regulations, activities, and impacts in a completely different way. In fact, it is as if the men and women who chose to "move in" with the company had translated the language of copartnership into the practice of coexistence with a powerful neighbor, reverting, along the way, to ideas that had marked early encounters between the oil industry and Huaorani warriors. As Paola Colleoni argues in her doctoral dissertation (in progress), war, that is, the willed, fierce, and targeted effort of obtaining something from someone, has played an increasingly important role in the harvesting of oil wealth, a wealth that is not so much a generous gift from the forest, but a victorious reward and the result of a hard-won battle.

Ompure and his wife Bogueney, the protagonists of the last chapter of *Petróleo, Lanzas y Sangre* (Viteri 2008), have continued to trek through the camps set up by Maxus and other companies, but they now pass through canteens and managerial staff dining halls rather than temporary tents as if still walking in forest groves. Some of their children and grandchildren, however, have specialized in mounting "war expeditions" against company offices; they install toll barriers on oil roads, or angrily threaten, spears on hand, whoever stands in their way. Like other Huaorani oil road activists, they have recently been accused by the government of being lawless terrorists who must be brought under control and held accountable for their actions (Rival 2015). As several of these road activists are currently in jail awaiting trial, I am rereading Huaorani words in a new light. For example, in the words of Babe and Mengatohue, two elders now dead, the oil frontier is a battlefield.

> BABE: I will not leave this land, this land is my territory, I will suffer, but I will go on defending the land of my forebears. Each day, the oilmen's long metal spears are perforating the earth's belly deeper. There will remain no more than an empty, dirty desert. This is why I feel as hot as fire. With my spears and my war cries, I shall defend the forest to my death. Look at my spears, I have tinted them with red *achiote*. The *cohuori* must leave my land at once, otherwise, I will sever their souls from their bodies, I will spear them, they will die. (Tagliani 1996: 194–95, my translation)
>
> MENGATOHUE: The spear is our law. I categorically do not want my people to be friends with The Company (Maxus). I am opposed to any deal or negotiation. Those of us who have learned the ways of cities

and are now living in cities sign agreements, which make us all look very bad. I do not agree. It has always been my position that they should not do anything of the sort. I really do not want oil companies around here. (Gondecki 2015: 438)

Such declarations are commonplace, but very few analysts interpret them as indicative of a determination to wage war on oil so that its riches can be obtained. The reason is simple. There seems to be an abyss between what the Huaorani say and what they do. I once saw Mengatohue, with spear in hand, stop cars on the Vía Auca and demand a tribute in exchange for the right to drive. But clearly he was unconcerned about the value of what he received from the drivers who indulged him. This show, after all, was part of the folklore of the frontier. When I, feeling rather ashamed and dismayed, asked Mengatohue why he was doing this, he simply laughed. Warriors tolling the oil roads have become legendary sources of jokes since the 2000s precisely because they are seen as childish rather than threatening. Their lack of interest in the real material benefits they could derive from their attempts at control is usually interpreted as a sign of silliness and powerlessness. As for Babe, he would call me to his house from time to time to show me with obvious pride and excitement the staggering quantities of plates, glasses, and other merchandise he had gradually piled up along the walls, transforming the main room into a kind of company warehouse. He would say: "*boto qui baacuu*" ("look at all my possessions, look at the quantity of stuff"). For the Ecuadorians and foreigners who were subjected to or who had witnessed the harassing demands of Huaorani men and women on the oil road, war talk is empty talk. "The Huaorani never have enough; they always want more; they have become dependent beggars." These are some of the disapproving remarks I have often heard from oil workers, missionaries, and other Ecuadorians. When Babe died, though, he was grieved by his kin as a great warrior, a warrior who knew how to channel wealth and make it available to his people. Moreover, and as Gondecki's (2015) careful recording of conflicts illustrates, one should not forget that any detection of greed or meanness from the part of The Company has led to protests, and, at times, violence.[13]

Vía Maxus, a 150-km-production road that cuts deep into the Yasuní National Park, is often mentioned in Ecuador as proof that oil exploitation and biodiversity conservation are entirely compatible. The road, which has caused no deforestation and brought no colonization, is used in arguments to support an "offshore inland model" for the future development of oil infrastructures in the Amazon Basin (e.g., Finer et al. 2015). According to this model, industrial development takes the form of an insulated enclave; the industry protects the forest and its inhabitants by guarding against intrusions and harmful connections with the outside. Offshore techniques were once explained to me by an Ecuadorian engineer, whose task was to oversee Conoco's public and community relations. I perused at leisure a promotional leaflet he had handed over to me while listening to his explanations.[14] A drawing caught my attention. The illustration centered on a naked brown body facing away into the forest, a spear on hand. A graceful macaw perched on the hunter's left shoulder. The Huaorani, it was explained in the leaflet, would work for Conoco in their quality of "guardians of the forest."

Twenty-five years have passed since the Vía Maxus was first opened, and one can clearly see that expanding the oil frontier in the Yasuní National Park has offered the Huaorani unique opportunities not only to revive their fierceness (Rival 2015), but also to exercise their talents as hunters in new and unexpected ways (Suárez et al. 2009; Suárez et al. 2012). The history of Gueyero, Timpoca, Peneno, Dicaro, Yarentaro, and Yoweweno, the Huaorani communities that have settled along Vía Maxus, remains to be written. What I gather from conversations with Huaorani friends, who live in these communities or who have visited them, is that the villagers of these communities consider themselves "The Company's guests."[15] The company delivers prepackaged meals by truck to each adult twice a day and offers free transport up and down the Vía Maxus, as well as all the way to towns such as Pompeya and Coca.[16] The pictures I was shown (often on mobile phones) indicate that people live in cement houses grouped next to a school, a health center, and a village hall. The houses are equipped with electricity, running water, showers, TVs, and other electronic equipment. Men have top-of-the-range rifles, and many own a motorcycle. Part of the population also receives monthly payments, which some equate to a *sueldo* (salary) and others to an *indemnización* (compensation). Additional research would be needed to establish the nature of the moral framings at work in the negotiation of such payments.

I have met and conversed with young men and women from these villages on more than one occasion. Their conversations left me with no doubt that obtaining the amenities and benefits mentioned above had been hard work, especially for the leaders, who had to organize numerous *hacer paro* (strikes), write many *informes* (letters), and file many *denuncias* (formal complaints). I also came to understand that demands and requests are structured around what people perceive as the "oil worker way of life." For example, when Ompure and Bogueney were killed in March 2013 (Rival 2015), villagers demanded that the company install a wire mesh around the whole community. They insisted that the mesh be identical to the one surrounding the wells. Nothing else, they were adamant, would protect them from attacks by Indians in voluntary isolation. Such anecdotes have helped me make sense of what continues to baffle Ecuadorians who have worked with the Vía Maxus communities, either for the oil industry or for the agencies ensuring the integrity and protection of the Yasuní National Park. Park officials, for instance, cannot comprehend the wild meat trade that men of the Vía Maxus communities have specialized in (Suarez el al. 2012). Why empty the park of its precious protected species and sell the meat at such low prices if accessing cash and modern amenities is not an issue given that people obtain these for free from Repsol? The hunters of Vía Maxus puzzle nationals and foreigners, oil engineers, and conservation scientists alike. How could they be more different from the representations condensed in images such as the Conoco drawing mentioned above? Making war on oil and hunting for *cohuori* are two sides of the same coin. In the economy of obtainability, controlling offers and demands is of upmost importance. There is no autonomy without control of the forces that shape the *monito omëre* (territory). Moreover, because the work of controlling is hard, the more one works hard for one's people, the more one controls, and the more one sees one's reputation and prestige increase.[17]

DEALING WITH THE "GREEN ECONOMY"

A colleague with research experience on indigenous rights and extractive industries once told me that he had written a consultancy report on the Huaorani case for a European nongovernmental organization. The Huaorani were perfectly aware that oil is dirty and polluting, he told me; they know it brings illnesses, kills fish, and forces the animals to flee. He recalled the words of an oil man who had worked for years in the oil camps blanketing his hunting territory and who later lived on the Vía Maxus road. "You can't possibly look after the forest well when the oil company works next door." My colleague added that every time the Huaorani had signed work contracts or community agreements, they had done so to get the benefits that come with oil, whether cash income, free flights, medical attention, or scholarships for their children. And every time these benefits were not forthcoming, or every time the levels of pollution and disruption became overwhelming, they protested. His conclusion was that the Huaorani people know and accept that forest conservation is not compatible with oil development. This analysis makes a great deal of sense, except that it does little to shed light on some of the conflicts I discussed earlier. To reduce Huaorani deals and protests to the pragmatics of cost/benefit analysis is, in my view, simplistic, if not misleading.[18] Moreover, such analysis misses the point that, as the Yasuní Initiative has shown, most people in Ecuador want the government to find ways of conciliating oil extraction and biodiversity conservation in the Yasuní National Park and elsewhere in the country (e.g., Barnard 2011). The analysis also fails to take into consideration the fact that the oil industry has consistently argued that its activities do not damage the park's biodiversity or the fact that large conservation organizations, which partly depend on oil funding, seek mediating policies that would reconcile extraction and conservation (e.g., Muradian and Rival 2012; Finer et al. 2015). This, to many, is what the green economy is all about. What we need to analyze, as I argue below, are the conflicts and tensions that structure Huaorani encounters with both the green economy (including tourism) and the oil industry, and we need to do this from the native point of view.

In the summer of 2005, Moi, whom I had not seen for a number of years, greeted me with the announcement, "Hi, Daoda, how are you? Everything is in turmoil! Come with me to see the caiman." He was referring to a company contracted by USAID (The United States Agency for International Development) to execute a project called CAIMAN (Conservation in Areas Managed by Indigenous Groups). When we arrived in the office, the employee who had offered to help the Huaorani was speaking with an Ecuadorian forester I knew well. My friend said, "Laura, we can hardly believe it. The Huaorani have sold their rights for thirty years to a North American environmental services company. The document is totally legal; we do not know how to remedy the situation." I heard much commentary about this mysterious and legally binding agreement in the following days. I copy below some of the remarks I kept in my field notes:

DIRECTOR OF A NORTH AMERICAN CONSERVATION NGO: This is a usufruct contract signed between the Huaorani ethnic organization (ONHAE) and an Ecuadorian NGO, FED (Fundación Fondo Ecuatoriano de Desarrollo Sustentable). The agreement is too general, this is the problem; it covers everything. The future of the Yasuní is darkening, Laura. The contract is totally legal and utterly immoral!

A HUAORANI LEADER *(talking about ONHAE's President and Vice-President, who, at the time, were parallel cousins, tonya [brothers or classificatory brothers])*: Daoda, it's simply a conflict of power and leadership between tonya.

A HUAORANI SCHOOL TEACHER: This conflict is between two *cohuori* companies!

A HUAORANI WITH LONG EXPERIENCE WORKING IN THE OIL COMPANIES: The conflict is not between Huaorani, Daoda. The conflict is between FED and YPF.[19]

A HUAORANI LEADER WORKING AS A TOURIST GUIDE: It's a conflict between BrasPetro's *Plan de Vida* (overall development program for the Huaorani nation) and the university created by FED for EcoGenesis. CAIMAN is with BrasPetro; they don't want EcoGenesis to come. ONHAE is not allowed to execute the two plans simultaneously.

I soon noticed that Huaorani interpretations tended to point to a conflict between two foreign entities. Both promised substantial financial investments over the medium term, not unlike the agreement with Maxus. The Huaorani who had followed the negotiations closely (many had come to Puyo to watch over their leaders and scrutinize their moves and dealings) wanted both agreements to go ahead (as long as neither jeopardized the agreement with Maxus). With two additional large contracts, there would be more cash incomes, more scholarships, more projects, and, in short, more benefits for everyone. Repsol, now in charge of administering the twenty-year agreement of friendship signed by Maxus with the Huaorani nation, gave at least $1,000,000 per year to ONHAE. The controversial environmental services company I had heard so much about since my arrival (EcoGenesis Development, LLC) had also invested close to $1,000,000 between September 2004 and July 2005 to develop the first phase of the feasibility project, with a plan to reinject the same amount through OHNAE every year for the duration of the thirty-year usufruct contract.[20] When adding up the funds invested by other oil companies (especially BrasPetro, which was developing its management plan for Block 31, including a life plan for the Huaorani nation), various companies funded by USAID (such as Chemonics International, executor of the CAIMAN program), and other donors, I realized that an additional $1,000,000 had also been paid to the Huaorani through ONHAE in 2005. In short, and to simplify slightly, during my visit that summer, ONHAE had administered an average of $1,000 per person for the tax year 2004–05.

What made the EcoGenesis project so attractive to the Huaorani who had benefited from it and with whom I had the opportunity to speak is that it offered them a full scholarship to study in Puyo for a university degree. Thanks to the scholarship, they told me, they could live in town with their spouses and children. Although they were instructed by Ecuadorian staff in Puyo, they were in fact enrolled with a Chilean university and preparing a degree in project management and business administration. When the program was suspended, following accusations that ONHAE leaders had sold Huaorani land to foreign companies, those benefiting from the training were very disappointed. It was very difficult to get a sense of what they were studying, what the purpose of the program was, or what they learned during the training. To this day, whenever I ask about EcoGenesis to check what people remember of the conflict that surrounded it, the clearest message that people share with me is of disappointment and nostalgia, as if details about lies, corrupt dealing, or the privatization of common lands have been forgotten. Several blame their predicament on the leaders "who were too greedy" and "cumulated salaries." "There's so much money here, Daoda, I mean in the Amazon," I was told by a young man, who had no choice but to go back to teach in his village, far from Puyo. "The leaders are fighting among themselves; we don't know where the money goes."

When I finally succeeded in triangulating information from a range of sources (interviews, conversations, reports, media coverage, and so forth), I became aware that harassing demands from the Huaorani had played no small part in precipitating the demise of EcoGenesis's environmental services project. The NGO in charge of "technical support," FED, had planned to train thirty-two men and women.[21] They soon had to accept fifty at their training center and to raise the value of the scholarships so that each of the trainees could afford living in Puyo with their families for the duration of the training. The Huaorani, who did not see these payments as scholarships, but as salaries, started to negotiate better rates. One of FED's managers recalled that "ONHAE leaders demanded to be paid $5,000 per month, but we managed to convince them to agree [to] a monthly payment of $1,500." Ordinary trainees, by contrast, received $350 per person, per month; a couple received $500, that is, less than two independent trainees. Ordinary trainees thus started to campaign against the unfair difference in salary between them and the leaders. Moreover, the wife of a well-known leader, Huiñame, protested against the rule of $350 per person and $500 per couple. She found it terribly unfair that her husband received a salary of $350, while she only received $150. In addition to these disputes over pay, FED had to face increased demands for flights, hospital bills, and other emergency expenses. "We had to comply with all their fancies" sighed an employee. "It became unworkable. The irony is that we really wanted to help them with a great project, a project that would put an end to their dependency on oil." The FED's employee in charge of dealing with these conflicts got increasingly annoyed, especially in the case of Huiñame, who was no longer attending classes. In retaliation, Huiñame's scholarship was cut by half on the understanding that full payment would be reinstalled as soon as attendance resumed. This decision infuriated Huiñame, who replied that she too was a leader (she had worked for the newly created women's association), and that she should in fact be paid $1,500 a month like the leaders working for ONHAE. A new dispute over salaries came as the straw that broke the camel's back. When FED employees realized that some of the leaders had received concurrent salaries (four or five, one for each of the projects they were enrolled with), they sought an agreement with the paying institutions so that each leader would receive only one joint salary. To the Huaorani leaders, this was an outright scandal. Outraged, they allied with Huiñame and her husband to form a faction that plotted against EcoGenesis. Having understood that the usufruct agreement could only be legal if it guaranteed total exclusivity to Eco-Genesis, they sought other companies interested in establishing a contract with ONHAE. Although this was contrary to the legal usufruct agreement signed between ONHAE and EcoGenesis, leaders thus went on to sign with at least four additional Ecuadorian consultants. These agreements granted them the Huaorani's legal powers to sell environmental services on their behalf. With its conviction that Huaorani people needed to find ways to use their territorial resources without depending on the oil companies, or that the Green Economy had the potential to transform them into entrepreneurs, FED had not envisaged that nonexclusivity was, in Huaorani eyes, the best weapon against dependency.[22]

To conclude, with the advent of the green economy, the Huaorani have become aware that they are no longer dealing with small deals but with big money. Using with flair their extraordinary talents for detecting conflicting influences and competing interests, and for perceiving changes in their environment, they have put all their energy into capturing, channeling, and controlling the new mysterious forces of capital. To face the predatory power of the oil industry and the green economy requires a new type of shrewdness and a new form of astuteness. Without astuteness, prey cannot overcome the physical superiority of predators. This message is encapsulated in a short myth, which essentially consists of a dialogue between almighty Jaguar and the little orphaned Turtle he wants to devour. In order to devour Turtle, Jaguar must get him to stick his head out of his carapace. The dialogue between Turtle and Jaguar is lengthy, for Turtle tries to gain time, while thinking about the best way to save his life. Once the turtle has figured out what to do, he tells Jaguar that he will stick his head out if Jaguar shuts his eyes closed, opens his mouth wide, and sticks his tongue out. Jaguar agrees, and Turtle jumps decisively into Jaguar's mouth, aiming for the root of the tongue, which he bites with all his might. In no time Turtle has reached down Jaguar's body all the way into the heart. This is how, the myth concludes, Turtle, although toothless, ends up devouring Jaguar, instead of being devoured by him. Armed with astuteness, a prey may reverse asymmetrical situations and neutralize a predator.

As I shall argue at greater length in the next chapter, astuteness is more important than ever in Correa's Ecuador. As they are discovering the new political regime and its *revolución ciudadana*, experiencing its effects on their lives and territory, and figuring out how best to respond to it, Huaorani people increasingly realize that more than ever, given the opacity and complexity of the situations they face, obtainability depends on fierceness and astuteness.[23]

9

INSIDE PRESIDENT CORREA'S CITIZEN REVOLUTION

"*TIÑE TIÑE* (FASTER, FASTER, WITH SPEED), hurry up, it's our turn!" In no time, my eight Huaorani companions had run down the stairs, disappeared behind the stage of the university lecture theater, and gathered in the small changing room. By the time I caught up with them, they had already stripped off their *cohuori* clothes. Yatehue, who had rushed outside and disappeared into the bush beyond the car park, reappeared with special leaves and balsa wood for the Huaorani adornments. He seemed impervious to the fact that the plants he had brought back were different from the ones normally used in Bameno, or in other Huaorani communities for that matter. We were ready for our first presentation to the Foro Saberes Ancestrales e Interculturalidad (Forum on Ancestral Knowledge and Interculturality).

The forum was designed as Universidad Estatal Amazónica's, ([UEA] Amazon State University) first official event in the build up to the launch of its new research and teaching program on *plurinacionalidades y Saberes Ancestrales* (plurinationalities and ancestral knowledge).[1] This program, the first in the social sciences and the humanities to be taught at the university, was developed in partnership with representatives of the indigenous "nationalities" present in the province of Pastaza with two aims: (1) to strengthen the *valores culturales* (cultural values) of each nationality; and (2) to promote a new *ciencia intercultural* (intercultural science). There is currently a *diálogo* (debate) as to whether the new program should be purely an anthropology program or whether it should be a mix of anthropology, sociology, linguistics, and legal studies. The debate illustrates interesting differences in the way participants understand the nature of anthropological knowledge and, therefore, its role in a region like Pastaza. During the consultation exercise, a majority of indigenous participants defined anthropology as the study of the past. Whereas some established a correspondence between anthropology and the study of the ways in which their ancestors and grandparents lived, others defined it more narrowly as "the study of a time before history." External consultants, by contrast, sought to widen the indigenous vision of anthropology by pointing to its role in increasing public awareness regarding the importance of cultural values in structuring intercultural relations among interacting human groups. The key role that anthropology could potentially play as the study of how indigenous communities use what they know in order to live better was also emphasized.[2]

After discussing the participation of Bameno in the forum on ancestral knowledge, I turn to other aspects of Huaorani engagements with the state and its citizen revolution to illustrate the ways in which ideas about culture, development, and the "good life" have shaped contemporary encounters between Ecuadorians and Huaorani people. I conclude with a few remarks on the diversity of indigenous responses to "civilization."

"THIS IS NOT A SHOW. IT IS OUR LIVES"

Cupe sat with her back to the audience in the hammock that Cahui had the wit to install while we were still offstage. It was one of the long and wide fiber hammocks that the women's association keeps with pride in its shop in the center of town. Its loan had taken some pleading and begging, as the women never fully trust the young men who come to "borrow" artifacts for events and meetings. Penti, at the center of the men's row, approached the hammock and, facing Cupe and the audience, struck up a welcoming chant traditionally sung at *eëmëiri* (drinking festivals). All the men on stage chanted, then the women, and then the men again. Penti, sharing his thoughts about the meaning and relevance of Huaorani ancestral knowledge, then addressed the audience in both Huaorani and in Spanish. "Huao guequene inpa" (*huao* means to be free), he started. "The Huaorani nationality, in its rebellious spirit," he continued, "shouts to the outside world in support for its cause. We will defend our forest world like our forebears have always done before us, since the beginnings of time; we love our ecology." He then added in Spanish, "My people basically asks one thing from the government, that it respect us. Let us be, this is what we ask. Allow us to be who we are. We want to be left in peace." After more chanting and dancing, he concluded, "No es un show, es nuestra vida" (This is not a show. This is our life).

A great deal was meant with this deceivingly simple statement. As I interpret it in the light of my conversations with Penti and his *nanicabo*, and of what I know about his community, this short declaration was meant both as a response to critiques and as a statement about the nature of ancestral knowledge.[3] Although they are the most filmed and the most photographed of all the Huaorani, Bameno people do not feel that they are acting *huaorani* for *cohuori* consumption. What they feel, rather, is that they love their way of life; this is why they do not want Huaorani culture or Huaorani life to disappear. Penti often repeats in meetings and public events that he and his people have been told that their culture is savage and sinful, and that they have been asked to abandon their traditions and to change their ways. He says, "we intend to continue to live the way of life we have chosen to live, whole, happy, proud, and free, and without interference." It is a statement he often uses in public. It is therefore not surprising that Bameno people are happy to share moments of their lives with those who admire and respect their traditions.[4] As far as Penti is concerned, spending time with his family on stage (or traveling with them all the way from Bameno to Puyo, for that matter) represents one moment in the ongoing life of his *nanicabo*, a moment he accepted on this occasion to share with university strangers in their strange house, a lecture hall. In short, far from being a crafted representation, their being on stage was, as it were, a sharing of conviviality, which itself was part of a wider field of social experience.

The anthropologists working with the Shuar, Shiwar, and the other nationalities that participated in the forum had already met their counterparts and agreed upon a program of work; I was still waiting for the organizers to tell me who my counterparts would be. As soon as Penti and his family arrived (a day before the forum), I tried to convince them—in vain—to hold a preparatory meeting. Not knowing what to do with myself, I ended up climbing the stairs to the large hotel room they were sharing. The TV was on (with no sound), and the shutters were half closed, making the room fairly dark. Men and women were lying or sitting on the beds and conversing softly. Each of them was busy making some ornament: feather crowns, woven cotton arm bands, palm leaf headbands, necklaces, and so forth. I sat for a while in silence, then took some palm fiber and started to twine it into thread as I listened to the conversations. Daboto smiled. Why did it take me so long to realize that this was the best way to get ready for the public event? The presentation would be neither improvised, nor rehearsed; it would simply happen, in the same way as now was occurring, the only difference being that there would be many more guests to receive on the morrow.

It is hard to say whether Penti and his people imagined themselves as guests or as hosts while on stage; perhaps a bit of both. In any case, their arrival on stage without clothes should in no way be confused with an act of self-exoticization. What they did, rather, was to take up one of the few opportunities afforded by Ecuadorian society to be, to act, and to behave as a true human being, that is, *huaorani*. If a *huaorani* body appears naked to *cohuori* eyes, such a body, in Huaorani eyes, is revealed as *a dentro* (an inside).[5] Let me illustrate this point with two examples: buying clothes for old Meñemo (Penti's mother-in-law) and being approached in the street by one of the young urbanites, who undressed and joined Bameno villagers on stage.

The day before the presentation, I took Meñemo and a few of her relatives to Puyo's covered market. I was concerned by the fact that she was barefoot (the streets are full of small pieces of broken glass and other dangerous things), and I worried about the horrible rags she was wearing. My intention was to buy new clothes for everyone, so that we would all look good on campus, where students, teachers, and administrative staff come each day in their smartest clothes. Our walking in procession toward the market stall after we came out of the taxi caused a sensation. People in Puyo are not accustomed to seeing villagers from Bameno, a faraway community. Their wild appearance was a source of both fascination and muted repugnance. I could feel the bemused looks of the crowd who was entertained by the efforts involved in trying to find the right garments; no size, width, or length seemed adequate. I could also feel Meñemo's boredom, as she could not see the point of swapping her familiar rags, with their reassuring feel and smell, for the strange and obnoxious ones I was presenting her with. The tension between the populace's secret desire to tame and beautify the *huaorani* body by covering it with brand new clothes, on the one hand, and the muted resistance of the *huaorani* body to its *cohuori* transformation, on the other, is something that people like Meñemo experience each time they leave their forest surroundings.[6] Huaorani persons such as Meñemo live deep *a dentro* (in the forest, far from human settlements), and their bodies have hardly any *a fuera* (outside) surfaces; they are intensely *huaorani*.

A few days after the forum, I heard Yatehue shout my name in the street. "Daoda, it's me, Yatehue. I'm here with this German tourist, over there." It might have been 6:30 pm. The sky was already dark, and I was coming back to my hotel from a visit to friends on the other side of town. I had taken a wrong turn and now found myself on a loud and bright street lined with bars, clubs, and discotheques. I did not recognize Yatehue's voice or face at first. The music was very loud; the neon lights made his permed hair stick out even more strangely than it did a few days before when I had joked with him about his *cohuori* hairdo. "Daoda, you who went through my people's land, through and through, all these years ago, before I even existed, you need to know something about me; *a dentro* I am *huaorani*." Why had he felt the urge to approach me and to tell me this? Yatehue had been living outside his community for some time now. He was in Puyo because he wanted to go to university, but he had no money to pay the entry fees. He had enjoyed the ancestral knowledge forum and had participated in the activities with no fear. He eagerly took his clothes off whenever it was required. Perhaps the presence of the Bameno group in Puyo had moved something deep inside him.[7] When Yatehue came up to me that evening, vivid memories of another young man I saw from time to time came to my mind. Huatene had spent several painful years in Quito trying to get through a university degree in environmental sciences, which was far too difficult for him. He once used a beautiful metaphor to explain to me what *cultura propia* (culture in Spanish) is all about.[8]

> It looks like I live a *cohuori* life, especially here in Quito, but the forest is within me; it's a territory, it cannot die. It is like one of these perfumes they advertise on TV. You watch the advertising, and you really want this perfume, you long for it, it remains engraved in your brain. It is as if you had smelled this perfume, and as if you could never forget the smell. I live in the city, alright, but there is no way I will ever forget my forest territory. It is a perfume I have incrusted in my brain. Even as a city dweller, I have my heart *omëre, a dentro monito omë* (within our territory).

On the second day, we were expected to discuss the impact of new technologies, and Penti had a harder time conveying the value of what he called Huaorani ancestral technology to the university audience.[9] He had brought a fire-making kit to illustrate the great simplicity and absolute efficacy of his forebears's *tecnologías de sobrevivencia* (best translated as life-saving technologies). With the fire-making kit, which was light and easy to carry, and which could be used over and over again to start a fire, even after having journeyed in water, we were in the presence of an indestructible and inexhaustible object, he told the public, far superior to *cohuori* matches or to lighters. His forebears, Penti added, did not need much equipment to know the world. Whereas an Ecuadorian scientist requires a battery of instruments and machines, a Huaorani who has learned to use his or her knowing body can scan, measure, and read the world accurately, without external aid from objects. This is why, he concluded, he wanted to speak about "ancestral science," not about technology. A young Shuar in the audience raised his hand to remark, rather reprovingly, that "Cada cultura tiene su momento, no puede pararse su desarrollo. No hay como detenerlo" (there is a time for each culture; its development cannot be stopped). Penti answered by saying that what he was showing were core techniques, techniques that, being about life and death, are timeless. This is why the Huaorani would never stop having the fire-making kit or the curare poison they are so famous for. These techniques, both nature and culture, or forest and body, are *a dentro*, which is why the Huaorani who make and use them will continue to remain Huaorani. Of course, the Huaorani, like other indigenous people, use a range of modern technologies. However, these bear no relation to *durani bai* knowledge, that is, to the indestructibility of the forest body within.

Whereas interculturality depends on communication and exchange across ethnic differences that have already mixed, *durani bai* ancestrality transmits an inalterable inner strength acquired through direct experience. At the UEA ancestral knowledge event, interculturality came face-to-face with a force it could not quite encompass, a force it did not wish, perhaps, to tame or to reduce. How else are we to comprehend the rapture with which the Bameno group's final dances and chants were received on the closing night? The Huaorani act came last after a series of carefully choreographed and innovative urban Indian dancing shows performed by well-known Shuar and Quichua cultural associations. The audience had by then left the lecture hall for the inner courtyard formed by the university's main buildings. We were sitting on the pavement at a distance from the crowds in a corner of the quadrangle. Just as on the first day of the forum, my companions seemed unprepared as they chatted and laughed away among themselves. Suddenly, the men stood up and ran to the small changing room and reappeared almost as quickly as they had disappeared. How had they sensed that their time had come? Once again, I marveled at their way of being so effortlessly attuned to their surroundings. It took a few circling tours of the quadrangle for the chanting men—in their full war regalia—to get the audience's full attention. The more they chanted, though, the more their voices echoed against the buildings, building up crescendo in a timeless Huaorani melody. It was simple, powerful, and beautiful. Happiness was glowing on Penti's face and on the faces of his *guirinani* (relatives and friends). At each completed circle, one or two men from the audience (young Huaorani at first, then others) would join the group, and each put one hand on the shoulder of one of the chanting and dancing warriors. Gregarious happiness is contagious, and so is the power of warriors whose pride is not to kill bodies, but to conquer hearts, or so it seemed. The crowd grew around the dancing and chanting group and moved along with it. Onlookers fired their cameras and went snap on their smartphones to the rhythms of the Huaorani performance, which felt as if it would never end. The crowd was delirious, and the echo expanded, latticed with many shades of laughter. Exhausted and thirsty, the warriors eventually stopped, each now bombarded with requests from young indigenous girls wanting to have selfies taken with them. Would these be part of the reflection on the impact of new technologies? I wondered.

When I came back to UEA the following morning for the final meeting (we were to discuss the format and content of a forthcoming book based on the forum's presentations and discussions), I saw policemen guarding the entrance of the university. To my surprise, they were checking the identity cards of those wishing to get in. It could very well have been just a simple coincidence, but I wondered still whether their presence had anything to do with the previous night's rapture. Perhaps the Huaorani war of seduction had been perceived as sufficiently subversive to demand in retort the deployment of force. Could it be that interculturality is an order that requires the presence of the police to become fully visible? The Bameno group was not present at the meeting. Sadly, I did not get a chance to say goodbye to Penti and his family. They had already left, not to go on a tour around Puyo and other regional towns (having received several offers to participate in programmed folkloric events) but to get back to their community. Their act had been a success; their mission was accomplished. Their presentation, one recalls, was not a show but a moment in life sharing, and this moment had now ended.

"OIL WILL HELP DEVELOP YOUR COMMUNITIES"

I had not seen Huareca in eight years, that is, since EcoGenesis had selected him for the Chilean university training program (see Chapter 8), which he loved as much as his life in Puyo. Unfortunately, the program had abruptly come to an end when his uncle decided to wage a campaign against EcoGenesis. After months of bitter disappointment and frustration, Huareca managed to find some funding to pursue his studies in Cuenca, south of Ecuador. Having completed a university degree in *licenciatura en educación bilingüe* (educational sciences), he was in charge of organizing a secondary school in his home village, QuehueireOno. He hoped that under the current government's ambitious educational program for the country's rural and indigenous areas, the school would soon be transformed into a *colegio del milenio* (millennium college). "Ecuador está en una Y" (Ecuador is at a crossroads), he told me that day as he pointed to two footpaths that joined QuehueireOno to the next village, Huentaro.[10] Both paths started equally from a single path that ran along the airstrip, but one was shorter than the other. What Huareca was trying to explain was that the country could achieve the level of social development people needed by choosing the longer path (without additional oil wells) or by choosing the shorter one (drilling new wells).

His analysis impressed me; it resonated with questions about Ecuador's future that had been bubbling in my mind for a while. What place should policies aimed at reducing poverty, protecting the Amazon rainforest, and developing the country sustainably give to cultural diversity? How will the country's diverse indigenous cultures help solve the enduring contradiction between economic development and biodiversity conservation? What steps are to be taken to get the country firmly on a post-oil development path? What concrete policies will best translate the official political commitment to change the country's model of development in the face of climate change? Once again, I became aware of the lucidity with which educated Huaorani come to understand the choices facing the country in which they live. Not only are they well aware of the national context, but they also analyze the divisions that have emerged in their communities in light of national priorities, not least because they are increasingly being told that there is no other choice but to develop with oil. "Even Penti is going to have to accept oil development," I was told recently by one of my oldest Huaorani friends. "President Correa is almighty. His power is maximal. Those who do not agree with him will be thrown out of the country."

Ima Fabian Nenquimo (2014) offers a cautious and nuanced position on Huaorani oil dependency. In his latest book, which vividly captures the conversations, disagreements, and accords that structure the various political economies of life in tension along the oil frontier, he portrays his people as *habituated* to the convenience and comforts of oil (Nenquimo 2014: 89–98). His people's combative anger, as he sees it, must be directed toward getting the best share of Ecuadorian citizenship they can possibly win in a world where greatness and abundance are obtained through education, paperwork, and projects, rather than through hunting and gathering. Moreover, he tells the readers, his people are pragmatic. They will necessarily be on the side of those who provide benefits, regardless of who the provider is, a private company or the state. Benefits are not subsidies, he adds, making clear that, from a Huaorani perspective, La Companía has to give to the Huaorani people because the authorization to operate on Huaorani land comes from the Huaorani people (Nenquimo 2014: 94). With the same reasoning, many of my friends and hosts have told me that they are compensated for "letting La Companía work." On April 14, 2006, for example, I wrote in my field diary the words of a young leader. "We have a claim on The Company, so they give us projects; we make demands, and they give us more projects; they give to stop us from pestering, at least for a while."[11]

However, making demands on the state is not as easy as addressing claims directly to a company. This became obvious to me in the spring of 2013 when I participated in two preparatory workshops that eventually led to the official signing of various agreements between the government and the Huaorani nation during 2014 and 2015. The second meeting, organized in Tena by the Secretaría de Pueblos (Peoples' Secretariat) was a perfect example of the kinds of problems, difficulties, and tensions that have resulted from the changes introduced by the current government in its relationship with indigenous nationalities in general, and with the Huaorani in particular. The priority for the Secretaría de Pueblos and its team of technical experts in social communication was to identify a number of needs (in education, health, infrastructural development, organizational strengthening, etc.) and to address burning issues, such as land legalization and the protection of the groups in voluntary isolation. For the Huaorani representatives present at the event, however, the workshop was mainly an opportunity to vent their frustration and to reaffirm their political commitment to Huaorani values: autonomy, independence, and territorial defense. Huaorani delegates grew increasingly impatient with the technical experts. The latter worked to identify very specific areas for intervention, which they spent time matching with the appropriate government bodies for speedy implementation. The former found it pointless to engage in talks of problem solving and policy implementation with consultants, who had no decision power or resources to execute the projects and the programs they were supposed to identify during the workshop. Their wish, they said repeatedly, was to negotiate directly with government officials; technical experts, in their view, were not real partners. The quote below is typical of the type of exchanges I heard in these workshops.

> CONSULTANT WORKING FOR THE SECRETARÍA DE PUEBLOS: There will be a new government on the 24th of May, and this is why we are here. The government will bring integral attention to the Huaorani nationality through the coordination of eight ministries. We are in a process of total transformation; the oil companies will no longer hand down resources directly to the communities; everything will be channeled through parishes, municipalities, provincial governments, and various ministries. In the future, and thanks to the government, oil will really help develop your communities.
>
> HUAORANI LEADER: We want to control our future and manage our own development directly; we want paid employment to do so. We are defending our territory, and demarcating our lands against invasions. We are in danger, and we will fight hard and to the end to defend our families and our land. There is too much dialogue and not enough action. What is needed right away is the budget to realize all the actions that we have identified as urgent. It is the funding we wish to settle, it is the funding we want to see.

These few examples illustrate the ways in which people create the conceptual space within which oil-community interactions will be apprehended. In the dynamic whirlpool so created, the dual opposition between conservation and development while being reaffirmed, is also constantly being destabilized. A myriad of nuanced positions is generated through this tension, none of which are easily reducible to either categorical refusal or unconditional approval. It is through this negotiation space that President Correa's power is encountered as a new power, which is measured against the older and more familiar power of La Companía.

Ecuador's heavy dependence on oil revenues has created a skewed regime of development with high levels of deforestation, indebtedness, unemployment, poverty, and inequality. Ecuador took a big step forward with the Yasuní-ITT initiative, which had the potential to generate new revenues to protect the country's ecological wealth and move it beyond its current economic dependency on oil. The National Development Plan has equally sought to move the country toward a new regime of wealth creation through greater investments in scientific research and technology, an increase in national energy efficiency and savings, a more integrated pro forest policy (with the prevention of deforestation, the protection of remaining original ecosystems, and the enhancement of natural regeneration in forests owned by small landholders and indigenous communities), and the promotion of social and environmental development in the Amazon region (Rival 2011). Since the government's decision to abandon the Yasuní-ITT initiative and to intensify oil extraction in the Amazon region, the direct policy involvement of indigenous communities affected by oil development has become a matter of priority. However, such involvement is constituted in terms of popular participation, that is, of unconditional support for the government of President Correa.[12] State institutions at the provincial and parochial level play an increasingly important role in the new, decentralized organization of the Ecuadorian state, especially since they were given the responsibility of administering the *renta petrolera* (oil rent), which represents a significant percentage of their overall budget. The immediate danger of this policy change is that development decisions (especially infrastructure ones) may be taken on the basis of clientelistic politics rather than after a measured examination of local needs. Decentralization also means that political legitimacy and success increasingly depend on gaining the support of the indigenous people and rural poor who live in the Amazon region, itself conditioned by their understanding and embracing of the policies presented to them.

This is especially true for the Huaorani, who occupy a vast ethnic territory that borders on the Yasuní National Park, and who are accustomed to negotiating directly with the oil companies. The ways in which oil interests are negotiated nationally in relation to other social and economic benefits is confusing to them. Moreover, recent changes to the constitution, to various laws, and to the style of government have all affected the ways in which people organize to demand improvements in their living conditions. Men and women I interviewed in 2013 told me that the new situation reminded them of what happened in the first years of the treaty of friendship signed with Maxus. Some communities had to negotiate with local authorities at the parish or at the canton levels, while others negotiated with higher-level state institutions. Changes in the regime of aid delivery have meant much uncertainty as to the source of community funding and the organization of basic social services. Moreover, promises of development (new roads, schools equipped with computer suites and internet connection, health centers, etc.) are increasingly contingent upon the acceptance of further oil development (for instance, new seismic research or the perforation of new wells). In response, Huaorani leaders have actively tried to understand the new rules of the game, and they have learned new ways to mobilize resources. Important issues of common concern, such as how to defend the homeland against encroachments or how to respond to key government policies, need to be discussed thoroughly by all, and people continue to value the General Assembly format.[13] However, such assemblies, which materialize the unity of the Huaorani nation, are imagined to require great investments in time, resources, and energy. As a result, most policy work takes place regionally in workshops, such as the one evoked earlier. Such consultation meetings foster the multiplication and the deepening of relations with *cohuori* nationals. In this light, the Huaorani have been granted a special legal status as *people of recent contact*, that is, with little understanding of state law and citizen obligations (e.g., Rival 2015). This is one of the ways through which interculturality gains new political meanings. Needless to say, such framings leave very little room for citizens to campaign for political reforms based on human rights (a safe environment, for instance) or cultural rights (the integrity of one's homeland and way of life).

CIVILIZATION, CITIZENSHIP, AND DEVELOPMENT

Defining development, a concept that emerged in the aftermath of WWII, is notoriously difficult. Most people find it hard to make sense of the controversies that surround the term, or to navigate the conflicting definitions of experts and academics. In Huaorani language, the concept of development is intimately linked to what people call *civilization*, a term used to refer to cultural changes linked to the work and presence of North American evangelical missionaries (High 2015). *Civilisación* (civilization), *desarrollo* (development), and *ciudadanía* (citizenship) are some of the key terms that Huaorani men, women, and children have learned to use when *a fuera*, that is, when contact with the *cohuori* world requires intercultural competence.

Literate Huaorani living in places like Puyo spend a good part of their days responding to *cohuori* requests for translations between Spanish and their mother tongue. It is thus no wonder that they have become experts in handling terms such as *civilización*, *desarrollo*, or *cultura*, even if they often find these abstract terms overwhelming. The individual creativity with which such words are translated hints to the fact that they are far from being culturally embedded. If the Spanish phrase "somos civilizados ahora" (we are now civilized) pops up from time to time in conversations, its Huaorani rendering (*betente quehuemonipa*, literally meaning "we now live all united, as one group") is only heard in political meetings or during translation exercises. As for the highly abstract substantive *civilización*, I have never heard it used. From a Huaorani point of view, civilization is a form of social development (literacy, learning the dominant language, the use of clothing, eating certain kinds of food, etc.) that occurred as a logical consequence of a new form of living together—that is, a new form of nonexclusive sociality. Spanish expressions such as *buen vivir* (good life), *bien estar* (well-being), or *desarrollo sustentable* (sustainable development) are not well understood (or not understood at all), even by political leaders. As most Huaorani see it, there is only one form of development (that is, of becoming civilized), which refers to people living well within a new type of social organization, and which keeps scarcity and illness at bay. Said differently, the ultimate goal of *huaponi quehuemonipa* (living well) and the values attached to the desire of living a good, happy life do not seem to be affected by *civilización*. When pushed to translate the expression *buen vivir* literally, an informant will use a synonym of *huaponi quehuemonipa*, such as, *waa quehuingui* (we live well). In other words, a different grammatical formulation is offered to articulate the same semantic content. Development is thus never conceptualized critically according to different values and priorities, such as greater efficiency vs. greater parity. As for the term *sustainable development,* no one seems to know or understand it, let alone to grasp it in terms of revealing disagreements between different forms of development (i.e., sustainable vs. unsustainable development).[14]

As no one I spoke with understood the Spanish terms *sustentable* or *sostenible*, I tried to explain them by referring to economic activities that do not destroy the environment while promoting social development (more and better schools, health centers, etc.). Having listened to my explanation, several young men decided to translate the notion of sustainability as *quegoki* (*ir trabajando*, "continuing the good work") or *quegoki cönwi* (*seguir trabajando hasta el fin*, "perform work actions until the objective is reached"). The emphasis was unambiguously on the continuity of actions rather than on rupture, change, or transformation. This became clear when I asked for some clarifications regarding *quegoki cönwi*. More than an idea of working until a given objective has been reached, the term, I was told, refers to the notion of "work that lasts forever." Interestingly, *quegoki* is closely related to the notion of *la lucha hasta siempre* (continued struggle). In this sense, sustainable development is understood in light of traditional political notions according to which leadership is conceptualized in terms of ongoing good work. Leaders "do development," for it is their responsibility to work well and hard, and to try their best. "Doing good work" is assimilated to *la lucha* (a struggle) considered essential to the continuity or, even, the perpetuation of the good work, as well as, and perhaps more fundamentally, of life itself. *Quegoki cönwi* also implies that leaders must be relentlessly *reclamando* (demanding). Without leaders who are continuously asking things of mean and greedy people (who would never give anything away without such harassment), Huaorani people would not live a good life. In other words, the more one is "civilized," the more one has to struggle with agents who control the flows of material goods and services. One of the young men with whom I discussed this added that sustainable development, then, should be *waa quegoki, ir haciendo bien* (to continue to work well). What makes his reflection particularly interesting is the fact that peace is said *waa quequi* (do well) or *waa quehuimi* (we live well). It can thus be deduced that peace, civilization, and development are closely related notions, all having to do with living happily without conflicts or problems. To be civilized, in other words, is to be able to achieve such harmony in larger groups that are constituted not only of pure kin, but also of friends, acquaintances, and persons not related through residence from birth. I should stress further that there is no contradiction between living peacefully and living in struggle; the two go on together all the time. Leaders build peace within their communities by becoming responsible for the harnessing of resources, which necessarily implies they struggle with the hostile outside forces that control wealth.[15]

Given current political debates within Ecuador on citizenship, development, well-being, nature, and other key notions, it is urgent to analyze indigenous understandings of good life, social change, betterment, or nature conservation carefully, and in much greater depth that I am able to do here.[16] Such analyses are crucial, given the ease with which relationships between the nation and the state, or between nature and culture are framed, both normatively and intellectually, through the direct appropriation of indigenous sociocosmological notions, which are rearticulated hegemonically according to the canons of interculturality. To illustrate the complexity of the task, I would like to share a story—a joke—I heard a leader tell his companions after a meeting in 2010.

> A man from a remote part of the Huaorani territory comes to visit Puyo. In the market, he sits at a table to eat; he does so, having been invited by a buxom waitress. She puts plate after plate in front of him, and he eats with gusto. He

does not know or realize that this is a pure sales technique. Every time the waitress asks him if he wants something else, he says yes. Full and satisfied, he gets up to leave the restaurant. The waitress stops him angrily, waving a paper under his nose. The man does not know that the meal is not free, and that he has a bill to settle. He has no money, and wants to leave. Getting angrier, the waitress calls the police. A big and strong policeman appears. The man too is armed; he has a knife in his pocket. Should he wound the policeman and run away? But the policeman has a revolver. While the man is thinking about what to do, the policeman questions the waitress. In the end, the man goes free because both the waitress and the policeman understand that the man is ignorant and penniless. He will not have to go to jail after all. He now knows that the next time he enters a restaurant, he will have to pay.

Analyzing this story is far from easy. I wrote it down in my diary from memory at the end of a long day. I know that the men and women who listened to the story found it extremely funny, and I also know that the story conveys a number of Huaorani ideas about money and *pedir centavo* (the act of asking for money).[17] What seemed to make this story so entertaining was the contrast between two different etiquettes. From a Huaorani perspective, it is rude to refuse an invitation to eat; it is alright to accept more food when it is offered and when one is with an appetite; it is polite to get up and to leave when one has eaten enough; and it is legitimate to want to fight and to defend oneself when aggressed by someone. The joke, thus, seemed to be constructed in such a way as to reveal both the moral worth of *a dentro*, and the inapplicability of *a dentro* norms in the urban context, that is, *a fuera*.

In addition to revealing these two contrasting moral systems, the joke also suggests that *centavo*, which has no value or worth in Huaorani villages, where exchanges are not mediated by money, has not much value either for those who know city rules. There are at least three basic ways of controlling cash flows and the material resources accessed through money: (1) *pedir centavo*; (2) *hacer plata* (make money) through a regular salaried job; and (3) *manejar proyectos* (manage projects) and be part of the project economy, which tends to be the exclusive turf of leaders. *Pedir centavo* (interpreted by outsiders as a form of begging) is characteristic of those who come from *a dentro* and are ignorant of *a fuera* ways. Leaders, by contrast, know all the rules (of both *a dentro* and *a fuera*), can organize life in towns, and execute projects. They have learned many tricks to intercept, channel, and divert the flows of wealth controlled by outsiders. Without an accurate record of the story and of the circumstances in which it was told and found so entertaining, I will never know for sure what the joke was about, or what messages it conveyed. It made me aware, however, of how much more research is needed on indigenous constructions of money and on the ways such constructions change over time, as people develop a new awareness of scarcity, poverty, and the mystery of money.

PATROLLING THE BORDERS OF CIVILIZATION

In May 2015, at a seminar I had been invited to give on my last day before leaving Ecuador, the celebrated historian Enrique Ayala thanked me for documenting in such detail the ways in which the Huaorani enrich the country with their unique vision of life, nature, and humanity. They are, he added, the heirs to Ecuador's last frontiers, frontiers historically produced time and time again through multifold inclusions and exclusions. I wonder what thoughts this powerful metaphor triggered in the minds of Waiwa and Hueica, who had come along. What it brought to my mind was the memory of a week-long seminar I attended in South Africa with colleagues from the University of Cape Town (UCT).

Like many Europeans, I considered myself reasonably well informed about postapartheid South Africa. Coming to Cape Town for this meeting was my first trip to the African continent, and it was a real shock. Nothing I had read or heard had prepared me for the jarring mix of politics and culture I was faced with. A quote that adorns one of the national gallery's walls encapsulates the reality of South Africa as it has become engraved in my memory, beautifully and painfully.

> In spite of the fact that the various peoples of South Africa have lived together in this part of the continent for more than three hundred years, the country as such has no objects that can be said national, no common myths, no common heroes, no war victories to commemorate together, and no statues or symbols of joint accomplishment. Instead, we have the memory and the scars of the suffering we have inflicted on each other. (Wiseman Nkhuhlu)

In response to the many questions I was putting to UCT colleagues on ethnicity and citizenship, I was advised to read J. M. Coetzee. I started with *Life and Times of Michael K*, which left me feeling as intrigued, moved, and disturbed as the above quote had. Michael K lived as a nobody, a refugee, and then a prisoner in his own country. The system made it impossible for him to leave the city, where he had grown up, or to return to the rural place where his mother was born and where she wanted to die. The only moments of peace and joy in the book are when Michael reconnects with nature: first as a sweeper in The Company's gardens, and then on an abandoned farm his mother knew. It is on this farm that he discovered the pleasures of growing crops and the promises of living off the land, as well as the system's absolute closure on his human freedom.

Could a Coetzee write a novel on the basis of the joke about the Huaorani man from *a dentro* who had no money or knowledge of *a fuera* customs? Probably not. The greatest difference between native Americans or Afro-Americans and poor South Africans, such as Michael K, relates to the latter's historical impossibility to take refuge in nature and live off the land. I have met some Chocóan Blacks down the Vía Auca on the outskirts of Huaorani settlements. Today, both the advancing agro-industrial frontier and armed conflicts continue to displace the rural dwellers of the Chocó. And their colonial history is every bit as traumatic and as violent as that of Black South Africans. However, there is room for the descendants of Latin American Black slaves to recreate a vital space, a place in which to live autonomously and develop the "art of not being governed" (Scott 2009). In the Ecuadorian Chocó, Black activists have articulated a project of territoriality to protect the cultural wealth of their people against capitalist development, as I was told in the late 1990s when I worked there for a while.[18] One of the leaders added, "the fight is not just about land ownership. . . . We're fighting for biological reproduction and social continuity; lore, norms and values; spiritual kinship and ancestral solidarity." He then explained how his people had been torn apart by rural migration, market integration, and rapid urbanization. Shrimp farming and oil palm plantations were destroying the mangrove forests and people's livelihoods; those who migrated to the coastal cities and ports were confronted with exploitation, alienation, violence, and crime. Urban dreams and the world of commerce lured men, women, and youth with promises of employment, money, and consumer goods. But the jobs never paid enough, or lasted long enough. There was never enough money for food, rent, or transportation.

> One gets into real trouble in the cities: drugs, crime, [and] prostitution. . . . So one needs to return to the rural communities, with their rivers and forests. One

has to go back to the safety of the village. Back in the village, money is not essential. There's always a piece of land to cultivate, a fish to catch, a rodent to trap, a house in which to sleep, and a consoling shoulder on which to cry. Survival depends on the gifts of rural folks, the curative hands of an aunt, and the soothing tales of the traditional storyteller.

Before concluding, he added, "the energy lost in commerce, exploitation, and consumption must be replenished through a counterflow of animation and hope."

As I have tried to show in this book, more than a refuge where it is still possible to live free from coercion and exploitation, the forest is a vital space the Huaorani call *monito omë* (our world). The durability and adaptability of Huaorani life, indeed its continued existence, depends on defending the forest as a territory to which people can always come back to live. Interdependency and autonomy are not antonyms in *monito omë*, where nothing preexists the relations that constitute life. The diversity of paths that are trodden in the defense of *monito omë* is staggering. If on the western border of the ethnic territory Huaorani and Quichua have chosen to intermarry and to mix, on the eastern side, *nanicaboiri* live in ways that are much closer to the ways of their forebears.[19] And along oil roads, such as the Vía Maxus and the Vía Auca, families make use of oil materialism to develop entirely new ethnic ways of living. Their modes of life, which have yet to be fully documented, will only last as long as oil companies continue to facilitate their material realization. As for the Taromenani (Rival 2015), they will have to find new interstices between islands of civilization, trekking their way to new horizons, unless they decide, one day, to settle as well. In any case, it is with such inner diversity that the Huaorani people have contributed to Ecuador's regional cultural systems and will—one can only hope—continue to do so, irradiating them from within, with their radical difference.

APPENDIX A

LETTER TO PRESIDENT CORREA

Oxford, 30 August 2013
Mister President,
I am taking upon myself to write personally to you and to do so in the language of my country of adoption, the United Kingdom, where you have many admirers (http://liberalconspiracy.org/2013/02/17/letter-celebrating-the-achievements-of-ecuadors-citizens-revolution/), including my person. I was vaguely aware of the Yasuní Initiative, which you embraced during your first electoral campaign, but it is the speech you gave at Chatham House in London on 27 October 2009 that swayed me. I translated your speech into English, and my students distributed it widely. I started my first publication about the Yasuní Initiative with direct quotes from your speech:

> Ecuador seeks to transform old notions of economics and the concept of value. In the market system, the only possible value is the exchange value, the price. The Yasuní-ITT Project is based on the recognition of use and service of non-chrematistic values of environmental security and maintenance of world biodiversity. The project ushers in a new economic logic for the 21st century, one in which what is compensated for is not just the production of commodities, but the generation of value.
>
> There are things which have a high value, but no price. Some things have very little value, yet fetch high prices; and things with great value may be priceless. Like friendship, happiness, and security, the environment is priceless. In our

well-being approach to the economy, an economy geared to generate well-being for all, we seek to generate value, to preserve value, and to compensate for the generation of value. This means changing the market logic through collective action, and seeking other logics beyond the profit logic through agreement, justice, and responsibility. This means not relying exclusively on a monetary scale of values. Things that do not have a price can be evaluated in value terms. Biodiversity has multiple values. The environment is not just natural resources, it's not just another factor of production along labour and capital. To conserve nature for future generations can be an end in itself. We need nature to live.

Being an Amazonianist anthropologist, I had little knowledge or understanding of climate change economics and politics, but the Yasuní Initiative, and the way it was so cynically received by many colleagues and specialists, both in Ecuador and in Europe in the build up to Copenhagen COP15, brought me to read extensively, to think deeply, to discuss its implications, and even to make changes to the way I live. I have observed and analysed the continuing evolution of the Yasuní proposal ever since. While in Ecuador last spring, I took stock of the planning transition and governance changes the Initiative brought forth, as well as its real popularity, especially in the Amazon region, where nationalist pride builds on protecting the forest and its biocultural diversity. I wrote in another publication:

> The Yasuní-ITT Initiative represents a novel institutional mechanism evolved out of conflict resolution and leading to transformative planning. Furthermore, the Yasuní-ITT Initiative proposes an innovative paradigm of regulation to tame the state's environmentally destructive potential, while enhancing its emancipatory potential. Whether the Ecuadorian state can live up to its proposal of becoming a core political institution capable of facilitating socially progressive environmental change and true sustainability remains to be seen. The challenge of developing economic activities that enhance the well-being of people while ensuring the maintenance of integrated social and ecological systems is daunting. However, the Yasuní-ITT Initiative has facilitated the popular debate on Ecuador's economic future. Many citizens are now busy challenging the oil lobby's motto "we're too poor a country to afford to leave the ITT oil in the ground" and arguing that a strong state is a state that knows when and where to stop the oil frontier.

Social and natural science research shows beyond doubt that (1) the Amazon is one of the worst places on earth to drill for oil, and (2) we must avoid extracting a large part of the world's exploitable fossil fuel reserves, if we are to remain under 2° C warming. Lord Professor Nicholas Stern tells us that we need urgently to limit the exploitation of fossil fuels, and to disinvest rapidly capital from the hydrocarbon industrial sector. Before presenting to the world the Yasuní Proposal, you fought within OPEC for another innovative policy, the Daly-Correa Ecotax, arguing that: "the Kyoto framework needs to include the concept of compensation for avoided pollution." In your speech at Chatham House, you further explained that the Yasuní-ITT proposal articulated a new economic logic: "In economic terms, what we would be doing is compensating for the generation of value." You have shown repeatedly that a small country endowed with ecological wealth and burdened by unjust debt like Ecuador can play an important role in international relations.

This is why, I guess, upon announcing on the national television your decision to sign an executive decree on 15 August 2013 that opens up the ITT fields to oil drilling, you said: "With great sadness, but absolute responsibility to our people and our history, I had to take one of the most difficult decisions of my administration."

I am not qualified—or even entitled—to judge whether this was the right decision. All I know is that the Yasuní Initiative is not a dream from which a strong country has to waken up; it is a way of valuing the Amazon region for its diversity rather than for the market value of its crude oil content; a way of valuing the national patrimony that opens new possibilities for redefining the forms of social consciousness, collective identity, and will to act through which both nationalism and internationalism get realized in practice. Exploiting the ITT fields will not deliver millions of dollars, if one counts all the destruction of human and non-human lives it will bring. As Jorge Viteri Toro, who worked all his life for the oil industry in the Oriente, wrote with profound sadness, this industry wrecked the lives of workers and their families, fuelled the destitution of many for the profit of a few, and despoiled local inhabitants not only from their lands, their forests, their dignity, but also of their ways of relating to each other and to nature (*Petróleo, lanzas and sangre*, 2008, pp. 355, 424).

Exploiting the ITT fields will not bring in many millions, and those will not put an end to local or national misery.

It will not facilitate the great transition you dreamt for your country, from an extractive type of economy to a new type of service economy. China will not use the oil extracted from the Yasuní—the quantities are too small, the quality too bad; how many Chinese bureaucrats will benefit from the deal? Why could not Chinese investments be put to financing Ecuador's energy transition?

It will not help Ecuador take its rightful place in the international combat against climate change. Rather, it will encourage mounting cynicism, either against your person, or against your country, and ruin the efforts of a seven years long campaign.

Having been won to the Yasuní Initiative, I shall be part of the movement that refuses to let it die. It has grown organically and evolved dynamically; a decree cannot put an end to it. It belongs both to the people of Ecuador, and to the people of the world. It belongs to the national Constitution, which guarantees the rights of nature. It still belongs to you, Mister President, and my only hope is that you will not forget this ownership in the democratically sanctioned battle of ideas that is now about to take place.

Respectfully yours,
Laura Rival, University of Oxford

NOTES

INTRODUCTION

1. Taromenani, like Tagaeri, are names used to refer to Huaorani groups in voluntary isolation.
2. The most commonly used is *Astocaryum chambira* (*chambira* in Spanish, *ōone* in Huaorani). The threaded palm fiber is worked into a wide range of bags, nets, hammocks, and many more items of material culture with today a multitude of new designs developed for the tourist market.
3. While the president of the AMWAE, Omari won Ecuador's Woman of the Year Prize for her leadership in the development of AMWAE's handicraft trading scheme. The scheme is close to becoming financially self-sufficient. The social enterprise generates an average monthly income of $4,000. I calculated that each item is worth $4 on average, and that about thirty-three items are sold every day. Local and regional government offices, such as *Consejos Provinciales*, buy a large proportion of the smaller items (especially bracelets), which are used in tourism promotion campaigns. Oil companies and other corporations also purchase AMWAE's products, but I have not investigated them. Women, who get 70 percent of the sales (the rest goes into financing the operational costs), can make from $1,000 to $1,500 a year (that is, if they make at least three hundred objects per year).
4. In 2003, Omari's *maapo* (father's brother) led an expedition that ended with the death of ten to twenty Huaorani in voluntary isolation. This is when she

acquired her first Taromenani necklace. In 2008, she led a campaign to prevent a conflict among colonists, Huaorani villagers, and Huaorani in voluntary isolation from escalating on the Vía Auca. In 2013, she personally intervened to convince villagers who had been attacked by Huaorani in voluntary isolation and who had lost two elders, not to retaliate. Her efforts were in vain; ten to twenty Taromenani were killed, and two little girls abducted (Rival 2015).

5. This happened in 1993. I thought that Omatoque was Tagaeri. The attempt to renew peaceful contacts and spouse exchanges failed, leading to the 2003 massacre (Rival 2015).

6. See endnote 4.

7. I have learned since that the order was canceled in the end. Muji, with over eighty stores around the world, needed a large volume of baskets, far too large for AMWAE to cope with. Moreover, Huaorani women did not like the basket's style, which did not allow them to insert threads of fiber colored with natural dyes. They found the baskets ugly and far too monotonous. Huaorani women often complain that, unlike what was the case when AMWAE started up, the objects currently made are no longer traditional. Some AMWAE members regard critically the demands of new niche markets. While they are happy to learn new weaving techniques, they lament what they see is a threat to the techniques they learned as children from their mothers and grandmothers. Some women are worried that the new handicrafts may actually work against passing on cultural heritage and devalue the work of elder women, whose traditional aesthetics and skills are seen as not well suited for the niche markets AMWAE is trying to produce for. "Real" products do not sell as well as the new macramé art that women have now learned to produce. One woman in particular voiced her frustration by explaining to me that traditional net bags are inspired from nature's designs, such as certain hanging bird nests. She concluded that AMWAE should work to preserve the authentic Huaorani traditions from dying out. Other women have expressed their discontent at what they see as the "exoticization" of Huaorani culture in AMWAE publications, advertising, calendars, and so forth. They also remark that many of the women who are most successful at new-style object making live *cohuori* lives *a fuera*, that is, in towns and along oil roads.

8. I was asked by the Ministry of Justice to be an expert witness and, in the terms officially used, to identify "the filiation or cultural origin of the spears that caused the death of Bogueney through a detailed analysis that will determine the characteristics of the manufacture, production, and decoration

among other peculiarities and specificities, which the expert may, according to her experience and knowledge, be able to establish" (my translation).

9. There is no denying that my descriptions of Huaorani sharing as a kind of ritualistic social game based on a principle of solidarity that privileges moments of consumption over moments of production have been obscured by neo-Marxist terminology and by pseudo-materialist concerns with infrastructure and superstructure.
10. See Rival (2002, xxii) on the rules adopted for the spelling and pronunciation of vowels, consonants, and nasalized vowels.
11. This review does not include works published before the early 1990s, which were reviewed in my doctoral dissertation (Rival 1992), or popular, journalistic accounts, a genre that would require a separate study. Recent publications on Huaorani genetic uniqueness (Baeta et al. 2009; Cardoso et al. 2008; Cardoso et al. 2012) have not been included either. For the same reasons, I have also excluded missionary publications, with the exception of works by Miguel-Angel Cabodevilla (from the Capuchin mission) and Jim Yost (who worked for SIL), whose scholarly writings have shed light on Huaorani ecology (Yost 1981, 1991; Yost and Kelley 1983; Davis and Yost 1983a, 1983b), history (Cabodevilla 1994, 1996), and relationships with groups who live in voluntary isolation (Cabodevilla 2004; Cabodevilla and Berraondo 2005; de Marchi, Aguirre, and Cabodevilla 2013).
12. A German student who learned hunting and men's forest knowledge in the communities where I (and Flora Lu) undertook field research also completed his PhD thesis in 1999 (Feser 1999).
13. Papworth, Milner-Gulland, and Slocombe (2013, 10) wrongly quote me as arguing that the Huaorani never hunt peccaries. What I was arguing instead is that peccaries, which are social animals displaying herd behavior, were less a source of social imagery than monkeys, who live more fluid, and sometimes even solitary, lives. I also noted that the consumption of peccary meat was imbued with much more ambivalent moral connotations than the consumption of monkey meat.
14. Today it is called Nacionalidad Waorani del Ecuador (Waorani Nationality of Ecuador).
15. Which I discuss in Chapter 8.
16. Unlike outside ethnographers, who are almost always perceived as potential allies, insiders are caught in relational webs that radically separate kin from enemy.
17. See Fawcett (2012) for details of the initial phase of the project.

CHAPTER 1

1. See also Lathrap (1970). Both Lathrap and Lévi-Strauss were influenced by cultural geographer Carl Sauer (1936, 1947).
2. Lévi-Strauss's early notice of the importance of the "developed exploitation of wild resources" is now given full recognition. Irvine (1989) argued that, given the extent of indigenous manipulations of wild, semidomesticated, or domesticated plants, swidden agriculture is best seen as the first stage of a larger agroforestry complex in which farming strategies (the selection and breeding of domesticated species in order to enhance their yields) are not distinguishable from manipulations, which can be very deliberate or almost unconscious. See also Posey (1984: 165) who, following a similar line of argument in his analysis of Kayapo resource management, states that "no clear cut demarcation between field and forest exists. Rather the more general reforestation process is reflected by a continuum between undisturbed and disturbed forest."
3. I do not know whether these forests are pristine from an archaeological and paleobotanical perspective. I have yet to collect field data on old fallows among the Yasuní communities. However, it is my guess that they would describe at least some areas of the Yasuní as *ahuene* rather than *omëre*, given that they have lived in the area for at least five generations.
4. I have seen women plant part of the vine they had brought for stunning fish near the stream before going home with their catch. One threw the seeds of *cuñi* (a bush whose leaves are mashed and mixed with clay to produce a stunning poison) along the stream where she had fished. She also threw some of the same seeds in her manioc plantation the previous day.
5. I could not establish whether it was truly wild manioc or some domesticated variety still growing in an old fallow.
6. There is no single term to translate the verb "to plant." To insert a manioc stalk into the ground is said *gay gati huiyeng*, a term which describes the action of digging an oblique hole and thrusting something into it. To plant a banana shoot is *penenca huote mi*, literally, "to fit the banana shoot in the hole with will." To sow (seeds of domesticated plants, such as corn or of semiwild plants) is *yamöi gaqui*, "to spread in the open."
7. Most Huaorani deny that they or their forebears made stone axes. Stone axes, which are thought to be gifts from the son of Sun, are always found already made in the forest.

8. These are unidentified species, probably of the *Bombacaceae* family. When a patch of forest is cleared for a house or a garden site, this slender, smooth, easy-to-climb, and fast-growing tree (it grows much faster than the peach palm) is protected. Young saplings are replanted at the side of old peach palm trees, or germinated peach palm are planted next to *macahuè* saplings.
9. Traditionally, and as just described, peach palm groves are not planted but result from symbiotic relations perpetuated through consumption. Despite the fact that the current practice in sedentarized villages is, like in many other Amazonian societies, to plant peach palms in swiddens and backdoor yards, the old cultural meanings have not completely died out. When, for example, families leave a village community after a dispute with its leader (a rare and dangerous undertaking), they never abandon their gardens without felling all their peach palms, a precaution never taken for other crops (large banana and manioc plantations, cacao, coffee, and groves of citrus trees are left behind). This practice indicates that peach palms do still stand for social continuity. Moreover, planted peach palms, which are like any introduced food crop, are still distinguished from the ancestral groves to which people continue to go every year.
10. I have interpreted (Rival 1993) the ritual beating of manioc stalks with large balsa leaves (mainly of *Ochroma pyramidale*, *Cecropia sciadophylla*, or *Cecropia* spp.) before planting as a transfer of energy between two categorically similar, fast-growing species. People know that manioc grows well whether this ritual beating is performed or not. Ritual beating is therefore performed for ceremonial purposes to ensure the symbolic transformation of manioc into balsa.
11. Today, pushed (under the pressures of missionaries and non-Huaorani teachers, and because of the constraints of sedentism) to cultivate more intensively, people have maintained a system of host-guest relations by which only one family out of four cultivates a garden and shares its production with its "guest" relatives. Recently, young educated men who need more garden products cope with the Huaorani women's resistance to cultivate by marrying Quichua women.
12. Whenever in season, fruit becomes the main staple. During the peach palm fruiting season, even hunting is discontinued.
13. For a review of some of the most influential explanations advanced for the transition from foraging to agriculture in the tropics and neotropics, see Piperno and Pearsall (1998: 10–26).
14. For Doyle McKey (person. comm. June, 2005), domestication is a coevolved mutualism, where coevolution is not purely genetic but the result of dynamic interactions between genes and culture. McKey's model is closely related

15. For Piperno and Pearsall (1998: 12), who note that "lowland [n]eotropics may have had the lowest population densities of any region shown to have supported the emergence of food production during the early Holocene," changes in food production and diet were not responses to population pressure, but rather to natural shifts in the abundance and distribution of resources.
16. Perhaps it was not until 1,000–2,000 years later in the New World, as humans arrived in North America by around 20,000 BP. By 12,000 BP, they had migrated to the tip of South America. By 9,000 BP, they had domesticated squash (*Cucurbita pepo*) in Mesoamerica (Piperno and Pearsall 1998: 168). "Systematic cultivation of back yard gardens was under way 10,000–9,000 BP in the humid, tropical lowlands of Panama, Peru, Ecuador, and Colombia. By at least 9,000–8,000 BP evidence of morphological and other changes (such as larger seed size) associated with systematic cultivation and probably indicating domestication is apparent in some economic plants" (Piperno and Pearsall 1998: 259).
17. Diamond, who does not accept that climate change caused the extinction of large mammals (previous glaciation ages did not bring about the same loss of species), favors the thesis of over-hunting by recently migrated humans. It is only in Africa that large mammals coevolved with humans and developed defense mechanisms to protect themselves from human predation. Winterhalder, Piperno, and Pearsall would not find Diamond's explanation satisfactory, for it assumes human population densities far higher than what they actually were in most parts of the world, that is, except for the Easter Islands on which Diamond bases his generalization.
18. See in particular Denevan (2001), Petersen, Neves, and Heckenberger (2001), Erikson (2000), and all the contributions in Lehman et al. (2003).
19. For a contrastive interpretation, see Heckenberger (2005).
20. The existence of Amazonian chiefdoms was either denied or explained away as failed or short-lived attempts by highlanders to establish civilization in the lowlands. See Rival (2002) for a review of these arguments. See also Wolf (1961).
21. Of proto-Arawak and proto-Tupí stock according to Clement (pers. comm. August, 2005). Proto-Arawak groups then moved north and west, and continued to perfect the domestication of sweet manioc and peach palm. Proto-Tupí groups moved east and south, and specialized in the domestication and improved diversification of bitter manioc.

22. Mithen (2006: 59) usefully reminds us that "human genetic diversity is highly constrained, with significantly greater differences between chimpanzees separated by a few kilometers in Africa than between humans living at the opposite ends of the earth and engaged in quite different lifestyles."
23. Similarly, changing alimentary markers are used to signify the choice of new political and economic alliances, particularly interethnic trade. For the Matsigenga who have controlled an important long-distance trade route for several centuries, to consume salt is to be human. Salt has also become an important ethnic marker among Ecuador's lowland Quichua and Shuar speakers. And when the missionized Huaorani speak of "civilizing" uncontacted Huaorani groups, such as the Tagaeri, they always mention that these wild Indians must now eat proper food like sugar and rice. Traditionally, the Huaorani identified as eaters of boiled monkey meat. Old Huaorani still refuse to eat salt or meat other than monkey and forest bird.
24. See *The Belem Declaration on Isolated Indigenous Peoples* signed on November 11, 2005, and the creation of the International Alliance for the Protection of Isolated Indigenous Peoples (http://www.ethnobiology.net/what-we-do/core-programs/global-coalition/declaration-of-belem/).
25. "The economy of any society always defines an important aspect of human relationships with the environment. Beliefs and values regarding the natural world and humanity's place within it provide powerful motivations both with regard to economic practices and other types of human actions" (Winthrop 2001: 205).
26. Or, rather, it was, at least until the advent of Mendelian science.
27. "All human 'others' can only be 'others' to the extent that they are the same in a very important way. But the search for that sameness involves us in a whole range of theoretical wrangles that most of us prefer to avoid. The result has been a single-minded emphasis on 'difference' as the factor defining our field" (Piña-Cabral 2005: 126).

CHAPTER 2

1. See, for instance, Nabhan (2001: 147):

   Salvage ethnobotany missions only scratch the surface of 'indigenous knowledge about the world' by simply recording indigenous names for plants and cataloguing their uses. Such descriptive, purely utilitarian, ethnobotanical surveys hardly tell us anything about how 'the natural world works' from an indigenous perspective because of the assumption of some that ethnobotanical fieldwork is no more than the elicitation of 'folk taxonomies,' which therefore allow correlations between indigenous names for plants and Linnaean species. In this way, ethnobotanists mirror 'biodiversity systematists,' who ignore ecological interactions while attempting to find regions of high species richness. . . . Commonly published inventories of useful plants named in native languages typically appear to be lacking any ecology or evolutionary context.

2. The authors that Berlin discusses include Turner's (1974) studies carried out among various Northwest Coast Indian populations of Canada, Whistler's (1976) study of Patwin speakers in California, Fowler's (1972) comparative work among the Numic peoples of the Great Basin (USA), Waddy's (1988) monograph on the Anindilyakwa of Groote Eylandt (Australia), Hunn's various publications on the Sahapatin of Washington State (especially Hunn 1977), and to illustrate the particular case of a once-foraging people, Hays's (1983) discussion of the Ndumba's taxonomic system (New Guinea).
3. "The human observer, psychologically endowed with innate capacities for categorization, almost spontaneously perceives the readily recognizable patterns inherent in the ways that evolution has worked. This unconscious recognition of nature's plan ultimately emerges as the cognitive structure that we know as a society's system of ethnobiological classification" (Berlin 1992: 286).
4. It is in the currently cultivated, as well as the fallow, areas that the highest rates of botanical diversity were found.
5. Taken from Table 8.1 in Balée (1994: 205).
6. For Davis and Yost (1983a; see also Davis 1997), the Huaorani are at once "exceptionally skilled naturalists" and "restricted pharmacologists." These authors were surprised, for example, to find that the huaorani use no more than thirty-five medicinal plants, and that, moreover, many of these plants are used for their sympathetic rather than chemical properties—that is, according to magical beliefs that seek to achieve an effect by performing an associated action or using an associated thing, such as, for instance, when a plant with leaves shaped like a stingray is sought out to treat stingray wounds. Davis and Yost (1983b) also noted with surprise that a plant species commonly used by Amazonian Indians to treat fever, *Brunfelsia grandiflora* D. Don. spp. schultesii Plowman, is only used as a source of wood by the Huaorani. "It seemed incredible to [us] that a people who had such a profound knowledge of the

forest would have failed to recognize the medicinal properties of the plant" (Davis 1997: 290). The two authors contrasted the Huaorani "limited and highly selective use of medicinal plants" with that of "neighboring tribes, such as the Canelo Quichua, a people who have been repeatedly ravaged by Western diseases for hundreds of years" (Davis 1997: 292).

7. The Paliyan of South India are compared with two different Dene groups (one in the Canadian Subartic and the other in Alaska), the !Kung of Botsawna, the Yup'ik of the western Alaskan coast, the Aka pygmies, and the Ulgunigamiut Inuit.

8. In a fascinating study documenting floristic diversity in Northwest Amazonia, Pitman et al. (2001) investigated the composition and structure of two tree communities located at the western margin of the Amazon Basin, the Yasuní National Park in Ecuador (where the Huaorani hunt and gather), and the Manu National Park in Peru. Pitman found that despite significant differences between these two moist lowland forests (Yasuní is considerably more diverse than Manu at three different spatial scales), their tree communities are surprisingly similar in composition and structure. Most notably, species in a few key families, including the palm *Iriartea deltoidea*, consistently dominate these two forests at identical densities. This led him to conclude that although undeniably complex and diverse, these forests are far from unpredictable. Consequently, a person able to identify one hundred tree species can identify a large proportion of the standing timber, even when these forests contain more than ten times as many species (Pitman 2000: 17).

9. One could say that their culture predisposes them to be "historical ecologists" (Balée and Erickson 2006).

10. From Davis 1997: 276–77:

> Wepe, like all the Waorani I met, turned out to be not only a keen observer but also an exceptionally skilled naturalist. He recognized such conceptually complex phenomena as pollination and fruit dispersal, and he understood and could accurately predict animal behavior. He could anticipate the flowering and fruiting cycles of all edible forest plants, list the preferred foods of most forest animals, and identify with precision the places where they slept. It was not just the sophistication of his interpretations of biological relationships that impressed me; *it was the way he classified the natural world*. He often could not give you the name of a plant, for every part—roots, fruits, leaves, bark—had its own name. Nor could he simply label a fruit tree without listing all the

animals and birds that depended on it. His understanding of the forest *precluded the narrow confine of nomenclature. Every useful plant had not only an identity but a story*: a pungent leaf used for fever, a poison capable of killing fish in half a mile of river, a solanum first planted by the jaguar, another employed as a treatment for scorpion bites. (emphasis added)

11. A total of 409 species were identified primarily as food for mammals and 384 as food for birds. One hundred fifty species were identified as food for humans, and 102 as having medicinal properties (Cerón and Montalvo 1998: 9). It cannot be overstressed that all the species that Cerón and Montalvo collected were named and used by the Huaorani. In fact, all plants in their environment are named and used directly or indirectly. By compiling all the plant names (including variants) reported by Ceron and Montalvo, Mondragón and Smith, Alarcón, Rival, and Davis and Yost, I have reached the total figure of 1,330 names. More research is needed to determine how many of these constitute primary folk biological taxa.
12. Of these, 408 species are tree species, 64 are treelets, 40 are grasses (herbacea), 32 are vines, 21 are creepers, 16 are lianas, 12 are herbaceous treelets, and 8 are parasite trees (Cerón and Montalvo 1998: 22).
13. Interestingly, of these 109 species, only 41 are also included in Cerón and Montalvo's inventory. The collection was made in 4 different communities (Bataboro, Ñoneno, Bameno, and Tigüino) and the forests surrounding them (Mondragón and Smith 1997: 21, 189).
14. No check has been made in these comparisons for synonyms.
15. Out of the 625 species listed, 409 were named as food for mammals, 384 as food for birds, and 150 as food for humans.
16. The Huaorani names have been left as spelled by informants. There are obvious synonyms. Quichua names provided here are taken from Lescure, Baslev, and Alarcón (1987).
17. However, *Aniba hostmanniana* (Nees) Mez is called *ocatoe* and *guememoyibe* (or *guememoyihue*); but *A. guianensis* Aublet, *A. hostmanniana* (Nees) Mez sp. Aff, and *Aniba* spp. are simply called *ocatoe*.
18. Similarly, a peach palm will be called *yengmokahue* if it is very young; *tehue* if it is slightly older (the stem fibers are still relatively soft in contrast to *dagenkahue*, the mature palm with hardwood), and *tehuemo* when it starts fruiting.
19. Although the descriptions given in this chapter concern trees, the argument equally applies to the classification of shrubs.

20. By this I mean the use of facts and properties pertaining to the biological world to derive structural relations metaphorically applicable to the social world and to articulate rules of exchange, in particular, kinship rules.
21. This has led Morris (1976: 556) to speak of a "totemic void" among the Hill Pandaram.
22. Lenaerts (2004) argues that the main objective of the taxonomic systems he studied in Peru and Brazil is not to achieve a complete and comparative description of animal and plant morphologies. Rather, it is to class the forms of sociability established between humans and nonhuman species and inventory all the types of intentional behavior found among living beings.
23. See Nabhan's (2000) study of O'Odham and Comcaac names for plant and animal species. Nabhan argues that the languages spoken by these groups encode their traditional knowledge of ecological interactions between plants and animals of the Sonoran Desert, a habitat where they have lived for centuries.
24. R. Alarcón (pers. comm. July, 2000).

CHAPTER 3

1. This latest collection of old and new essays, which covers the various strands of Balée's unique interdisciplinary research, gives an excellent overview of the evolution of his thought. It demonstrates the power of anthropology to establish a fruitful intellectual junction between the biological, sociological, and historical sciences (Balée 1998a, b).
2. Sauer's position contrasted sharply with that of Julian Steward for whom culture increasingly created its own artificial environment. Whereas Sauer was critical of modernism, Steward embraced modern change as not only inevitable but also as inherently progressive. He saw the adaptive responses of modern societies as very unlike those of tribal societies, the latter being much more dependent on nature for their physical survival than the former. Complex societies, for Steward, adapted predominantly to the built and artificial environments they constructed. He even imagined forms of future human adaptation to permanent space stations circling the earth (Kerns 2003: 112, 233, 246–47, 282, 299). The fascinating intellectual and political differences between Berkeley anthropologists and geographers during this formative period are yet to be fully explored.
3. Primary succession refers to the initial colonization of a substrate that had no life on it before, such as the succession of organisms in areas of former

glaciation. Secondary succession refers to the replacement of organisms by other types of organisms on a substrate that has been disturbed, such as the replacement by humans of one type of vegetation for another through slash-and-burn cultivation (Balée 2006: 83). For a refutation of Balée's thesis, see Barlow et al. (2012) and McMichael et al. (2014).

4. He sometimes calls the Amazon's cultural forests "vegetational artifacts" or "living artifacts" (Balée 2013: 80–85).

5. Through years of pioneering studies, Darrell Posey established that the Kayapó model is based on six main principles: (1) overlapping and interrelated ecological categories; (2) an emphasis on ecotone utilization; (3) the modification of "natural" ecosystems to create ecotones; (4) the extensive utilization of "semidomesticates"; (5) the transfer of biogenetic materials between similar ecozones; and (6) the integration of agricultural practices with forest management practices. He stressed the fact that the Kayapó transfer "useful plants across distances into managed concentrations" (Posey 1998: 112), and he argued that Kayapó ecological engineering constitutes a blueprint to restore and conserve degraded forests in the Brazilian Amazon. Posey's assertion that the Kayapó consciously plant and propagate a wide range of useful domesticated, semidomesticated, and nondomesticated plants in *apêtê* was challenged by various researchers, who argued that what appeared to Posey as having been planted was in fact occurring naturally in transitional environments. Parker insisted, for instance, that it is more accurate to say that *apêtê* result from "natural processes along the dynamic frontier between forest and savannah" (Parker 1992: 424).

6. In his response to his critiques, Posey stressed the difficulties encountered in researching indigenous knowledge. To start with, there are issues of translation. The verb *to plant* does not coincide with any single Kayapó word, phrase, or concept, and the Kayapó expression translated as "plantable" is inherently ambiguous; it refers to a plant that could be planted or to a plant that Kayapó cultivators in some way propagate or encourage to grow (Posey 1998: 112–13). Then, there is the issue of acknowledging indigenous knowledge in its integrity, which for Posey requires taking Kayapó landscape metaphysics seriously. Kayapó ethnoecology (the knowledge of relations between plants, animals, and humans) is often expressed through the highly symbolic codes of myth and ritual (Posey 1998: 105). It is also enacted in ceremonies that punctuate both the agricultural cycle and the human life cycle. Shamanic notions, such as *karon* (plant-diffused energies) and *x-karon* (spiritually defined

energies), play a central role in explaining "ecological-social relationships and the changes that occur within them" (Posey 1998: 106–7). For Posey, therefore, the forces and energies enacted in Kayapó myths illustrate the nonlinearity of indigenous ecological concepts. These concepts, which link consciousness to cultural choice, clash with Western concepts of time and space (Posey 1998: 110).

7. These primary landscape formations "were designed, engineered, and built in prehistory, and not just in Amazonia" (Balée 2013: 184).

8. See Balée (2013: 105–6) for a discussion of whether the Tupian Sirionó were historically "Guaraní-ized."

9. See Balée (2013: 73) who said "I am convinced the Guajá and many other foragers of Amazonian tropical forests lost agriculture—they did not give it up willingly." Or note his comment "full-time hunting and gathering does not appear to be an option that a horticultural society freely chooses. Warfare, epidemic disease, and depopulation evidently can make horticulture and semisedentism less rewarding than foraging for some societies" (Balée 2013: 78).

10. "Contemporary characterizations of indigenous societies are primarily the products of recent history and serve, for the most part, as inaccurate portraits of the pre-Columbian past" (Stahl 2008: 7).

11. Clement (2014: 4389) defines landscape domestication as "a process in which human intervention in the landscape and manipulation of the landscape components result in changes in landscape ecology and in the demographics of its plant and animal populations, resulting in a landscape more productive and congenial for humans."

12. The Tupí-Guaraní form a large family of at least 33,000 peoples and 21 languages dispersed over distant countries. They show minimal linguistic differentiation, maximal geographical dispersion, the propensity to adapt to very different ecological contexts, and a predilection for migration (Politis 2014: 1052). These unique features deserve explanations that go beyond the examination of causal historical events.

13. See Ima Fabian Nenquimo (2011, 2014) and Chapter 9 for a discussion of historical movements up and down small rivers south of the Napo River and north of the Curaray River, and of perhaps longer-term southeast/northwest historical treks.

14. I agree with Clement (2014) that hunting and gathering lifestyles actively promote landscape formations. However, I am wary of his evolutionary (and developmental?) sequence: pristine > promoted > managed > cultivated >

swidden > settlements. This does not leave sufficient room, in my view, for non-Western landscape imaginaries.

15. Typing communities along this spectrum in distinct, pre-established categories is a vain exercise. The Huaorani do not categorize their communities in terms of bundled criteria that set arbitrary and impoverishing limits on the possibilities that they see civilized life opens to them.
16. New Dayuno was created where Dayuno stood thirty years ago. Tepapare was created on the hunting grounds of a number of families from Zapino.
17. She chooses to use "agriculture" as a generic term to refer to cultivated plots, regardless of their size or of the techniques used to cultivate them (Zurita 2014: 14).
18. The species mentioned include *Rynchophorus palmarum R.*, *R. barbirostris*, and *Metamasius hemipterus sericeus*.

CHAPTER 4

1. Da Matta (1982) was the first anthropologist to stress the importance of *substance relationships* in native Amazonia and to discuss the concomitant belief that parents influence the physical appearance and health of their children according to the foods they eat or avoid.
2. This is generally the case. Butt Colson (1975), Da Matta (1982), and Guss (1989) note that their informants refer to perinatal restrictions with the same generic term they also apply to other periods of fasting and confinement. To my knowledge, only the Wayapi studied by Grenand (1984), who use a similar term to refer to both parental birth observances and a bird sitting on top of eggs, view the couvade as a kind of human brooding. High (2015: 137) has found out that a man following couvade restrictions receives the name *gerempo* (literally, "babyfather"), while a pregnant woman is referred to as *geremara* ("babymother").
3. Comparative sources can be found in Rival (1998a).
4. See Rival (1998a: 637, footnote 9) for a list of food taboos.
5. A *wegõnhuè* is a small mouse-like rodent that comes in the kitchen at night to feed on manioc and sweet potato.
6. Kapamo is a root similar to manioc in appearance but has a juicy sweet white flesh that can be eaten raw like a fruit. It is still given to babies and young

children as a complement to breast milk. Other versions mention that fathers raised their children on woolly monkey brain.
7. Huegongui, the original ancestor, "our grandfather" (*monito mëmë*), is at the origin of all animal and human life on earth.
8. See Rival (1998a: 628–30) for a discussion of anthropological approaches to the couvade. Munroe, Munroe, and Whiting (1973: 68–69) note that most cases of "intensive couvade" in their cross-cultural survey belong to South and Central America, a fact they attribute to "large-scale diffusion."
9. This is the sense in which I interpret Lévi-Strauss's (1962: 258–59) remark that both parents respecting couvade restrictions imitate the child.

CHAPTER 5

1. In conversations I have had the opportunity to have with them over the years, old Huaorani, such as Guiketa, Quimo, or Dabo, used the same reasoning to justify their decision to follow Dayuma and the Summer Institute of Linguistics (SIL) missionaries and live in the first mission bases. Their dear relatives had been killed off by the enemy, and they felt deeply lonely and abandoned; they say "Nemo (missionary Rachel Saint) loves us, God loves us, and we live well again." The mission village, with its church, health center, and North American-style log cabins, had become the enlarged symbolic equivalent of the longhouse. And the Huaorani who left the SIL Protectorate, fleeing as far as they could from missionary influences, did so for the very same reason: to live well. They resented having to live on Guiketa's land and hunt his game, having their marriage alliances overseen by Dayuma, and being forced to abide by strict evangelical rules. They also found Dayuma and the missionaries particularly stingy and unfair in their distributions of outside goods.
2. The *nanicabo* (plural form, *nanicaboiri*) constitutes the basic social unit of Huaorani society. Huaorani people prefer to marry close. Preferred marriage is between bilateral cross-cousins, giving rise historically to a high degree of endogamy. Marrying close is especially valued by women (see Chapter 6). A child may have more than one biological father (see Chapter 4). Compared with other Amazonian societies, the Huaorani have been, and to some extent still are, remarkably mobile, autarkic, and endogamous. The Huaorani's fierce egalitarianism, present-oriented ethos, and rejection of elaborate gardening

have led them to avoid interethnic contact and exchange. Their hunting and gathering economy is matched by a close-knit egalitarian social organization based on strong ties and shared communal patterns (Rival 2002).

3. Men behave particularly boisterously while building the house frame and preparing the outer roof. Sexual jokes cover a wide range of topics from adulterous adventures to suggestions of incestuous matches between, for instance, parallel cousins or men and women separated by a wide age gap. Bachelors, the favored targets of such jokes, are subjected to the double entendres of their adult male kin. Women tend to ignore male banter and bawdy laughs. They impassively weave the inner roof while singing in chorus. A woman may occasionally engage in rapid verbal jousting with a male companion to everyone's delight.

4. In Chapter 13 of his *History of Human Marriage*, Westermarck (1921: 455–76) marshals as much ethnographic evidence as was available at the time in support of Darwin's thesis that male sexual desire is stronger than the female one and that males initiate courtship. The counterexamples he gives (e.g., women initiating courtship) are almost all from South America.

5. Lévi-Strauss (1983: 195) wrote that "the house is the objectification of a relationship," and Bloch (2005) fruitfully applied this insight to the Zafimaniry context. He showed how the centrality of the monogamous marriage finds material expression in the elaborately carved wooden houses for which the Zafimaniry are so well known. See also Malinowski (1927:182); "the hearth and the threshold not only symbolically stand for family life, but are real social factors in the formation of kinship bonds."

6. Often left behind by hosts gone trekking, I had many opportunities during fieldwork to evaluate the extensive forest knowledge, economic skills, and resourcefulness of Huaorani children.

7. There is an exception in the case of orphans, whose survival and welfare depend on the protection they receive from individuals who choose to take them under their wing. A protégé is considered a member of his or her protector's house group only as long as the latter is able to take on this responsibility.

8. It is misplaced to mistake such behavior for homosexuality, defined in the *Oxford English Dictionary* as "sexual attraction only to persons of the same sex." Both Catholic and Evangelical missionaries have spread rumors of homosexual behavior among the Huaorani on flimsy evidence. Archbishop Alejandro Labaca, who was speared to death in 1987 by a group of noncontacted Huaorani, wrote in his diary that on several occasions he had to share his blanket with Huaorani men, who caressed his genitals (Labaca 1988: 63). The

behavior in question concerns masturbation and nothing else. Although I did not discuss this directly with my Huaorani friends, such caressing seems to me of the same nature as the sensuality described in this chapter. It consists of a mixture of great curiosity for new bodily forms, and a response to felt bodily needs for mutual pleasure. Our own experience of sexual attraction (either hetero- or homo-) does involve the same elements of curiosity and pleasure of giving pleasure, but these aspects are, it seems to me, greatly overshadowed by our Western ideological obsession with sexual desire, possession, and orgasm.

9. Gregor (1985:33) mentions the case of a woman who made love with her lover in her own hammock not far away from where her husband was sleeping. His Mehinaku informant told him, "a little danger is pepper for sex."
10. She is referring to the male youth of her local group.
11. I was also unable to establish this fact in discussions with women. Gregor (1985: 33, 86) experienced the same difficulty in establishing the existence of female orgasm.
12. Huaorani material culture is made up of a few basic artifacts perfectly adapted to nomadic life and freedom of movement. Everything can be easily made, packed, and replaced.
13. Several men told me that they would not however sleep with a one-night-stand lover before hunting or making curare poison. I was also told that before making spears, one had to sleep absolutely *alone*, with no one else.
14. For Paz, Western romantic love represents a historical synthesis of Arab erotic influences, Tantric ecstatic experiences, and Provençal *amour courtois*.
15. Elwin (1947: 102) reports similar beliefs among the Muria, who regard the sexual organs, whether male or female, as living things with an independent life of their own.
16. This giant worm is an unidentified species of the genus *Andiorrhinus*. Gregor (1985: 53–54) found a very similar myth among the Mehinaku of Brazil. In August 2008, I was having dinner with Omari and other AMWAE representatives in a pizzeria in Shell-Mera. Omari had recently been elected as President of AMWAE, and Hawaiian pizzas were her most favorite *cohuori* food. She made everyone laugh by saying, "You know of course why I work so hard and stay such long hours in the AMWAE office? Cuica is hiding under the waste paper basket!"
17. There is an equivalent myth about male sexual pleasure, but I did not hear it as often. In one version I know, a married man goes fishing. He is called by a *bufeo* (Amazon dolphin, *Inia geoffrensis*), who wants to seduce him. Her genitals

are very similar to a woman's, only deeper, softer, and moister. After making love for the first time with the she-dolphin, the man finds her so desirable that he cannot stop himself from copulating with her over and over again. Never has he experienced such intense pleasure. He ends up wasting all his semen and blood; he drowns and dies in his animal lover's dwelling at the bottom of the river. In another version I heard, the man was having a sexual liaison not with a dolphin but with a giant otter (nutria, *Pteronura brasiliensis*). However, the story was identical. Mehinaku men also fantasize about having voluptuous but lethal embraces with the feared anaconda (Gregor 1985: 183).

18. Patrice Bidou (2001: 32) reminds us that when Didier Eribon asked Claude Lévi-Strauss "what is a myth?" he answered that for an Amerindian, a myth is a story about the time when humans and animals were not yet distinct [my translation].

19. Lévi-Strauss (1983: 83–84) explains very well the dangers of autarky and closed endogamy using Tylor's (1888: 267) famous rendering of the choice between "either marrying out or being killed out." It is quite clear that Lévi-Strauss's firsthand ethnographic experience in Amazonia has influenced his general understanding of early marriage strategies.

20. This literally means "brother-in-law (in Spanish), brother-in-law (in Huao), I am going to fool around (in Huao) with your sister (in Spanish), fool around (in Huao), my potential affine (in Huao)."

21. The description of the Shuar *tsantsa* (shrunken head) celebrations offered by Michael Harner (1972) leads the reader to interpret them as a kind of virtual sex encounter between the killer and the *muisak* (avenging soul) trapped in the *tsantsa*, as well as between his wife and the *muisak*.

22. Elwin (1947: 97) makes similar remarks about the Muria's "simple, innocent, and natural attitudes to sex," which is all the more remarkable given the institution of the *ghotul* (village dormitory) where boys and girls sleep together and are emotionally and erotically involved with a series of partners before marriage (they marry their cross-cousins). Moreover, the choice of sexual partner in the *ghotul* obeys taboos broadly similar to those operating in Amazonia. Although Gell (1992: 190) is critical of what she sees as Elwin's romanticization of the *ghotul* as a model institutionalization of adolescent free sexual love, her ethnography is consistent with Elwin's. Both Elwin's and Gell's ethnographies demonstrate that the mixed village dormitory works at creating intimate physical closeness between adolescent boys and girls before marriage. Relational exclusivity and sexual jealousy cannot develop inside the *ghotul*,

which reinforces collective harmony, interdependence, and autonomy from the adult world. The kind of "innocent" sexual pleasures the two ethnographers describe recall the ones I have just described among the Huaorani. Here too the give-and-take of bodily pleasures is not obsessively focused on penetration or ejaculation. As Elwin (1947: 433) notes, "a diffused affection does not promote sexual potency."

23. If we are to believe Napoleon Chagnon, this would not be the case in Yanomami society where sexual jealousy is the prime cause of warfare.
24. No wonder that the loving practices of the Londoners studied by Miller (1998) tend to center on consumer goods, which materialize everyday practices of attachment, identification, care, and concern for one's coresidents. These Londoners "make love" while shopping, an activity which best expresses their long-term commitment to each other.
25. "Avoiding the primal scene" is the main reason the Muria give to explain why they prefer to send their growing children to the *ghotul* (Elwin 1947: 322–25). Kenyatta (1953: 161) explains that in the bachelor huts of the Gikuyu, where sexual indulgence is governed by rules not unlike those found in the *ghotul*, brothers and sisters avoid the deep embarrassment that witnessing each other's erotic acts would cause by not meeting their sweethearts in the same huts.
26. See Uchiyamada (1999) for a telling description of sexual relations between unequal partners.
27. Erikson further uses the anti-Freudian distinction between sexual and asexual bonds to differentiate incest avoidance as biological adaptation from incest as pathological manifestation.

CHAPTER 6

1. See High (2015: 143, 149) for a discussion of changing meanings of shared substance in mixed couples (Quichua-Huaorani).
2. There is no separate term for *husband* or *wife*, just a term for *spouse, nanoongue*. All the husband's brothers are referred to as *nanoongue* and so are all the wife's sisters. One may sleep with anyone one calls *nanoongue*. In this way, the rights and obligations contracted upon marriage extend to a whole set of same-sex siblings.
3. See Rival (2002: 143–44) for a discussion of present-day marriages between Napo Quichua and Huaorani.

4. After the great flood that destroyed everything the Creator had caused to exist, the only survivors were a brother and a sister who traveled upriver inside a hollow log until they reached a dry land where they married and gave birth to the first Huaorani people. The other myth is linked to the creation of the moon (Rival 2002: 125, 204–5).
5. For both men and women, social maturity comes only with marriage.
6. Additionally, 11 percent were between cross-sex sibling sets, and 15 percent were between same-sex sibling sets.
7. Rivière n.d. states:

> In Guiana there are no enduring social units involved in the exchange of women and no mechanism other than prescription embedded in the relationship terminology itself through which an exchange can take place. There is nothing to ensure that the giving of a woman in this generation will bring about a return in the next, and the only secure course of action is to effect an immediate exchange. Under such conditions, virilocal residence represents considerable risk, for when control over a woman is surrendered there is no mechanism that assures replacement. The alternative strategy is to maintain control over all human resources through endogamy or female resources through uxorilocal residence. However, because the actual means by which uxorilocal residence can be enforced are weak, [potential affines] are regarded as a threat. The relationship between inside and outside, to which the fictional notion of a coresident endogamous kindred and the denial of reciprocity are responses, is one of danger because the mechanisms of exchange are inadequate to mediate the opposition.

8. A somewhat similar conclusion was reached by Brian Ferguson (1988: 149), who further remarked that his survey of the ethnographic literature on the relationship between conflict patterns and postmarital residence could find no evidence of a man bringing an outside wife into a matrilocal household. Arhem (1987: 165–66) also argued that Makuna bride capture, which defines and expresses political relations between groups, may be the cause, as well as the result, of conflicts.
9. Henrietta Moore supervised my doctoral work for a few months in 1991.
10. It might be true that in modern Western societies women share, beyond their differences, a common identity based on their equal subjection to male sexual violence. However, I have yet to be convinced that "male sexual violence" constitutes a unitary, empirically verifiable phenomenon. In any case, to speak of male sexuality (then qualified as violent) presupposes the prior existence of

sexuality as a separate domain, which is not the case among the Huaorani (see Rival, Slater, and Miller 1998).

11. Throughout their married life up to this point, they had woven the conjugal hammock together.

12. The most important nongendered terms are: *toniya* (sibling); *huï* (child, offspring); *nanomoco* (grandchild); *nanoongue* (spouse); *guiri* (kin). They all have a plural potential and are often used to refer to a class of people: *toniyari, huiñenani, nanomoco, guirinani, nanicabo, huaomoni,* and *huarani*. *Memeiri,* derived from the male term GF for grandfather, refers to both male and female forebears.

13. The left leg of one is tied to the right leg of the other.

14. A woman can hunt with the blowpipe of a brother, father, or son.

15. To make curare, sections of the poison vine are cut in the forest by men or women when needed and brought back to the longhouse. Men prepare the poison by scraping the *oonta* vine (*Curarea tecunarum*) into a funnel of palm leaves (*mö*) from the forest. Mö leaves are intrinsically feminine. They are collected by women to line the inner roof of the longhouse and render it perfectly impermeable and hermetically closed. Mö leaves are also associated symbolically with the womb's blood lining. The funnel is placed above a small clay pot called *caanta*. Small quantities of water are slowly run over the funnel; when the *caanta* pot is full with black liquid, it is placed over the embers of the cooking hearth for several hours. Curare poison, simmered over the conjugal hearth, where all cooking takes place, is prepared in the midst of other domestic activities. No marked taboo or ritualized behavior relates to the preparation of curare, and there is no particular behavior expected from women (not even when menstruating) or from children (Rival 1996b). However, a man will not sleep with a woman other than his wife the night preceding curare making. Although men today have on the whole stopped hunting with blowguns and curare poison, they continue to make curare as a sign of malehood.

16. For an exhaustive critique of the inconsistencies in Collier and Rosaldo's (1981) argument, see Kelly (1993).

17. Other, rarer, forms of polygyny involve men with many sisters ending up taking several wives to ensure that all their sisters get married, or male orphans, who, finding it particularly difficult to find a spouse, mount a raid to capture wives. Captured wives will only remain with their abductor if several of them (i.e., sisters) are captured together and if their entire natal *nanicabo* was exterminated.

18. This is perhaps why Huaorani marriage is ritualized before the parents-to-be start procreating. By contrast, the common Amazonian practice is to a marital union official after a period of cohabitation and after the birth of one child.
19. *Affinity* in French and English has the similar connotation of proximity. According to my *Petit Bordas* dictionary, *affinité* has been used since the twelfth century to mean neighborhood. Incidentally, uxoriality (the condition of being a wife) has the same connotation. The *Oxford English Dictionary* states that "uxorial connection" has been used to mean neighborhood, a fact that further illustrates the semantic overlap between proximity, wifehood, and neighborhood. For the Huaorani, however, female cross-cousins are all but close neighbors. Interestingly, they could never be thought to be enemies either. Affinity as the closing distance between a man and the group in which he marries corresponds to the expectation of sharing substance and becoming alike. Alterity, or pure difference, which characterizes the unbreachable distance that seperates female cross-cousins, or, in other words, the nonrelationship between sisters-in-law, also characterizes the impossibility of alliance with *cohuori*.
20. This is exactly what occurs in situations of extreme autarky, as among the noncontacted Tagaeri group, for instance.
21. To this day, *pïï* men kill men, women, and children with spears made by themselves for this specific purpose.
22. Killing raids are always told by the victims and their kin, never by the instigators.
23. My classificatory sisters once showed me how this was done, and as they were putting a young infant on the pretend grave, they explained to me that the body soul of a buried speared victim who dies by suffocation does not go back to its birth place but stays right there.
24. "We call Huègöngui, our God, the Creator, *meme* (grandfather) and his spouse *Ñeñe* (grandmother)." Cahuitipe Wepe Baihua told me this myth on July 13, 1997.
25. An old widow is sheltered in a small house (not unlike that built by a bachelor who has passed the age of sharing a hammock with his younger siblings) built next to her *nanicabo*'s longhouse.
26. When a *nanicabo* moves to another site without leaving an old kin behind, men burn the house immediately in fear that it might be used as an abode by malevolent spirits.
27. In an often-told myth, the deity Sun is said to have sent his son to the Huaorani to give them the peach palm and stone axes and to teach them how

to carve hardwood in blowpipes and spears. In some versions, the Huaorani receive from Sun a magical tree that releases weapons already made.
28. They may also be omnivorous, but never carnivorous like the species involved in the predatory model.
29. *Huaorani* (true people) encompasses all the speakers of *huao terero* (Huaorani language) at the "tribal" level. *Huaomoni* (we-people) corresponds to endogamous networks.
30. In the doxic sense of accepted or given common sense used by Yanagisako and Delaney (1995).
31. I use Strathern's (1988: 228) expression, although she uses it to talk about women marrying virilocally.
32. To continue with the Melanesian parallel, would it be that the Amazonian uxorilocal husband is extractable from his natal kin by virtue of being owed to predatory cosmic forces? (Strathern 1988: 228).

CHAPTER 7

1. I revisited Toñampari in 2006 for the first time in twelve years to collect additional data for my study of Huaorani palm (*Bactris gasipaes*) management (Clement, Rival, and Cole 2009). During my doctoral fieldwork, more than half of the Huaorani population lived in Toñampari, where a *colegio* (a high school) opened in 1993 to offer secondary education to youth between fourteen and twenty-two who wished to further their studies beyond primary education. See High (2015) for ethnographic descriptions of Toñampari villagers.
2. *Astrocaryum chambira* is used to make many nets and, today, handicrafts for tourists.
3. Here are some examples taken from my field notes. **Color**: Huaorani prefer red, Quichua yellow fruit. **Consistency**: Huaorani prefer oily, Quichua starchy. **Festival styles**: Huaorani have many chonta palms and make big chonta-dinking festivals, but Quichua plant the palm only for their household needs. Zurita (2014: 162, 299) shows that in other villages, where the Quichua influence is less pronounced, people talk about contrasting practices, such as the fact that Huaorani prefer monocultures, while Quichua prefer polycultures. They also stress that their practices are better or more efficient than those of Quichua cultivators and say, for example, that mulching a new field is more efficient (and better) than burning it.

4. Tocari (cultural hero shaped as a red-crested woodpecker) plays an important role in one of the versions of the myth about the rebirth of the world I once recorded. In the aftermath of the big flood that killed everything except for a brother and a sister who escaped together in a hollow log, Tocari saves the world by creating hills out of the flat land prone to flooding. He does this by flying up and down piercing palm trees that stand in his way.
5. This includes, above all, birds, especially toucans and parrots; but it also includes agoutis, deer, peccaries, tapir, squirrels, and monkeys.
6. Amo stressed how this was unusual in Toñampari. Most other Huaorani preferred to follow the Quichua ways by planting fewer palms and felling them after seven or eight years. People had learned to appreciate the *palmito* (palm heart) and the grubs that develop on cut palms (see also Zurita 2014: 256).
7. Zurita (2014: 251) notes the importance of plants that know no seasonality in Huaorani culture, as these species, always available, allow them to survive when on the run from enemies. She mentions in particular a palm fruit, petomo (*Jessenia bataua*), on which I have also written (e.g., Rival 2009a), and obiyenka, young seedlings of *Astrocaryum chambira*.
8. See Wasserstrom and Bustamente (2015). Their synthesis of ethnohistorical data for the Ecuadorian Amazon focuses on the progressive role of the modern state and tends to simplify processes of tribalization and detribalization.
9. *Myoprocta pratti*, see also Zurita (2014: 240).
10. Zurita (2014: 240, 326) discusses the contrast of old/young and parent/child used in the conceptualization of such clumps. Her informants showed her examples of a "plant parent," from which "plant children" had developed naturally.
11. See Zurita (2014: 166–67) for other examples of planting rituals still practiced today. See Zurita (2014: 287) for examples of old village sites used as seed banks. And see Zurita (2014: 240) for examples of what she calls human/animal "alliances," that is coupled human and animal activities that foster natural abundance.
12. Lévi-Strauss gives interesting hints on the etymology and origin of the word *bricole*. In the fourteenth century, it meant *harness*, as it had come from the Italian word for a catapult with straps. During the sixteenth century, the word acquired a metaphorical meaning, and people used it to refer to the play of ducks and drakes; it became a synonym of zigzag, deceit, and fraud. The verb *bricoler*, which was coined during this period, took on all these metaphorical meanings. In the eighteenth century, *bricoler* was used to mean to throw or to manipulate with great dexterity. The word *bricolage* is a much more recent

invention that dates to the 1940s. It is used to mean more or less the same as the contemporary English abbreviation DIY (do-it-yourself). The anthropological definition recorded by the Petit Robert (work according to improvised techniques, and adapted to materials at hand and circumstances) appears to come straight from *La Pensée Sauvage* (Lévi-Strauss 1962).

13. "Monito memeiri mani omë quenquëre iñomo tomami quëgonanitapa mani omë yequene nangui impa quehuenani beye." (Our grandparents had a large territory; their territory was expansive; they worked and lived their forested land; they lived and worked well.) In this shorter expression, the anonymity of those whose past activities have transformed the land into high forest is emphasized: "durani huarani ahuene tei tei què." (Those who lived in ancient times worked the forest; they worked, worked, and this is why the forest today is ancient.").

14. Food sharing at feasts and *nanicabo*-food sharing are of a difference nature. The latter is characterized by repetitive giving away that crystallizes enduring social units. Feast goers do not share food; they jointly and liberally consume products from a natural source, such as a tree (see Rival 2002, Chapter 6).

15. The word for guest is *ne eñaca* (the one who is born), while the word for host is *ne ocöinga* (the one who is at home); see Chapters 4 and 6.

16. Dayuma, who died recently, worked for years alongside missionary Rachel Saint.

17. See Miller (2015) for an excellent example.

18. See Rival (2005) and Rival (2014). Rival (2015: 273) offers a critical discussion of the role attributed to scarce and circulating cosmic energy in the constitution of Amazonian personhood.

19. The Spanish term *pura familia* (exclusively kin) was used in conjunction with the Huaorani term *huaomoni*, which is discussed in Chapter 6.

20. There were at this particular moment in time a deer, monkeys of various species, and a baby peccary, which I did not see. My reactions to their presence were scrutinized, and my obvious pleasure at their sight taken as a sign that the system of attraction was working.

21. Toñampari is known for being the Huaorani community with the greatest number of interethnic marriages (see High 2015).

22. Toñampari's community center, by far the largest in Huaorani land, was built at great cost, as all the materials had to be transported by plane. It is an exact copy of the warehouses where planes are parked near Puyo in the airport that serves Huaorani communities.

23. Now that people travel to towns more frequently and often spend extensive periods of time away from their home communities, they often talk of being

a dentro (inside) or *a fuera* (outside). These Spanish expressions are inserted in Huaorani sentences, the former to inform that one is back home (i.e., living in one's community) and the latter to specify that one has moved to town. By contrast, when someone is planning to visit Bameno, the expression *omëre* (in the forest) is used.

24. Penti has a hard time convincing journalists and other cynics that Bameno's project "no es un show, es nuestra vida" (is not a show, it's our lives). See Chapter 9.
25. Quemperi, Penti's father-in-law, is a powerful shaman (Rival 2002: 78–79, 198).
26. By "intact" I do not mean unchanged. Bameno is not built on a hilltop but along the Cononaco River. Hunting is no longer restricted to the few animal species traditionally eaten, and crop cultivation is not tied to ceremonial life. What I mean by "intact," rather, is change that allows for the continuity of a certain type of relationship with the forest and a concerted refusal of missionary and oil influences.

CHAPTER 8

1. Manioc drinking ceremonies result from *created*, rather than *natural* abundance. As first noted in Chapter 4, the Huaorani word for guest is *ne eñaca* (the one who is born), while the word for host is *ne ocöinga* (the one who is at home). The host-guest relationship creates dynamic interactions between providers of natural abundance and consumers who request it. It operates in everyday social situations, as well as in the ritual context. See Chapter 6 for further details.
2. They are called *patas coloradas* (red feet) by the populace, after the color of their feet, which they painted with *achiote* (*Bixa orellana*).
3. Moipa was credited for many of the raids on outsiders that took place in the 1940s and 1950s. His fierceness also caused many internal dissensions and much intraethnic violence. Infuriated by the frontier, he enlarged his group, stole other men's women, refused to let his sons marry out, and forced his allies to support longer and more frequent war campaigns. He was finally killed during a festival over disagreements on marriage exchanges (Rival 1996a).
4. The term *tabado* (from the Spanish *trabajo*) was only used to refer to long-term or stable salaried occupations, such as teaching positions or the jobs young, schooled men got through their ethnic association.
5. The astonishing demand to be incorporated into the company delivery schedules clearly distinguished Huaorani dealings with the oil companies from

those of other indigenous groups. A Quichua, Shuar, or poor colonist community would approach the company to obtain funding to create a community hall, a school, or any other small development project. Requesting regular food deliveries was, to them, an absurd proposition. See Muratorio (1991: 133–40) for an account of Napo Runa work experience in prospecting for oil on Huaorani land.

6. See Nenquimo (2014: 88), who explains that the company felt that it had to deal with the entire nation to prevent intraethnic conflicts, as well as massive migration to the vicinity of its wells.

7. The quotes are from the *Orientation Manual* that was distributed to all Maxus employees in the 1990s (Maxus 1994). The "practical cases" discussed in Chapter 3 of the manual are aimed to alert Maxus employees to cultural differences and to the need to avoid creating dependent relations. For example, in Case # 4 (entitled "Miguel and the Turtle"), Maxus employees are asked to reflect on trade relations:

> CASE #4. MIGUEL AND THE TURTLE
>
> "Near a community, there was a Waorani who wanted to sell me a turtle," Miguel tells. He spoke a little Spanish, and I understood that he was selling it in order to buy food. I smiled and told him no. I felt rather guilty because I wasn't helping him to eat if I didn't buy the turtle, but I thought it was better not to give him any money. I didn't want to exchange the turtle for the jack knife I had in my pocket. Why didn't Miguel help the Wao?
>
> ANSWERS TO CASE #4.
>
> 1. Miguel knows that Maxus prohibits buying or trading with the indigenous people. Maxus has very well-defined programs to aid the Waorani, such as in matters of health, education, and community development.
> 2. Miguel could have been fired if he carried out the purchase or barter with the Waorani, also if he helped to transport live or hunted animals to sell.
> 3. The best way to help the Waorani is by respecting their culture and not buying objects or animals from them.

8. Studies funded and/or approved by Maxus included, among others, biodiversity surveys, archaeological research, ecological restoration projects, and anthropological and life history projects. It is now publicly known that blood

samples for DNA and human genome research were also collected without prior informed consent under Maxus's scientific research program.

9. This historical event was filmed by Chris Walker as part of his 1996 prize-winning documentary *Trinkets and Beads*. The documentary, which tells the story of how Maxus set out to convince the Huaorani people to allow drilling on their land, is one of the films the Huaorani most relish viewing. I have watched it with them on a number of occasions. They still regard the ceremony in which the agreement was signed as one of their great victories.

10. See Nárvaez (1996) for an analysis of the Maxus-ONHAE agreement from the perspective of Ecuador's petroleum development legislation. Nárvaez (2009) analyzes Repsol's annual report on corporate responsibility for the year 2010, which states that the company's goal is to help the Huaorani "to find the best ways of making use of their resources."

11. Gondecki's (2015, 641–60; 669–720; 727–28) recently completed doctoral thesis is especially commendable for its comprehensive approach to the complex representations of Huaorani culture, industrial pollution, and rainforest biological diversity that have emerged both in Ecuador and in the rest of the world over the last forty years. By using a conflict-resolution approach grounded within German political anthropological traditions, he shows how a detailed ethnography of conflicting understandings of industrial development and its sociocultural and environmental impacts may shed new light on the moral evaluations, political activism, and actions of a wide range of actors. Gondecki is particularly successful at showing the role of the media and of new communication technologies in linking actors at different scales and in creating unexpected and novel actor networks. In addition to a very comprehensive bibliography, Gondecki provides an impressive filmography, as well as comprehensive lists of documentaries, TV shows, webpages, multimedia documents, and so forth (pp. 641–660). He also provides a chronological list of conflicts from 1878 to 2013. The many activist documents reproduced are insightful, especially the letter to Maxus written during a Huaorani General Assembly a few months before the signature of the Maxus-ONHAE agreement.

12. The chapter concluded with the following remark. "The Huaorani consider themselves the guests of Maxus. Their inflated demand sharing requests cannot be fulfilled, as demand is what keeps natural abundance going. They may have little power over the future development of the oil industry in the Oriente, but by naturalizing the industry and denying all forms of exchange or trade with its numerous subsidiaries, contractors, and subcontractors, they

have reduced the power the oil companies may have over them to the precarious power of a feast giver whose generosity can only be artificial and short lived" (Rival 2000: 260).

13. For example, in April, 2014, a family traveled in haste from Bataboro to Tiguino (some 20 km away) to get their son, who was suffocating, checked by the medical doctor. The surgery was empty, and the doctor was absent. The little boy died. In grief, they returned to their village. The father, accompanied by male relatives, grabbed a bundle of spears and rushed back to Tiguino where they spear killed two highland workers and seriously injured a third one. The other workers fled in a panic and barricaded themselves in the oil pumping station. An infuriated crowd then proceeded to ransack the station. The workers were employed by a new state enterprise called Ecuador Estratégico, whose mission is to deliver aid directly funded by oil revenues under a new government social development program. The highland workers had been sent to these two Huaorani villages to build cement houses for Huaorani families, which are worth thousands of dollars each. Although families in Bataboro and Tiguino receive substantially more financial and material rewards than many other Huaorani communities (given their proximity to sizeable wells), any hint that the company is failing to respond to claims and requests triggers conflict.

14. The company was preparing a campaign to get the right to develop Block 16.

15. Further research would establish whether this perception constitutes a calculated equivocation. As mentioned in footnote 7, employees of Maxus Ecuador Inc. insisted that "MAXUS is a guest in the home of the Waorani, the rainforest. For this reason we must respect their culture, customs and territory" (Maxus 1994: 1). Section II.B.1 a few pages later specifies:

> II.B.1. HOW TO SHOW RESPECT TO THE WAORANI AND TO THEIR TERRITORY.
>
> 1.1. By respecting the people, their customs, their traditions, and ways of living the forest.
>
> You work for Maxus. You are a guest in Waorani territory. They expect you to show absolute respect to their customs, their belongings, their families, and, especially, their women. There are three important points that you should know:
>
> a) *We are guests*: The Waorani have allowed us to come into their home only for the purpose of working in the fields where oil is present. All

the trees, all the fruits that grow wild or that have been planted, all the animals, belong to the Waorani. Because you work for Maxus, you are not entitled to appropriate them.

b) *Avoid contacts with the indigenous population*: As mentioned in Maxus Ecuador Inc.'s Environmental Management Plan, you must try to avoid contacts with the indigenous population as much as possible. The officer in charge of Community Relations in the area is authorized to establish contacts. You must give immediate notice to your Supervisor about any attempted contacts by the Waorani.

c) *Respect their women*: Like all human beings, the Waorani are jealous with women. They marry very young, as of 12 or 13 years of age. Any insinuation could be interpreted as flirting. You must avoid these situations so that a cordial relationship can be maintained with your hosts.

16. "Some communities even receive prepared food three times a day as is the case in Dikaro (i.e., Dicaro), by way of the distribution of individual 'lunchboxes'" (Henningsen 2006: 66, 70).

17. The following anecdote provides further insight on Huaorani constructions of control. I once talked with the son of a Huaorani chief who was deeply involved in logging the Yasuní National Park with Colombian trade partners. The young man justified his family's dealings by saying that "the government controls oil; I control the timber." As for prestige, and although I have yet to speak personally with the Huaorani men who were jailed in 2013 and 2014, I suspect that they see their ordeal as an experience that enhances their fierceness and reputation, hence their prestige.

18. A social development expert from a U.S. nongovernmental organization (NGO), who had worked several years in poverty alleviation programs in Guayaquil and Quito before working with the Huaorani, told me that he saw no difference between the ways in which the poor in urban slums "handle their situation" and the Huaorani. He said that "the problems are the same, the people are the same, their expectations are the same." However, later on in the conversation, he mentioned he was at a loss with Huaorani expectations, which made his work very difficult. "I really don't understand their society.... They think that all the whites are glamorous and rich, with endless supplies of money and merchandise to give away.... It is as if they did not understand that they are poor.... And they don't know what it means to be wealthy either."

19. The YPF was an Argentine company that operated Block 16 for some years after Maxus and before Repsol.
20. This company was expressly created for the Huaorani feasibility project by Genesis Eurasia, an environmental services company specializing in new recovery technologies for old oil fields. Examples include trading projects linked to the Clean Development Mechanism and the development of wind farms on abandoned or reclaimed mine lands in the United States. Promotional materials that were given to me in 2008 describe the carbon credits trading activities developed by the Genesis Group for 2007–08:

    > In lieu of the global warming threat and the need for environmentally safe initiatives worldwide, Genesis developed various opportunities in the environmental sector.
    >
    > "One of the opportunities with tremendous potential is the carbon (CO_2) emission credits trading market.
    >
    > "In 2004 Genesis established Eco-Genesis Development Ltd. (EGD), a British Virgin Island Corporation. EGD has exclusive rights for 30 years to develop the resources located over 1.77 million acres of land owned by the Huaorani Indians in the Ecuadorian forest. EGD intends to certify and sell the carbon credits contained in the Huaorani rainforest to companies in need of carbon credits to offset emissions. EGD believes that this carbon credit investment opportunity is substantial both in scope and scale.
    >
    > "Ecuador is recognized as one of the twelve most diverse countries in the world with a tremendous varieties of trees. It is estimated that 20% of the world's plant species can be found in Ecuador, and this is largely due to its geographical and climatic diversity.
    >
    > "We believe that the Huaorani rainforest is a good target for forested sequestration of carbon credits. In addition, there is opportunity to create CDM projects once development begins. No significant commercial development has been done to date on the Huaorani land. The Clean Development Mechanism has recognized some forested land projects for certification."

21. Technical support consisted primarily of helping the Huaorani candidates prepare a portfolio of commercial and social projects. In their first year of training, the Huaorani would put together a number of business ideas for the building of green value chains in agriculture, fisheries, wood and non-timber forest products and ecotourism, as well as of carbon trading schemes, payments for ecosystem services mechanisms, and bioprospection projects, leading to their qualification as project planners (having received a *diploma*

en planificación de proyectos [diploma in project management]). Once this pre-university course was completed, in the second phase of the project, they would work toward a career in *gerencia empresarial* (business management) and receive a *diploma superior en diseño de empresas sustentables* (advanced diploma in the design of sustainable enterprises). They would then travel to the U.S. to present their project portfolio, and to create business partnerships. Among the investors EcoGenesis hoped to interest was the Chickasaw Nation, a North American tribe with, I was told, a business turnover of fifteen million dollars.

22. A Genesis Eurasia shareholder told me that "oil is no longer viable in Ecuador," while the director of FED said that "oil money is temporary."
23. See, for example, Conaghan (2011) and Ellner (2014).

CHAPTER 9

1. The UEA opened in the mid-2000s in Puyo, a small jungle town at the foothills of the Andes (e.g., Whitten 1985). At present, UEA has four programs: *ciencias agropecuarias* (agricultural sciences); *ingenierías de agroindustria* (food sciences); *ciencias ambientales* (environmental sciences); and *turismo* (tourism). See http://www.uea.edu.ec/, accessed on June 11, 2015.
2. These consultants also informed indigenous participants of new governmental norms that provide a framework for teaching anthropology; they referred to articles 57, 298, 344, 350–53, and 356–57 of Ecuador's most recent constitution. See http://www.educacionsuperior.gob.ec/proyecto-nacional-de-dialogo-de-saberes/ and http://ecuadoruniversitario.com/de-instituciones-del-estado/senescyt/la-senescyt-cuenta-con-una-coordinacion-de-saberes-ancestrales/, accessed on June 11, 2015.
3. "Gompote omë memeiri nëente quehuegaimamo" may be literally translated as "our land is our forebears' land; it is not to be taken away from us; we defend our land; it is where we always come back to live." This translation of ancestral knowledge is the one that those present at the event chose, though there are other ways of expressing such an abstract notion in Huaorani, or even to translate the expression reported here back into English or Spanish. The term *gompote* is particularly difficult to translate. It refers at once to the ethic of demand sharing (see Introduction), and to the right to refuse to share. *Gompote* means that the ethnic territory is not something Huaorani

people can let go of or readily share with non-Huaorani. It means that the Huaorani will defend their territory and will not let non-Huaorani invade or grab their homeland. As discussed in the introduction, a sociolinguistic study of contemporary Huaorani-Spanish bilingualism, especially in the context of interculturality translation work, is long overdue.

4. On the whole, such people tend to be ecotourists, journalists, writers, and artists rather than government officials, oil engineers, or missionaries.

5. The Channel 4 Tribal Wives Program filmed in Bameno is a popular hit with both young and old. People's favorite moment in the film is when Karen Morris-Lanz takes off her European clothes and appears in front of the camera *durani bai* (see Chapter 7 for a discussion of this term). See Rival (2015: 287–88) for a discussion of Taromenani bodies, and the fear they instill.

6. The only *cohuori* adornment Meñemo wanted was her bead necklace. When we met in the hotel where she was staying, she caressed my silver ring, and I passed it onto her finger as a sign of friendship. After I left, she took the ring off her finger to attach it onto her necklace. She wore the new clothes I had bought for the duration of the event; perhaps they protected her from the cold. However, she discarded the shoes as soon as we reached the university grounds.

7. Urban youths are usually ashamed of their Huaorani looks, and parents often fear that their children are turning *cohuori*. Huaorani youths spend a lot of time and energy on their appearance. From what I could judge, they work at looking "cool" according to specific aesthetic criteria, and it would be very interesting to understand their logic. Some young people aspire to look thin, beautiful, and dressed up, as other Ecuadorian urban middle-class young people do. Young women tend to keep their hair long and floating or gathered in chignons. They seem to value the practice of eating very little, and they seem to prefer what they perceive as healthy foreign food, such as packaged juices, nuts, or low-calorie biscuits. They also like sports clothing and equipment, white shoes, and stylish color combinations. On the whole, I have found that Huaorani youths look better dressed than other indigenous youths. The fact that they eat little and want to look thin goes hand-in-hand with their rejection of hunting, collecting, and agricultural activities. Many young women prefer not to have to prepare or drink manioc beer. Young men have no real hunting experience. They do not go to the forest as often as their parents do, and their mobility seems restricted to urban areas or other Huaorani villages. They want salaried jobs they find cool, such as tourist guides or project managers. I heard many adults comment that youths are ashamed of their parents

and of their ethnic origins. Several middle-aged men have told me that they do not wish to see young people at political meetings or involved in important decisions, as "they have no idea of how to defend the territory, given that they want to be *cohuori*." A study of aspirations and values among Huaorani youths, who form the majority of the population, is long overdue.

8. Some people translate culture as *moni quehuemano* (this is the way we live our lives) and traditional culture (*cultura típica* or *tener lo nuestro* in Spanish) as *monito nè, onko nè, monikinè* (the way we are at home, what we do, and have when at home). I have also heard people translate culture as *monito eya* (literally, "our clothes") when the meaning intended is material culture.

9. Presenters for the other nationalities essentially discussed the use of new communication technologies (such as writing, Facebook, or YouTube videos) to preserve their native languages and traditions.

10. Many of the Huentaro villagers had left their community for Gareno, which is located on one of the distant northern oil roads.

11. "Nos dan proyectos, reclamamos, nos dan otros proyectos, nos dan para que no jodemos." The original sentence does not have Spanish words for what I translated as "at least for a while." However, this is what is implied, given that the give-and-take implied (receiving, claiming, receiving) is conceived as an ongoing, unbreakable chain of demands.

12. I was told recently by a young Huaorani that the president of the ethnic organization NAWE (Nacionalidad Waorani del Ecuador, the new name for the Huaorani ethnic organization that replaced ONHAE [Organización Huaorani de la Amazonía Ecuatoriana] in 2008) "es hijo de Correa, no de las organizaciones no-gobernamentales" (a son of Correa, not a son of nongovernmental organizations).

13. The most burning policy issues concern the expansion of oil extraction, the generalization of forest conservation programs, and the multiplication and diversification of conditional social welfare schemes.

14. If people readily speak of divisions in Huaorani communities between those who are pro-oil and those who are proconservation or, for that matter, of those who are pro-Correa and those who are *en contra* (oppositional), such division is often presented in relational terms rather than in terms of substantial content. What matters is the existence of a polarization between camps, which the Huaorani will do everything to avoid, but which they recognize as an inherent characteristic of those they interact with who try to get them on their side.

15. To be civilized increasingly involves living with people who are not only non-kin, but also members of other (and competing) ethnic groups, such as the Shuar and the Quichua. People must express their civilized identity through complex forms of peace building and struggle; they learn to cope with new forms of illness, misery, and misfortune, in particular interethnic sorcery and witchcraft (see High 2015).
16. See Santos-Granero (2015) for a recent discussion of indigenous ideas about well-being and public wealth in lowland South America.
17. Both an abstract notion and a concrete reality, money is *centavo* (cent), or *tucuri* (*tocodi*), a derivative of *sucre*, Ecuador's former currency. Money is what foreigners use to access goods that people would rather access directly through barter or gift exchange. Money does not change the fact that wealth continues to be wealth in people, not accumulation of material wealth. The major concern, by far, is health as a form of individual and collective wealth, and much of the money people want and need is used to pay hospital bills and other health-related costs.
18. I was working with a large USAID-funded conservation program, which covered the Yasuní National Park and the Cotacachi-Cayapas Ecological Reserve (e.g., Rival 2003).
19. This process is reckoned inevitable by some of my Ecuadorian friends who point to the fact that there are on average fifty Quichua for each Huaorani. I still think that the "Quichuasization" of a village, such as Toñampari, is better explained through the life histories of its leaders than through demographics (Rival 1992). When she returned to Huaorani land in the company of North American missionaries, Dayuma (Toñampari's great leader) was as much a Quichua as she was a Huaorani. A few weeks before she died, I was told by a Huaorani friend that she no longer spoke Huaorani, and only communicated in Quichua and in Spanish.

REFERENCES

Acosta, Alberto. 1996. *El Fracaso de los Contratos de Prestación de Servicios.* Quito, Ecuador: ILDIS.

Aguirre, Milagros. 2007. *¡A Quién le Importan Esas Vidas!: Un Reportaje sobre la Tala Ilegal en el Parque Nacional Yasuní.* Quito, Ecuador: Cicame.

Albán, Dayuma. 2008. "Parto y Terapia entre los Waorani de Tigüino." BA thesis. PUCE, Quito, Ecuador.

Albert, Bruce. 1985. "Temps du Sang, Temps des Cendres: Représentation de la Maladie, Système Rituel et Espace Politique chez les Yanomami du Sud-Est (Amazonie Brésilienne)." PhD diss., Université Paris Ouest Nanterre La Défense, Nanterre.

Alvarez, Katy. 2005. "Relaciones de Poder entre Comunidades Indígenas y Compañías Petroleras en el Pororiente Ecuatoriano. Una Lectura desde Michel Foucault." BA thesis. Ecuador's Central University, Quito.

———. 2009. "El Efecto del Contacto de la Sociedad Nacional en las Practicas Culturales Entorno a la Muerte en los Waorani." MA thesis. FLACSO Sede Ecuador, Quito, Ecuador.

———. 2012. "Investigación Pueblos Aislados. Situación del Grupo Armadillo-Cononaco Chico-Vía Tigüino." Report for Fundación Pachamama. Quito, Ecuador.

Arcand, Bernard. 1981. "The Negritos and the Penan Will Never Be Cuiva." *Folk* 23: 37–43.

Arhem, Kaj. 1981. *Makuna Social Organization: A Study in Descent, Alliance, and the Formation of Corporate Groups in the Northwest Amazon.* Uppsala: Acta Universitatis Upsaliensis.

———. 1987. "Wives for Sisters: The Management of Marriage Exchange in Northwest Amazonia." In *Makuna Natives and Neighbors in South America: Anthropological Essays*, edited by O. Skar and F. Salomon, 130–177. Göteborg: Etnografiska Museum.

Astuti, Rita. 1998. "It's a Boy, It's a Girl! Reflections on Sex and Gender in Madagascar and Beyond." In *Bodies and Persons: Comparative Perspectives from Africa and Melanesia*, edited by Michael Lambek and Andrew Strathern, 29–52. Cambridge: Cambridge University Press.

Atran, Scott. 1999. "Itzaj Maya Folkbiological Taxonomy: Cognitive Universals and Cultural Particulars." In *Folkbiology*, edited by D. Medin and S. Atran, 119–203. Cambridge, Mass.: The MIT Press.

Atran, Scott, D. L. Medin, and N. O. Ross. 2005. "The Cultural Mind: Environmental Decision Making and Cultural Modeling Within and Across Populations. *Psychological Review* 112(4): 744–76.

Avilés, M. D. 2008. "Narratives of Resistance. An Ethnographic View of the Emergence of the Huaorani Women's Association in the Ecuadorian Amazon." MA thesis, University of Florida, Gainsville.

Baeta, Miream, Carolina Núñez, Fabricio González-Andrade, C. Sosa, Y. Casalod, and Miguel Bolea. 2009. "Mitochondrial Analysis Revealed High Homogeneity in the Waorani Population: The Last Nomadic Group of Hunter-Gatherers from Ecuador." *Forensic Science International: Genetic Supplement Series* 2: 313–14.

Bahuchet, Serge, D. McKey, and I. de Garine. 1991. "Wild Yams Revisited: Is Independence from Agriculture Possible for Rainforest Hunter-Gatherers?" *Human Ecology* 19(2): 213–43.

Bailey, R., G. Head, M. Jenike, B. Owen, R. Rechtman, and E. Zechenter. 1989. "Hunting and Gathering in a Tropical Rain Forest: Is It Possible?" *American Anthropologist* 91: 59–82.

Bailey, R., and T. Headland. 1991. The Tropical Rainforest: Is It a Productive Environment for Human Foragers?" *Human Ecology* 19: 261–85.

Balbus, I. 1982. *Marxism and Domination: A Neo-Hegelian, Feminist, Psychoanalytic Theory of Sexual, Political, and Technological Liberation*. Princeton, NJ: Princeton University Press.

Balée, William. 1988a. "The Ka'apor Indian Wars of Lower Amazonia, ca. 1825–1928." In *Dialectics and Gender*, edited by R. R. Randolph, D. Schneider, and M. N. Diaz, 155–69. Boulder, Col.: Westview Press.

———. 1988b. "Indigenous Adaptation to Amazonian Palm Forests." *Principes* 32 (2): 47–54.

———. 1988c. "Indigenous Adaptation to Amazonian Palm Forests." *Principes* 32 (2): 47–54.

———. 1989. "The Culture of Amazonian Forests." In *Resource Management in Amazonia: Indigenous and Folk Strategies*, edited by D. Posey and W. Balée. Bronx, NY: New York Botanical Garden. *Advances in Economic Botany* 7: 1–21.

———. 1992. "People of the Fallow: A Historical Ecology of Foraging in Lowland South America." In *Conservation of Neotropical Forests—Working from Traditional Resource Use*, edited by K. Redford and C. Padoch, 35–57. New York: Columbia University Press.

———. 1993. "Indigenous Transformation of Amazonian Forests: An Example from Maranhão, Brazil." In *La Remontée de l'Amazone*, edited by A. C. Taylor and P. Descola. *L'Homme* 126–28 XXXIII (2–4): 235–58.

———. 1994. *Footprints of the Forest. Ka'apor Ethnobotany—The Historical Ecology of Plant Utilization by an Amazonian People*. New York: Columbia University Press.

———. 1995. "Historical Ecology of Amazonia." In *Indigenous Peoples and the Future of Amazonia: An Ecological Anthropology of an Endangered World*, edited by L. Sponsel, 97–110. Tucson: University of Arizona Press.

———. 1996. "On the Probable Loss of Plant Names in the Guajá Language (Eastern Amazonian Brazil)." In *Ethnobiology in Human Welfare*, edited by S. K. Jain, 473–81. New Delhi: Deep Public.

———, ed. 1998a. *Advances in Historical Ecology*. New York: Columbia University Press.

———. 1998b. "Historical Ecology." In *Advances in Historical Ecology*, edited by W. Balée, 13–29. New York: Columbia University Press.

———. 1999. "Sirionó." In *The Cambridge Encyclopedia of Hunters and Gatherers*, edited by R. Lee and R. Daly, 77–85. Cambridge: Cambridge University Press.

———. 2006. "The Research Programme of Historical Ecology." *Annual Review of Anthropology* 35: 75–98.

———. 2013. *Cultural Forests of the Amazon: A Historical Ecology of People and Their Landscapes*. Tuscaloosa: University of Alabama Press.

———. 2014. "Historical Ecology and the Explanation of Diversity: Amazonian Case Studies." In *Applied Ecology and Human Dimensions in Biological Conservation*, edited by L. M. Verdade, M. C. Lyra-Jorge, and C. I. Piña, 19–33. Berlin Heidelberg: Springer-Verlag.

Balée, William, and Clarke Erickson, eds. 2006. *Time and Complexity in Historical Ecology: Studies in the Neotropical Lowlands*. New York: Columbia University Press.

Balée, William, Denise Schaan, James Whitaker, and Rosangêla Holanda. 2014. "Florestas Antrópicas no Acre: Inventário Florestal no Geoglifo Três Vertentes, Acrelândia." *Amazônica* 6(1): 140–69.

Barker, Graeme, and Monica Janowski, eds. 2011. *Why Cultivate? Anthropological and Archaeological Approaches to Foraging-Farming Transitions in Southeast Asia.* Cambridge: McDonald Institute for Archaeological Research.

Barlow, J., T. A. Gardner, A. C. Lees, L. Parry, and C. A. Peres. 2012. "How Pristine Are Tropical Forests? An Ecological Perspective on the Pre-Columbian Human Footprint in Amazonia and Implications for Contemporary Conservation." *Biological Conservation* 151(1): 45–49.

Barnard, Alan, ed. 2004. *Hunter-Gatherers in History, Archaeology, and Anthropology.* Oxford: Berg.

———. 2012. *Genesis of Symbolic Thought.* Cambridge: Cambridge University Press.

Barnard, Alexander Vosick. 2011. "We Are the Lungs of the World: Popular Environmentalism and the Local Politics of Climate Change in the Ecuadorian Amazon." MPhil thesis. University of Oxford.

Barsh, R. L. 1994. "Indigenous Peoples in the 1990s: From Object to Subject of International Law." *Harvard Human Rights Journal* 7: 33–86.

Basso, Ellen. 1973. *The Kalapalo Indians of Central Brazil.* New York: Holt, Rinehart, and Winston.

Beckerman, Stephen, P. I. Erickson, J. Yost, J. Regalado, L. Jaramillo, and C. S. Sparks. 2009. "Life Histories, Blood Revenge, and Reproductive Success among the Waorani of Ecuador." *Proceedings of the National Academy of Science of the USA* 106(20): 8134–39.

Beckerman, Stephen, and James Yost. 2007. "Upper Amazonian Warfare." In *Latin American Indigenous Warfare and Ritual Violence*, edited by Richard J. Chacon and R. G. Mendoza, 142–79. Tucson: University of Arizona Press.

Belaúnde, Luisa. 2000. "The Convivial Self and the Fear of Anger Amongst the Aropai of Amazonian Peru." In *The Anthropology of Love and Anger: The Aesthetics of Conviviality in Native Amazonia*, edited by Joanna Overing and Alan Passes, 209–20. London: Routledge.

Bellier, Irène. 1991. *El Temblor y la Luna. Ensayo sobre las Relaciones entre las Mujeres y los Hombres Mai Huna.* Quito: Abya Yala.

———. 1993. "Réflexion sur la Question du Genre dans les Sociétés Amazoniennes." *L'Homme*, 126–28: 517–26.

Bellwood, Peter. 2005. *First Farmers: The Origins of Agricultural Societies.* Oxford: Blackwell.

Berlin, Brent. 1992. *Ethnobiological Classification: Principles of Categorization of Plants and Animals in Traditional Societies.* Princeton, NJ: Princeton University Press.

———. 1999. "How a Folkbotanical System can be both Natural and Comprehensive: One Maya Indian's View of the Plant World." In *Folkbiology*, edited by D. Medin and S. Atran, 71–89. Cambridge, Mass: MIT Press.

Bessire, Lucas. 2014. *Behold the Black Caiman: A Chronicle of Ayoreo Life.* Chicago: University of Chicago Press.

Beuchat, Henri, and Marcel Mauss. (1906) 1979. *Seasonal Variations of the Eskimo: A Study in Social Morphology.* Translated by J. Fox. London: Routledge and Kegan Paul.

Bidou, Patrice. 2001. *Le Mythe de Tapir Shamane. Essai d'Anthropologie Psychanalitique.* Paris: Odile Jacob.

Bird-David, Nurit. 1990. "The Giving Environment: Another Perspective on the Economic System of Gatherer-Hunters." *Current Anthropology* 31: 183–96.

———. 1992a. "Beyond 'The Original Affluent Society': A Culturalist Reformulation." *Current Anthropology* 33(1): 25–47.

———. 1992b. "Beyond 'the Hunting and Gathering Mode of Subsistence': Culture-Sensitive Observations on the Nayaka and Other Modern Hunter-Gatherers." *Man* 27: 19–44.

———. 1999. "'Animism' Revisited: Personhood, Environment, and Relational Epistemology." *Current Anthropology* 40(Supplement): S 69–91.

Blaser, Mario. 2004. "Life Projects: Indigenous Peoples' Agency and Development." In *The Way of Development: Indigenous Peoples, Life Projects, and Globalisation*, edited by M. Blaser, H. Feit, and G. McRae, 26–45. London: Zed Books.

Bloch, Maurice. 1986. *From Blessing to Violence: History and Ideology in the Circumcision Ritual of the Merina of Madagascar.* Cambridge: Cambridge University Press.

———. 1992. "Birth and the Beginning of Social Life Among the Zafimaniry of Madagascar." In *Coming into Existence: Birth and Metaphors of Birth*, edited by A. Göran, 71–91. Gothenburg: Institute for Advanced Studies in Social Anthropology.

———. 2000. "A Well-Disposed Social Anthropologist's Problems with Memes." In *Darwinizing Culture: The Status of Memetics as a Science*, edited by R. Aunger, 189–204. Oxford: Oxford University Press.

———. 2005. "Questions Not to Ask of Malagasy Carvings." In *Essays on Cultural Transmission*, edited by M. Bloch, 39–44. Oxford: Berg.

Bloch, Maurice, and Susan Guggenheim. 1981. "Compadrazgo, Baptism, and the Symbolism of a Second Birth." *Man NS* 16(3): 376–86.

Bonilla, Oiara. 2007. "Des Proies si Desirables. Soumission et Prédation pour les Paumari d'Amazonie Brésilienne." PhD diss., Ecole des Hautes Etudes en Sciences Sociales (EHESS), Paris.

Boster, James, James Yost, and Catherine Peeke. 2004. "Rage, Revenge, and Religion: Honest Signalling of Aggression and Nonaggression in Waorani Coalitional Violence." *Ethos* 31(4): 471–94.

Bourdieu, Pierre. 1977. *Outline of a Theory of Practice*. Translated by R. Nice. New York: Cambridge University Press.

Boyer, Pascal. 1993. "Cognitive Processes and Cultural Representations." In *Cognitive Aspects of Religious Symbolism*, edited by P. Boyer, 1–47. Cambridge: Cambridge University Press.

Bristow, Joseph. 1997. *Sexuality. The New Critical Idiom*. London: Routledge.

Brown, Cecil H. 1985. "Mode of Subsistence and Folk Biological Taxonomy." *Current Anthropology* 26(1): 43–64.

———. 1986. "The Growth of Ethnobiological Nomenclature." *Current Anthropology* 27(1): 1–18.

Busby, Cecilia. 1995. "Permeable and Partible Persons: A Comparative Analysis of Gender and Body in South India and Melanesia." *Journal of the Royal Anthropological Institute* 3(2): 261–78.

Butler, Juliet. 1993. *Bodies that Matter: On the Discursive Limits of "Sex."* New York: Routledge.

Butt Colson, Audrey. 1975. "Birth Customs of the Akawaio." In *Studies in Social Anthropology: Essays in Memory of E. E. Evans-Pritchard*, edited by J. Beattie and G. Lienhardt, 285–309. Oxford: Clarendon.

Cabodevilla, Miguel Angel. 1994. *Los Huaorani en la Historia de los Pueblos del Oriente*. Coca: CICAME.

———. 1996 Coca. *La Región y sus Historias, Vicariato Apostólico del Aguarico*. Coca: CICAME.

———. 2004. *El Exterminio de los Pueblos Ocultos. Vicariato Apostólico del Aguarico*. Coca: CICAME.

———. 2013. *La Massacre . . . Qué Nunca Existió? En Una Tragedia Ocultada*, edited by Massimo de Marchi, M. Aguirre, and M. A. Cabodevilla, 21–140. Coca: CICAME.

Cabodevilla, Miguel Angel, and M. Berraondo, eds. 2005. *Pueblos no Contactados ante el Reto de los Derechos Humanos. Un Camino de Esperanza para los Tagaeri y Taromenani*. Quito: CICAME and CEDES.

Canguilhem, George. 1975. *La Connaissance de la Vie*. Paris: Librairie J. Vrin.

Cardoso, S., M. A. Alfonso-Sánchez, F. González-Andrade, L. Valverde, A. Odriozola, and A. M. Pérez-Miranda. 2008. "Mitochondrial DNA in Huaorani (Ecuadorian Amerindians): A New Variant in Haplogroup A2." *Forensic Science International: Genetic Supplement Series* 1: 269–270.

Cardoso, S., M. A. Alfonso-Sánchez, L. Valverde, D. Sánchez, M. T. Zarrabeitia, A. Ordriozola, B. Martínez-Jarreta, and M. M. de Pancorbo. 2012. "Genetic Uniqueness of the Waorani Tribe from the Ecuadorian Amazon." *Heredity* 108: 609–15.

Carlstein, Tommy. 1982. *Time Resources, Society, and Ecology: On the Capacity for Human Interaction in Space and Time.* Vol. 1. London: George Allen and Unwin Hymen.

Carsten, Janet. 1995. "The Substance of Kinship and the Heat of the Hearth: Feeding, Personhood, and Relatedness Among Malays in Pulau Langkawi." *American Ethnologist* 22(2): 223–41.

Carruthers, Peter. 2002. "The Cognitive Functions of Language." *Brain and Behavioral Sciences* 25: 657–726.

Cepek, Michael. 2012. "The Loss of Oil: Constituting Disaster in Amazonian Ecuador." *Journal of Latin American and Caribbean Anthropology* 17(3): 393–412.

Cerón, Carlos E., and C. G. Montalvo. 1998. *Ethnobotánica de los Huaorani de Quehueiri-Ono, Napo, Ecuador.* Quito: Abya Yala.

Chase, A. K. 1989. "Domestication and Domiculture in Northern Australia: A Social Perspective." In *Foraging and Farming: The Evolution of Plant Exploitation*, edited by D. R. Harris and G. C. Hillman, 42–54. London: Unwin Hyman.

Cipolletti, María Susana. 2002. "El Testimonio de Joaquina Grefa, una Cautiva Quichua entre los Huaorani (Ecuador 1945)." *Journal de la Société des Américanistes* 88: 111–35.

Cleary, David. 1993. "After the Frontier: Problems with Political Economy in the Modern Brazilian Amazon." *Journal of Latin American Studies* 25: 331–49.

Clement, Charles. 1988. "Domestication of the Pejibaye (*Bactris gasipaes*): Past and Present." *Advances in Economic Botany* 6: 155–74.

———. 1992. "Domesticated Palms." *Principes* 36(2): 70–78.

———. 1999. "1492 and the Loss of Amazonian Crop Genetic Resources: I (The Relation Between Domestication and Human Population Decline) and II (Crop Biogeography at Contact)." *Economic Botany* 53(2): 177–216.

———. 2014. "Landscape Domestication and Archaeology." In *Encyclopedia of Global Archaeology*, edited by C. Smith, 4388–94. New York: Springer.

Clement, Charles, L. Rival, and D. Cole. 2009. "Domestication of Peach Palm (*Bactris gasipaes* Kunth): The Roles of Human Mobility and Migration." In *The Ethnobiology of Mobility, Displacement, and Migration in Indigenous Lowland South America*, edited by Miguel Alexiades, 117–40. Oxford: Berghahn Books.

Colchester, Marcus. 1984. "Rethinking Stone Age Economics: Some Speculations Concerning the Pre-Columbian Yanoama Economy." *Human Ecology* 12: 291–314.

Colleoni, Paola. "The Self and the Other in Amazonia: Indigenous Encounters with the 'Frontier.'" Graduate School of International Development Studies. Rolskinde University, Denmark. PhD diss., in progress.

Collier, Jane, and Michelle Rosaldo. 1981. "Politics and Gender in Simple Societies." In *Sexual Meanings: The Cultural Construction of Gender and Sexuality*, edited by S. Ortner and H. Whitehead, 275–329. Cambridge: Cambridge University Press.

Comaroff, Jean, and John Comaroff. 1992. *Ethnography and the Historical Imagination*. Chicago: Chicago University Press.

Conaghan, Catherine M. 2011. "Ecuador: Rafael Correa and the Citizens' Revolution." In *The Resurgence of the Latin American Left*, edited by Steven Levitsky and Kenneth M. Roberts, 260–83. Baltimore: Johns Hopkins University Press.

Costa, Luiz. 2009. "Worthless Movement: Agricultural Regression and Mobility." *Tipití* 7(2): 151–80.

Crawley, E. (1902) 1927. *The Mystic Rose: A Study of Primitive Marriage and of Primitive Thought in Its Bearing on Marriage*. Vol. 2. London: Methuen and Co. Ltd.

Crocker, Christopher. 1969. "Reciprocity and Hierarchy Among the Eastern Bororo." *Man NS* 4(1): 44–58.

———. 1985. *Vital Souls: Bororo Cosmology, Natural Symbolism, and Chamánism*. Tucson: University of Arizona Press.

Da Matta, Roberto. 1982. *A Divided World: Apinayé Social Structure*. Translated by A. Campbell. Harvard: Harvard University Press.

Davis, Wade. 1997. *One River—Science, Adventure, and Hallucinogenics in the Amazon Basin*. London: Simon and Schuster.

Davis, Wade, and James Yost. 1983a. "The Ethnomedicine of the Waorani of Amazonian Ecuador." *Journal of Ethnopharmacology* 9(2): 272–97.

———. 1983b. "The Ethnobotany of the Waorani of Eastern Ecuador." *Botanical Museum Leaflets* 3: 159–211.

Dayot, Julie. 2014. "Beyond Indigenous People's Responses to Oil Extraction: The Analysis of a Struggle of Valuation in the Ecuadorian Amazon." MPhil thesis. University of Oxford.

De Marchi, Massimo, Milagros Aguirre, and Miguel Angel Cabodevilla. 2013. *Una Tragedia Ocultada*. Quito: CICAME.

Denevan, William. 1992. "The Pristine Myth: The Landscape of the Americas in 1492." *Annals of the Association of American Geographers* 82: 369–82.

———. 1996. "A Bluff Model of Riverine Settlement in Prehistoric Amazonia." *Annals of the Association of American Geographers* 86: 654–81.

———. 2001. *Cultivated Landscapes of Native Amazonia and the Andes*. New York: Oxford University Press.

Descola, Philippe. 1986. *La Nature Domestique. Symbolisme et Praxis dans l'Écologie des Achuars*. Paris: Ed. de la Maison des Sciences de l'Homme.

———. 1993. "Les Affinités Sélectives: Alliance, Guerre et Prédation dans l'Ensemble Jivaro." *L'Homme* 126–28: 171–90.

———. 1996. "Constructing Natures: Symbolic Ecology and Social Practice." In *Nature and Society: Anthropological Perspectives*, edited by P. Descola and G. Pálsson, 82–102. London: Routledge.

Diamond, Jared. 1997. *Guns, Germs, and Steel: A Short History of Everybody for the Last 13,000 Years*. London: Vintage.

Diamond, Jared, and Peter Bellwood. 2003. "Farmers and Their Languages: The First Expansions." *Science* 300(April 25): 597–603.

Dickinson, Connie. 2002. "Complex Predicates in Tsafiki." PhD diss., University of Oregon.

Doughty, C., F. Lu, and M. Sorensen. 2010. "Crude, Cash, and Culture Change: The Huaorani of Amazonian Ecuador." *Concilience, the Journal of Sustainable Development* 3(1): 18–32.

Durkheim, Emile. 1898. "La Prohibition de l'Inceste et ses Origines." *L'Année Sociologique* 1: 1–70.

Elden, Stuart, and Eduardo Mendieta, eds. 2011. *Reading Kant's Geography*. Albany: State University of New York Press.

Elias, Marianne, Laura Rival, and Doyle McKey. 2000. "Perception and Management of Cassava (Manihot esculenta Crantz) Diversity Among Makushi Amerindians of Guyana (South America)." *Journal of Ethnobiology* 20(2): 239–65.

Ellen, Roy. 1994. "Modes of Subsistence: Hunting and Gathering to Agriculture and Pastoralism." In *Companion Encyclopedia of Anthropology: Humanity, Culture, and Social Life*, edited by T. Ingold, 197–225. London: Routledge.

———. 1999. "Models of Subsistence and Ethnobiological Knowledge: Between Extraction and Cultivation in Southeast Asia." In *Folkbiology*, edited by D. L. Medin and S. Atran, 91–117. Cambridge, Mass: MIT Press.

Ellner, Steve, ed. 2014. *Latin America's Radical Left: Challenges and Complexities of Political Power in the Twenty-First Century*. Lanham, MD: Rowman and Littlefield.

Elwin, Verrier. 1947. *The Muria and Their Ghotul*. Oxford: Oxford University Press.

Erikson, Clarke. 2000. "An Artificial Landscape-Scale Fishery in the Bolivian Amazon." *Nature* 408: 190–93.

Erikson, Mark. 2005. "Evolutionary Thought and the Current Clinical Understanding of Incest." In *Inbreeding, Incest, and the Incest Taboo: The State of Knowledge at the Turn of the Century*, edited by A. Wolf and W. H. Durham, 161–89. Stanford: Stanford University Press.

Erikson, Philippe. 1984. "De l'Apprivoisement à l'Approvisionnement: Chasse, Alliance, et Familiarisation en Amazonie Amérindienne." *Techniques et Cultures* 9: 105–40.

———. 2004. "La Face Cachée de l'Ancestralité: Masques et Affinité chez les Matis d'Amazonie Brésilienne." *Journal de la Société des Américanistes* 90(1): 119–142.

Escobar, Kelly. 2012. "Cuando los Limites de las Ciencias y los Senderos de Cacería se Entrecruzan: Una Etnografía de Laboratorios Científicos Amazónicos en Asocio con Comunidades Autoctonas Locales." PhD diss., Université de Liège, Belgium.

Evans-Pritchard, E. E. 1940. *The Nuer*. Oxford: Clarendon Press.

Ewart, Elizabeth. 2013. *Space and Society in Central Brazil: A Panará Ethnography*. London: Bloomsbury.

Fausto, Carlos. 2001. *Inimigos Fiéis. História, Guerra e Xamanismo na Amazônia*. São Paulo: EDUSP.

———. 2007. "Feasting on People." *Current Anthropology* 48(4): 497–530.

———. 2008. "Donos Demais: Maestria e Dominio na Amazonia." *Mana* 14(2): 329–366.

Fawcett, A. Z. 2012. "Documenting Language, Culture, and Cognition: Language and Space Among the Waorani." BA thesis. Bryn Mawr College.

Feely-Harnick, Gillian. 2002. "'Communities of Blood': The Natural History of Kinship in Nineteenth-Century America." *Journal of the Society for Comparative Study of Society and History* 41: 215–62.

Ferguson, Brian. 1988. "War and the Sexes in Amazonia." In *The Dialectics of Gender*, edited by R. Randolph and D. M. Schneider, 136–55. Boulder, Col: Westview Press.

———. 1995. *Yanomami Warfare: A Political History*. Santa Fe: School of American Research.

Ferret, Carole. 2012. "Vers une Anthropologie de l'Action. André-Georges Haudricourt et l'Efficacité Technique." *L'Homme* 202: 113–40.

Feser, Heiko. 1999. "Die Huaorani auf den Wegen ins neue Jahrtausend." PhD diss., University de Friburgo. Publicada en Münster por Lit Verlag.

Fine-Dare, Kathleen. 2013. "(Neo) Indigenismo and the Transculturative Praxis of Ethnogenesis: A Case Study from Urban Ecuador." In *Indigenous and Afro-Ecuadorians Facing the Twenty-First Century*, edited by Marc Becker, 7–33. Cambridge: Cambridge Scholars Publishing.

Finer, Matt, B. Babbitt, S. Novoa, F. Ferrarese, S. E. Pappalardo, M. de Marchi, M. Saucedo, and A. Kumar. 2015. "Future of Oil and Gas Development in the Western Amazon." *Environmental Resources Letter* 10 (2015, 024003): 1–7. doi: 10.1088/1748-9326/10/2/024003.

Fock, Niels. 1963. *Waiwai: Religion and Society of an Amazonian Tribe*. Natural Museum of Denmark Ethnographical Series 8.

Foucault, Michel. 1978. *The History of Sexuality. Vol. I: An Introduction*. New York: Random House.

Fowler, C. S. 1972. "Comparative Numic Ethnobiology." PhD diss., University of Pittsburgh.

Franzen, M. 2006. "Evaluating the Sustainability of Hunting: A Comparison of Harvest Profiles Across Three Huaorani Communities." *Environmental Conservation* 33: 36–45.

Franzen, M., and J. Eaves. 2007. "Effect of Market Access on Sharing Practices Within Two Huaorani Communities." *Ecological Economics* 63: 776–85.

Frazer, James. 1910. *Totemism and Exogamy*. London: MacMillan.

Freud, Sigmund. (1950) 1983. *Totem and Taboo*. London: Ark Paperbacks.

Fuentes, Berta. 1997. *Huaomoni, Huarani, Cowudi. Una Aproximación a los Huaorani en la Practica Politica Multi-étnica Ecuatoriana*. Quito: Abya Yala.

Gardner, Paul. 1966. "Symmetric Respect and Memorate Knowledge: The Structure and Ecology of Individualistic Culture." *Southwestern Journal of Anthropology* 22: 389–415.

———. 2001. "Rethinking Foragers' Handling of Environmental and Subsistence Knowledge." Paper presented at the 7th CHAGS Conference, Edinburgh, July 2001.

Gell, Simeran. 1992. *The Ghotul in Muria Society*. London: Harwood Academic.

Gentry, A. H. 1988. "Tree Species Richness of Upper Amazonian Forests." *Proceedings of the National Academy of Sciences* 85(1): 156–59.

Godelier, Maurice. (1973) 1982. *La Production des Grands Hommes*. Paris: Fayard.

Gondecki, Philip. 2006. "Huaorani, Öl, and Umweltschutz: Steteguen und Allianzen im Sozio-Ökologischen Konflikt der Erdölförderung im Ecuadorianischen Oriente." MPhil thesis. University of Bonn.

———. 2015. "Wir Verteidigen Unseren Wald: Vom lokalen Widerstand zum Globalen Medienaktivismus der Waorani im Konflikt Zwischen Erdölförderung und Umweltschutz im Yasuni im Ecuadorianischen Amazonastiefland." PhD diss., University of Bonn.

Gordillo, Gastón. 2014. *Rubble: The Afterlife of Destruction*. Durham, NC: Duke University Press.

Gow, P. 1991. *Of Mixed Blood: Kinship and History in Peruvian Amazonia*. Oxford: Clarendon Press.

Gregor, Thomas. 1985. *Anxious Pleasure: The Sexual Lives of an Amazonian People*. Chicago: University of Chicago Press.

Grenand, Françoise. 1984. "La Longue Attente ou la Naissance à la Vie dans une Société Tupi." *Journal de la Société Suisse des Américanistes* 48: 13–27.

Griffiths, Thomas. 2001. "Finding One's Body: Relationships Between Cosmology and Work in North-West Amazonia." In *Beyond the Visible and the Material: The Amerindianization of Society in the Work of Peter Rivière*, edited by L. Rival and N. Whitehead, 247–62. Oxford: Oxford University Press.

Grinker, Roy. 1994. *Houses in the Rainforest: Ethnicity and Inequality Among Farmers and Foragers in Central Africa*. Berkeley: University of California Press.

Gudeman, Stephen. 1971. "The Compadrazgo as a Reflection of the Natural and Spiritual Person." *Proceedings of the Royal Anthropological Institute*, 45–71.

Guillaumin, C. 1996. "The Practice of Power and Belief in Nature." In *Sex in Question: French Materialist Feminism*, edited by D. Leonard and L. Adkins, 72–108. London: Taylor and Francis.

Guss, David. 1989. *To Weave and to Sing: Art, Symbolism, and Narrative in the South American Rainforest*. Berkeley: University of California Press.

Guzmán Gallegos, María A. 1997. *Para que la Yuca Beba Nuestra Sangre. Trabajo, Género y Parentesco en una Comunidad Quichua de la Amazonía Ecuatoriana*. Quito: Abya Yala.

Hancock, J. F. 1992. *Plant Evolution and the Origin of Crop Species*. Englewood Cliffs, NJ: Prentice Hall.

Hardesty, D. L., and D. D. Fowler. 2001. "Archaeology and Environmental Changes." In *New Directions in Anthropology and Environment*, edited by C. Crumley, 72–89. Walnut Creek: Altamira Press.

Harner, Michael. 1972. *The Jívaro People of the Sacred Waterfalls*. Berkeley: University of California Press.

Harris, David. 2012. "Evolution of Agroecosystems: Biodiversity, Origins, and Differential Development." In *Biodiversity in Agriculture: Domestication, Evolution, and Sustainability*, edited by Paul Gepts et al., 21–56. New York: Cambridge University Press.

Harris, Marvin. 1968. *The Rise of Anthropological Theory*. New York: T. Y. Crowell.

———. 1984. "Animal Capture and Yanomamo Warfare: Retrospect and New Evidence." *Journal of Anthropological Research* 40(1): 183–201.

Hays, T. E. 1983. "Ndumba Folkbiology and General Principles of Ethnobiological Classification and Nomenclature." *American Anthropologist* 85: 592–611.

Heckenberger, Michael. 2005. *The Ecology of Power: Culture, Place, and Personhood in the Southern Amazon AD 1,000–2,000*. New York: Routledge.

Henningsen, Maria. 2006. "Indigenous People and External Actors in the Ecuadorian Amazon: The Creation of Spaces and Strategies in the Meeting between Two Different Worlds. A Case Study with Special Focus on the Huaoranis." PhD diss., Roskilde University, Denmark.

Henry, Jules. 1941. *Jungle People: A Kaigang Tribe of the Highlands of Brazil*. New York: Vintage Books.

Héritier, Françoise. 1979. "La Symbolique de l'Inceste et de sa Prohibition." In *La Fonction Symbolique: Essais d'Anthropologie*, edited by M. Izard and P. Smith. Paris: Gallimard.

Héritier, Françoise, B. Cyrulnick, and A. Nouri, eds. 2000. *De l'Inceste*. Paris: Odile Jacob.

High, Casey. 2006. "From Enemies to Affines: Conflict and Community Among the Huaorani of Amazonian Ecuador." PhD diss., London School of Economics, University of London.

———. 2009. "Remembering the Auca: Violence and Generational Memory in Amazonian Ecuador." *Journal of the Royal Anthropological Institute* 25(4): 719–36.

———. 2010. "Warriors, Hunters, and Bruce Lee: Gendered Agency and the Transformation of Amazonian Masculinity." *American Ethnologist* 37(4): 753–70.

———. 2012. "Shamans, Animals, and Enemies: Human and Non-Human Agency in an Amazonian Cosmos of Alterity." In *Animism in Rainforest and Tundra: Personhood, Animals, Plants, and Things in Contemporary Amazonia and Siberia*, edited by Olga Ulturgasheva, Marc Brightman, and Vanessa Elisa Grotti, 130–41. Oxford: Berghahn.

———. 2015. *Victims and Warriors: Violence, History, and Memory in Amazonia*. Urbana: University of Illinois Press.

Hill, Jonathan. 1993. *Keepers of the Sacred Chants: The Poetics of Ritual Power in an Amazonian Society*. Tucson: University of Arizona Press.

Hill, Jonathan, and Fernando Santos-Granero. 2002a. "Introduction." In *Comparative Arawakan Histories: Rethinking Language Family and Culture Area in Amazonia*, edited by J. Hill and F. Santos-Granero, 1–22. Urbana and Chicago: University of Illinois Press.

———, eds. 2002b. *Comparative Arawakan Histories: Rethinking Language Family and Culture Area in Amazonia*. Urbana: University of Illinois Press.

Hladik, A., and E. Dounias. 1993. "Wild Yams of the African Forest as Potential Food Resources." In *Tropical Forests, People, and Food*, edited by C. M. Hladik, A. Hladik, O. F. Linares, H. Pagezy, A. Semple, and M. Hadley, 163–76. Paris: UNESCO and Grupo Editorial Partenón.

Holmberg, Allan. 1969. *Nomads of the Long Bow*. Garden City, NY: Natural History Press.

Homans, G. 1941. "Anxiety and Ritual: The Theories of Malinowski and Radcliffe-Brown." *American Anthropologist* 43: 164–72.

Hornborg, Alf. 2005. "Ethnogenesis, Regional Integration, and Ecology in Prehistoric Amazonia: Toward a System Perspective." *Current Anthropology* 46(4): 589–620.

Houck, K., M. V. Sorensen, F. Lu, D. Alban, K. Alvarez, D. Hidobro, C. Doljanin, and A. I. Ona. 2013. "The Effects of Market Integration on Childhood Growth and Nutritional Status: The Dual Burden of Under- and Over-nutrition in the Northern Ecuadorian Amazon." *American Journal of Human Biology* 25(4): 524–33.

Houseman, Michael. 1988. "Towards a Complex Model of Parenthood: Two African Tales." *American Ethnologist* 15(4): 658–77.

Hugh-Jones, Stephen. 1979. *The Palm and the Pleiades: Initiation and Cosmology in Northwest Amazonia*. Cambridge: Cambridge University Press.

———. 1995. "Inside-Out and Back-to-Front: The Androgynous House in Northwest Amazonia." In *About the House: Lévi-Strauss and Beyond*, edited by J. Carsten and S. Hugh-Jones, 226–52. Cambridge: Cambridge University Press.

Hugh-Jones, Christine, and Stephen Hugh-Jones. 1996. "La Conservation du Manioc chez les Indiens Tukano: Technique et Symbôlique." In *L'Alimentation en Forêt Tropicale: Interactions Bioculturelles et Perspectives de Développement*, Vol. 2, edited by C. M. Hladik, A. Hladik, H. Pagezy, O. Linares, G. Koppert, and A. Froment, 897–902. Paris: UNESCO.

Hunn, Eugene. 1977. *Tzeltal Folk Zoology: The Classification of Discontinuities in Nature*. New York: Academic Press.

Hunter, D., and P. Whitten. 1976. "Couvade." In *Encyclopedia of Anthropology*. New York: Holt, Rinehart, and Winston.

IACHR (Inter-American Commission on Human Rights). 2006. *Informe Annual de la Comisión Interamericana de Derechos Humanos.* http://www.cidh.oas.org/annualrep/2006sp/cap3.1.2006.sp.htm, accessed on September 9, 2013.

Ingold, Tim. 1988. "Notes on the Foraging Mode of Production." In *Hunters and Gatherers: History, Evolution, and Social Change,* edited by T. Ingold, D. Riches, and J. Woodurn, 269–84. Oxford: Berg.

Irvine, Dominique. 1989. "Succession Management and Resource Distribution in an Amazonian Rain Forest." In *Resource Management in Amazonia: Indigenous and Folk Strategies,* edited by D. Posey and W. Balée. *Advances in Economic Botany* 7: 223–237.

Izquierdo Peñafiel, J. 2000. *La Ecoarquitectura. Asentamientos Humanos Huaorani.* Quito: Abya Yala.

Jackson, Jean. 1983. *The Fish People: Linguistic Exogamy and Tukanoan Identity in Northwest Amazonia.* Cambridge: Cambridge University Press.

James, Wendy. 1997. "Placing the Unborn: On the Social Construction of New life." The Kaberry Memorial Lecture 1997, manuscript in possession of the author.

Journet, Nicolas. 1995. *La Paix des Jardins. Structures Sociales des Indiens Curripaco du Haut Rio Negro (Colombie).* Paris: Musée de l'Homme.

Kane, Joe. 1995. *Savages.* New York: Alfred A. Knopf.

Kelley, Patricia. 1988. "Issues for Literacy Materials Development in a Monolingual Amazonian Culture: The Waodani of Ecuador." MA thesis. Centre for the Study of Curriculum and Instruction. University of British Columbia, Vancouver, Canada.

Kelly, Raymond. 1993. *Constructing Inequality: The Fabrication of a Hierarchy of Virtue Among the Etoro.* Ann Arbor: University of Michigan Press.

Kendall, Gavin, Ian Woodward, and Zlatko Skrbis. 2009. *The Sociology of Cosmopolitanism: Globalization, Identity, Culture, and Government.* Basingstoke: Palgrave Macmillan.

Kensinger, Kenneth. 1995. *How Real People Ought to Live: The Cashinahua of Eastern Peru.* Prospect Heights, Ill: Waveland Press.

———, ed. 1984. *Marriage Practices in Lowland South America.* Illinois Studies in Anthropology No. 14. Urbana: University of Illinois Press.

Kenyatta, Jomo. 1953. *Facing Mount Kenya: The Tribal Life of the Gikuyu.* London: Secker and Warburg.

Kerns, Virginia. 2003. *Scenes from the High Desert. Julian Steward's Life and Theory.* Urbana and Chicago: University of Illinois Press.

Keyeux, G., C. Rodas, N. Gelvez, and D. Carter. 2002. "Possible Migration Routes into South America Deduced from DNA Studies of Colombian Amerindian Populations." *Human Biology* 74: 211–33.

Kimerling, Judith. 2012. "Huaorani Land Rights in Ecuador: Oil, Contact, and Conservation." *Environmental Justice* 5(5): 236–51.

———. 2013. "Oil, Contact, and Conservation in the Amazon: Indigenous Huaorani, Chevron, and Yasuni." *Colorado Journal of International Environmental Law and Policy* 24(1): 43–115.

Kirsch, Stuart. 2012. "Juridification of Indigenous Politics in Law against the State." In *Ethnographic Forays into Law's Transformations*, edited by J. Eckert, B. Donahoe, and C. Strümpell, 23–42. Cambridge: Cambridge University Press.

Kohn, Eduardo. 2002. "Natural Engagements and Ecological Aesthetics Among the Avilá Runa of Amazonian Ecuador." PhD diss., University of Wisconsin, Madison.

———. 2013. *How Forests Think: Toward an Anthropology Beyond the Human*. Berkeley: University of California Press.

Labaca, Mons Alejandro. 1988. *Crónica Huaorani*. Pompeya: CICAME.

Larrea, Carlos. 2011. "La Iniciativa Y-ITT: Una Opción Factible Hacia la Equidad y Sustentabilidad." In *La Iniciativa Yasuní-ITT desde una Perspectiva Multicriterial*, edited by M. C. Vallejo, C. Larrea, R. Burbano, and F. Falconí, 12–34. Quito: PNUD and FAO.

Lathrap, Donald. 1970. *The Upper Amazon*. London: Thames and Hudson.

Lea, Vanessa. 1992. "Mebengokre (Kayapó) Onomastics: A Facet of Houses as Total Social Facts in Central Brazil." *Man* 27(1): 129–53.

———. 1995. "The Houses of the Mebengokre (Kayapó) of Central Brazil: A New Door to Their Social Organization." In *About the House: Lévi-Strauss and Beyond*, edited by Janet Carsten and Stephen Hugh-Jones, 206–225. Cambridge: Cambridge University Press.

Leach, Edmund. 1954. *Political Systems of Highland Burma: A Study of Kachin Social Structure*. London: Athlone Press.

Lee, Richard, and I. DeVore, eds. 1968. *Man the Hunter*. Chicago: Aldine.

Leeds, A. 1961. "Introduction." In *The Evolution of Horticultural Systems in Native South America: Causes and Consequences*, edited by J. Wilbert, 1–12. Caracas: Ed. Sucre.

Lehman, John, D. Kern, B. Glaser, and W. Woods, eds. 2003. *Amazonian Dark Earths: Origins, Properties, and Management*. Dordrecht: Kluwer Academic Publisher.

Lenaerts, Marc. 2004. *Anthropologie des Indiens Ashéninka d'Amazonie. Nos Soeurs Manioc et l'Étranger Jaguar*. Paris: L' Harmattan.

———. 2006. "Ontologie Animique, Ethnosciences et Universalisme Cognitive. Le Regard Ashéninka." *L'Homme* 179(3): 113–39.

Lescure, Jean-Paul, H. Baslev, and R. Alarcón. 1987. *Plantas Útiles de la Amazonia Ecuatoriana*. Quito: Orstom, Puce, Incrae.

Lévi-Strauss, Claude. 1943. "Guerre et Commerce chez les Indiens d'Amérique du Sud." *Renaissance* 1: 122–39.

———. 1948. "La Vie Familiale et Sociale des Indiens Nambikwara." *Journal de la Société des Américanistes de Paris* 37: 1–132.

———. 1950. "The Use of Wild Plants in Tropical South America." In *Handbook of South American Indians. Vol. 6: Physical Anthropology, Linguistics and Cultural Geography of South American Indians*, edited by J. H. Steward, 465–86. Smithsonian Institution, Bureau of American Ethnology. Washington DC: US Government Printing Office.

———. 1955. *Tristes Tropiques*. Paris: Librairie Plon.

———. 1962. *La Pensée Sauvage*. Paris: Librairie Plon.

———. 1966. *The Savage Mind*. Chicago: University of Chicago Press.

———. 1983. "La Famille." In *Paroles Données*, by C. Lévi-Strauss, 65–92. Paris: Librairie Plon.

———. 2001. "Productivité et Condition Humaine." *Etudes Rurales* 159–60: 129–44.

Liedloff, Jean. (1975) 1986. *The Continuum Concept*. London: Penguin Books.

Little, Paul. 2001. *Amazonia: Territorial Struggles on Perennial Frontiers*. Baltimore, Md: Johns Hopkins University Press.

Londoño Sulkin, Carlos. 2012. *People of Substance: An Ethnography of Morality in the Colombian Amazon*. Toronto: University of Toronto Press.

Lu, Flora. 1999. "Changes in Subsistence Patterns and Resource Use of the Huaorani Indians in the Ecuadorian Amazon." PhD diss., North Carolina University, Chapel Hill.

———. 2001. "The Common Property Regime of the Huaorani Indians of Ecuador: Implications and Challenges to Conservation." *Human Ecology* 29(4): 425–47.

———. 2007. "Integration into the Market among Indigenous Peoples: A Cross-cultural Perspective from the Ecuadorian Amazon." *Current Anthropology* 48: 593–602.

———. 2010. "Patterns of Indigenous Resilience in the Amazon: A Case Study of Huaorani Hunting in Ecuador." *Journal of Ecological Anthropology* 14: 5–21.

———. 2012. "Petroleum Extraction, Indigenous People, and Environmental Injustice in the Ecuadorian Amazon." In *International Environmental Justice: Competing Claims and Perspectives*, edited by F. Gordon and G. Freeland, 71–95. Hertfordshire: ILM Publishers.

———. 2013. Comentario sobre el Artículo "Response Diversity and Resilience in Socio-ecological Systems" by P. Leslie and J. T. McCabe. *Current Anthropology* 54(2): 133–35.

Lu Holt, Flora. 2005. "The Catch-22 of Conservation: Indigenous Peoples, Biologists, and Cultural Change." *Human Ecology* 33(2): 199–215.

Lu Flora, R. E. Bilsborrow, and A. I. Oña. 2012. *Modos de Vivir y Sobrevivir: Un Estudio Transcultural de Cinco Etnias de la Amazonía Ecuatoriana*. Quito: Abya Yala.

Lu, Flora, and Ciara Wirth. 2011. "Conservation Perceptions, Common Property, and Cultural Polarization Among the Waorani of Ecuador's Amazon." *Human Organization* 70(3): 233–43.

Macía, Manuel. 2004. "Multiplicity in Palm Uses by the Huaorani of Amazonian Ecuador." *Botanical Journal of the Linnean Society* 144: 149–59.

Macía, Manuel, H. Romero-Saltos, and R. Valencia. 2001. "Patrones de Uso en un Bosque Primario de la Amazonía Ecuatoriana: Comparación Entre dos Comunidades Huaorani." In *Evaluación de Recursos Vegetales no Maderables en la Amazonía Norroccidental*, by J. Duivenvoorden et al., 225–49. Amsterdam: IBED, Faculty of Science, University of Amsterdam.

Maffi, Luisa. 2001. "Linking Language and the Environment: A Co-evolutionary Perspective." In *New Directions in Anthropology and Environment*, edited by C. Crumley, 24–48. Walnut Creek: Altamira Press.

Malinowski, Bronislaw. 1927. *Sex and Repression in Savage Society*. London: Routledge and Kegan Paul.

———. (1948) 1954. *Magic, Science, and Religion*. New York: Doubleday Anchor Books.

Mauss, Marcel. 1979. "Body Techniques." In *Sociology and Psychology: Essays by Marcel Mauss*, translated by B. Brewster, 95–123. London: Routledge and Kegan Paul.

Maxus Ecuador Inc. 1994. *Procedural Manual for the Waorani Territory*. Quito: Maxus Ecuador Inc.

Maybury-Lewis, David. 1979. *Dialectical Societies: The Gê & Bororo of Central Brazil*. Oxford: Oxford University Press.

———. 2009. "Indigenous Theories, Anthropological Ideas: A View from Lowland South America." *Anthropological Quarterly* 82(4): 897–928.

McCallum, Cecilia. 2001. *Gender and Sociability in Amazonia: How Real People Are Made*. Oxford: Berg.

McKey, Doyle, Marianne Elias, Benoit Pujol, and Anne Duputié. 2012. "Ecological Approaches to Crop Domestication." In *Biodiversity in Agriculture: Domestication, Evolution, and Sustainability*, edited by Paul Gepts, T. R. Famula, R. L.

Bettinger, S. B. Brush, A. B. Damania, P. E. McGuire, and C. O. Qualset, 377–406. New York: Cambridge University Press.

McMichael, Crystal, Mark B. Bush, Dolores R. Piperno, Miles R. Silman, Andrew R. Zimmerman, and Christina Anderson. 2012. "Spatial and Temporal Scales of Pre-Columbian Disturbance Associated with Western Amazonian Lakes." *The Holocene* 22(2): 131–41.

McMichael, Crystal, M. W. Palace, M. B. Bush, B. Braswell, S. Hagen, E. G. Neves, M. R. Silman, E. K. Tamanaha, and C. Czarnecki. 2014. "Predicting Pre-Columbian Anthropogenic Soils in Amazonia." *Proceedings of the Royal Society B* 281: 20132475. http://dx.doi.org/10.1098/rspb.2013.2475.

Medin, Douglas L., and Scott Atran, eds. 1999. *Folkbiology*. Cambridge, Mass: MIT Press.

———. 1999. "Introduction." In *Folkbiology*, edited by Douglas Medin and S. Atran, 1–16. Cambridge, Mass: MIT Press.

Meillassoux, Claude. 1981. *Maidens, Meal, and Money: Capitalism and the Domestic Community*. Cambridge: Cambridge University.

Mena, P., J. R. Stallings, J. Regalado, and R. Cueva. 2000. "The Sustainability of Current Hunting Practices by the Huaorani." In *Hunting for Sustainability in Tropical Forests*, edited by J. G. Robinson and E. L. Bennett, 57–78. New York: Columbia University Press.

Menget, Pierre. 1979. "Temps de Naître, Temps d'Être: La Couvade." In *La Fonction Symbolique: Essais d'Anthropologie*, edited by M. Izard and P. Smith, 245–64. Paris: Gallimard.

———, ed. 1985. Special Issue on Amazonian Warfare: "Guerre, Société et Vision du Monde dans les Basses Terres de l'Amérique du Sud" of *Journal de la Société des Américanistes*, LXXI.

Métraux, Alfred. 1946–50. "The Couvade." In *Handbook of South American Indians*, Vol. 5, edited by J. Steward. Washington DC: Smithsonian.

Mignolo, Walter, and M. Tlostanova. "The Logic of Coloniality and the Limits of Postcoloniality." In *The Postcolonial and the Global*, edited by Revathi Krishnaswamy and John C. Hawley, 109–23. Minneapolis, Minn: University of Minnesota Press.

Miller, Daniel. 1998. *A Theory of Shopping*. Cambridge: Polity Press.

Miller, Geoffrey. 2001. *The Mating Mind: How Sexual Choice Shaped the Evolution of Human Nature*. London: Vintage.

Miller, Theresa. 2015. "Bio-sociocultural Aesthetics: Indigenous Ramkokamekra-Canela Gardening Practices and Varietal Diversity Maintenance in Maranhão, Brazil." PhD diss., University of Oxford.

Mithen, Stephen. 1996. *The Prehistory of the Mind.* London: Thames and Hudson.
———. 2006. "Ethnobiology and the Evolution of the Human Mind." In *Ethnobiology and the Science of Humankind: A Retrospective and a Prospective*, edited by R. Ellen, 55–75. Special issue of *Journal of the Royal Anthropological Institute.*
Mondragón, Marta L., and Randy Smith. 1997. *Bete Quiwiguimamo: Salvando el Bosque para Vivir Sano.* Quito: Abya Yala.
Moore, Henrietta, and Megan Vaughan. 1994. *Cutting Down Trees: Gender, Nutrition, and Agricultural Change in the Northern Province of Zambia, 1890–1990.* Oxford: James Currey.
Morris, Brian. 1976. "Whither the Savage Mind? Notes on the Natural Taxonomies of Hunting and Gathering People." *Man* 11: 542–57.
Munroe, Robert L., Ruth H. Munroe, and John W. M. Whiting. 1973. "The Couvade: A Psychological Analysis." *Ethos* 1(1): 30–74.
Muradian, Roldan, and Laura Rival, eds. 2012. *Governing the Provision of Ecosystem Services.* Dordrecht: Springer.
Muratorio, Blanca. 1991. *The Life and Times of Grandfather Alonso: Culture and History in the Upper Amazon.* New Brunswick, NJ: Rutgers University Press.
Murphy, Robert. 1960. *Head Hunter's Heritage.* Berkeley: University of California Press.
Murphy, Yolanda, and Robert F. Murphy. 1974. *Women of the Forest.* New York: Columbia University Press.
Nabhan, Gary P. 2000. "Interspecific Relationships Affecting Endangered Species Recognized by O'Odham and Comcáac Cultures." *Ecological Applications* 10(5): 1288–95.
———. 2001. "Cultural Perceptions of Ecological Interactions: An 'Endangered People's' Contribution to the Conservation of Biological and Linguistic Diversity." In *On Biocultural Diversity: Linking Language, Knowledge, and the Environment*, edited by L. Maffi, 145–56. Washington DC: Smithsonian Institution Press.
Narváez, Ivan. 1996. *Huaorani vs. Maxus. Poder Étnico, Poder Transnacional.* Quito: Ed. Porvenir.
———. 2007. "La Política Ambiental del Estado: ¿Hacia el Colapso del Modelo de Conservación?" In *Yasuní en el Siglo XXI. El Estado Ecuatoriano y la Conservación de la Amazonia*, edited by G. Fontaine and I. Narváez, 33–73. FLACSO, Quito.
———. 2009. *Petróleo y Poder: El Colapso de un Lugar Singular Yasuní.* Quito: FLACSO and GTZ.
Nenquimo, Ima Fabian. 2011. *Tome Waorani Ponino.* Quito: Ministerio del Ambiente del Ecuador.

———. 2014. *Tagaeri Taromenani. Guerreros de la Selva*. Quito: Fundación Apaika Pee.
Omene Ima, and Omari Manuela. 2012. *Saberes Huaorani y Parque Nacional Yasuní. Plantas, Salud y Bienestar en la Amazonía del Ecuador*. Quito: PNUD and FNAM.
Ortiz, Pablo, and Ana María Varea. 1995. "Introduction." In *Marea Negra en la Amazonia. Conflictos Socioambientales Vinculados a la Actividad Petrolera en el Ecuador*, 15–24. Quito: ILDIS.
Overing, Joanna. 1991. "A Estética da Produção: O Senso de Comunidade Entre os Cubeo e os Piaroa." *Revista de Antropologia* 34 (2): 7–33.
Overing, Joanna, and Alan Passes, eds. 2000. *The Anthropology of Love and Anger: The Aesthetics of Conviviality in Native Amazonia*. London: Routledge.
Pappalardo, S. E., M. de Marchi, and F. Ferrarese. 2013. *Uncontacted Waorani in the Yasuní Biosphere Reserve: Geographical Validation of the Zona Intangible Tagaeri Taromenane (ZITT)*. PLoS ONE 8 (6): e66293. doi:10.1371/journal.pone.0066293.
Papworth, Sara, E. J. Milner-Gulland, and K. Slocombe. 2013. "The Natural Place to Begin: The Ethnoprimatology of the Waorani." *American Journal of Primatology* (11): 1117–28.
Parker, Eugene. 1992. "Forest Islands and Kayapo Resource Management in Amazonia: A Reappraisal of the Apêtê." *American Anthropologist* 94(2): 406–28.
Paz, Octavio. 1993. *La Llama Doble. Amor y Erotismo*. Barcelona: Editorial Seix Barral.
Peeke, Catherine. 1973. *Preliminary Grammar of Auca*. Quito: ILV.
Peirano, Mariza. 2008. "Brazil: Otherness in Context." In *A Companion to Latin American Anthropology*, edited by Deborah Poole, 56–71. Oxford: Blackwell Publishing.
Petersen, J., E. Neves, and M. Heckenberger. 2001. "Gift from the Past: Terra Preta and Prehistoric Amerindian Occupation in Amazonia." In *Unknown Amazon: Culture in Nature in Ancient Brazil*, edited by C. McEwan, C. Barreto, and E. Neves, 50–85. London: British Museum Press.
Peterson, Nicholas. 1993. "Demand Sharing: Reciprocity and the Pressure for Generosity among Foragers." *American Ethnologist* 4(95): 860–74.
Piña-Cabral, João. 2005. "The Future of Social Anthropology." *Social Anthropology* 13(2): 119–128.
Piperno, Dolores, and Deborah Pearsall. 1998. *The Origins of Agriculture in the Lowland Neotropics*. San Diego: Academic Press.
Pitman, Nigel. 2000. "A Large-Scale Inventory of Two Amazonian Tree Communities." PhD diss., Duke University, Durham, North Carolina.
Pitman, Nigel C., J. Therbgorg, M. Silman, P. Nunez, D. A. Neill, C. Cerón, W. Palacios, and M. Aulestia. 2001. "Dominance and Distribution of Tree Species in Upper Amazonia *Terra Firme* Forests." *Ecology* 82(8): 2101–17.

Politis, Gustavo. 2007. *Nukak: Ethnoarchaeology of an Amazonian People*. Walnut Creek, CA: Left Coast Press.

———. 2014. "Regional Hunter-Gatherer Research Traditions: South America." In *The Oxford Handbook of the Archaeology and Anthropology of Hunter-Gatherers*, edited by Vicki Cummings, P. Jordan, and M. Zvelebil, 1031–54. Oxford: Oxford University Press. doi 10.1093/oxfordhb/9780199551224.013.045.

Posey, Darrell. 1984. "Native and Indigenous Guidelines for New Amazonian Development: Understanding Biological Diversity through Ethnoecology." In *Change in the Amazon Basin*, vol. 1 of *Man's Impact on Forests and Rivers*, edited by John Hemming, 156–181. London: Royal Geographical Society.

———. 1985. "Indigenous Management of Tropical Forest Ecosystems: The Case of the Kayapo Indians of the Brazilian Amazon." *Agroforestry Systems* 3: 13–58.

———. 1998. "Diachronic Ecotones and Anthropogenic Landscapes in Amazonia: Contesting the Consciousness of Conservation." In *Advances in Historical Ecology*, edited by W. Balée, 104–18. Columbia: Columbia University Press.

Radcliffe-Brown, Alfred R. 1965. "Taboo." In *Structure and Function in Primitive Society*, by A. Radcliffe-Brown, 133–52. New York: Free Press.

Ramos, Alcida. 1980. *Hierarquia e Simbiose: Relações Intertribais no Brasil*. São Paulo: Editora Hucitei.

Rappaport, Roy. 1999. *Ritual and Religion in the Making of Humanity*. Cambridge: Cambridge University Press.

Reeve, Mary, and High, Casey. 2012. "Between Friends and Enemies: The Dynamics of Interethnic Relations in Amazonian Ecuador." *Ethnohistory* 59(1): 141–62.

Reichel-Dolmatoff, Gerardo. 1971. *Amazon Cosmos: The Sexual and Religious Symbol of the Tukano Indians*. Chicago: Chicago University Press.

Reid, Howard. 1979. "Some Aspects of Movement, Growth, and Change among the Hupdu Maku Indians of Brazil." PhD diss., Cambridge University.

Renard-Casevitz, France-Marie. 2002. "Social Forms and Regressive History: From the Campa Cluster to the Mojos and from the Mojos to the Landscaping Terrace-Builders of the Bolivian Savanna." In *Comparative Arawakan Histories: Rethinking Language Family and Culture Area in Amazonia*, edited by J. D. Hill and F. Santos Granero, 123–46. Urbana: University of Illinois Press.

Richards, Audrey I. 1932. *Hunger and Work in a Savage Tribe: A Functional Study in Nutrition Among the Southern Bantu*. London: Routledge.

Rindos, David. 1984. *The Origins of Agriculture: An Evolutionary Perspective*. Orlando: Academic Press. London: Routledge and Kegan Paul.

Rival, Laura. 1992. "Social Transformations and the Impact of Formal Schooling on the Huaorani of Ecuador." PhD diss., University of London.

———. 1993. "The Growth of Family Trees: Huaorani Conceptualization of Nature and Society." *Man* 28(4): 635–52.

———. 1996a. *Hijos del Sol, Padres del Jaguar, los Huaorani Hoy*. Quito: Abya Yala.

———. 1996b. "Blowpipes and Spears: The Social Significance of Huaorani Technological Choices." In *Nature and Society: Anthropological Perspectives*, edited by Philippe Descola and Gisli Pálsson, 145–64. London: Routledge.

———. 1998a. "Androgynous Parents and Guest Children: The Huaorani Couvade." *Journal of the Royal Anthropological Institute* 5(4): 619–42.

———. 1998b. "Domestication as a Historical and Symbolic Process: Wild Gardens and Cultivated Forests in the Ecuadorian Amazon." In *Principles of Historical Ecology*, edited by William Balée, 232–50. New York: Columbia University Press.

———. 1998c. "Preys at the Centre: Resistance and Marginality in Amazonia." In *Lilies of the Field: Marginal People Who Live for the Moment*, edited by S. Day, E. Papataxiarchis, and M. Stewart, 61–79. Boulder, Col: Westview Press.

———. 1999. "Introductory Essay on South American Hunters-and-Gatherers." In *The Cambridge Encyclopedia of Hunters and Gatherers*, edited by R. Lee and R. Daly, 77–85. Cambridge: Cambridge University Press.

———. 2000. "Marginality with a Difference: How the Huaorani Remain Autonomous, Preserve Their Sharing Relations and Naturalize Outside Economic Powers." In *Hunters and Gatherers in the Modern Context: Conflict, Resistance, and Self-Determination*, edited by Megan Biesele and Peter Schweitzer, 244–62. Providence, Rhode Island: Berghahn Books.

———. 2001. "Seed and Clone: A Preliminary Note on Manioc Domestication, and Its Implication for Symbolic and Social Analysis." In *Beyond the Visible and the Material: the Amerindianization of Society in the Work of Peter Rivière*, edited by L. Rival and N. Whitehead, 57–80. Oxford: Oxford University Press.

———. 2002. *Trekking Through History: The Huaorani of Amazonian Ecuador*. New York: Columbia University Press.

———. 2003. "The Meanings of Forest Governance in Esmeraldas, Ecuador." *Oxford Development Studies* 31(4): 479–501.

———. 2005. "Soul, Body, and Gender Among the Huaorani of Amazonian Ecuador." *Ethnos* 70(3): 285–310.

———. 2006. "Amazonian Historical Ecologies." In *Ethnobiology and the Science of Humankind: A Retrospective and a Prospective*, edited by R. Ellen, S79–S94. Journal of the Royal Anthropological Institute Special Issue.

———. 2010. "What Sort of Anthropologist Was Paul Rivet?" In *Out of the Study, into the Field: Ethnographic Theory and Practice in French Anthropology*, edited by Robert Parkin and Anne de Sales, 164–204. Oxford: Berghahn Books.

———. 2011. "Planning Development Futures in the Ecuadorian Amazon: The Expanding Oil Frontier and the Yasuní-ITT Initiative." In *Social Conflict, Economic Development, and Extractive Industry: Evidence from South America*, edited by A. Bebbington, 155–73. New York: Routledge.

———. 2014. "Encountering Nature Through Fieldwork Experiments: Indigenous Knowledge, Local Creativity, and Modes of Reasoning." *Journal of the Royal Anthropological Institute* 20(2): 218–36.

———. 2015. "Huaorani Peace: Cultural Continuity and Negotiated Alterity in the Ecuadorian Amazon." *Common Knowledge* 21(2): 270–304.

Rival, Laura, and Doyle McKey. 2008. "Domestication and Diversity in Manioc (Manihot esculenta Crantz ssp. esculenta, Euphorbiaceae)." *Current Anthropology* 49(6): 1119–28.

Rival, Laura, Don Slater, and Daniel Miller. 1998. "Sex and Sociality: Comparative Ethnography of Sexual Objectification." *Theory, Culture, and Society* 15(3–4): 294–321.

Rival, Laura, and Neil Whitehead. 2001. *Beyond the Visible and the Material: The Amerindianization of Society in the Work of Peter Rivière*. Oxford: Oxford University Press.

Rivas, Alexis. 2003. "Sistema Mundial y Pueblos Indígenas Aislados en la Amazonía: A Propósito del Ataque a los Tagaeri." *Íconos* 17: 21–30.

———. 2005. "Gobernabilidad Democrática, Conflictos Socioambientales y Asistencialismo." *Íconos* 20: 101–6.

———. 2006. *Los Pueblos Indígenas en Aislamiento Desde los Derechos Humanos y la Conservación de la Biodiversidad*. Unión Mundial para la Naturaleza, Oficina Regional para América del Sur. Text Prepared for the 8th Conference of the Parties, Biodiversity Convention, Curitiba, Brazil.

———. 2007a. "Los Pueblos Indígenas en Aislamiento: Emergencia, Vulnerabilidad y Necesidad de Protección. Cultura y Representaciones Sociales." *Electronic Journal of the Social Sciences* (México, DF)1 (2): 73–90 (www.culturayrs.org.mx/revista).

———. 2007b. *Informe Sobre la Situación de los Pueblos Indígenas Aislados y la Protección de los Conocimientos Tradicionales*. International Union for the Conservation of Nature and Biodiversity Convention, Gland.

———. 2012. "Los Pueblos Indígenas Aislados y la Conservación de los Ecosistemas en la Amazonía. Hacia una Estrategia de Educación Ambiental para la

Protección de sus Derechos, Territorios y Ecosistemas. Estudio de caso en la Región de Yasuní, Ecuador." In *News Investigaciones Iberoamericanas en Educación Ambiental*, edited by L. Cano, M. Junyent, J. Benayas, and Meira, 457–81. Madrid: Siren Edición del Organismo Autónomo de Parques Nacionales. Spanish Ministry of Agriculture, Nutrition, and Environment.

Rivas, Alex, and P. Rommel Lara. 2001. *Conservación y Petróleo en la Amazonía Ecuatoriana, un acercamiento al caso Huaorani*. Quito: Ecociencia and Abya Yala.

Rivière, Peter. 1974. "The Couvade: A Problem Reborn." *Man* 9(3): 423–35.

———. 1984. *Individual and Society in Guiana: A Comparative Study in Amerindian Social Organisation*. Cambridge, Cambridge University Press.

———. n.d. "Bride Exchange, Bride Capture, and Bride Service: Problems of Substitution." Manuscript in possession of the author.

Robarchek, Clayton, and Carole Robarchek. 1998. *Waorani: The Contexts of Violence and War*. Orlando, Fl: Harcourt Brace.

Roe, Peter. 1982. *The Cosmic Zygote*. New Brunswick, NJ: Rutgers University Press.

Roosevelt, Anna. 1998. "Ancient and Modern Hunter-Gatherers of Lowland South America: An Evolutionary Problem." In *Advances in Historical Ecology*, edited by W. Balée, 190–212. New York: Columbia University Press.

Salick, Jan. 1995. "Toward an Integration of Evolutionary Ecology and Economic Botany: Personal Perspectives on Plant/People Interactions." *Annals of Missouri Botanical Garden* 82: 25–33.

Sanjek, Roger. 1991. "The Ethnographic Present." *Man* 26(4): 609–28.

Santos-Granero, Fernando. 2009. *Vital Enemies: Slavery, Predation, and the Amerindian Political Economy of Life*. Austin: Texas University Press.

———, ed. 2015. *Images of Public Wealth or the Anatomy of Well-Being in Indigenous Amazonia*. Tucson: Arizona University Press.

Santos-Granero, Fernando, and Frederica Barclay. 2000. *Tamed Frontiers: Economy, Society, and Civil Rights in Upper Amazonia*. Boulder: Westview Press.

Sauer, Carl. 1925. "The Morphology of Landscape." *University of California Publications in Geography* 2: 19–54.

———. 1936. "American Agricultural Origins: A Consideration of Nature and Agriculture." In *Essays in Anthropology in Honor of A. L. Kroeber*, edited by R. H. Lowie, 279–98. Berkeley: University of California Press.

———. 1947. "Early Relations of Man to Plants." *Geographical Review* 37: 1–25.

———. 1950. "Grassland Climax, Fire, and Man." *Journal of Range Management* 3(1): 16–21.

Schurr, T. G. 2004. "The Peopling of the New World: Perspectives from Molecular Anthropology." *Annual Review of Anthropology* 33: 551–83.

Scott, James. 2009. *The Art of Not Being Governed: An Anarchist History of Upland Southeast Asia.* New Haven, CT: Yale University Press.

Seeger, Anthony. 1981. *Nature and Society in Central Brazil: The Suya of Matto Grosso.* Harvard: Harvard University Press.

Seeger, A., R. da Matta, and V. de Castro. 1987. *Sociedades Indígenas & Indigenismo no Brasil.* Rio de Janeiro: UJRJ, Editora Marco Zero.

Sirén, A. 2012. "Festival Hunting by the Kichwa People in the Ecuadorian Amazon." *Journal of Ethnobiology* 32(1): 30–50.

Sperber, Dan. 1996. *La Contagion des Idées.* Paris: Eds Odile Jacob.

Stahl, Peter. 2008. "The Contributions of Zooarchaeology to Historical Ecology in the Neotropics." *Quaternary International* 180: 5–16.

Steward, Julian, and L. Faron. 1959. *Native Peoples of South America.* New York: McGraw-Hill.

Strathern, Marilyn. 1988. *The Gender of the Gift: Problems with Women and Problems with Society in Melanesia.* Berkeley: University of California Press.

———. 2001. "Same-Sex and Cross-Sex Relations: Some Internal Comparisons." In *Gender in Amazonia and Melanesia,* edited by Thomas Gregor and Donald Tuzin, 221–44. Berkeley: University of California Press.

Suárez, E., M. Morales, R. Cueva, V. Utreras Bucheli, G. Zapata-Rios, E. Toral, J. Torres, W. Prado, and J. Vargas Olalla. 2009. "Oil Industry, Wild Meat Trade and Roads: Indirect Effects of Oil Extraction Activities in a Protected Area in Northeastern Ecuador." *Animal Conservation* 12(4): 364–373.

Suárez, E., G. Zapata-Ríos, V. Utreras, S. Strindberg, and J. Vargas. 2012. "Controlling Access to Oil Roads Protects Forest Cover, but Not Wildlife Communities: A Case Study from the Rainforest of Yasuní Biosphere Reserve (Ecuador)." *Animal Conservation* 16(3): 265–274.

Symons, Donald. 1979. *Evolution of Human Sexuality.* New York: Oxford University Press.

Tansley, Arthur. 1935. "The Use and Abuse of Vegetational Concepts and Terms." *Ecology* 16(3): 284–307.

Taylor, Anne-Christine. 1996. "The Soul's Body and Its States: An Amazonian Perspective on the Nature of Being Human." *Journal of the Royal Anthropological Institute* 2(2): 201–15.

Taylor, Douglas. 1950. "The Meaning of Dietary and Occupational Restrictions Among the Island Caribs." *American Anthropologist* 52(3): 343–49.

Ter Steege, H., D. Sabatier, H. Castellanos, T. van Andel, J. Duivenvoorden, A. Adalardo, P. Maas, and S. Mori. 2000. "An Analysis of the Floristic Composition and Diversity of Amazonian Forests, Including Those of the Guiana Shield." *Journal of Tropical Ecology* 16(6): 801–28.

Tededanipa. 2009. *Las Voces de las Mujeres.* Quito: Corp. Humanas, AMWAE, and Ministerio de Cultura del Ecuador.

Tsing, Anna L. 2013. "More-than-Human Sociality: A Call for Critical Description." In *Anthropology and Nature*, edited by K. Hastrup, 27–42. London: Routledge.

———. 2014. "Strathern Beyond the Human: Testimony of a Spore." *Theory, Culture, & Society* 31(2/3): 221–41.

Turner, Nancy. 1974. "Plant Taxonomic Systems and Ethnobotany in Three Contemporary Indian Groups of the Pacific Northwest (Haida, Bella Coola, and Lillooet)." *Sysis* 7: 1–107.

Tylor, E. B. 1865. *Researches into the Early History of Mankind and the Development of Civilization.* London: J. Murray.

———. 1888. "On a Method of Investigating the Development of Institutions, Applied to Laws of Marriage and Descent." *Journal of the Royal Anthropological Institute* XVII: 245–72.

Uchiyamada, Yasushi. 1999. "Two Beautiful Untouchable Women: Processes of Becoming in South India." In *Lilies of the Field: Marginal People Who Live for the Moment*, edited by S. Day, E. Papataxiarchis, and M. Stewart, 96–116. Boulder, Colorado: Westview Press.

Uzendoski, M. A., and E. F. Calapucha-Tapuy. 2012. *The Ecology of the Spoken Word. Amazonian Storytelling and Chamánism among the Napo Runa.* Urbana: University of Illinois Press.

Vilaça, Aparecida. 2002. "Making Kin Out of Others in Amazonia." *Journal of the Royal Anthropological Institute* 8(2): 347–65.

Viteri Toro, J. 2008. *Petróleo, lanzas y sangre.* Quito: La Palabra.

Viveiros de Castro, Eduardo. 1992. *From the Enemy's Point of View: Humanity and Divinity in an Amazonian Society.* Chicago: Chicago University Press.

———. 1995. "Pensando Parentesco Ameríndio." In *Antropologia do Parentesco. Estudos Amerindios*, edited by E. Viveiros de Castro, 7–24. Río de Janeiro: UFRJ.

———. 1998. "Cosmological Deixis and Amerindian Perpectivism." *Journal of the Royal Anthropological Institute* 4(3): 469–88.

———. 2001. "GUT Feelings about Amazonia: Potential Affinity and the Construction of Sociability." In *Beyond the Visible and the Material: The Amerindianization of Society in the Work of Peter Rivière*, edited by Laura Rival and Neil Whitehead, 19–43. Oxford: Oxford University Press.

Waddy, J. A. 1988. *Classifications of Plants and Animals from a Groote Eylandt Aboriginal Point of View* (2 vol.). Darwin: Australian National University.

Wagley, Charles. 1977. *Welcome to Tears. The Tapirape of Central Brazil.* New York: Oxford University Press.

Walker, Harry. 2013. *Under a Watchful Eye: Self, Power, and Intimacy in Amazonia.* Berkeley: University of California Press.

Wasserstrom, Roberto, and Teodoro Bustamente. 2015. "Ethnicity, Labor, and Indigenous Populations in the Ecuadorian Amazon, 1822–2010." *Advances in Anthropology* 5(1): 1–18.

Weeks, Jeffrey. 1995. *Invented Moralities: Sexual Values in an Age of Uncertainty.* Cambridge: Polity Press.

Werbner, Pnina, ed. 2008. *Anthropology and the New Cosmopolitanism: Rooted, Feminist, and Vernacular Perspectives.* London: Berg.

Westermarck, Edward. 1921. *The History of Human Marriage.* Vol. 1. London: Macmillan and Co.

Whistler, Karl. 1976. "Patwin Folk-Taxonomic Structures." MA thesis, University of California, Berkeley.

Whitmore, T., and B. L. Turner. 2001. *Cultivated Landscapes of Middle America on the Eve of Conquest.* New York: Oxford University Press.

Whitten, Norman. 1985. *Sicuanga Runa: The Other Side of Development in Amazonian Ecuador.* Urbana: University of Illinois Press.

———. 2008. "Interculturality and the Indigenization of Modernity: A View from Amazonian Ecuador." *Tipití* 6(1): 3–36.

Widlok, Thomas. 2013. "Sharing: Allowing Others to Take What Is Valued." *Hau: Journal of Ethnographic Theory* 3(2): 11–31.

Wierucka, A. 2012. "The Changing Understanding of the Huaorani Chamán's Art." *Anthropological Notebooks* 18(3): 47–56.

Wilbert, Johannes, ed. 1961. *The Evolution of Horticultural Systems in Native South America: Causes and Consequences.* Caracas, Venezuela: *Antropológica* Supplement 2.

Winterhalder, Bruce. 1981. "Optimal Foraging Strategies and Hunter Gatherer Research in Anthropology: Theories and Models." In *Hunter-Gatherer Foraging Strategies*, edited by B. Winterhalder and E. A. Smith, 13–35. Chicago: University of Chicago Press.

Winterhalder, Bruce, and C. Goland. 1993. "On Population, Foraging Efficiency, and Plant Domestication." *Current Anthropology* 34: 710–15.

Winthrop, K. 2001. "Historical Ecology: Landscapes of Change in the Pacific Northwest." In *New Directions in Anthropology and Environment*, edited by C. Crumley, 203–22. Walnut Creek: Altamira Press.

Wolf, Arthur. 1993. "Westermarck Redivivus." *Annual Reviews of Anthropology* 22: 157–75.

———. 2005. "Explaining the Westermarck Effect, or What Did Natural Selection Select For?" In *Inbreeding, Incest, and the Incest Taboo*, edited by A. Wolf and W. H. Durham, 76–92. Stanford: Stanford University Press.

Wolf, Arthur, and William H. Durham, eds. 2005. *Inbreeding, Incest, and the Incest Taboo: The State of Knowledge at the Turn of the century*. Stanford: Stanford University Press.

Wolf, Eric. 1961. "Concluding Comments." In *The Evolution of Horticultural Systems in Native South America: Causes and Consequences*, edited by J. Wilbert, 111–16. Caracas: Editorial Sucre.

———. 1982. *Europe and the People without History*. Berkeley: University of California Press.

Woodburn, James. 1982. "Egalitarian Societies." *Man* 17: 431–51.

Yanagisako, S., and Carole Delaney. 1995. "Naturalizing Power." In *Naturalizing Power: Essays in Feminist Cultural Analysis*, edited by S. Yanagisako and C. Delaney, 1–22. London: Routledge.

Yen, David. 1989. "The Domestication of the Environment." In *Foraging and Farming: The Evolution of Plant Exploitation*, edited by D. R. Harris and G. Hillman, 55–75. London: Unwin-Hyman.

Yost, James. 1981. "Twenty Years of Contact: The Mechanisms of Change in Wao (Auca) Culture." In *Cultural Transformations and Ethnicity in Modern Ecuador*, edited by N. Whitten, 677–704. Urbana: University of Illinois Press.

———. 1991. "People of the Forest: The Waorani." In *Ecuador in the Shadow of the Volcanoes*, edited by M. Acosta-Solis, 95–115. Quito: Libri Mundi.

Yost, James, and Patricia Kelley. 1983. "Shotguns, Blowguns, and Spears: An Analysis of Technological Efficiency." In *Adaptive Responses of Native Amazonians*, edited by R. B. Hames and W. T. Vickers, 189–224. New York: Academic Press.

Zent, Englee, and Stanford Zent. 2004. "Los Jödi: Sabios Botánicos del Amazonas Venezolano." *Antropológica* 97: 3–43.

Ziegler-Otero, Lawrence. 2004. *Resistance in an Amazonian Community: Huaorani Organizing against the Global Economy*. New York: Berghahn Books.

Zurita, María Gabriella. 2014. "De la Gestion de la Forêt à la Gestion de l'Abattis: La Construction du Système Agricole Waorani, Amazonie Équatorienne." PhD diss., National Museum of Natural History, Paris.

INDEX

achiote (*Bixa orellana*), 292n2
adaptation, 48, 65, 98
after birth, 133
agency, 98, 110
agouti (*Agouti paca*), 80, 208, 209
ahuè, 51, 54
ahuene, 30, 50, 51, 205, 207, 216, 270n3, 291n13
Amazon dolphin (*Inia geoffrensis*), 283n17
amotamini, 177, 216
AMWAE (Asociación de Mujeres Waorani del Ecuador), 5, 32, 267n3, 268n7, 283n16
anaconda (*Eunectes* spp.), 284n17
animals, relations with, 124, 126, 157, 206, 219, 290n11
anthropocentrism, 218
anthropogenic forests, 18, 38, 49, 51–53, 61, 93, 97, 101, 104
anthropological knowledge, 24, 135–41, 164, 168, 211–12; and Amazonianist anthropology, 12, 39, 113, 114, 210, 217; and values, 21, 64, 66, 69, 210, 213
Arawak cultural complex, 63, 68, 69

Arawete, 162
aroboqui baön anobain, 125, 150
arome mö, 124
Asociación de Mujeres Waorani del Ecuador. *See* AMWAE
autonomy, 14, 27, 112, 121, 150, 197, 216, 220, 223
ayahuasca (*Banisteriopsis muricata* or *B. caapi*), 49, 185, 186, 219
ayeromonque quehuemoni, 150

baacuu, 210, 236
Balée, William, 12, 61, 64, 75, 76–77, 91, 92–102, 108, 110, 112, 279n7
balsa (*Ochroma pyramidale*, *Cecropia sciadophylla*, or *Cecropia* spp.), 271n10
Bameno, xi, 33, 199, 207, 208, 221, 222, 244, 245, 246, 247, 248, 249, 250, 276n13, 292n26, 299n5
bananas and plantains (*Musa* spp.), 43, 48, 55, 80, 105, 128, 170, 232, 270n6
bara, 135, 153
barè. *See* curassow
bark cloth, 85

Barnard, Alan, 17
baromipa, 127, 214, 215
Berlin, Brent, 73, 74, 75, 88
binary ideologies, 31
Bird-David, Nurit, 211–12, 217
birth, 115, 123, 127, 128, 129, 135
bobeca tëre, 207
böyego. *See* agouti
buyo aquequi, 159

caanta, 129, 187, 287n15
cacao (*Theobroma*), 84
Canguilhem, George, 71–72
capibara (*Hydrochaeris hydrochaeris*), 80
Capuchin mission, 22
Cerón, Carlos and Montalvo, 82–83
chambira (*Astrocaryum chambira*), 51, 267n2, 289n2; *chambira* palm fiber, 5
Cipoletti, María Susana, 27, 228–29
civilization, 31, 66, 68, 70, 100, 106, 107, 108, 109, 156, 218, 221, 245, 255–57, 259, 261, 272n20, 273n23, 301n15
Clastres, Pierre, 20
Clement, Charles, 47, 53, 60–61, 69, 103, 272n21, 279n11
Coca (Francisco de Orellana), 5, 10, 225, 237
cohuori (*cowodi*), 3, 23, 25, 50, 105, 149, 171, 172, 184, 186, 189, 190, 205, 217, 220, 222, 223, 235, 238, 240, 244, 246, 247, 248, 249, 255, 268n7, 288n19, 299nn6–7, 300n7
compensation, 21, 231, 237
couvade. *See* birth
cuica, 157
cumi, 177
cuñi. *See* fish poison from unidentified vine
curare (*Curarea tecunarum*), 52, 287; curare poison, 45, 52, 109, 129, 156, 173, 178, 249, 283n13, 287n15
curassow (Cracidae), 127

daboca. *See* *Solanum sessiflorum*
daguenkahue. *See* peach palm
daguenka tëre, 207

Dayuno, 104, 108, 232, 280n16
death, 11, 16, 27, 101, 138, 142, 145, 157, 158, 172, 183–84, 186, 188, 189, 190, 191, 194, 217, 235, 249
Denevan, William, 62, 96, 272n18
Descola, Philippe, 18, 19, 47, 68, 69
determinism, 103–5; environmental, 14, 18, 48, 59, 63, 102, 110; historical, 14, 57, 60–62, 100
development and pluriculturalism, 244–45, 249; and interculturality, 198, 248; and the plurinational state, 35; and political subjectivity, 35, 249, 258–59; and poverty, 259
Diamond, Jared, 57, 59, 64, 272n17
dicago, 229
DINEIIB (Dirrectión Nacional de Educación Indígena Intercultural y Bilingüe), 22, 23
Dirrectión Nacional de Educación Indígena Intercultural y Bilingüe. *See* DINEIIB
durani ahuè, 54
durani bai, 107, 109, 205, 206, 208, 219, 220, 221, 222, 249, 299n5

ecological relations, 12, 39, 86, 87, 89, 209, 279n6
Ecuadorian Chocó, 260–61
ECY (Estación Científica Yasuní). *See* Yasuní Scientific Station
ëëmë(iri), 120, 205, 206, 207, 208, 216, 219, 220, 231, 245
èèquète ante nètohuenga, 126
Ellen, Roy, 73, 78, 81, 88
environmental services, 239–42
Estación Científica Yasuní. *See* Yasuní Scientific Station
ethnographic present, 24

Fausto, Carlos, 18, 30, 68
fish poison from unidentified vine (*cuñi*), 51, 270n4

food taboos, 128
foragers: Amazonian, 18, 58, 61, 78, 93, 101, 102; and foraging ethos, 18, 63, 65, 89, 103; and forest societies, 34, 49, 79; Northwest Amazonian trekkers, 12, 59, 87, 89

Gardner, Paul, 78–79
gata tèquè guèpempa tēre, 207
gay gati huiyeng, 270
gender relations, 121, 171; and childhood, 152, 153; and conjugality, 178–79; and co-parenthood, 127, 131, 143, 169; and division of labor, 55; and host-guest relationship, 132, 180–81; and polygyny, 127, 179, 180; and postmarital residence, 13, 129–30, 182; and sensuality, 125, 149, 154, 156; and sex, 125, 147, 155, 161, 162
giant river otter or nutria (*Pteronura brasiliensis*), 284n17
Guajá, 46, 76–77, 86, 93, 98
guiri(nani), 183, 207, 250, 287n12
guiyitèhue ayè, 208
guumbè imba, 221

High, Casey, 25, 27, 30, 33, 285n1, 289n1
historical ecology, 12, 16, 19, 46, 91–94, 96; and agricultural regression, 39, 61, 69, 100, 101, 105; and Anthropocene, 91, 94–95; and Holocene, 59, 65, 106; and late Paleolithic, 58, 59; and plant domestication, 47–48, 53, 57
homicidal rage, 185
horticulture, 12, 14, 18, 48–49, 54–56, 64, 77, 88, 89, 104
huaarete pone, 163
huaca, 155, 182, 184
huañoö imba, 124
huaocä, 151
huaomoni, 50, 53, 54, 188, 191, 219, 287n12, 289n29, 291n19
huaorani, 16, 25, 150, 171, 172, 184, 189, 190, 217, 222, 223, 246, 247

Huaorani language, 21–23, 32, 50; and bilingualism, 21; and dictionary, 22, 32; and language standardization, 22; and linguistic variation, 34
Huaorani Organization of the Ecuadorian Amazon. *See* ONHAE
huaponi (*waponi*), 125, 149, 150, 151, 153, 210, 219, 256
huaponi quehuemonipa (*waa quehuimi*), 125, 149, 151, 153, 257
huarani, 50, 56, 183, 287n12, 291n13
huarique, 155
huatapè, 55
huati huati, 158
Huègöngui, 186, 187, 188, 195, 281n7
huene (*huine*), 158, 159
hueno tenongui, 183
huentey, 214–15, 218
huento. *See* stinging nettles
huihua aquequi, 159
huiñègäncoo, 132, 176
huiñeme, 51
human condition, 68, 70, 149, 164, 198
hunting, 51, 64, 68, 80, 81, 104, 109, 127, 156, 178, 198, 205, 206, 221, 238
hunting and gathering, 12, 14, 16, 17–20, 24, 38, 57, 64, 101, 198, 211–12
huyenco, 51

indigenous knowledge, 29, 93, 97; and ethnobiology, 71, 73, 77; and ethnobotany, 39, 46, 52, 62, 87, 93; and ethnoecology, 69, 278; and folkbiology, 73, 86; and hunter-gatherer taxonomies, 74–76
insider/outsider dialectics, 13, 247–48, 258, 292n23
intermediate subsistence systems, 100, 102
isolationism, 27, 217; and autarky, 27, 49–50, 51, 68, 172, 284n19; and language, 21, 22
Itzaj Maya, 89

jacaratia digitata, 109
jaguar, 219, 221

Ka'apor, 46, 75–77, 84, 86, 93, 98, 99
kapamo, 131, 280n6
Kayapó, 98, 99, 181, 270n2, 278n5
kinship terminology, 287n12
Kohn, Eduardo, 16

landscape domestication, 39, 66, 70, 95, 98, 99, 103, 110
Lee, Richard, 17
Lévi-Strauss, Claude, 47, 48, 50, 68, 69, 88, 168, 211, 212–13, 270n2, 281n9, 282n5, 284nn18–19, 290–91n12
life force, 15, 56, 127, 146, 192, 202, 217
life projects, 13, 24, 25, 31, 71, 240, 245, 246; and values, 20, 27, 28, 29, 33, 111–12, 210–13, 222, 252
lowland Quichuas, 55, 66, 81, 84, 89, 109, 148, 206, 229, 249, 273n23, 285n1, 285n3, 289n3, 290n6, 292n5, 301n19
Lu, Flora, 27–28

maapo, 11, 267
macahuè (Bombacaceae), 54, 271
maeñe. See parrots
Makú, 67, 68
maney, 127
manioc (*Manihot esculenta*), 51, 53, 55, 56, 65, 70
masculinity, 25, 121, 169–72, 206; and body and soul, 121, 143, 182–85, 192; and fatherhood, 133–35, 193; and humanity, 189; and malehood, 31; and partible paternity, 127; and shamanism, 134–35, 185–86
materialism, 21, 46, 54, 71, 95, 97
matrimonial alliances, 50, 53, 54, 111, 121, 145, 170–74; and feasting, 56, 105
Maybury-Lewis, David, 31, 32
Mehinaku, 160–63, 283
memeiri, 209, 219, 287n12, 291n13, 298n3

meñera, 44, 135
menqui, 158
mento, 187
mii. See ayahuasca
mina pa, 124
miñe, 135
mö, 124, 187, 287n15
mobility, 16, 19, 20, 27, 46, 61, 62, 69, 86, 104, 105, 108, 109, 111, 205; and abandonment, 111–12, 206, 218; and nomadism, 12, 38; and residence, 15, 49, 81, 106, 205; and trekking, 38, 39, 46, 49, 64, 79, 81, 105, 111, 198
monito eya, 300n8
monito omë, 221, 238, 261
monkeys, 80, 151, 209, 210
morete (*Mauritia flexuosa* L.f., Arecaceae), 80, 109
Mundurucú, 160–62, 182
Muratorio, Blanca, xi
myths (Huaorani): childbirth, 131; creator (Huègöngui), 186–87; giant earth worm, 157–58, 283; great flood, 286n4, 290n4; jaguar and turtle, 242–43; moon, 126; son of the sun, 190, 270n7, 288–89n27

Nacionalidad Waorani del Ecuador. See NAWE
nanicabo (*nanicaboiri*), 114, 115, 126, 133, 140, 144, 145, 148, 151, 153, 155, 156, 169, 170, 171, 173, 174, 177, 178, 179–81, 184, 190, 205, 215, 216, 218, 219, 220, 222, 246, 261, 281n2, 287n12, 287n17, 288nn25–26, 291n14
nano tohue nono, 126
nanoongue, 145, 154, 285n2, 287n12
nantohue. See morete
National Directorate of Bilingual Intercultural Indigenous Education. See DINEIIB
natural abundance, 19, 29, 30, 103, 109, 145, 189, 190, 209–11, 218, 222, 223, 224; and giving environment, 14, 198, 217

NAWE (Nacionalidad Waorani del Ecuador), 269n14, 300n12. *See also* ONHAE
ne eñaca, 132, 180–81, 291n14, 292n1
ñemebo. See *jacaratia digitata*
ñeñe, 187, 188
ne ocöinga, 132, 180–81, 291n15, 292n1
niñcopa, 124
niñe, 124

oil industry, 13, 224–30, 292n26, 292–93n5; CGG: 230, 231; "la companía," 230, 232, 235, 237, 252, 253; Maxus, 13, 233–34, 240, 293–94nn7–12, 295–96n15, 297n19; oil camps, 229; oil companies, 80, 107, 267n3; oil frontier, 11, 29–30, 106, 112, 202, 203, 224, 225, 230; oil workers, 226
omëre, 51, 238, 248, 270n3, 292n23
ömere (äante) gobopa, 1, 102, 111, 214
ömere gomonipa, 14, 38
ömere quëqui, 214, 231
onco(iri), 170, 218
oñè, 176
oñetahue, 85
onguèngö, 176
onguiyè, 176
ONHAE (Organización Huaorani del la Amazonía Ecuatoriana), 13, 30, 129, 233, 240, 241, 242, 294nn10–11, 300n12. *See also* NAWE
onohuoca, 185
onomastics, 23
ononqui, 125, 155
onquiyè, 176
ontabepo, 187
ontologies, 11, 18, 114; and cosmology, 33, 222; and native metaphysics, 22, 32, 39, 223; and nature/society dualism, 16, 46, 47, 91, 114, 217, 218; and perspectivism, 13, 19, 114, 115; and relationship epistemology, 15, 89. *See also* predation
oömena, 186
oönempa, or *öone*. See *chambira*
oönta (oonta). See curare

Organización Huaorani del la Amazonía Ecuatoriana. *See* ONHAE
Oriente, 10, 36, 225

pambil (*Iriartea deltoida*), 109
parrots, 152
Paz, Octavio, 147–48, 156, 166, 283n14
peaceful contact, 26, 27
peach palm (*Bactris gasipaes*), or chontaduro, 49, 53–54, 65, 80, 110, 205, 206, 207, 208, 271nn8–9, 271n12, 272n21, 276n18, 288n27; and viewpoint of prey, 16, 19–20
peccaries, 210, 211
Peeke, Catherine, 21, 25
petohuè, or *petöhue*. See *ungurahua*
pii (inte), 4, 182, 184, 194, 195, 258, 288n21
Piperno, Dolores and Deborah Pearsall, 47, 57, 58–60, 63, 271–72nn13–17
plant phenology, 89
Posey, Darrell, 98, 99, 270n2, 278–79nn5–6
pre-Columbian chiefdoms, 62
predation, 13, 16, 19–20, 121, 170, 190, 198, 223, 242, 243, 289n28

quegokicönwi, 256–57
QuehueireOno, 4, 104
queremene, 187

Rappaport, Roy, 70
Rivière, Peter, 138, 162, 174–75, 286n7
rubber boom, 20, 207

sacrifice, 25, 134–35, 197
Santos-Granero, Fernando, 20
Sauer, Carl, 95–96, 277n2
sharing economy, 14, 15, 17–18, 19, 125, 171, 216, 234; and demand sharing, 19, 20, 80, 170, 224; and substance sharing, 13, 115, 125, 153, 171, 190
SIL (Summer Institute of Linguistics), 4, 21, 22, 23, 25, 124, 127, 214, 226, 240, 269n11, 281n1

Solanum sessiflorum, and/or *Solanum jamaicense*, 53, 208
Sperber, Dan, 40
Steward, Julian, 97, 277n2
stinging nettles (*Urera bacifera*), 129
Summer Institute of Linguistics. *See* SIL

Tagaeri, 4, 21, 33, 50, 267n1, 268n5, 273n23, 288n20
tapaca huenonte (*hueni*), 183
tapey, 124, 127
tapir (*Tapirus*), 51, 52, 126, 157, 290n5
Taromenani, 3–5, 8, 21, 23, 27, 33, 107, 267n1, 268n4
tedenanipa, 32
tehuè, 54, 176
tepa. *See* pambil
tëpë, 55
tèquè eñaringa, 131
terero (also *tededo*), 50
terra firme, 79
tey, 54, 127
tome waorani ponino, 32
Toñampari, 23, 27, 206, 220, 289n1, 290n6, 291nn21–22, 301n19
totequehue, 150, 155
toucan (*Ramphastos cuvieri*), 127
transformations, 16, 25, 27, 112, 198, 247; and development process, 16, 202; and landscape, 97, 98, 99, 102, 103, 108–9, 112; and pre-Columbian history, 61; and transfiguration, 18
trekking. *See* mobility
tribal zone, 20
Tukano, 49, 67, 68
Tupi-Guaraní, 12, 68, 75, 89, 93, 94, 99, 103, 279n12

ungurahua (*Jessenia bataua* or *Oenocarpus bataua*), 52, 80, 86, 109
urban migration, 26

uxorilocality, 50, 121, 127, 175, 180, 189, 194, 195

Vía Auca, 236, 261, 268n4
Vía Maxus, 236, 237, 238, 261
vital energy. *See* life force
Viteri, Jorge, 224–28, 230, 235, 264
voluntary isolation, 14, 21, 27, 107, 238, 252; and Zona Intangible Tagaeri Taromenane, 5

Waodani Documentation Project. *See* WDP
wao tededo, 23
warfare, 27, 41, 55, 67, 68, 90, 101, 134, 145, 156–58, 159, 162, 164, 174, 182, 185, 228, 235, 236, 250, 279n9, 285n23
WDP (Waodani Documentation Project), 33, 34
wegönhuè, 131, 280n5
Westermarck, Edward, 166–68, 282n4
Woodburn, James, 20
wood peckers, 206
woolly monkeys (*Lagothrix lagotricha*), 52
work ethics, 210, 212, 214–15

yamöi gaqui, 270n6
Yanomamo, 25
yarëcare, 105
Yasuní, 51, 79, 207, 239, 270n3; Biosphere Reserve, 29, 31; Yasuní Initiative, 31, 239, 253–54, 262–65; Yasuní National Park, 5, 10, 19, 27, 28, 80, 221, 236, 237, 238, 239, 254, 275n8, 296n17, 301n18. *See also* Yasuní Scientific Station
Yasuní Scientific Station, 29. *See also* Yasuní
Yost, James, 25

Zaparo, 21, 49, 50, 186
Ziegler Otero, Lawrence, 30

ABOUT THE AUTHOR

Laura Rival is associate professor at the University of Oxford where she convenes and teaches courses developing her unique approach to the anthropology of nature, society, and development. She has worked with various indigenous communities in Ecuador, Guayana, and other Latin American locations where she goes back as often as she can. She combines academic research with actions aimed at highlighting the value of distinct indigenous ways of inhabiting the world. Her research interests include Amerindian conceptualizations of nature and society; historical and political ecology; indigenous peoples, development, and environmental and conservation policies in Latin America. She has written numerous articles on these topics and edited a number of books, including *Governing the Provision of Ecosystem Services* (Springer, 2012), *Beyond the Visible and the Material* (Oxford University Press, 2001), and *The Social Life of Trees* (Berg, 1998). Her extensive publications on the Huaorani include *Hijos del sol, padres del jaguar* (Abya-Yala, 1996), and *Trekking through History: The Huaorani of Amazonian Ecuador* (Columbia University Press, 2002).